CHRISTIANITY AND THE HUMAN BODY

A THEOLOGY OF THE HUMAN BODY

Proceedings of the ITEST Workshop
October, 2000

ITEST FAITH/SCIENCE PRESS
3601 Lindell Boulevard
St. Louis, Missouri 63108

BT
741.2
· I 84
2000

Published by:
ITEST Faith/Science Press
3601 Lindell Boulevard
St. Louis, Missouri 63108

PHONE   (314)-977-2703
FAX   (314)-977-7211
E-MAIL   postigm@slu.edu
WEB SITE   http://ITEST.slu.edu

Printed in the United States

ISBN   1-885583-09-5

Cover: This cover is an original design by Mr. Leonard E. Buckley of Damascus, Maryland. Mr. Buckley, retired foreman of Designers at the Bureau of Engraving and Printing, designed among other stamps the issue commemorating the Apollo 8 Flight as well as the mineral issues. Many of the Duck Stamps issued by the government are his design. Many of his paintings grace the Smithsonian. He and his wife, Janet, have been longtime members of ITEST.

CONTENTS

FOREWORD

What is the fleshly human body? What is the corporeal human body? What is the relationship between them? These and other questions were treated at a Workshop held at Mercy Center in Saint Louis county in October, 2000. Twenty-seven members of The Institute for Theological Encounter with Science and Technology (ITEST) met to discuss *A Theology of the Human Body*. This was a rare meeting in that there was only a theological theme running through the meeting. However, the science and technology aspects of the topic were lying just beneath the surface.

The discussion, it must be admitted, ranged rather widely through many areas of theology — from a long discussion of Subordinationism through long arguments about the Fall and Original Sin and the body/soul distinction to the place of science, technology and philosophy. The result was not so much a discussion of *the* theology of the human body as hints at building such a theology. These suggestions include the necessary elements from which such a theology can (and maybe should) be constructed. In other words, the meeting reported in this volume gives bits and pieces of a theology, not a finished picture of that theology. It is preliminary, but necessary, to a fully evolved sense of the body in Christian thought and practice.

In dealing with a theology of the human body (or the human anything) some sense must be made of the Fall and Original Sin. This will highly color any statements about the human. For instance, can we say anything about the Fall without starting with the Incarnation and Resurrection/Ascension of Jesus the Christ and working our way backwards? Would we even know we were fallen without the Incarnation? Would we know our original destination and our resurrected direction if Christ had not come? Or could it be revealed independently of the mission of the Christ? If so, how? The Genesis story was (and is) applicable here, but can it really be "understood" apart from the *posterity* promised in Genesis 3?

Pastor Steven Kuhl at one point raised an extremely interesting idea: the whole purpose of the Incarnation, life, death, resurrection and ascension of Christ is our re-embodiment. Is our salvation precisely our re-embodiment? Are they in reality co-terminus? Does one really mean (or at least imply) the other? Is Revelation itself directed to this end? For a long, long time the Church has proclaimed as doctrine that we shall rise, identifiably ourselves, to heaven or hell. I could not identify myself if I rose as a fourth century BC Asian woman. Will I not be raised as an American male of the 20th-21st century? Otherwise, how will I know myself?

We examined the body/soul distinction. One of the essayists suggested that the notion of "soul" needs a lot more work. Neuroscience, for one, has located in the body many of the functions that were once ascribed to soul. The brain is far better understood now than it was in the twelfth or thirteenth century and more work is being done on it. The body has been seen (and will be seen) as more and more important in our salvation, or in our re-embodiment.

After all, everything about our actions, on which we shall be judged, originates in the body. It is certainly partly in the body that we are angry and hateful or patient and loving. This in turn leads into the question of corporeality and *flesh*liness. Is there anything corporeal (*soma*) that does not partake in the fleshly (*sarx*)? Are not even our thoughts and desires "fleshly"? Even our service of the Lord is at least in part fleshly. As Saint Paul writes: "Who will deliver me from this body of death?" We should in passing note the passage immediately following: "Thanks be to God through Jesus Christ our Lord." But, whenever we deal with the body on an intellectual level, we must realize the part that *flesh* plays in our being. It cannot be ignored — simply because we are fallen creatures living in a fallen world. The darkening of the mind is an ongoing phenomenon. For instance, philosophers still contend with the mind/body split, even though we know that we are one. Could this inability to approach unity be a sign of our fallenness?

Another theme dealt with the "separated soul" on death. "Soul" can and will be separated from "body (sarx)." Inasmuch as a personal judgment is ours immediately (*mox*) after death, it must be inferred that our death cannot be understood as that separation of the soul from the body which would transform us into "separated souls" in that impersonal Thomist sense commonly taken for granted, without annulling the immediacy of that judgment. (To describe the Thomistic separation of soul and body, I generally think of a cosmic file cabinet filled with "immaterial separated souls" waiting until the end to be united somehow with some form of body, the more immaterial the better.) This is not at all the case. "Spiritual" for a Christian does not mean "immaterial"; it means immortal. We don't know what happens when we die, but we know that we will rise again, body and soul, identifiably ourselves.

Another theme was our interconnectedness with all other living beings. The knowledge of this was often connected with the discovery and subsequent elucidation of DNA (deoxyribonucleic acid). But we have known for a long time that we are related to all living things; we depend on at least some of them for sustenance and life. If only implicitly we were aware of that dependency and that relationship. DNA merely tells us how we are related, what the physical situation is. Even God, without the "benefit" of DNA, is relational. The Father sent the Son to reveal the Spirit. God could not have done this if Father were not related to Son and Holy Spirit. We are monotheists; we believe in one God. But that God is Trinitarian. Christianity is a "relational religion." We are not somehow divine freelancers. Nonetheless, the consciousness of our interconnectedness is a very necessary part of our humanity. It is an idea which cannot be overstressed. We live in the body for each other. Jesus Christ meant it when he told us to "love one another." The example of the vine and the branches, an example he used at the Last Supper (John 15) leaves no doubt of our relationality with Christ and with each other.

As Sister Carla Mae Streeter pointed out in the discussion, those at the meeting were all Westerners. The East has insights into the meaning of the body that we might well learn from. Maybe we won't get much of value from such a discussion, but we should still try to learn what might be helpful. It is a different tradition.

Dr. Jitse van der Meer's paper is different from the rest. He is trying in his essay to present a model for bridging the gap between science and theology. This is especially urgent in dealing with the human body. That's where we live. That is the area of massive work in the life sciences. He builds two pillars (represented by Theodosius Dobhzansky and Rudolph Bultmann) to show various hermeneutical levels. Then he constructs a bridge between them. He concludes that each science demands its own methodology — and Biblical revelation is an essential source for Christian theology.

Finally, the essays and discussion do not constitute a definite theology of the body. They do contain many of the elements thereof. Much of this requires greater reflection and inflection. This volume, however, does contain many occasions for meditation, many items that need further thought. It is not the end of the search; it is a mere continuance of the quest. It is offered in this spirit.

Robert Brungs, SJ
Director: ITEST
April 2, 2001

A Theology of the Body: Body, Genes, and Culture
Who's Holding the Leash?

The Reverend Dr. Michael Hoy is the Academic Dean of the Lutheran School of Theology, St. Louis and Pastor of Holy Trinity Lutheran Church, St. Louis. He holds a Master of Divinity from Christ Seminary-Seminex, a Master of Theology from Lutheran School of Theology at Chicago and a PhD in Theology and Ethics from Lutheran School of Theology at Chicago. Dr. Hoy has taught theology and ethics at Valparaiso University, Capital University and at the Lutheran School of Theology. Past president of the Board of Directors, (1995-1999), Crossings Community, St. Louis, he continues to serve as a board member. In addition to his many talks and papers he has authored the book *The Faith that Works: The Relationship of Faith and Works in the Theology of Juan Luis Segundo, S.J.* (1995).

"What are human beings that you are mindful of them, mortals that you care for them?" (Psalm 8:4)

In the center of the paleontology hall of the Smithsonian's National Museum of Natural History, at the top of the long vertical pole depicting the epochs of geological time and the evolution of life, there is a final, small segment depicting the most recent installment: "man." The query of the psalmist above overwhelms me with both with a sense of wonder and awe, as well as humbling insignificance in the larger picture of life.

From the perspective of the humanities, the beginnings of human history start with the emergence of "culture," traced no earlier than the first forms of art by the Cro-Magnons of the late Paleolithic Period, less than 35,000 years ago.[1] Still, the origins of life itself are at least a hundred-thousand times older, with the first mammals appearing some 200 million years ago, *Homo sapiens* ("wise man") 500,000 years ago, and the first ceremonial rituals "recognizing mortality" during the period of the Neanderthals.[2]

Evolutionary theorists may affirm with the humanities that the beginning of "modern man," of the "real human," comes with culture.[3] But they would find little to celebrate in the "cultured" human being. "I think nature red in tooth and claw' sums up our modern understanding of natural selection admirably," Richard Dawkins concludes.[4] And while some, like the Gifford lecturer Holmes Rolston, chastise how by such claims the "the natural world is being negatively judged,[5] perhaps we should not be so quick to judge the radical biological evolutionists in their depiction of nature. Respected though divergent theories on human justice, like the social-contract theory of Rawls and the entitlement theory of Nozick, seem to take the human propensity toward survival and self-interest as a given.[6] And an earlier Gifford lecturer, Reinhold Neibuhr, would seem to throw weight in their direction by claiming that, "For all the centuries of experience, men have not yet learned how to live together without compounding their vices and covering each other with mud and with blood.'"[7]

Genes and culture frame our understanding of the human. To examine the human strictly on the basis of its genes, which is the science of the current Human Genome Project, is to ignore the cultural implications of life. I do not believe that the scientists themselves are interested in doing that, and that they are making every effort to "share" their knowledge with as many as possible. This suggests a cultural direction. On the other hand, one cannot understand the human body only by examining the human being in culture. This has been the tendency of the humanist sciences, including theology, at the expense of not giving enough consideration, until recently, to the natural sciences.

While the headlines are still captivated by the debate between the evolutionary biologists and the Creationists, that is not the focus here. Though unquestionably the latter have exerted undue political and legal pressure, it is yet another reminder of the tragic and lamentable history of the persecution of science by religion. The evolutionary sociobiologists, for their part, are to be commended for not only perceiving what is at the root of the Creationist argument, but also for superseding the Creationist argument by providing their own evidence for a "sincerely articulated world picture" and their own well-reasoned response to the supposed "beauty and complexity of the living world."[8]

The real critical debate is among those who already embrace the biological understanding of human life. The divergence and differences, however, are in regard to the premises of those biological understandings. On the one hand, there are the Darwinian sociobiologists who advocate genetic determinism; on the other hand, there are those of more humanist persuasion who would contend for a position that ascribes greater freedom and transcendence to human beings and their culture, without denying the biological bases.[9] The contention of this paper is that the Darwinian sociobiologists may actually have a more solid *theological* ground in their understanding of the human, with its genes and culture, than they are given credit for by their opposition. What Aubrey Moore once said about evolutionary biology may be true once more, "under the disguise of a foe, [it] did the work of a friend."[10]

Genes and the Genome: Selfish or Self-Actualizing?

Genetic studies are clearly dominating scientific analysis today, and point toward developments that will change our future.[11] Many are hailing the work of the Human Genome Project as "the Holy Grail of modern biology" and on par with our landing on the moon.[12] Others (perhaps a minority) are more skeptical, seeing the fascination as "genomania" and "fetishizing DNA."[13] The project has raised a whole host of questions still waiting to be answered: What will be the "ethical, legal, and social implications" (ELSI) of the project? Who will really benefit from its results? Can health care providers and the general public become genetically literate in time? In addition, there have been the distractions of competition, even feuding, among the scientists and corporate executives involved — "differences over who should get credit for this scientific milestone; over whose genome sequence was more complete, more accurate, more useful; over the free exchange of what may be mankind's most important data versus the exploitation of what may also be its most valuable."[14]

These differences and disputes were glossed over in the landmark announcement that was made from the White House lawn on June 26, 2000. But the ethos that has surrounded the project, together with the subject matter of the project itself, may have a connection. Will our having an informational booklet by 2003 (if not sooner) of the three billion pairs of genes that comprise the human genome tell us all that we really need to know about the human body? Or will we still need to understand more about what makes us human, including our bodies, than our genes alone can tell us? Is there more to understanding our genes than being able to properly sequence the single nucleotide polymorphisms (A, C, T, and G) in our genome?

Richard Dawkins, in his enduring landmark tome *The Selfish Gene*, adopts the more formal definition of gene from G. C. Williams: "A gene is defined as any portion of chromosomal material that potentially lasts for enough generations to serve as a unit of natural selection." For Dawkins, this means that the gene is ruthlessly "selfish" toward the goal of its own survival.[15] His understanding of the nature of the human organism is consistent with this genetic composition: "We are survival machines—robot vehicles blindly programmed to preserve the selfish molecules known as genes."[16]

Holmes Rolston takes issue with Dawkins' assessment. How can genes be selfish, Rolston queries, and still lead to the eventual *cooperation* toward an organism? "The feature of any gene is not so much that it must be selfish' as that it contributes' to other genes, supplying information that they lack, and they do likewise."[17] Instead, Rolston adopts an understanding of genes as "loci of *intrinsic value*, expressed and defended in individuals and also inclusively present and distributed in family, population, and species lines."[18] Genes are therefore more "creative" in their basic design, "searching," "struggling toward more diverse and more complex forms of life," "shares in a whole."[19] Correspondingly, Rolston's understanding of the basic nature of the organism is in keeping with his value-directed appraisal of the gene: "an organism is self-actualizing.'It pursues its integrated, encapsulated identity; it conserves its own intrinsic value, defends its life. The organism does this in both competition and symbiosis with other organisms of the same and other species in its biotic community."[20]

Nevertheless, Rolston's "self-actualizing" organism does not preclude "selfish behavior."[21] In fact, what Rolston dismisses in Dawkins, "selfishness" in the genes, he seems to take back in his discussion of the phenomenon of sin. "There is something original' about sin, something in human origins that produces sin perennially, something in human biology, in the flesh, that makes it inevitable for humans to lapse into sin."[22] For Rolston, sin *is* selfishness, and this selfishness is due to the failure of human beings to "break out of their animal nature."[23] But if " original' sin" is so "perennial," who's to say that the selfish quality may not still be in the genes of *our* nature, even as it is in *animal* nature?

In his assessment of the specific nature of human beings, Rolston contends: "Humans are made godward, to turn toward God, but shrink back and act like beasts." Hence, Roltson can argue that "self-actualizing is a good thing for humans as well as animals. Self-interest is godly; the commandment, we remember is to love others as we do ourselves.... But concupiscence, the desire to possess and enjoy inordinately, is *not* a fitting form of life in the world."[24] In fact, natural selection, says Rolston, will even ward against it.[25] But Dawkins can also affirm that in order to survive, organisms will adopt their own "evolutionary stable strategy" that will both help to maximize their own success as well as penalize any deviance. In effect, selfishness itself can be shrewd enough to accept or adapt to a strategy of reciprocity and cooperation, something that will "put on hold" an all-out selfish behavior that may eliminate a predatory species, because that would reduce its chances for survival. Organisms may need other organisms in order to survive, and in their selfishness toward survival, may *not* seek to exert their own natural preferences.[26]

That there are predatory organisms seeking their own survival, however, does seem to be an observable datum. Even the Human Genome Project has, at least as one of its objectives, a functional genomics that seeks to determine "how individual genes work together in health and disease," and not simply with objective interest but with the intent of sharing that information with the medical community in the hopes of finding ways to address problems in this area. President Clinton in one paragraph affirms how "we are learning the language in which God created life," but in the next paragraph speaks of how we will use this language in "attacking the genetic roots" of diseases.[27] The human species is in a battle for its own survival. But it is not only our genes that are under the microscope. So are we in our efforts toward survival.

To further the questioning of Rolston, what evidence would support that human beings are "*made* godward, to *turn toward* God" as long as this "inevitable" problem of our sinful selfishness persists? Couldn't it just as reasonably be argued that "all human beings who are propagated according to nature are born with sin, that is, without fear of God, without trust in God, and with concupiscence"?[28] Might the "evil lusts and inclinations" be already possessed in our "mother's wombs," such that our human body and human being is off to a problematic start (origin), and that the inevitability be reflective of "the continual inclination of nature"?[29] Indeed, might our own drives toward survivalism be influenced by that inclination?

To be sure, there may a worthwhile argument that would not simply be splitting theological hairs (or biological chromosomes) on whether human beings are sinful in their "nature and essence" or whether their nature reflects a "horrible, deep-seated, and indescribable corruption" through sin.[30] Perhaps that is what lies behind Rolston's complaint that "the natural world is being negatively judged," though that doesn't seem to be the real thrust of his argument. Rolston, as we will see, is more interested in placing the *Homo sapiens* on a pedestal of evolutionary achievement different from what one might encounter in the rest of nature. That is Rolston's basic presupposition, and it informs his understanding of the gene.

As presuppositions go, perhaps it is just as defensible as Dawkins' Darwinianism. Even Dawkins will acknowledge that "there is no universally agreed definition of a gene."[31] Given Dawkins concession, we might also be able to question whether Dawkins is himself reading back into the gene something that may not have originally been there in the gene, say in some pre-fallen state. Would that be esoteric? In any event, one of the things that commends Dawkins analysis of our genes is that he is not afraid of recognizing their propensity toward "selfishness" and "survival of the fittest;" nor is he content to accept that quality. He just recognizes its validity, and offers his own best suggestions to address what he himself sees as a problem: "Let us try to *teach* generosity and altruism, because we are born selfish. Let us understand what our selfish genes are up to, because we may then at least have the chance to upset their designs, something that no other species has ever aspired to."[32] But that does not change the nature—nature as we now have it—in our genes, with their orientation toward selfishness and survival.

In summary, Rolston's depiction of the value-enhanced gene is influenced by his desire to paint a more optimistic picture of the human species and, especially, their culture; but perhaps the more pessimistic depiction in the biologist's perspective may be more useful for upping-the-ante for our theological considerations. Indeed, the real appreciation and even redemption of our human body may depend on our understanding exactly what the genes are up to.

Human Bodies in the Balance of Genes and Culture

In the now classic statement for the evolution of culture, Theodosius Dobzhansky exclaimed, "Human genes have accomplished what no other genes succeeded in doing. They formed the biological basis for a super-organic culture, which proved to be the most powerful method of adaptation to the environment ever developed by any species."[33] Human beings are distinguished by, among other things, the evolution of their central nervous system and the brain; the brain gives rise to the capacity for language; and language is central to the establishment of culture.[34]

Philip Hefner defined the human being as "a two natured creation ... a coalition and symbiosis of genes and culture."[35] His definition is influenced in part by Ralph Wendell Burhoe's suggestion that "genes" and "culture" are "two organisms" that have co-adapted in the human species as a "symbiosis."[36] Hefner's own coined descriptor of the two-natured creation is "created co-creator": "a creature of nature and its processes of evolution — hence the *created* — and who at the same time is created by those very processes to be a creature of freedom and culture — hence *co-creator*."[37]

But why "two" natures? For Hefner, the two natures seem necessary in order to allow for the recognition of the dynamic of our genetic determinism, while also opening the door to cultural freedom. There is, therefore, a disjunctive quality that comes with the emergence of culture: "Culture is defined ... as learned and taught patterns of behavior and the symbol systems that contextualize those behaviors, both interpreting and justifying them. *Unlike genetic information, cultural information is not programmed*, but rather discovered, learned, taught, interpreted, and justified."[38]

Rolston seems to be making a similar claim about our dual nature, though perhaps he adopts a little less cavalier perspective about our "programming." "In computer imagery, the same hardware' (biology) supports diverse programs of software' (culture), even if there are many repeated subroutines."[39] Again, the human brain is the evolved instrument that makes possible the cultural innovations. Human beings are equipped with "a unique genius'" in the human mind.[40] The Latin word "*genius*" itself means "spirit" (the German equivalent is *Geist*). Human beings are above the higher animals in that they have "conscious self-awareness," which is their unique genius or *Geist*.[41] Higher animals possess a different kind of "spirit," or "soul" (*anima*), with only rudimentary conscious experience. "These animals have psychology beyond biology; they have points of view. But only in the human world does spirit become recompounded through the compounding of transmissible cultures; that is the particular genius of the human spirit. Superposed on biology, spirit is nurtured within culture and takes on a life of its own, *not free from its world but free in it*."[42]

The evolutionary biologists, by contrast, disagree with the suggestion of a real cultural break from nature's patterns. Dawkins has argued that culture arises from the "imitation" of ideas (Dawkins coins the word, "meme," from the Greek root *mimeme*); but memes are just as selfish and survival oriented as genes. "When we die there are two things we can leave behind us: genes and memes.... Our genes may be immortal but the collection of genes that is any one of us is bound to crumble away.... But if you contribute to the world's culture, if you have a good idea, compose a tune, invent a sparking plug, write a poem, it may live on, intact, long after your genes have dissolved in the common pool."[43]

Missing from Dawkins, as Rolston is quick to point out, is a sense of how genes and memes are truly connected.[44] Edward O. Wilson and Charles Lumsden have attempted to make that bridge clear by contending that *Homo sapiens* are the only species to achieve the highest form of culture. Nevertheless, culture itself is formed through the processes of genes and their organisms playing by certain "epigenetic rules" that direct their biases toward selecting some traits (artifacts, behaviors, or mental constructs) over others. These traits are called "culturgens," the "basic units of culture."[45] Far from seeing the hardware of biology distinct from the software of culture, genes and culture co-evolve together.[46] Perhaps the best sense of a "natural" connection between genes and culture comes from the explanation of Michael Ruse. Ruse affirms the importance of "language" in the formation of culture, but underscores that "language" is itself a product of evolutionary biology, and the thought and action that language seeks to direct is governed by the "epigenetic rules" (à la Wilson and Lumsden) of natural selection. Nature and nurture are connected, and this through the Darwinian process of natural selection, survival of the species.[47]

Leashed or Unleashed?

The question really before us, therefore, is whether the human body, with its genes and culture, is "leashed" by our genes, or whether these are somehow "unleashed" through the cultural *Geist* of the human spirit. Wilson has framed well the position of the evolutionary biologists:

> The genes hold culture on a leash. The leash is very long, but inevitably values will be constrained in accordance with their effects on the human gene pool. The brain is a product of evolution. Human behavior — like the deepest capacities for emotional response which drive and guide it — is the circuitous technique by which human genetic material has been and will be kept intact.[48]

Interestingly, Wilson's classic statement here appears in his chapter on "Altruism," which begins with a citation from Tertullian: "The blood of martyrs is the seed of the Church." Wilson calls this a "chilling dictum," viewing it as "an intimation that the purpose of sacrifice is to raise one human group over another."[49] While I hardly think that Tertullian had that kind of reasoning in mind — and whether he did or did not, I suspect, Wilson would regard it as beside the point — I can nonetheless appreciate the consistency that would leave no human action, statement or thought beyond the parameters of addressing goals of "survival." More poetically, Wilson expresses, "we are biological and our souls cannot fly free."[50] Similarly, Dawkins speaks of "the long reach of the gene," and Ruse will admit that "culture soars beyond biology, but I suspect its roots are firmly within biology."[51]

The biologists' perspective of a "leashed" environment is precisely what the humanist perspective seeks most to eradicate from the human. Richard Lewotin, for example, has contended that "genes, in making possible the development of human consciousness, have surrendered their power both to determine the individual and its environment. They have been replaced by an entirely new level of causation, that of social interaction with its own laws and its own nature."[52] Hefner has also affirmed, "The human species has been unleashed within the ecosystem and defined by its working, but the species, bestowed with self-awareness and the ability to act upon it, must actively *discover* its bounds and its definition — thus it is driven to self-definition within the context of its already having been defined.... Human survival requires this act of self-defining and the responsible action that flows from it."[53] Finally, we have the claims of Rolston. Given his perception of genes as searching, creative, and sharing, creative minds can be unleashed in the cultural milieu. "The genesis of culture is as remarkable as the genesis in nature; it is nature's most remarkable genesis. The genes outdo themselves."[54] And again, "the leash is not just loose: there is some release from biological determinism."[55] Indeed, Rolston will offer his own defiant counter-manifesto:

> The leash is broken; biology and culture are two dramatically different events—even though culture is superposed on biology, and even though they both can be subsumed under a formal selection theory."... [There is reason to think that] culture has overleaped genetics. Each develops his or her own abilities to the fullest and, where ability is lacking, benefits when the specialized abilities are culturally shared. There is nothing new or controversial in the claim that different people have different abilities and that we enjoy the community of talents. There is nothing suspect ("selfish") about a heritage of life-sustaining information being discovered, selected, and transmitted culturally (in crafts, politics, philosophy, art, religion, and so on), any more than there is anything immoral in a heritage of information being discovered, selected, and transmitted genetically.[56]

Remember that it is in Rolston's examination of culture that we perhaps see most clearly the division, the separation, of human beings from the mere animals: humans have "*Geist*," animals have "*anima*." We may want to affirm and embrace the fact that human beings are higher forms of life, even theologically see it as a basis and a reason for our difference and even dominance vis-à-vis the rest of creation (Gen. 1:26). But recall Rolston's earlier point about the human cultural spirit: "not free from its world but free in it."

Still, no matter how much we may seek to exonerate the freedom of the human spirit, it cannot be freed from its *body* in the world. "Minds are   leashed' to bodies ... and that is inescapable,"[57] says Rolston. Rolston wants to affirm human freedom, but also cannot move far beyond the truly existent "hardware" of our bodies that would allow the luxury of letting that spirit (*Geist*) soar.

The same could be said about Hefner's "two-natured creature." On the one

hand, Hefner is affirming how (culturally) "the human species has been unleashed within the ecosystem," but (genetically) "human survival requires this
act." So also to Lewotin, we must ask, what exactly does it mean for social interaction to proceed "with its own laws and its own nature"? How are those
"laws" and "nature" radically different from their natural environment?

Rolston claims that when it comes to God, the biologists "stutter over the
origins of the information that generates complexity and diversity."[58] But when
it comes to nature, he seems to be doing the same. Maybe he, too, is tripping
over the theological threshold.

Theological Leashing

To be sure, Rolston is more interested in arguing for a transcendent God. And
he is also savvy enough to realize that he cannot advocate for a God who is
ethereal, unattached from nature, and still have credibility in his argument
with the biologists. Notice, it is the biologists who are keeping his feet to the
ground — and to the attached body.

Hence, his first point is that "God lies in, with, and under the forces" of our
creation.[59] The biological evolutionists would not necessarily dispute this claim.
"Deity can still be sought in the origin of the ultimate units of matter," says
Wilson. "Hans Kung was right to ask atheists why there is something instead
of nothing."[60] It is just that, to the evolutionists, this God is not all that visible
— maybe not all that necessary, since the evolutionary process seems to go
along with or without God. The fact that God may not be all that visible, in
fact, may be the first datum of theological leashing. Luther called this the
"*Deus absconditus*," the "hidden God."[61]

This leads to Rolston's second point. God is more than the set-up of creation.
God is also "the lift-up that elevates the creatures along their paths of cybernetic and storied achievement. God introduces new possibility spaces all along
the way. What theologians once termed an established order of creation is
rather an order that dramatically creates, an order for creating."[62] There is no
question that theologians understand the order of creation, or perhaps better
the Creator's order, as a dynamic process by which God does God's creating.
But the question is, how does God create in the natural world? What processes
are at work in the creation? How, exactly, does God "lift-up" or "elevate the
creatures along their paths of cybernetic and storied achievement"?

The Darwinian biologists can perceive only one process at work: that of natural
selection, survival of the fittest. The human body, complete with all its genes
and culture, finds itself in a competitive environment. This is where Rolston
objects that "the natural world is being negatively judged." But maybe Rolston

was on to more than he realized, theologically, when he made that claim. Rolston wants to advocate that God is doing something truly creative in the natural world, but he wants to see that creativity in a positive light—a "lift-up." But Rolston also realizes that "the life epic is lived on in the midst of perpetual perishing, life arriving and struggling through to something higher."[63] Knowing that God is "superintend[ing] the possibilities"[64] behind the created orders — with all its perishing and struggling — may not necessarily leave room for theological comfort. Maybe it is not only the biologists that are seeing to it that "the natural world is being negatively judged." Maybe the way that God is doing God's good creating, keeping it lifted-up and elevated, is by considering it worthy of God's judgment, holding it accountable, criticizing it into being. Perhaps the biologists, with their keen sense of "survival" are aware that a critical process is going on. They can't see it — not as God, at least — but they know it's there. The drive to survive, to be judged some way other than negatively (i.e., dead), can indeed lift us up and elevate us to dimensions that we might otherwise never achieve. But that critical, creational judgment or accountability may be the second datum of theological leashing, also very much in, with, and around our bodies.

Now we arrive at Rolston's third and final point. God will lure "autonomous individuals" toward God's kind of creating through the natural orders, and still be "slipping information into the world." "God could sometimes also be in the details. The general picture is not one of divine micromanagement; rather of secular integrity and creaturely self-organizing. The extent to which divine inspiration enters into particulars might be difficult to know, especially if God operated with the resolve to maximize the creaturely autonomy, to prompt rather than to command."[65] This point is consistent with Rolston's humanist argument, and is in fact the culmination of where Rolston has been wanting to lead us. When all is finally said and done, the human beings must themselves take up the ownership of their destiny. There is the teleology in God's lure, the occasional (though undefined, at least naturally) means by which God can "sometimes" slip information into our world, but ultimately we "autonomous individuals" must be the ones left to lead our origin and destiny to its fruition.

Of course, among the main challenges for the human species is how it will deal with its own "ambiguity."[66] This purports to Rolston's basic understanding of the function of religion: "to deal with many aspects of human nature that need to be curbed if optimal social cooperation is to be achieved."[67] And what specifically needs to be "curbed"? Rolston answers, "selfishness, pride, greed, dishonesty, covetousness, anger, jealousy, sloth—aspects of human nature that are not genetically specific but are ubiquitous problems of *Homo sapiens*. These problems indisputably have some roots in our genetic past, but these shortcomings are common to all flesh. The religions that have stood the test of time

12

have unanimously taught that humans must discipline and inhibit many tendencies in human nature.... Values — now valuable answers — are getting shared again, rather than being something selfishly defended."[68]

As far as humanist arguments go, Rolston's is just as noble and inviting as any other. That the human being is in a struggle for its own survival, even with those "ubiquitous problems" that are so deeply in our human nature, and that we do well to "curb" them, is readily affirmed by many, including the biologists in their educational approaches to make us aware of our human selfishness. And should we not work toward that goal? Absolutely. In fact, it may be the best option available to us apart from faith. Rolston's project is ambitious, to be sure, but also one that is worthy of our applause.

What is problematic with Rolston's point, however, is that it assumes that we are, in fact, autonomous, independent, living by our own laws. Does the natural environment allow for such, or is nature perpetually calling us to *its* laws, whereby we perpetually and inevitably find that we cannot seem to get very far from the "clumsy, wasteful, blundering, low, and horribly cruel" evolutionary environment (Darwin), maybe also our bodies.[69] This does not negate that what we do, also with our bodies, is all important. But it does mean, as I indicated earlier, that not only our genes come under scrutiny, but all our bodily acts, even our culture.

St. Paul's complaint was that no matter how much we may seek to use our bodies for good, we are humbled by our own propensity toward evil. Not even with the best resources that God had slipped into the world could he find a way to escape his own "body of death" (*somatos tou thanatou*, Romans 7:24). There is no escape from the striving, the struggle, the perpetual and inevitable failures, but also the accountability. That is the third datum of our theological leashing. The biological evolutionists, for all their pessimism of selfish survivalism in the body, may actually have a better handle on that theological leashing, even though they could never define it as theological. Nonetheless, it preferable, if for no other reason, to set the stage for any new leashing that can come, also for our bodies.

A New Leash on Life

To be sure, the theological leashing we have described thus far is hardly optimistic. The Greek world had the seeming advantage of escaping the entrapment, but at the expense of leaving the body behind. The Judeo-Christian faith is not so ethereal. The question is how to hold on to the "paradox" of a sinful body while also at the same time claiming that the body itself is redeemed.[70]

The real truth about the survival of the human body is that no body has survived the accountability of nature's critique — not even Jesus' body. The New Testament, therefore, does not endorse any set of "ascetic rules for the body" as being finally effectual; but it *does* advocate "the reconciliation effected in the crucifixion of Christ's body of flesh' [*to somati tes sarkos autou*, Col. 1:22]."[71] While it is true that we are unable to escape the (theological) leashing of nature, what is *new* is that Jesus the Christ himself became "leashed" with our nature. The results were that He shared completely in our death (*contra* docetism). This, too, was under the divine microscope. But what is distinctive here is not some new "information" that God had slipped into the world, but a new being, a new body, God generating Godself in the flesh (*sarx egeneto*, John 1:14).

The mystery of the atonement is that Jesus' flesh shares our own; but we, in the happy exchange, we get to share his flesh as our own. Nowhere is this more evident than in Jesus' invitation to share *his body*, even eat *his flesh*, than within the context of the Eucharist (*Touto mou estin to soma [to huper humon]* 1 Cor. 11:24; Mark 14:22, Matt. 26:26; Luke 22:19; *trogon mou ten sarka*, John 6:54). There is no separation of this event from the context of the event that would take place in the death of Jesus on the cross. There is this positive symbiosis that takes place in that event, linking our identity (even our bodily identity) with that of Jesus. Hence St. Paul can exclaim, "I have been crucified with Christ; and it is no longer I who live, but it is Christ who lives in me. And the life I now live in the flesh [*nun zo en sarki*] I live by faith in the Son of God, who loved me and gave himself for me" (Gal. 2:19-20). Note: I "live (*zo*)," not simply I "survive" (biologically, *bios*).

The *new* leashing that takes place, therefore, is not only that Jesus "leashes" himself with our nature, but that we, in turn, become "leashed" to Jesus, even in our bodies. There are several references to "body" in the Pauline corpus that underscore this new leashing: the body redeemed, as we have seen above in Galatians, but also the body in its sexuality in 1 Corinthians 6:13-20; the (ecclesiastical) body of Christ, in several places in Paul's correspondence; and hope of the resurrection of the body in I Corinthians 15, the basis also of our creedal acclamation, *carnis resurrectionem*. All of these underscore the nature of our new leashing, already by faith in the context of our current nature. But it is a "leashing" with Christ: "you are not your own" (1 Cor. 6:20). Through the new leashing, Christ is our owner; but that is all counted joy because of the way He leashes us into forgiveness, freedom, wholeness.

There is a line that Robin Williams cites in the film, *Bicentennial Man*. Here Williams plays the role of a futuristic robot seeking to become totally human, eventually turning in all his robotic components for bodily organs. In his journey, he asks the question, "How does one obtain freedom? One has studied

14

your history. Terrible wars have been fought where many have died for one idea: freedom. And it seems that something that means so much to so many people would be worth having."

The joy of faith is that under this new ownership, this new leashing, there is "freedom" from the only trajectory available to us in our natural determinism. There is no *Geist* of our own that can adequately capture it. It is ours only by faith, through the working of the Holy Spirit (*der Heilige Geist*), in the promising gospel of Christ's new leashing.[72]

ENDNOTES

[1]   Jack A. Hobbs and Robert L. Duncan, *Arts, Ideas and Civilization*, Second Edition (Englewood Cliffs, N.J: Prentice Hall., 1992) and William Fleming, *Arts and Ideas*, Ninth Edition (Fort Worth: Harcourt Brace College Publishers, 1995).
[2]   Michael Ruse, *Taking Darwin Seriously: A Naturalistic Approach to Philosophy* (Oxford: Basil Blackwell Inc., 1986), 7, 123. Cf. also Leonel L. Mitchell, *The Meaning of Ritual* (New York: Paulist Press, 1977), 1-2.
[3]   Ruse, *Taking Darwin Seriously*, 123.
[4]   Richard Dawkins, *The Selfish Gene*, New Edition (Oxford: Oxford University Press, 1989), 2.
[5]   Holmes Rolston, III, *Genes, Genesis and God: Values and the Origins in Natural and Human History* (Cambridge: Cambridge University Press, 1999), 83,
[6]   John Rawls, *A Theory of Justice* (Cambridge, Mass.: Harvard University Press, 1971) and Robert Nozick, *Anarchy, State, and Utopia* (New York: Basic Books, Inc., 1974). Cf. also Edward O. Wilson, *On Human Nature* (Cambridge, Mass.: Harvard University Press, 1978), 5-6. Wilson criticizes Rawls and Nozick for not really getting beyond "human emotional responses," which are themselves "programmed to a substantial degree by natural selection." Nevertheless, Wilson's critique does not discount that Rawls and Nozick were essentially on target, even if not exploring the biological roots of their theories.
[7]   Reinhold Neibuhr, *Moral Man and Immoral Society*, (New York: Charles Scribner's Sons, 1960), 1. First published in 1932.
[8]   See Ruse, who depicts his own trials with Creationists, but also speaks highly in this regard, in *Taking Darwin Seriously*, xi-xii; also Richard Dawkins, *River Out of Eden: A Darwinian View of Life* (New York: Basic Books, 1995), 59. I concur with the point made by Steve Kuhl, "Darwin's Dangerous Idea. . . and St. Paul's: God, Humanity, Responsibility, Meaning in the Light of Evolutionary Findings," in *Creation and Evolution*: Proceedings of the ITEST Workshop, October 1997 (St. Louis: ITEST Faith/Science Press, 1998), 78, that the battle has already been won, and by the biological evolutionists.
[9]   Cf. Philip Clayton, "Biology meets theology," *Christian Century* (January 19, 2000):61-64.
[10]   Leading quote by Arthur Peacocke, "Biological Evolution — A Positive Theological Appraisal," in *Evolutionary and Molecular Biology: Scientific Perspectives on Divine Action*, edited by Robert John Russell, William B. Stoeger, S.J., and Francisco J. Ayala (Berkeley, CA: Center for Theology and the Natural Sciences, 1998), 357.

[11] Cf. Dr. Francis Collins, "The Human Genome and the Future of Medicine," public lecture at Georgetown University <www.ncbi.nim.nih.gov/genome/seq>.

[12] Kevin Powell, "A Basic Guide: Facts and Issues," in *Genetic Testing & Screening: Critical Engagement at the Intersection of Faith and Science* (Minneapolis: Kirk House Publishers, ELCA, 1998), 17; Dorothy Nelkin and M. Susan Lindee, *The DNA Mystique: The Gene as Cultural Icon* (New York: W. H. Freeman, 1995), 39; Ted F. Peters, "Why Genes and Theology?" *dialog* Vol. 33, No. 1 (Winter 1994): 2.

[13] Richard Lewotin, *It Ain't Necessarily So: The Dream of the Human Genome and Other Illusions* (New York: New York Review Books, 2000).

[14] Frederic Golden and Michael D. Lemonick, "The Race is Over," *Time* (July 3, 2000): 19.

[15] Dawkins, *The Selfish Gene*, 28, 2-3. That Dawkins work is still enduring is affirmed by Michael Ruse, *Mystery of Mysteries: Is Evolution a Social Construction?* (Cambridge, Mass.: Harvard University Press, 1999), 124, and more begrudgingly, but nonetheless evident, in Rolston, *Genes, Genesis and God*, 70.

[16] *Ibid.*, v.

[17] Rolston, *Genes, Genesis and God*, 80.

[18] *Ibid.*, 38. The italics are mine.

[19] *Ibid.*, 34, 70.

[20] *Ibid.*, 84.

[21] Rolston, *Genes, Genesis and God*, 81, 84.

[22] *Ibid.*, 300.

[23] *Ibid.*

[24] *Ibid.*, 301.

[25] *Ibid.*

[26] Dawkins, *The Selfish Gene*, 69.

[27] Remarks by the President, et al., on the Completion of the First Survey of the Entire Human Genome Project, June 26, 2000, <http://www.nhgri.nih.gov/NEWS/sequencing_consortium2.html>.

[28] Augsburg Confession, Article II, in *The Book of Concord*, edited by Robert Kolb and Timothy J. Wengert (Minneapolis: Fortress Press, 2000), 37, 39. The Latin original reads, "*secundum naturam propagati, nascantur cum peccato, hoc est, sine metu Dei, sine fiducia erga Deum et cum concupiscentia.*"

[29] Apology of the Augsburg Confession, Article II, in *The Book of Concord*, edited by Theodore G. Tappert (Philadelphia: Fortress Press, 1959), 100-101. Tappert provides a more faithful translation of the German original, "*dass sie alle von Mutterleibe an voll boeser Lueste und Neigung sind.*"

[30] Solid Declaration, Formula of Concord, Article I, Kolb and Wengert, *The Book of Concord*, 531-532. The German original for the quoted phrases are "*Natur order Wesen*" and "*eine greuliche, tiefe, unaussprechliche Verderbung.*"

[31] Dawkins, *The Selfish Gene*, 28.

[32] Dawkins, *The Selfish Gene*, 3.

[33] Theodosius Dobzhansky is from *Biological Basis of Human Freedom* (New York: Columbia University Press, 1956), 121.

[34] Rolston, *Genes, Genesis, and God*, 109.

[35] Philip Hefner, "Determinism, Freedom, and Moral Failure," *dialog* Vol. 33, No. 1 (Winter 1994): 25.

[36] Philip Hefner, "Biocultural Evolution: A Clue to the Meaning of Nature," in

16

Evolutionary and Molecular Biology, 331.
[37] *Ibid.*, 338.
[38] *Ibid.*, 335. The italics are mine.
[39] Rolston, *Genes, Genesis and God*, 136.
[40] *Ibid.*, 140.
[41] *Ibid.*
[42] *Ibid.*, 140-141.
[43] Dawkins, *The Selfish Gene*, 199.
[44] Rolston, *Genes, Genesis and God*, 146.
[45] Charles J. Lumsden and Edward O. Wilson, *Genes, Mind, and Culture: The Coevolutionary Process* (Cambridge, Mass.: Harvard University Press, 1981), 7, 368, 370.
[46] Rolston, Genes, *Genesis and God*, 126.
[47] Ruse, *Taking Darwin Seriously*, 126-147.
[48] Edward O. Wilson, *On Human Nature* (Cambridge, Mass.: Harvard University Press, 1978), 167.
[49] *Ibid.*, 149.
[50] *Ibid.* 1.
[51]. Dawkins, *The Selfish Gene*, 234-266; Ruse, *Taking Darwin Seriously*, 126.
[52] Richard Lewotin, *Biology as Ideology: The Doctrine of DNA* (New York: HarperCollins, 1991), 123.
[53] Hefner, "Biocultural Evolution," 331.
[54] *Ibid.*, 112.
[55] *Ibid.*, 141.
[56] *Ibid.*, 147-148.
[57] Rolston, *Genes, Genesis and God*, 124.
[58] *Ibid.*, 368.
[59] *Ibid.*, 364.
[60] Wilson, *On Human Nature*, 1.
[61] *LW* 33, 139. The concept of the "hidden God" is traced throughout Luther's theology by Walther von Lowenlich, *Luther's Theology of the Cross*, translated by Herbert J. A. Bouman (Minneapolis: Augsburg Publishing House, 1976), 27-49.
[62] Rolston, *Genes, Genesis and God*, 364-365.
[63] *Ibid.*, 362.
[64] *Ibid.*, 364.
[65] *Ibid.*, 367.
[66] *Ibid.*, 302.
[67] *Ibid.*, 333.
[68] *Ibid.*
[69] *Ibid.*, 27.
[70] S.V. McCausland, "Body," in *The Interpreter's Dictionary of the Bible*, Vol. 1, (Nashville: Abingdon Press, 1962), 452.
[71] R. Jewett, "Body," in *The Interpreter's Dictionary of the Bible*, Supplementary Volume, (Nashville: Abingdon Press, 1976), 118.
[72] Small Catechism, Kolb and Wengert, *Book of Concord*, 355.

Theological Meaning in Genetic Research and Evolutionary Theory

Dr. Carolyn Schneider teaches theology courses at Texas Lutheran University in Sequin, Texas. She specializes in courses related to the history of Christianity and Christian thought. She earned her BA in history from Concordia College, Bronxville, NY in 1985, her MDiv from the Lutheran School of Theology at Chicago in 1992 and her PhD from Princeton Theological Seminary in 1999. Her dissertation topic was "The Connection between Christ and Christians in Athanasius and Luther."

Dr. Schneider was born and grew up attending international schools in the Philippines, where her father was a pastor and seminary professor for the Lutheran Church in the Philippines. She served as the pastor of Atonement Lutheran Church in Staten Island, NY from 1996-1998. She is on the Board of Directors of "Crossings, Inc.," an organization devoted to bringing the Gospel as told in the weekly lectionary readings into conversation with what is happening in the world, both in individual lives and on a broader scale.

Introduction

In light of our theme for this conference, I have been asked to examine the new things that the discipline of biology is teaching us, especially through the Human Genome Project, and to run these insights through the classical loci of Christian theology to discern their theological meaning. I was asked to leave questions of ethics outside of my limits (which was not so easy). I want to make some acknowledgments before I begin. I am not a biologist. I am a theologian specializing in the history of doctrine. Therefore, I am very grateful to be on a faculty with helpful colleagues in the biology department. Mark Gustafson and Robert Jonas were especially generous with their help when I asked for it, explaining basic things to me and pointing to further resources.

What are we learning from the Human Genome Project? In many ways, what scientists have learned so far has more to do with details than with new theoretical constructs. They are learning about particular genes, gaining the ability to locate them and to discern their functions. The Human Genome Project is reinforcing existing scientific theories and providing tools for researchers to work within those paradigms. The real challenge is not to biology, but to other disciplines, such as theology, to make sense of those scientific views of humanity that are now supported with an immense amount of useful data.

This is rather humbling. First of all, it means that the conversation we are having here is not absolutely avant garde. We are really talking about ideas that have been around for quite some time. But Garrison Keillor told a story once on *Prairie Home Companion* that I think is apropos. He was talking about a town hall meeting held one night in Lake Woebegon, Minnesota. There was only one issue on the table and everything that could have been said about it was said in the first ten minutes. But it wasn't until two hours later that it had been said *by everyone*. Only then could Mayor Eloise Krepsbach adjourn the meeting. The basic issue of what it means to be human is on the table here, as it has been on many tables before, and even on this table on prior occasions. Even if one or several other people have said brilliant, thoughtful and accurate things about it, this conversation is not over until everyone has joined it. It is not the kind of conversation that can be had by a panel of experts once and for all, and this is precisely because of what it means to be human.

One of the biology textbooks to which I referred, listed the following as characteristic of and unique to humans:[1]

1) They can walk upright.
2) They have stereoscopic color vision.
3) They have hands with opposable thumbs.
4) They have consciousness.
5) They have speech and language.
6) They have culture.

These are obviously arranged in the order in which they evolved in the genus *Homo* and the species *Homo sapiens.* I will be concerned mainly with the last three characteristics, although I also want to add one more from my colleague Robert Jonas: Human beings can breed with each other to produce fertile offspring. Human sexuality is a major question in the complex of questions regarding what it means to be human, especially when the practical implications of genetic research are considered.

In my naiveté, I pointed out to Dr. Jonas that these characteristics are not true of every human in reality, though they may be in theory. I wish to revisit that naiveté because it is precisely these details that trouble people about the Human Genome Project and the scientific taxonomies that underlie it. It is not insignificant that not everyone can walk upright; not everyone can see in color; not everyone has hands; not everyone has a consciousness that is functional enough for them to live safely without the special care of others; not everyone can talk; and some have great difficulty living in a society. Furthermore, not every human couple is able to produce offspring. Yet, it is repulsive to most of us to say that these people are not fully human.

Laying out a normative humanity, or a normative genome for that matter, is deeply troubling to people. One of the most frequently asked questions on the website for the Human Genome Project is: "Whose genome is being sequenced in the Human Genome Project?"[2] There is fear that what has happened in the past may be repeated, and the genome of a healthy white male will be held up as *the* human genome against which all others will be measured. The website assures us that women's blood cells are also being used. I found out from the *New York Times* that Celera has included the cells of people of both Asian and African descent as well.[3] This deep suspicion of defining a normative humanity increases the further one goes beyond North America and Europe. This is especially obvious in the responses of church bodies to genetic research. For example, J. Robert Nelson has summarized the statements on genetics by various denominations, by the National Council of the Churches of Christ in the U.S.A., and by the World Council of Churches. The statement by the National Council of the Churches of Christ in the U.S.A. is largely favorable in its judgment. As long as research does not violate "the sanctity of human life," the National Council sees it opening "awesome possibilities ... to the human race for joining in the evolutionary process, using still unsuspected ways of modifying physical and psychological properties over coming generations and centuries."[4] The World Council of Churches, on the other hand, lists eleven practical recommendations for its member churches. All eleven of them contain warnings about genetic research and urge that it be leashed in various ways to prevent "unrestrained exploitation."[5] Who is going to define what a proper human is? In his African American systematic theology entitled, *We Have Been Believers,* James Evans notes that for peoples who have been told for a long time that they are sub-human, the question of anthropology, and theological anthropology in particular, is not an abstract one, but is a matter of life and death, and has been the source of deep reflection. Evans gives excellent summaries of these reflections, and in my reflections, I will include these as well as the thoughts of Martin Luther King, Jr. Another theologian on whom I will lean heavily was also of African descent, namely, Athanasius of Alexandria, Egypt.

The theological loci that will frame my remarks are as follows:
1) Creation, focusing on human creatures
2) Evil
3) Salvation
4) The sacrament of the Lord's Supper
5) The new creation

This is obviously not a complete list of all possible loci, but these topics seemed to me to be the first points of connection to the issues raised by genetic research.

II. Creation

Part A: Human Bodies in the Image of God

In his remarks at a symposium on genetics held at Texas Lutheran University in 1996, Maynard Olson, professor of molecular biotechnology at the University of Washington, said that the big revolution in thought brought about by Watson and Crick's model of the double helix in 1953 is the idea that genetic information is digital. The Human Genome Project, then, is simply the printing out of these base numbers.[6] Holmes Rolston highlights one implication of the observation that DNA is not substance or matter but information: With genes, life and information came into the world together.[7] Rolston insists that this information encodes what he calls a "pro-life principle."[8] He refers here to all life, not merely to human life. One can say that all life is valued because the DNA common to all living things carries a basic message, or even a command: Duplicate and divide, in other words, multiply and fill the earth.

Paul Nancarrow has found a biblical equivalent to this kind of information in the concept of wisdom.[9] After supporting the observation of mathematician Rudy Rucker that in postmodernity "'reality is a pattern of information,'"[10] Nancarrow shows how this plays out genetically. He writes,

> Some gene sites along the DNA chain, as is well known, provide the coded information for the production of proteins that are the necessary building blocks of living tissue. These genes function as data, as structural patterns of differences that yield a given deter-

minate content. The DNA molecule has other gene sites that do not themselves code for proteins, however, but instead regulate how the protein-coded genes behave. These genes act, in effect, as rules for the activation of other genes: they serve as algorithms for the transformation of the genetic data.[11]

The figure of Wisdom, Nancarrow continues, functions like an algorithm in creation, especially as described in Proverbs 8:22-36 and Wisdom 7:15-8:1.

The role of Wisdom has been debated at various points in the history of Christianity. More recent debates concern the use of Wisdom as a feminine metaphor for God, but there were ancient debates as well, not the least of which was the one between the Arians and Athanasius. This debate concerned precisely the role of Wisdom in creation as described in Proverbs 8, particularly verse 22, where Wisdom says, "The Lord created me at the beginning of his work, the first of his acts of long ago.[12] The verses following this one describe the subsequent creative acts in which Wisdom was active with the Lord. From our perspective, there was significant agreement between the Arians and Athanasius because both believed that the world was created by God and that Wisdom was from God and in creatures, guiding their development and setting their limits. However, the Arians understood this creative Wisdom not to be divine in itself, but to be merely a gift mirroring God for the sake of creation. Athanasius, in contrast, argued that this creative Wisdom was of the very essence of God, so that all creatures participated in their own way in God. (For Athanasius, by the way, this was not limited to living creatures.) What made creatures different from God for Athanasius was that they were receptors of Wisdom rather than essentially generative of Wisdom.[13] Athanasius saw creaturely participation in God as a gift of grace. Arius considered it blasphemy to draw God so closely into creation; for Arius, if God were to touch creatures directly, they would be destroyed by God's holiness. After a hard and prolonged struggle, the Church went with Athanasius on this.

But how did Athanasius reconcile the words, "The Lord created me" in Wisdom's mouth, with Wisdom's essential divinity? By a circuitous route, a way that could only pass through Jesus Christ. According to Athanasius, Proverbs 8:22 was visionary poetry trying to articulate the intuition that God's eternal Wisdom would fashion for itself a created form. In other words, for Athanasius, Proverbs 8:22 referred to Wisdom's incarnation in Jesus. But the person of Jesus Christ was clearly created in time and was not present "in the beginning." Athanasius explains that by saying that human participation in Wisdom from the beginning was also a proleptic participation in Jesus because the incarnation was God's purpose for humanity from the beginning.

This intricate line of argument is smoothed out when Athanasius turns from the language of Wisdom, which was chosen by the Arians, to the language of Word, which was Athanasius' own choice. His primary text was John 1:1-3 and 14: "In the beginning was the Word, and the Word was with God, and the Word was God. He was in the beginning with God. All things came into being through him, and without him not one thing came into being.... And the Word became flesh and lived among us, and we have seen his glory, the glory as of a father's only son, full of grace and truth." Word functioned in the same way as Wisdom for Athanasius, so it relates in the same way as Wisdom to our current understanding of information. But the concept of "Word" opened up many possibilities for conversation with traditional Middle Platonism.

What Athanasius says about the connection between Christ and Christians revolves around the central concept of "participation." This is the concept that Plato uses to describe how individual, earthly, time-bound realities relate to the eternal Forms or Ideas. Briefly, for Plato, the Forms are utter reality, and tend to be abstract mathematical, moral or aesthetic concepts, such as Justice, Beauty, Wisdom, Similarity, Unity, etc. Things that exist in the less real world of the senses approach the more real world of the Forms when they are "participating" in the Forms, that is, when they are just, beautiful, wise, alike, whole, etc. Plato's student, Aristotle, rejected Plato's theory of Forms as existing outside of any particular things. Aristotle taught that the Forms are embedded in particular things, which can be grouped into species and genera according to what Forms they exhibit. Later, the Middle Platonists, synthesizing Plato, Aristotle and the Stoic philosophers united all the Forms in the Mind of the One, whom the Jewish philosopher Philo of Alexandria identified as the God of Moses. God's Mind (or Reason or Word [Logos]) contains the pattern for the world, writes Philo, and the genus for each particular thing. In the Logos, all things cohere in an orderly way and each rational thing participates in the divine Logos.[14] Elements of each of these views infuse Athanasius' use of the notion of participation, yet they are transformed Christologically.

As Athanasius sees it, it is the nature of created things to participate in external Forms because the Word of God, in whom all Forms cohere, orders all things and connects them to himself, so that they reflect the Word's unity and participate in the Word's life. The Forms of created things spring from the eternal Form, but that we are given this participation in eternal Form is always a gift of grace given to us in the realm of time; eternity is not natural to us. What the Word creates is a genus, actualized in an individual prototype. Adam is the prototype of "humanity." God made humans reflect the Word in their minds and see the Word rereflected in the rest of creation, called into being through the Word.

Charles Kannengiesser points out that in Athanasius' work, *Contra Gentes*, especially in section 2, Athanasius describes Adam and Eve in ecstatic contemplation of God with their reasonable minds, their *nous*. With the onset of sin, however, Athanasius no longer speaks of a human *nous* because humans cannot perceive spiritual things anymore; they are no longer *logikoi* (rational, "worded") since they have turned away from participation in the Logos. In the time of sin (and not before) Athanasius speaks of the human soul, the *psyche*, which is the part of us that experiences constant change and suffers because it is not always influenced by what is good.[15] E.P. Meijering calls attention to Athanasius' *Letter to Marcellinus*, in which he says that the soul has three "movements" or "functions": being reasoned, being desirous and being passionate. When the soul is functioning in the first way, Athanasius calls it a *nous*. It is only when it is not functioning in the first way that he calls it a *psyche*, a soul that has been disconnected from its Form, the Logos (Word or Reason) of God. Real humanity, for Athanasius, has something of the divine in it. It is when people lose their realness and their humanity that they lose what is divine. But this divine gift is always, emphatically, seen as a *gift*.

There is one important element that I have not yet discussed, and that is spirit, *ruach* in Hebrew, *pneuma* in Greek. For Athanasius, the activity of the Holy Spirit in creation is what enables creatures to receive and express the Word. Humans, who are made uniquely according to the Image of God, have a spirit of their own that participates in God's Spirit.[16]

Now to return to science. Has Athanasius taken us beyond any point of connection with a genetic view of the human, rooted as it is in an evolutionary understanding of human emergence? One thing that is clear from scientific research is that humanity did not descend from two individuals named Adam and Eve who lived in a state of innocence in a benign world centered around the Tigris and Euphrates Rivers. One of the things that is useful about Athanasius' view of creation by the Word is that it does not depend on this particular interpretation of the first chapters of Genesis.

For Athanasius, every genus embodies some aspect of God's Wisdom or Word. (The genus was the level at which things were truly defined in Middle Platonism.) What marked the human genus in particular was that it was made to be an embodiment of the total Wisdom/Word of God itself. Discerning what that life code is saying in the human body, therefore, is a worthy goal. One of the things we are now learning from that code is that creatures are all linked, not only socially but also compositionally. We are indeed made of earth. It is not our genes, but the sequence of our genes that distinguishes humans from other species, and even that is not so very different. Of the five pairs of chromosomes on which humans differ significantly from primates, the difference is in merely inverted or translocated gene sequences.[17] The basic information of life exhibits the same pro-life message, or the same Wisdom, in all living beings. Furthermore, when living beings die, they decompose into the same chemicals found also in things that have never been alive.

Martin Luther King, Jr., takes this thought and carries it further. This is from *The Measure of a Man*, which was written in 1959:

> Some years ago a group of chemists who had a flair for statistics decided to work out the worth of man's body in terms of the market values of that day. They got together and did a lot of work, and finally they came to this conclusion: The average man has enough fat in him to make about seven bars of soap, enough iron to make a medium-sized nail, enough sugar to fill a shaker, enough lime to whitewash a chicken coop, enough phosphorus for about 2,220 match tips, and enough magnesium for a dose of magnesia. When all of this was added up in terms of the market values of that day it came to about 98 cents.... But can we explain the whole of man in terms of 98 cents?... Can we explain the mystery of the human soul in terms of 98 cents? Oh, no. There is something within man that cannot be explained in terms of dollars and cents. There is something within man that cannot be reduced to chemical and biological terms, for man is more than a tiny vagary of whirling electrons. He is more than a wisp of smoke from a limitless smoldering. Man is a child of God.[18]

What Martin Luther King, Jr., says here squares both with Athanasius and with current biology. *Homo sapiens* is so named for its self-conscious creation of culture, with all that implies, especially language, the ability to speak words in a meaningful way so that ideas may be passed on from person to person and generation to generation. When Athanasius says that humans are all in Adam because the principles of the succession of the whole human race were in Adam,[19] or that humans are in Mary because she "is our sister,"[20] he means not only that we are in the same body but also that we are in the same spirit. These go together. For many years theologians have been banging their heads against the wall trying to understand this ancient and biblical language of being in a common body, which did not seem possible without adopting some form of Platonic metaphysics. Now biologists are handing to us on a golden platter a way to speak of common embodiment of form that can be held with all of our current intellectual integrity.

Part B: Human Persons in the Image of God

In an interview with the magazine *Science & Spirit* at the beginning of this year, British geneticist Steve Jones said that since the evolution of *Homo sapiens*, the species has undergone very little change physically. Our further evolution has all been in our consciousness. He says, "If Cro-Magnon man got onto the tube at Camden Town, you wouldn't change seats. Physically, he's identical to you and I [me]. But mentally, we're unutterably different: he himself would be terrified on the tube...."[21] What Jones is getting at is what Reinhold Niebuhr tried to capture by the term "self-transcendence." Humans have the capacity to be self-transcendent, which means that they can make themselves both subject and object. Niebuhr calls this capacity for self-transcendence "the basis of discrete individuality, for this self-consciousness involves consciousness of the world as 'the other.'"[22] There is no individuality in non-organic life, and as Niebuhr says, "In animal life it is the species rather than the individual which is really unique."[23] Holmes Rolston traces human ethics back to this ability to see oneself as if from outside and to distinguish between one's self and others. Animals do not really have ethics, he says, because they "are unaware that there are mental others, that is, other minds, who might be held responsible, to whom one might be held responsible.[24]

Ethicist Roy Enquist claims that humans interacting within these webs of relationships become persons, and it is difficult to pin personhood down biologically. This is because it is part of our subjectivity, which always remains, even when we objectify our subjectivity itself. My biology textbook agrees with the assertion worded well by Alice Hayes at last year's ITEST conference: "Science cannot answer questions like: What is a human person? Can a cell be considered a person? Does life have a meaning, and if so, what is the meaning of life? What is the value of a life? What is our purpose on earth? Why is there evil in the world? Will there be anything after this life?"[25]

African American theology has put a great deal of stress on personhood. This is partly due to traditional African anthropology, summed up as "'existence in relation'...."[26] This is the recognition that one's social and spatial environment is part of one's identity. This thought is not far from the recognition among biologists that evolution, whether of genes or memes, takes place in the interaction of organisms with their environment and the recognition that the passage from genotype to phenotype is not direct and may be influenced at many points and in many ways by environmental factors. To forcibly remove people from their land and rip them out of every social context is to warp their personhood and to disfigure one's own as well. (This is an argument that has been raised, by the way, also in regard to creating life with an unclear and insufficient social context in the laboratory.)

This total dislocation is what happened to those who were captured, enslaved, and brought to America, where the economics of slavery meant that no stable family life could be achieved. Furthermore, using evolutionary theory many understood those of African descent to be from a precursor species to *Homo sapiens*. Writing in the 19th century, W.E.B. Du Bois articulated a deep distrust of biological definitions of humanity that has endured in the African American community. In more recent years James Cone identified the main characteristic of human beings as freedom. Freedom involves fighting against whatever would hinder one from becoming what one was created to be, namely, a human person. It also involves joining with others, such as Jesus, who are suffering in the exercise of such freedom. Love and responsibility can be carried out only by those who are free persons. In conversation with Nathan Wright, Jr., James Evans writes: "Power is the animus of human existence because people need the ability to individuate — that is, to exercise freedom — and the ability to relate — that is, to exercise love."[27] The argument about whether morality is biologically determined or culturally determined really makes no difference here. What matters is that we need to be part of a moral community in order to live both as humans and as persons. It may be that, as sociobiologists suggest, morality is simply an adaptive behavior to which humans are genetically disposed, rather than a realm in which pure spirits act undetermined by physical realities. If that is so, then we are indeed wired with a Wisdom that preserves life.

I think it is significant to note here that this clarity among theologians about nature and person in mutual interaction in the human and between humans seems to have evolved at least in part under the influence of Cappadocian thought about the Triune God. The Cappadocians solidified the language of *ousia* and *hypostasis*, which had been rather fluid and conceptually fuzzy before their work. Catherine Mowry LaCugna has explained the emergence and the importance of the doctrine of the Trinity superbly in her book, *God for Us*, to which I refer now. God was not perceived as Triune prior to Jesus, and because the doctrine of the Trinity rose out of attempts to understand Jesus, perhaps it properly belongs in the locus on new creation. But I am here applying the insights gained through Christian reflection retrospectively to the doctrine of the original creation in order to understand better what it means to say that humans are made in the image of God.

The Trinitarian doctrine worked out by Gregory of Nazianzus, Gregory of Nyssa and Basil the Great was basically this: God is three persons (*hypostases*), Father, Son and Spirit. It is their specific relations toward one another that constitute them as persons. These relations point to the source of their common nature (*ousia*). I quote from LaCugna: "The three *hypostases* manifest the unknowable *ousia* of God. The basis for our knowledge of the divine *ousia* is the *hypostases*, and we know the *hypostases* through the economy of salvation: the sending of the Son and Spirit by the Father."[28] Jürgen Moltmann has filled many pages with the content of what we may learn about God from the way the persons of the Trinity interrelate. I managed to find a sentence that encapsulates this content: "The trinitarian Persons do not merely exist and live in one another; they also bring one another mutually to manifestation in the divine glory.... The Persons of the Trinity make one another shine through that glory...."[29] Human participation in the Trinity, as Athanasius points out, is in the Son by means of the Spirit. In other words, it is specifically the second person of the Trinity, the Word and Wisdom of God, who later became flesh, who identifies with us. If it were not for God the Son, there would be no economic Trinity, but only an immanent Trinity. Because it is the *Son* who makes God God toward us, we are *children* of God. It is the Spirit who allows us to know this. If human beings are in the image of God not only because they bear the Wisdom of God in their DNA but also because they are conscious and can interrelate as persons sharing a common nature, then the quality of those interrelationships should match the mutually uplifting quality of the divine interrelationships.

Genetic research has revealed very little to us about love. However, for years sociobiologists have been tracking down the evolution of altruism. Edward Wilson has found altruism to be an adaptation by which social cooperation contributes to the survival of individuals and of groups. In other words, it enhances the preservation of DNA, life's information.[30] Research has shown that when a person does something that is consistent with what a group values, the brain releases endorphins, which give that person a pleasant feeling of belonging.[31] Humans need to feel that they are approved of and accepted by an Other that is bigger than themselves and thereby be given permission to identify with this Other.

What we know about DNA now creates the possibility of expanding our sense of self-identity in wider and wider circles. Breaking down the "us-them" gaps between groups of humans and even between human and other living species will surely bring great benefits for the world. But, who, then, is the "other" who will validate our collective value? Even the most hard-nosed scientific materialists seek a positive evaluation from beyond themselves. Richard Dawkins tells a touching story about such a plea by astronomer Carl Sagan. Sagan designed a message being carried on an unmanned capsule into deep space.

> The message is adorned with the picture of the species that created it, the image of a naked man and woman.... In what is designed to be a universally understandable iconic language, the plaque records its own genesis in the third planet of a star whose coordinates in the galaxy are precisely recorded. Our credentials are further established by some iconic representations of fundamental principles of chemistry and mathematics. If the capsule is ever picked up by intelligent beings, they will credit the civilization that produced it with something more than primitive tribal superstition.[32]

No matter how much further our boundary extends, we will continue not only to need to be loved by another, but to need to know that we are loved by another. That comes with the territory of self-transcendence. As Niebuhr put it, "To understand [one's humanity] truly means to begin with a faith that [one] is understood from beyond [oneself], that [one] is known and loved...."[33]

III. Evil

Now I have arrived at the unavoidable hitch in all of this, namely, evil. As Arthur Peacocke has pointed out, one of the developments that comes along with the evolution of consciousness is the ability to feel pain and suffering.[34] Pain and suffering and their causes become a problematic complex that we call evil when beings with a central nervous system evolve into beings with a central nervous system and a sense of self-transcendent personhood.

When looked at on a purely natural level, pain and suffering are not a problem but are a necessary fact. This is most accurately stated by Richard Dawkins, who points out that the universe operates to preserve DNA and it has no sense of a moral right or wrong. Pain happens in this effort, without justice.[35] This is undeniably true. The world's environment cannot sustain everything that comes to life in it, yet every life seeks to survive and to regenerate. In order for some to survive, others have to die. Which live and which die has more to do with power or with contingent environmental factors than with justice. However, although living things that are not self-conscious do feel pain and avoid it, they are not troubled by questions of fairness, and they don't take it personally.

The first humans, having reflected on life, did take their pain and suffering personally. Neanderthal and Cro-Magnon people, for instance, buried their dead, and the graves contain not only the bodies but also flowers, tools, and weapons. The faith of our ancestors seems to have been that death could not have permanent power over a person's life. The individuals they loved would live in some form after death.

We actually do not know very much about why the human body dies. Perhaps the tools of genetic research will yield more discoveries in this area. Research by Paul Moorhead and Leonard Hayflick on mitotic cells from human embryos suggests that, even apart from any kind of attack or mutation, cells may be programmed to divide a certain number of times and then simply stop. In other words, the command to shut down may be part of the information that we carry.[36] Although American life expectancy is now slightly over three score years and ten, the natural longevity of humans appears to be six score years, 120 years.[37] Perhaps the tree of life is indeed off limits.

The inevitability of death may not call into question the belief that life per se is valuable, because life per se continues in each generation. But it does call into question the belief that my life is valuable. The life process in general values itself more than it values my life in particular. There is a flowing Absolute of which I am a part but which goes beyond me. Cloning one's unique DNA fingerprint does not address this concern. It sidesteps it, on the one hand, by ignoring environmental factors that contribute to one's person and one's health; and it postpones the concern, on the other hand, if indeed it is true that cells will not divide indefinitely.

I think Christians often tend to think that when the so-called secular aspects of life present a really hard problem, all we need to do is to introduce God into the conversation and the problem will be resolved. I submit that if we introduce God into this conversation, the problem is compounded and plunges us into the depths of theodicy, where it is dark and scary. If, as I have suggested, the Holy Spirit enables creatures to be formed by the Word and Wisdom of God, and if human beings are formed as the very Image of God itself, then the shutting down of our cells signifies the withdrawal of the Holy Spirit from us. If my life has been "hasty, brutish and short," then the question becomes even more acute. Does God really love me? Am I merely here to serve some larger purpose that I cannot discern but for which my part is to suffer until I die? This is not fair.

Reinhold Niebuhr has called this anxiety over human finitude the root of sin. I think that Judith Plaskow has rightly corrected this view. She has suggested that anxiety over human finitude is the root of sin for the powerful, but not for the weak. I would call anxiety over human finitude the root of faith for the weak. I argue that the word of finitude is meant to be understood differently by those who have much power, on the one hand, and those who have little power, on the other hand. As Niebuhr explains it, for those who have much power, the human finitude inherent in the Word of God stands as a Law, a limit to their whole lives. Anxiety over this finitude becomes sin when it becomes the will to conquer by regarding oneself or one's group as the Absolute. In his book, *Racism and the Christian Understanding of Man*, George Kelsey shows how this is the essence of racism.[38] Refusing to differentiate between their purposes and those of God (if they are theists) or those of the cosmic life force (if they are not), the powerful then proceed to structure society toward their own continuity. The resources and the laws will be skewed in their favor. This concentration of energy will weaken those whom the powerful have chosen to exclude, perhaps those who have a different set of genetic possibilities from their own. Those who have been weakened in this way will either die or be subjugated. If they rebel, they will be killed. This has happened again and again and again in human history. In this way the highest development will be accompanied by the highest sin. I find it interesting to note that, although he is speaking in a different context, Richard Dawkins writes that nature itself does not work like this to favor a part at the expense of the whole.[39]

The will thus becomes both unnatural and irrational, a-logos, as Niebuhr (and Athanasius) point out.[40]

Liberation theologians of all varieties have brought the flipside of this into focus. Those who are subjugated live as if the powerful were indeed the Absolute. The weak ones absorb the negative judgment of others or of a whole society and follow a course of self-punishment and self-destruction, ostensibly for their own good. Theology labels both of these attitudes "sin" because they are the two sides of one and the same coin, namely, idolatry.

In this context, biological determinism ceases to be neutral. To show how an overemphasis on nature as opposed to nurture actually fosters a particular political agenda, Jeremy Rifkin quotes Jonathan Beckwith, professor of microbiology and genetics at Harvard:

> The focus on genetics alone as explanatory of disease and social problems tends to direct society's attention away from other means of dealing with such problems.... Genetic explanations for intelligence, sex role differences, or aggression lead to an absolving of society of any responsibility for its inequities, thus providing support for those who have an interest in maintaining these inequities.[41]

But what are the weak to do? If they are not compliant with the will of the powerful, they will suffer for it. Here is why I say that anxiety over one's finitude is the root of faith for those who are weak: To be anxious because one's finitude calls into question the value of one's own life is to realize the possibility that one's own life might be of value. This is to begin to deny authority to those who claim that one's life is of value only so long as it serves theirs. This little faith begins to believe the first article of the Creed, the article on creation. This is the tireless work of the Holy Spirit sustaining life and making one attentive to the Word of God. It is these people who recognized Jesus not as a lawgiver but as a savior.

Those who are not in positions of power and who lose anxiety over their finitude succumb to despair. This is true not only of individuals, but also of groups. The highest suicide rates in the world are among native tribes whose land is being taken from them and whose ways of life are being threatened. In the interests of bio-diversity, a proposal has been made to preserve sperm and ova from these endangered groups.[42] But I think it would be hard to convince them (and wrong to convince ourselves) that because their genes are thereby surviving, they are thereby surviving and we need not worry about the ongoing destruction of their cultures. If their cultures are destroyed, any future fertilization of their gametes will not result in Yanomamo, BaMbuti or

Guarani people, but in people of whatever the researchers' culture is at the time.

IV. Salvation

As we have seen, Athanasius teaches that it is possible to learn to know God from created things. But he goes on to observe that humans are perverse and do not worship the God whom they may see by means of this God's creation *as* God. Instead, they glorify creatures. So, this is what God does about that, in Athanasius' words:

> [N]o longer, as in the previous ages, did God want to be known through an image and shadow of Wisdom, which was in the creatures; but He made the true Wisdom itself take flesh and become a human, and be patient under the death of the cross so that, on account of their faith in him, finally all the faithful will be able to be saved.[43]

> For He was not a human before this, but became human in order to save the human. And the Word was not flesh in the beginning, but afterward became flesh, in which He both changed the hostility toward us, according to the Apostle, and "abolished the law with its commandments and ordinances, that He might create ... one new humanity in place of the two, thus making peace, and might reconcile both groups to [the Father] in one body." (Ephesians 2:15 1-6a)[44]

It is important that the Word of God should come in a body of his own. I like the words that the Lutheran Formula of Concord uses to explain why: "for safekeeping." Because of our weakness, God put our salvation "for safekeeping into the almighty hand of our Saviour, Jesus Christ, out of which no one can pluck us (John 10:28)."[45] As Paul says in Romans 8:39: Nothing "will be able to separate us from the love of God in Christ Jesus our Lord." This phrase, "the love of God *in Christ Jesus*" is very significant. The love of God that is *in us* is ambiguous, as we have seen. Our finitude makes it unclear to us whether we as self-conscious persons are loved by God or whether it is only the living flow of our collective genes that God loves, and not even all of those.

Jesus was a human in the flesh. This means that He shared our genome. But it also means that He was a person in his own right. He lived in his own body, in his own environment, in his own time, place, family and culture. If He had been allowed to die of old age, his cells, like ours, would have shut down, but that is not what happened. To those of his own time and of any time whose anxiety over their finitude takes the form of aggregation of power, Jesus stands outside of them as an embodiment of their finitude, the law that limits them. Jesus refused to be subject to them and consequently He was killed.

Those who were pushed to the margins experienced the same Jesus in a different way. They experienced him as a person of power, but who opened that power up to people. He inspired hope in them until it appeared that his own life was going to be a dead end. It was certainly a genetic dead end. He had no children and He did not even live out the full life encoded for himself. It was clear that his person and lineage were going to be extinct, and Jesus expressed anxiety at his finitude. "My God, my God, why have you abandoned me?," He shouted. Among other things, this means, "I matter!"

After Jesus' death, those who had loved him began to express hope about their own lives. They could have explained this by saying that Jesus had provided for them a good example of faith in the face of trial, but this is not how they explained it. They said that Jesus had appeared to them, recognizably human and recognizably Jesus, though transformed in some way that made him not immediately recognized. He had told them not to be afraid. He said that He was giving them his own Spirit and his own power, which they in turn were to open up to everyone. They would reach their limit and would die, as He had, but when the whole world had reached its limit, He would be there alive beyond the limit to receive all those related to him spiritually and bodily. They were indeed of value, both as a whole and individually. The Word of God that created them outdid itself to save them.

V. The Lord's Supper

The Christian creed asserts that it is not only information that matters, but also that which is informed. DNA is valuable, but so is the person with the body that is informed by DNA. Matter matters. The basis of this claim is that by faith in Jesus, God draws humanity informed by the Word through the power of the Spirit into the personal life of the Trinity, which is unlimited in mutual praise. This process, however, refuses to be abstracted from bodies and histories. It is a story of the Incarnation. The Word that Christians as well as everyone else carry in their bodies places limits on them. Only the Word that carries people in his body has overcome these limits because in Jesus God has chosen to supersede God's own Word and do a new thing. Jesus lived under the law that limits all people, but in him it was not God's last Word.

The Lord's Supper is a very effective way to illustrate this. I think its meaning is clearest in Paul's remarks in 1 Corinthians 11:17-34. Here Paul is angry with the Corinthians for their abuse of the Lord's Supper. To show to them what the problem is, Paul recalls the words used in the ritual eating and drinking, which clearly indicate that the body of Christ with which they are incorporated by the bread and wine that they eat and drink is the one that was crucified, the one that bled and hurt and died. But the Corinthians are skipping over this body and discerning only the exalted body of Christ, Paul says. He says this to one particular faction among those into which the Corinthian Church was apparently divided. Paul is speaking to the rich. They come to church to socialize with those who have equally abundant resources, it seems, and they use the worship space as a private picnic area. Those who come to worship with no resources must remain hungry as they watch and wait for the Lord's Supper. This is the old problem of power-hoarding that has its roots in the desire to live without limits. Paul argues that if these Christians paid attention to the Christ they received in the Lord's Supper, they would see the poor in their midst, who are sharing in Christ's body more truly than the others because they, like Christ, cannot ignore their limits. Paul makes an interesting diagnosis as he considers the rich Corinthians. He says that their failure to discern the body is the reason that so many of them "are weak and ill and some have died." (1 Corinthians 11:30) In other words, he tells them that if their failure to discern the suffering body of Christ has resulted in their failure also to discern the suffering bodies of their fellow humans, then let them be forced to discern their own suffering bodies. Maybe then they will come to realize that the only way to the exalted body of Christ is through the crucified body of Christ.

Yet it is true that the Lord's Supper also carries the promise of the exalted body of Christ. Current science is showing that what it means to be human is malleable. DNA can be transferred from one body to another, even between human and non-human substances. If we properly discern the body of Christ crucified, then somatic gene therapy that is done to help the person who is receiving the therapy is an excellent thing. Yet DNA as a carrier of information appears to have a self-imposed stop sign. Christian doctrine is that the resurrected Word and Wisdom of God incarnate does not have an end. Why should this Word of God in the person of Jesus be less flexible than its more limited image in us? This would mean then, that Jesus may choose any body that He wishes as his own. It is as if Jesus were saying, "The Lord's Supper is where I am going to be alive for you after my death. I want to come to you so that you can share my life with its final sentence and with its infinite post-script. It is both to your consciousness and to your body that I want to come. So I come to you in words and in digestible bread and wine." Jesus does not replace our DNA with his now transformed genes. If we are to rise with Christ we must also first die with Christ. Yet it is the whole of each of us that will die and rise. So that we may know that Christ is with us wholly in this dying and rising, Christ comes in a way that forms our faith and mingles with the chemicals that feed our bodies.

VI. New Creation

John Habgood, a biologist and Archbishop of York of the Church of England has written this:

> One of the most striking characteristics of human life, as actually lived and experienced, is its open-endedness. To be human is to be unfinished and free. This is a theme well-explored in Christian theology. "It does not yet appear what we shall be, but we know that when He appears we shall be like him, for we shall see him as he is" (1 John 3:2).... All the different dimensions of what it is to know a human being, from knowing their DNA sequence to knowing their personality, meet in this all-encompassing relationship with God. To see them this way sets them in perspective. The peril in not seeing them this way lies in imagining that we know more than we do.[46]

I wonder if sometimes the things Christians say sound crazy because they are searching for language in which to describe the future. Teilhard de Chardin has very correctly called Christianity a religion of the future. Christian teaching claims to have something to say about what the world's future will be. Theologian Peter Scott notes that "the irreversibility of time and the temporality of the universe according to the Big Bang model" itself "invites attention to the future of nature," since it means that nature is neither "fixed by a static metaphysics nor caught up in cycles of endless return."[47] Christ himself is the picture of the future that Christians hold up. One of the things that this means, as Robert Brungs mentioned at the ITEST Conference in 1997, is that the future includes those who would be considered failures in the race for the survival of the fittest. Jesus spent a great deal of time with the sick and those who were not favored by the shapers of society. The two primary things that Jesus did with these people were to forgive their sin and to heal them. In the language of the Gospel of John, this is the result of Jesus' drawing people to himself, so that they were no longer idolatrous and could begin to experience the future. This was perceived as a threat by those in power. I think this may be because disease is partly defined socially, and to tell those who feel the stigma of the diseased that God does not regard this stigma is to challenge those who make the labels. With the advances in medical technology that genetic research has opened up for us, we will need to listen much harder to those whom society now considers intolerably diseased to hear how they themselves experience their disease.

Why did Jesus not heal everyone? Why did the healing that He did not permanently alter people and make then immortal? Maybe Jesus was not trying to initiate a divine program of eugenics with cosmic proportions. Maybe Jesus healed some to show what the future would be like for them beyond earth's final limit. In an interview with Brent Waters and Ron Cole-Turner, Francis Collins, director of the Human Genome Project, was asked whether one of the results of the project might be that parents will "be blamed if they allow a child enduring 'unnecessary' suffering to be born?" Collins answered,

> The disability community is quite concerned about this issue. For example, if I have *achondroplasia* [a birth defect resulting in dwarf-ism], and if science now has an understanding of that gene which makes it possible to identify all the fetuses that have *achondroplasia* and make sure they don't get born, does that diminish my value in the eyes of society? It's a very significant issue. At the same time, it's another one of those possible scenarios that should not lead to the sweeping statement, "and therefore we should *not* be doing this research," because then you have doomed all the people with *achondroplasia* who are looking for some potential answers to their current medical problems to a future without hope. It comes down to trying to focus on the positives of genetics *and* trying to avoid some of the negatives. When Christ healed the lame and the blind, did those who didn't get healed complain that somehow they were now being considered as less contributory to society than before? I don't think so. I think they were amazed and hopeful.[48]

VII. Conclusion

In his book, *On the New Frontiers of Genetics and Religion*, J. Robert Nelson has drawn up a helpful chart summarizing and comparing the views of those la-beled "Scientific Materialist," "Questioning Believer," and "Confirmed Believer" on various topics related to genetics. It is no surprise that scientific materialists (which by no means includes all scientists) consider irrelevant such theological loci as I have discussed today, such as the Trinity, divine creation, and the atonement. But there are points of connection and agreement between the three groups, which could be the starting points for fruitful conversation, deci-sion and action. All approve the work of the Human Genome Project and agree that genetic research should continue to be supervised by the govern-ment. All agree that DNA research points to the interrelationships of all organ-isms and that some of the consequences of this knowledge should be a strong ban on the use of genetic information for biological weapons of any sort and a strong push for equitable access to the use of genetic information for medical advances. As long as there is no discrimination, all approve of genetic testing and public screening as well as somatic gene therapy. All disapprove of eugen-ics and enhancement of traits.[49]

36

References

1.   Clinton Benjamin, Gregory Garman and James Funston, *Human Biology* (New York: McGraw-Hill Companies, Inc., 1997), 588-91.
2.   Human Genome Management Information System, "Facts about Genome Sequencing," <http:www.oml.gov/hgmis/faqtseqfacts.htTnl#whose>, 28 July 2000.
3.   J. Craig Venter, quoted in "White House Remarks on Decoding of Genome," *The New York Times*, 27 June 2000, D8.
4.   J. Robert Nelson, *On the Frontiers of Genetics and Religion* (Grand Rapids, Michigan: William B. Eerdmans Publishing Company, 1994), 177-78.
5.   *Ibid.*, 173-74.
6.   Speech by Maynard Olson at the 1996 Krost Symposium held at Texas Lutheran University in Seguin, Texas. A video of this speech is held in the archives of the Krost Center on the campus of Texas Lutheran University.
7.   Holmes Rolston III, *Genes Genesis and God: Values and Their Origins in Natural and Human History*, The Gifford Lectures, University of Edinburgh, 1997-1998 (Cambridge: Cambridge University Press, 1999), 355-59.
8.   *Ibid.*, 367.
9.   Paul S. Nancarrow, "Wisdom's Information: Rereading a Biblical Image in the Light of Some Contemporary Science and Speculation," *Zygon* 32 (March 1997).
10.   *Ibid.*, 52.
11.   *Ibid.*, 53-54.
12.   All biblical quotations are from the New Revised Standard Version.
13.   The bulk of Athanasius' second discourse against the Arians concerns Proverbs 8:22. See Philip Schaff and Henry Wace, eds., *A Select Library of Nicene and Post-Nicene Fathers of the Christian Church*, second series, vol. 4, *St. Athanasius: Select Works and Letters*, translated by John Henry Newman, revised by Archibald Robertson (Edinburgh: T&T Clark, 1991; Grand Rapids, Michigan: Wm. B. Eerdmans Publishing Company, 1991), 357-93. (Hereafter cited as NPNF.)
14.   Philo, *On the Creation*, §§16-25, in *The Works of Philo*, trans. C.D. Yonge (Peabody, Massachusetts: Hendrickson Publishers, 1993), 4-5; and *The Special Laws*, I, §§45-50, in *ibid.*, 538.
15.   Charles Kannengiesser, *Le Verbe de Dieu selon Athanase d'Alexandrie*, Jésus et Jésus-Christ 45 (Proost, France: Desclee, 1990), 124-29.
16.   Athanasius, *The Letters of Saint Athanasius concerning the Holy Spirit*, translated by C.RB. Shapland (London: The Epworth Press, 1951), 108-33.
17.   Cecie Starr and Ralph Taggart, *Biology: The Unity and Diversity of Life*, 8th edition (Belmont, California: Wadsworth Publishing Company, 1998), 211.
18.   Martin Luther King, Jr., *The Measure of a Man* (Philadelphia and Boston: Pilgrim Press, 1968), 22-24.
19.   *Discourse II against the Arians*, NPNF, 375.
20.   *Letter to Epictetus*, NPNF, 573.
21.   Steve Jones, "Updating Our Origins: Biology, Genetics and Evolution," interview by Kate Prendergast, *Science & Spirit*, January/February 2000, 26.
22.   Reinhold Niebuhr, *The Nature and Destiny of Man: A Christian Interpretation* (New York: Charles Scribner's Sons, 1949), 55.
23.   *Ibid.*
24.   Rolston, *Genes, Genesis and God*, 222.

25.   Alice Hayes, "Education in Biotechnology and in Faith/Science," in Robert Brungs and Marianne Postiglione, eds. *The Genome: Plant, Animal, Human* (St. Louis, Missouri: ITEST Faith/Science Press, 1999), 171.

26.   James Evans, *We Have Been Believers: An African-American Systematic Theology* (Minneapolis: Fortress Press, 1992), 101.

27.   *Ibid.*, 110.

28.   Catherine Mowry La Cugna, *God for Us: The Trinity and Christian Life* (San Francisco: HarperSanFrancisco, a Division of Harpercollins Publishers, 1973), 68.

29.   Jürgen Moltmann, *The Trinity and the Kingdom: The Doctrine of God*, translated by Margaret Kohl (San Francisco: Harper & Row, Publishers, 1981), 176.

30.   Edward O. Wilson, *On Human Nature* (Cambridge, Massachusetts and London, England: Harvard University Press, 1978), 153-59.

31.   Camilo Cela-Conde and Gisele Marty, "Beyond Biological Evolution: Mind, Morals, and Culture," in Robert John Russell, William Stoeger and Francisco Ayala, eds., *Evolutionary and Molecular Biology: Scientific Perspectives on Divine Action* (Vatican City State: Vatican Observatory Publications, 1998; Berkeley, California: Center for Theology and the Natural Sciences, 1998), 445-62.

32.   Richard Dawkins, *River out of Eden: A Darwinian View of Life*, Science Masters (New York: Basic Books, a Division of HarperCollins Publishers, 1995), 160-61.

33.   Niebuhr, *Nature and Destiny*, 15.

34.   Arthur Peacocke, "Biological Evolution - A Positive Theological Appraisal," in Russell et al., eds., *Evolutionary and Molecular Biology*, 357-76.

35.   Dawkins, *River out of Eden*, 131-33.

36.   Starr and Taggart, *Biology*, 758.

37.   Benjamin, et al., *Human Biology*, 97.

38.   Evans, *We Have Been Believers*, 104-107.

39.   Dawkins, *River out of Eden*, 127.

40.   Niebuhr, *Nature and Destiny*, 115.

41.   Jeremy Rifkin, *The Biotech Century* (New York: Jeremy P. Tarcher/Putnam, a member of Penguin Putnam Inc.,1998), 158.

42.   H. Tristram Engelhardt, Jr., "Persons and Humans: Refashioning Ourselves in a Better Image and Likeness," *Zygon* 19 (September 1984): 288.

43.   My translation, from *Discourse II against the Arians*. See also NPNF, 392.

44.   My translation from *In Illud Omnia*. See also NPNF, 88.

45.   Formula of Concord, Solid Declaration, in Theodore Tappert, ed. *The Book of Concord* (Philadelphia: Fortress Press, 1959), 624.

46.   John S. Habgood, quoted in Nelson, *On the New Frontiers of Genetics and Religion*, 93-94.

47.   Peter Scott, "The Technological Factor: Redemption Nature, and the Image of God," *Zygon* 35 (June 2000): 382.

48.   Francis Collins, "Reading the Book of Life: Francis Collins and the Human Genome Project," interview by Brent Waters and Ron Cole-Turner, *Science & Spirit* (January/February 2000): 43.

49.   Nelson, *On the New Frontiers of Genetics and Religion*, 195-98.

INTERPRETING NATURE AND SCRIPTURE
A NEW PROPOSAL FOR THEIR INTERACTION

Jitse M. van der Meer was born in 1947 in The Netherlands. Nicolaas Rupke, now a professor in the history of science at the University of Göttingen, sparked his interest in religion and science by acquainting him with the controversies in creation and evolution. His interest in the philosophy of science sharpened during his undergraduate study in biology at the State University of Groningen (1966-69). Ludwig von Bertalanffy's *Die Philosophie des Lebendigen* represented another pivotal experience, confirming a suspicion that he was a philosopher/biologist. The mysteries of embryonic development reported by von Bertalanffy led him into graduate studies at the State University of Utrecht under Christiaan Raven and at The Hubrecht Laboratory under Pieter Nieuwkoop, then performing experiments that led to the discovery of an embryonic control centre known as the *Nieuwkoop Centre*. He did PhD work (1978) under Sander (Freiburg i. Br.) and Denucé and postdoctoral work in developmental biology at the University of Heidelberg (1978-79) and Purdue (1979-82).

Introduction

Almost half a century ago, Bernard Ramm (1954) in his *The Christian View of Science and Scripture* gave a systematic treatment of the questions raised by science for the interpretation of Scripture. They included the traditional questions about the creation narratives, the story of Noah's flood, reports of miracles etc. There has been no follow up. I think this is due mainly to the view that the religious language of the Bible does not refer to nature and history in a rational manner. Ramm's questions may have been seen as assuming those kinds of reference and perhaps that is why his questions were considered irrelevant.

Today the split between the sensible and the supersensible, between religion as emotion and science as knowledge, between knowledge and faith is being challenged. Reliable knowledge has more dimensions than scientifically controlled experience and reason. This has opened the door for science to raise once again questions for the interpretation of Bible texts. Yet little attention is given to the meaning of Scripture for the interpretation of nature in science even though this is the other side of the coin. In relating what we understand of Scripture and nature we continue to suffer from the errors of biblicism on the one hand and liberal theology on the other. The challenge for biblical hermeneutics as I see it is to chart strategies for taking the Bible into account that do not suffer from these errors, but instead respect the integrity both of the interpretation of Scripture and of nature. One such strategy consists in acknowledging that interpretation is as much involved in the study of nature both pre-scientific and scientific as it is in the study of Scripture. This approach was proposed by Vern Poythress (1988) in his *Science and Hermeneutics*. He concludes that the interpretation of the Bible must include a critique of the background beliefs of both theology and science. This approach has not been implemented probably because it requires an understanding of the role of background beliefs in science and theology. Since this understanding has grown recently (van der Meer, 1996, 1999a, b, Brooke, Osler and van der Meer, 2001), Poythress' proposal can be further developed. This contribution is a small step in that direction.

The human body is an ideal meeting place for theology and science because it displays the fullest spectrum of the manifold wisdom of God. If anywhere, it is in the study of the human body that "Science can purify religion from error and superstition" and "religion can purify science from idolatry and false absolutes...." (John Paul II, 1988: M13). My objective is to offer a hermeneutical procedure for the operation of these two types of purification by focussing on questions about body, soul, and resurrection. This procedure is intended to embody the vision that "Only a dynamic relationship between theology and science can reveal those limits which support the integrity of either discipline, so that theology does not profess a pseudo-science and science does not become an unconscious theology." (John Paul II, 1988: M14).

A clarification of terms is called for beginning with the terms nature' and
 science.' I use the term interpretation of nature' in the broadest possible
sense including the interpretation of natural phenomena in science unless
otherwise indicated. The pre-scientific and scientific interpretation of nature
are often difficult to distinguish because science is a systematic form of pre-
scientific problem solving. The focus of this paper is on the engagement of the
interpretation of nature in science with the interpretation of Scripture in theology. Also, in using the terms religion' and theology,' I have already introduced much material for reflection. However, I have chosen to focus neither
on religion nor on theology, but on the source of both, that is the Scriptures.
The Bible claims to be a spiritual and moral guide in life. For centuries, Christians have participated in the life of scholarship, and for centuries they have
assumed that the Bible is relevant for understanding both God and nature.
The question is: how can the Bible be such a guide in a culture shaped by science and technology as we know it? How can it be such a guide in a culture
that has gone through higher criticism' as well as through biblicism? A focus
on the Scriptures is warranted by the development of new doctrine informed
by contemporary interpretations of nature and by the questions these new doctrines raise for the interpretation of the Scriptures. Let me give some examples
which concern the human body.

The first example originates in process theology and concerns *the illnesses of
body* (and spirit). According to process philosophy the universe is eternal and
its constituents down to elementary particles have the ability of perception
however small. God providentially guides this universe toward the greatest possible realizable value, not by determining or coercing creatures through efficient causality, but by luring' them with the persuasive power of the good.
This approach does not ask what can be said exegetically about God's power
in nature. This is not a theoretical question. In the Bible God's power over nature warrants the trust people have in Him. Christians trust God with their
own life in the body as well as their expectation of a life after the body has
died on the conviction that someone with the power to create this cosmos and
heal sicknesses has the power to forgive sin. But how does one do pastoral
work in the cancer ward when God is seen as luring cancer cells with the persuasive power of the good, however powerful a lure God may present to the
natural processes in this world? In sum, there are important pastoral reasons
for raising exegetical questions about God's power in nature, specifically in the
human body.

My second example raises the question whether the *redemption of the human body*
(and spirit) might be understood in terms of continuous evolutionary progress
rather than a catastrophic discontinuity at the end of time. The evolutionary
process by which God is taken to create the cosmos has been interpreted as
grace (Gregersen, 2002). In this interpretation, grace refers to evolutionary

progress towards a world without natural and moral evil. That is, nature' is considered as grace.' The view of grace as evolutionary creation is a theological proposal inspired by evolutionary biology. How does this view engage the interpretation of Scripture? Several questions could be raised. If the history of Israel can be redemptive, and if this redemptive history can be discerned in an hermeneutical procedure called redemptive-historical analysis, could an evolutionary history of nature including the human body be redemptive in that same sense? Could there be a redemptive history of nature? That is, could evolution as process be interpreted that way? What kind of hermeneutical procedure might this suggest? How would it be evaluated? The classical Christian understanding of providence as God acting in both nature and history means that grace can be both natural and supernatural. Does this hold when natural grace is interpreted in terms of the neo-Darwinian theory of evolution? Can God be a Darwinian? What are the hermeneutical challenges implied in a move from a discontinuous to a continuous eschatology?

My final example of the development of new doctrine that is informed by science and raises questions about the interpretation of Scripture is about *the resurrection of the human body*. Physicalism is the view that there is no other matter in the world than physical matter. Emergent physicalism is the view that mental activity and religious experience have emerged from physical matter. Theologically, this means that between this life and the next people may not exist except in the form of dust (Cooper, 1989, Anderson, 1998, Murphy, 1998: 23). One challenge for biblical hermeneutics is whether it can discriminate between monistic and dualistic anthropologies. The same texts have been interpreted monistically (Green, 1998) and dualistically (Cooper, 1989). Is biblical hermeneutics capable of providing boundaries for the interpretation of these passages? Further, in traditional Christian belief, the world to come is characterized by a life as recreated persons in a new creation. In process theology this is transformed to life' as a memory in the mind of God. Can biblical hermeneutics narrow down the options?

Clearly, these are questions that require reflection on the interpretation of Scripture as well as of nature specifically as offered in science, and on interaction between the two. I will suggest that both interpretations proceed stepwise through a hierarchy of levels with each lower level being a prerequisite for the existence of the next higher level. Due to the technical nature of the lower levels of interpretation, there may not be much reason for interaction between the interpretation of Scripture and nature although in the case of science this remains to be seen in light of what the hermeneutical philosophy of science has argued is the constituting effect of conceptions of reality on experimentation and instrumentation. However, at the higher levels the interpretation of both Scripture and nature has links with the cultural and religious context. Each interpretative hierarchy will be illustrated with a brief case study.

In the first case study we will see how the Bible influenced the interpretation of nature via the religious world view it created in the geneticist Theodosius Dobzhansky. The second case study focuses on the theologian Rudolf Bultmann and shows that scientific naturalism as a worldview has shaped his interpretation of Bible passages. In my proposal, a person's worldview links the interpretation of nature and Scripture. On each side, worldview has potential effects down the levels of interpretation. Conversely, each hierarchy of interpretation has bottom up effects that can cross over to the other hierarchy via the world view level that links the two hierarchies.

BUILDING BRIDGES FROM THE SIDE OF SCIENCE: THEODOSIUS DOBZHANSKY

Let me begin with a case study of the role of religious belief in biology. The Russian American geneticist Theodosius Dobzhansky was born in 1900 and moved to the U.S.A. at 27. That is, he experienced the Communist Revolution during his formative years and this had a psychological and spiritual impact. Ruse (1996) has argued this impact entered his science in two forms. First, he came to see the relationship between the individual and society as one of conflict and this was translated into a view of the relationship between organism and environment. Second, as a Russian Orthodox Christian he struggled with the evil and suffering brought upon family and friends by the Russian Revolution. "The urgency of finding a meaning of life grew in the bloody tumult of the Russian Revolution, when life became most insecure and its sense least intelligible." (Dobzhansky, 1967). The justification of God in the face of evil and the question of freedom became enduring religious quests for Dobzhansky who suffered from survivor's guilt.

In the United States he became famous for his work on the genetics of microevolution and is known as one of the so-called architects of the synthesis between Darwinian evolution and the role of mutation. He believed that:

> "evolution, like everything in the world, is a manifestation of God's activity." "I see no escape from thinking that God acts not in fits of miraculous interventions, but in all significant and insignificant spectacular and humdrum events. Pantheism, you may say? I do not think so, but if so then there is this much truth in pantheism" (Letter to J. Greene, November 23, 1961; Dobzhansky papers).

Further:

> "Christianity is basically evolutionistic. It affirms that the meaning of history lies in the progression from Creation, through Redemption, to the City of God" (Dobzhansky, 1967: 112). "Evolution (cosmic and

biological and human) is going towards something, we hope some city of God" (letter to J. Greene, November 23, 1961; Dobzhansky papers).

The meaning of evil was that it is a condition for progress towards organisms with the greatest freedom and adaptability. Evil and biological progress were two sides of the same coin.

"On the human level, freedom necessarily entails the ability to do evil as well as good. If we can do only the good, or act in only one way, we are not free. We are slaves of necessity. The evolution of the universe must be conceived as having been in some sense a struggle for a gradual emergence of freedom." (Dobzhansky, 1967: 120).

One could call this a free process defense of natural evil along the line of what is known as the free will defense of moral evil (Polkinghorne, 1989: 66-67; 1994: 83).

Levels of Interpretation of Nature in Dobzhansky

The interpretation of natural phenomena in science involves a number of levels of generality. In order of increasing generality they include the collection of data, the construction of theories both at low, intermediate and high levels of generality, the guidance by a research tradition, and by a worldview (Laudan, 1977, van der Meer, 1999a, b, Wykstra, 1996, Eger, 1999). In what follows I will describe the levels that operate in the work of Dobzhansky and then analyse inter-level effects with a view to understanding the links between his religious beliefs and his biological thought.[1]

The lowest level discernable in Dobzhansky is that of the *construction and choice of theories*. The challenge was to explain how organisms could survive the accumulation of mutations which tended to be harmful in homozygotes, but which were also the source of adaptability. Two theories of natural selection were available, viz., the balance theory and the selection theory. The balance theory explains how a population maintains its adaptability in the face of natural selection. The answer is that it has a store of genetic variability hiding from selection in the form of recessive alleles in heterozygotes. These alleles are produced by mutation. In every new generation some of these alleles are exposed to selection as homozygotes. These homozygotes offer the population an opportunity to adapt to a new environment if required while keeping the same alleles in hiding from selection in heterozygotes. Over time a population

---

1. In Dobzhansky the pre-scientific and scientific interpretation of nature are unified so that it is difficult to distinguish between them.

accumulates a record of its exposures to a variety of environments in the form of a stock of successful alleles which provided adaptation in the past and can do so again in the future. Thus the balance theory explains that a population has the freedom to adapt to new environments because natural selection favours heterozygotes (Dobzhansky, 1937: 126-127). This theory incorporates a synthesis of Darwinian evolution and mutation. In the so-called selection theory or gradualist theory of evolution every allele is held to be subject to natural selection. This, Dobzhansky believed, reduces the freedom of a population to exist in different environments (adaptability) on the ground that natural selection removes genes.

The next level is that of the *research tradition*. "A research tradition is a set of general assumptions about the entities and processes in a domain of study, and about the appropriate methods to be used for investigating the problems and constructing the theories in that domain." (Laudan, 1977: 81) At this level theories and their concepts are interpreted and the meaning of theoretical concepts and the type of acceptable theories are determined. In Dobzhansky this concerns the concepts of adaptability, mutation and natural selection, and the balance and selection theories. Mutation is the source of conflict between organism and environment because it is random with respect to the environment (Dobzhansky, 1937: 126-127). Natural selection was a negative force under both theories because it removes alleles from populations. The balance theory explains how a population can have adaptability despite this negative effect of natural selection. Dobzhansky developed the balance theory because he saw adaptability as a positive force driving evolutionary progress. The selection theory did not provide adaptability because all alleles were assumed to be subject to natural selection so that they would be lost from the population.

Finally, at the *worldview* level we find Dobzhansky's religious belief that everything occurs under divine providence including mutation, natural selection, extinction and genocide. Dobzhansky thought about the relationship of organism to environment in terms of the relationship of individual to society as he had experienced it in his youth, viz., in terms of conflict. It was clear to Dobzhansky that God inflicted evil in the form of mutation, natural selection and extinction. He justified God by the traditional free will defence of moral evil and a free process defence of natural evil.

Effects of Dobzhansky's worldview
across the levels of interpretation of nature

The *worldview* level provides the context for the interpretation of theories in research traditions. By interpreting nature and society as the theatre of divine providence, Dobzhansky engaged religion, metaphysics and science in the same way as Newton who saw natural phenomena as manifestations of divine action, and whose concept of nature expressed this view. This fulfills a classic condition for the merger of thought about God and nature. Both Newton and Dobzhansky thought about nature in terms of what they knew about God and *vice versa*. Such mergers make it impossible to separate religion and science into entities that interact (Brooke, 1996: 3). Dobzhansky thought about the relationship of organism to environment in terms of the relationship of individual to society because he believed that both natural and social evolution were similar forms of divine providence. The negative content of this relationship originated in his experience of moral evil in the Russian Revolution and of natural evil' in mutation, natural selection and extinction. Social and biological evolution were one of a kind. The metaphorical analogy is between society eliminating individuals and the environment eliminating genes (natural selection). Thus Dobzhansky's negative interpretation of the concept of natural selection in his *research tradition* was a bottom up effect of his experience of society eliminating individuals *combined* with a top down effect of his religious view that social and biological evolution are similar manifestations of divine providence. It followed that the relationship between organism and environment is one of conflict. Hence, the prescription that theories explaining the relationship between organism and environment should do this in terms of conflict. The effect of this prescription was Dobzhansky's belief that natural selection eliminates genes.

Both the balance and selection theories satisfied this criterion. The choice between them is a second top down effect of worldview at the level of research tradition. Given that reality was the theatre of divine providence, it was clear for Dobzhansky that God inflicted evil in the form of mutation, natural selection and extinction. As a Christian, he had a religious need to explain evil and justify God, and he did so with the traditional free will defence of moral evil and a free process defence of natural evil. For Dobzhansky, mutation, natural selection and extinction were justified only because they provided the freedom for organisms to adapt to new environments. That is, mutation, natural selection and extinction were necessary consequences of God's desire to create adaptable organisms. The balance theory explained how that freedom was provided. Thus the ultimate ground for the balance theory was that it justified God in the face of natural evil by providing a free process defence of natural evil.

This top down effect was mediated by the concepts of freedom, adaptability and natural selection which received their biological interpretation at the level of the research tradition. Natural selection was a negative force. The biological interpretation of the conflict relation between society and individuals was a conflict relation between environment and organism. The role of the environment was to eliminate genes. Hence natural selection was incapable of explaining evolution. Dobzhansky rejected the selection theory because he concluded that natural selection gradually eliminates all alleles leaving the population no freedom to adapt to new environments. This effect on theory construction is a top down effect originating in Dobzhansky's *research tradition*. The warrant for this conclusion was that the freedom to adapt gives meaning to the evil of mutation, natural selection and extinction. This warrant is a top down effect originating in his religious belief at the level of worldview.[2]

In contrast, the balance theory incorporates natural selection as the price for the freedom to adapt. The biological interpretation of the concept of freedom as adaptability betrays the influence of religious belief operating at the worldview level that evolution is progressive under divine guidance. Hence, adaptability was a positive force guaranteeing variability and, therefore, capable of explaining evolution. The concepts of freedom and adaptability *constitute* the balance theory of population genetics (Ruse, 1996) because the balance theory explains how a population can be free to adapt to new circumstances.

The constitutive effect of these concepts in biology is mediated by the metaphorical analogy between nature and society, specifically between the free process defence of natural evil and the free will defence of moral evil. Belief in divine providence explains why Dobzhansky thought about the relations between environment and organism as well as between society and individuals in terms of what he believed about divine providence, namely that God had accepted evil as the price of adaptability, freedom and progress. Moreover, his perception of reality in terms of conflict informed a research tradition which prescribed theories of conflict as an acceptable type of theory. The immediate source of this constitutive effect appears to be Dobzhansky's experience of the relationship between individual and society in terms of conflict. Yet the ultimate source is his religious belief that evil is the price for freedom because in the balance theory mutation and selection are the price for adaptability. The religious priority of human freedom over evil informed the biological priority of adaptability over natural selection as the force driving the evolution of nature and culture. One can, therefore, say that his religious need to explain evil constituted the very content of his balance theory of evolution via the metaphorical analogy between nature and society.[3]

---

2   The constitution of the balance theory was accompanied by theory choice because theory construction involves making choices along the way.

3.   Obviously, bottom up effects are also possible. For instance, the balance theory affords maximum adaptability and freedom to a population because natural selection favours heterozygotes. That is why Dobzhansky could not keep

In the balance theory, Dobzhansky used the concepts of adaptability and freedom to refer to the ability of a population of organisms including human organisms to adjust to a variety of environmental circumstances. This did not explain the uniquely human freedom to make moral choices. Therefore, these concepts did not refer to human freedom of choice. But Dobzhansky believed that this human freedom evolved somehow in the processes explained by the balance theory (Dobzhansky, 1967: 120 quoted above).

What is the epistemological nature of the link between the religious belief in divine providence and the explanation of progressive evolution in the balance theory? Obviously, the link is causal, not logical. A belief in divine providence itself does not entail a conflict view of the relationship between organism and environment. The conflict view also requires the experience of conflict. Nor does belief in divine providence entail adaptability, freedom or evolutionary progression from simple to complex. A further reason why the balance theory is not entailed by a free process defence of natural evil lies in the complexity of religious beliefs.

In offering a free process defence of natural evil analogous to the free will defence of moral evil, a variety of other religious beliefs are implicit including (i) that one can think about God in human terms, particularly in terms of a human conception of love which excludes coercion, and (ii) that the origin of evil was not an event involving the Fall of angels and humans, but that evil was inevitable, given God's desire to create a progressively evolving cosmos. This in turn involves the view that God is subject to the order of things as we know it, specifically that he is unable to bring about progress and freedom without natural and moral evil. Modifying any of these auxiliary beliefs undermines simplistic notions of the balance theory being entailed by a free process defence of natural evil. Despite this complex entanglement of religion and science, a safe conclusion can be made. The religious belief in divine providence in which social progress is paid for by moral evil and suffering has informed the balance theory of evolution in which freedom to adapt is paid for with natural evil of mutation and extinction. Knowledge about society has been transformed into a specific testable hypothesis in biology with the help of the metaphor of progress. The content of evolutionary biology is not entailed by the idea of providential progress, but evolutionary biology has been informed by it. That is, the link is causal and can be broken. This is why the idea of evolutionary progress has the status of an interpretation of evolutionary theory. As Ruse puts it in characterizing Dobzhansky's work: "Those who liked the religion could keep it, and those who did not could drop it."

---

the idea of biological and cultural progress out of his evolutionary theory.

To conclude, three levels of interpretation characterize Dobzhansky's biology. They are linked with his religion via his worldview. The balance theory was constructed and the selection theory rejected on the ground that natural selection reduces freedom to adapt. The warrant for this conclusion originated at the level of worldview and was mediated by his research tradition. Via the world view level, religion had four functions in Dobzhansky's biology: (i) it informed the interpretation of the concepts of natural selection and adaptability, (ii) via these concepts religious belief constituted the balance theory, (iii) excluded the selection theory, and (iv) thereby informed theory choice. Secondly, scientific explanations of a particular phenomenon cannot be constructed without external support. Sometimes specific religious beliefs provide this support by contributing cognitive content to the explanation. Thirdly, the external support can be removed when the theory has become self-supporting, i.e., has received empirical support. This is possible because explanations are logically independent of the external source and can be made causally independent. Finally, explanations are logically independent of the external source of support because the support comes from a network of ideas rather than from one idea. The conjunction of ideas in the source network can entail an explanation of a target phenomenon, but the entailment changes when one of the source ideas is replaced.

BUILDING BRIDGES FROM THE SIDE OF SCRIPTURE: RUDOLF BULTMANN

Perhaps the best-known theologian whose exegesis has been developed in interaction with the world view of the Enlightenment, and more specifically with that of the natural sciences is Rudolf Bultmann (1884-1976). Bultmann's primary concern was with the meaning of the Gospel for modern believers. But as a scholar, he also addressed unresolved questions about the relationship of the Bible to our knowledge of nature, history and morality that were the legacy of the tradition of Liberal Theology in which he worked (Johnson, 1987: 11-13). He has written much on the meaning of New Testament passages about body and soul. I will focus on Pauline texts traditionally taken to refer to the resurrection of the body including that of Jesus. I will begin with the way historical and scientific research provided Bultmann with an understanding of the Bible text in terms of human reasons and natural causes. Next I introduce his conceptions of myth, knowledge and language. Then follows a description of the levels of interpretation operating in Bultmann's exegesis and an analysis of how his worldview has affected each level.

Understanding the Bible in terms of human reasons and natural causes

First, one question raised by Liberal Theology was how the Church can proclaim a faith based on the historical figure of Jesus, when evidence that would satisfy the requirements of objective historical enquiry is not available. Bultmann was a scholar in the tradition of Enlightenment naturalism and Liberal Theology. Accordingly, the text of any book including the Bible must be made intelligible in terms of reasons and natural causes. As for historical reasons, Gospel claims made about the body that are based on the action of supernatural forces in the natural world and on the duality of body and soul, can be understood as originating in Gnostic Christianity rather than in what happened in the Resurrection and the resurrections. Take a text such as II Corinthians 5: 1-4 (RSV):

[1] For we know that if the earthly tent we live in is destroyed, we have a building from God, a house not made with hands, eternal in the heavens. [2] Here indeed we groan, and long to put on our heavenly dwelling, [3] so that by putting it on we may not be found naked. [4] For while we are still in this tent, we sigh with anxiety; not that we would be unclothed, but that we would be further clothed, so that what is mortal may be swallowed up by life.

According to Bultmann (1952) Paul uses words such as *soma* (body), *psyche, pneuma, zoe,* mind, conscience, heart and flesh usually to refer to the whole person, the self. In this Paul is said to be consistent with the meaning of these words both in the Old and New Testaments. But there are exceptions in which Paul according to Bultmann separates body and soul dualistically. For instance, his words in II Cor. 5: 1-10 are dualistic ".... not merely in form of expression, by speaking of the *soma* under the figure of the "tent-dwelling" and "garment," but also in the thought itself." The *soma* is presented not as ruled by sin from which the self desires to be freed, but as an inappropriate physical tent-dwelling from which the Christian will be redeemed. The expressions *being naked'* and *to put on the heavenly dwelling'* (vs. 2, 4) indicated a deep and genuine dualism to Bultmann (Bultmann 1952: 169n, 201-02). He also saw traces of body-soul dualism in other Pauline texts such as I Cor. 7: 1-7. "For here, in keeping with ascetic tendencies of dualism, he evaluates marriage as a thing of less value than not touching a woman' (v. 1); indeed he regards it as an unavoidable evil (on account of fornication,' v. 2, tr.)." A dualism between the natural and the supernatural was spotted in texts which described the supernatural entering the natural world (Bultmann, 1952: 132, 136, 295). These include (i) Heb. 2: 10 in which Christ as son of God was said not only to be the one who saves, but also the one "through whom all things are and through whom we exist," (ii) I Cor. 15: 29, where he takes baptism as a form of magic that literally removes of sins, (iii) I Cor. 15: 5-8 where the resurrected Jesus is depicted as a visible fact in the realm of history, and (iv) Rom. 8: 38, Eph. 6: 12, Col. 2: 15, Gal. 4: 9, Col. 2: 8, 20 where the principalities and powers' are seen as supernatural powers acting in the natural world. In sum,

Paul presents a largely unitary view of the person with some apparent exceptions.

Bultmann explained both the unitary view and the dualistic exceptions as a result of Paul's attempts to express a unitary view of the person in the dualistic terminology of Hellenistic and Gnostic Christianity, and getting trapped occasionally in the content of dualistic thought. According to Bultmann, "...., Paul did not dualistically distinguish between man's self (his "soul") and his bodily *soma* as if the latter were an inappropriate shell, a prison, to the former; ..." (Bultmann, 1952: 201). He saw in the dualistic texts the influence of Hellenistic Gnosticism on early Christianity because the action of supernatural forces in the natural world is a dominant feature of Gnosticism. On those occasions Paul was seen as arguing against "the Gnostic view that man's self at death will be released from the body (and from the 'soul') and will soar in the state of nakedness' into the heavenly world. [ ] The Christian does not desire, like such Gnostics, to be unclothed,' but desires to be further clothed' ....; he yearns for the heavenly garment, for we will not be found naked when we have divested ourselves (of our present physical body).'" That is, he interpreted Paul as adopting the dualistic terminology of Gnostic-Hellenistic Christians for the sake of arguing against them that following death, disembodied persons are incomplete until they have put on a newly created heavenly body. An instance where Paul gets trapped in the content of the Gnostic terminology is I Cor. 15: 5-8 where according to Bultmann the Gnostics who denied any resurrection forced Paul to depict the resurrection of Jesus as a visible fact in the realm of history.

The Gnostic hypothesis sometimes led Bultmann to force the interpretation of the text to conform to the cultural role of Gnosticism as he saw it. For instance, in I Cor. 15: 12. Paul asks: "how can some of you say that there is no resurrection of the dead?" The addressees according to Bultmann (1952: 168-169) are Gnostic Christians. For them death releases the real heavenly self from the earthly prison. Bodily resurrection would have meant a return to the earthly prison. In support of the Gnostic beliefs of Paul's addressees Bultmann pointed to the practice of baptism on behalf of the dead (I Cor. 15: 29) because it was done on behalf of the disembodied spirits of Christian Gnosticism. But this evidence depends on the Gnostic hypothesis that he was trying to support and must, therefore, be rejected. In sum, historical research led Bultmann to conclude that Paul's dualistic texts reflect the influence of Christian Gnosticism and that faith in Jesus cannot be based on historical evidence because the Bible was not written with the intent to provide documentation that satisfies contemporary criteria for historical research.

The legacy of Liberal Theology also included the question: how can God act in a meaningful way in the life of the believer whose thought and action are shaped by the experience of the uniformity of nature? Working in the tradition of the Enlightenment, Bultmann was concerned not only to provide historical reasons for the text, but also to understand the text in terms of natural causes. He believed that God does not alter the laws of nature at any given moment. The uniformity of nature is not even an experience peculiar for the scientific age. "[T]he simple decision to work includes the thought that the things with which we wish to work will follow a conformity to law which our thoughts can master." (Bultmann, 1933, quoting Herrmann). This means that divine action in the world is manifest only in natural phenomena:

"We cannot use electric lights and radios and, in the event of illness, avail ourselves of modern medical and clinical means and at the same time believe in the spirit and wonder world of the New Testament. And if we suppose that we can do so ourselves, we must be clear that we can represent this as the attitude of Christian faith only by making the Christian proclamation unintelligible and impossible for our contemporaries." (Bultmann, 1984: 4-5).

God cannot be found in miracles because miracles are incompatible with the uniformity of causation (Bultmann, 1933). In sum while a supernatural spirit may act in a natural body or God act in nature, these actions will manifest themselves as natural events. There can be no resurrection of the body because it contradicts our experience of nature.

Myth

Bultmann defines myth as a story that has supernatural forces acting as if they were natural forces. Such stories should not be taken objectively nor rejected because this would presuppose that supernatural acts can be known. Rather, their meaning in the lives of contemporary people must be determined. This determination requires demythologization, i.e. explanation in terms of human reasons and natural causes combined with interpretation in terms of faith. Only this interpretation has to have meaning for modern man (existential interpretation). This excludes miracles because they contradict the experience of the regularity of nature. Miracle stories must be reinterpreted as natural events that represent God's action in the world because God cannot be portrayed as a natural cause inserted in the causal chains of the natural world. There can be no description of God as if he is a natural being. Thus, demythologizing consists of interpreting Gnostic and New Testament myths existentially, i.e., in terms of their message for contemporary humanity. Bultmann saw Paul as offering an existential interpretation of Gnostic cosmology for the New Testament Christians. Likewise, Bultmann himself offered an existential interpretation of the New Testament for contemporary Christians. Existential interpretation makes historical analysis of the New Testament possible because it sees the

New Testament in terms of human rather than divine action (Henderson, 1966: 30). The resurrection of the body as understood in classical Christianity was naturalized by interpreting it as a development in a person's spiritual life. Finally, Bultmann also offered an existential interpretation of Christian theology in its interpretation of the expression son of god.' Demythologization here meant stripping the expression from its Greek interpretation as the union of a divine with a human nature, and interpreting it existentially as the meeting of two persons (Henderson, 1966: 34).

Finally, historical analysis in the tradition of Liberal Theology had left unresolved the question how the Church can proclaim a future reward for submission to divine moral standards when the New Testament is filled with expectations for an end of history that never happened? Also, faith seen as fulfilment of divine command fails to account for the fact that believers are concerned with self-fulfilment. The failure for the paroesie to occur in Paul's lifetime made it necessary for Bultmann to reinterpret Paul's expectations by moving the paroesie into the future. The work of his mentor in New Testament studies, Johannes Weiss, suggested that an eschatological perspective on the New Testament might reveal the meaning of faith for modern people. But the paroesie (*parousia*) also had to be moved out of the realm of natural events because it assumed the action of supernatural forces in nature. This was achieved by an existential interpretation of descriptions of supernatural forces acting in nature on the basis of the existentialism of his friend Heidegger. Positively, existentialist interpretation or demythologization is interpretation that reveals the meaning of the myth for human existence. Negatively, it is criticism of the mythological world picture insofar it conceals the real intention of myth which is to talk about human existence as grounded in and limited by a transcendent, unworldly power, which is not visible to objectifying thinking. When the meaning of the text for my existence becomes clear it demands of me a decision between the mythological world picture with its objectifying knowledge and ideal of control and the existential surrender of all securities with its ideal of being unreservedly free for the future (Bultmann, 1941; in Ogden, 1984: p. 23). In this way existential interpretation delivers eschatological facts because according to it we exist ever in the moment of decision between the past and the future.

As for the resurrection of the body of Jesus he wrote "That the meaning of Jesus' resurrection is not that He is translated into the beyond, but that He is exalted to the status of Lord (Phil. 2:11) ...." [Bultmann, 1952: 306]. Thus the resurrection of Jesus was seen as referring to a change in the status of his life preceding his death in the eyes of his followers, not to a transition from an earthly to a heavenly existence or a return to an earthly existence.

The resurrection cannot - in spite of I Cor. 15: 3-8 - be demonstrated or made plausible as an objectively ascertainable fact on the basis of which one could believe. But insofar as it or the risen Christ is present in the proclaiming word, it can be believed — and only so can it be believed. [ ] For in the proclamation Christ is not in the same way present as a great historical person is present in his work and its historical after-effects. For what is here involved is not an influence that takes effect in the history of the human mind; what does take place is that a historical person and his fate are raised to the rank of the eschatological event. The word which makes this proclamation is itself a part of this event; and this word, in contrast to all other historical tradition, accosts the hearer as personal challenge. If he heeds it as the word spoken to him, adjudicating to him death and thereby life, then he believes in the risen Christ. (Bultmann, 1952: 305-306).

As for the body of others, Paul's usual anti-dualism led Bultmann to conclude that Paul did not "expect a release of the self from its bodily prison but expects instead the bodily' resurrection — or rather the transformation of the *soma* from under the power of flesh into a spiritual *soma*, i.e. a Spirit-ruled *soma*." (Bultmann, 1952: 201). The distinction made by Bultmann is between a physical resurrection which could be ascertained objectively by the methods of historical science and an existential resurrection from a sinful to a redeemed life. "For the resurrection, of course, simply cannot be a visible fact in the realm of human history. When Paul is pushed to do so by Gnosticizing objections to belief in any resurrection whatever, he does, I grant, think he can guarantee the resurrection of Christ as an objective fact by listing witnesses who had seen him risen (I Cor. 15: 5-8, §15, 2)." This, however, is not Paul's considered understanding of the resurrection. Rather Christ's death is "the means of release from the powers of this age: Law, Sin, and Death." Paul reinterpreted the cosmic unity between Redeemer and redeemed in Gnostic mythology because it enabled him to interpret the salvation-occurrence "as happening actually to and for and in man." (Bultmann, 1952: 300).

Language and knowledge

Bultmann worked with the view that language either refers to phenomena or expresses meaning. Referential language refers to the world objectively as in mythological or scientific language. There is no referential language that refers to phenomena in the world in a pre-scientific way. As a result, descriptions of phenomena that have occurred and events that have happened, but that are not accessible scientifically must be taken to express the original meaning given to them by the reporter in terms of his or her world view. This is because language according to Bultmann has a fixed meaning determined by its cultural origin. An example is Bultmann's contention that Paul believed in divine action in the natural world and the associated cosmology because of his adoption of Gnostic terminology. Bultmann assumed that Paul could not help adopting the Gnostic meaning because he had adopted the Gnostic terminology. This literalistic understanding of language kept him from considering that Paul could have held his beliefs quite apart from the Gnostic origin of his terminology — a plausible option because the terminology was shared by Gnosticism and Christianity. Existential language on the other hand expresses meaning. Bultmann put his distinction between objective and existential language as follows:

> There is in fact a language in which existence naively expresses itself, and, correspondingly, there is a science that talks about existence without objectifying it into being within the world."

This language is other than the objectifying language of science and of myth and contains such expressions as I love you.' (Bultmann, 1984: 101). Since the world view of the New Testament reporters is false, the meaning of the events reported must be separated from the context in which it has been expressed. For instance, the description of Jesus' resurrection cannot be taken to refer to an event in a pre-scientific way, and since it is not accessible for scientific analysis it must be taken to express a meaning for his followers. This meaning must be recovered for modern believers by removing the mythological context which would make it unbelievable in a naturalistic context. Bultmann saw Paul attempting to separate the meaning of Jesus' resurrection from the dualistic terminology in which it was cast by Gnostic-Hellenistic Christians. Bultmann thought that Paul was successful in this attempt insofar as he maintained the unity of the person characteristic for orthodox Judaism. However, while a physical resurrection was an acceptable interpretation in Paul's time, this had become unacceptable within the scientific world view. Bultmann saw himself, therefore, as continuing Paul's reinterpretation of the disciples' report. For Bultmann the report of Jesus' resurrection was meant by his disciples to express Jesus' call to a conversion from a fleshly to a spiritual life to occur in this biological life.

Finally, these examples illustrate that Bultmann defined *knowledge* as scientific knowledge. Take this definition of myth. He defined myth as a story that mistakes supernatural forces for natural ones. This definition is informed by his conception of knowledge as scientific knowledge or more precisely as knowledge in the service of human control over the world. Knowledge is that which can be known under the rule of naturalism. Therefore, stories about supernatural forces must be reinterpreted existentially, not objectively.

Levels of Interpretation of Scripture in Bultmann

Interpreting a passage of the Bible may involve a range of activities in which

Wolters (2000) discerns some nine levels. Some of these occur in the work of Bultmann and I will now identify them as possible levels for interaction with the interpretation of natural phenomena. Each preceding level is required for the next to operate properly.

Diachronic literary analysis or analysis of text history refers to "all the critical methodologies which seek to trace the pre-history of the canonical text as it stands. It includes such approaches as source criticism, redaction criticism, and tradition history." (Wolters, 2000). For instance, I and II Cor. indicate that Paul had written four letters to the Corinthians. Since internal criteria indicate that each of the current letters has two parts, Bultmann suggested that the original four letters must have been combined into two when the Corinthians circulated them (Bultmann, 1976: 22-23). One might think that this theory has no further consequences because all four letters have the same author who can be expected to present the same ideas about body, soul and resurrection. However, according to Bultmann, one can see an improvement in Paul's understanding of Gnosticism between the first and the second letter. This improvement will be discussed below under *Ideological criticism of the author*. Theories about the text can also have more substantial implications. In the case of the three synoptic gospels (Mark, Matthew and Luke), for instance, it was the presence of several different layers of oral tradition manifest in literary form that led Bultmann to conclude: "The analysis of the synoptic gospels has shown more and more clearly how little we know for certain about Jesus." (Bultmann, 1968: 223). This led to the conclusion that faith in Jesus must be based on something else than historical facts.

In *synchronic literary analysis* or analysis of the literary form of the final text, the kind of literary form (e.g., myth or history) will influence opinions on whether or not cognitive engagement between Bible and science is appropriate or possible. Bultmann (1984: 2) held that texts about bodily resurrection both of Jesus and others are myths, i.e., "the report of an occurrence or an event in which supernatural, superhuman forces or persons are at work ... [ ]. Myth actually talks about transcendent powers or persons as though they were immanent and worldly — contrary to its real intention." This intention is "to talk about human existence as grounded in and limited by a transcendent, unworldly power, which is not visible to objectifying thinking." (Bultmann, 1984: 95, 98, 99). In putting things this way, Bultmann granted the possibility that God acts in the world, but that this act cannot be known objectively (scientifically) because it cannot be manipulated in experiment. There can only be natural phenomena interpreted as divine action in the world. For instance, an accident which happened to us may be interpreted as a divine act in our life and explained as the result of a faulty brake or someone else's carelessness. He limited divine action to what is intelligible in terms of the world picture of the natural sciences and in terms of our self-understanding as modern persons

(Bultmann, 1984: 5). An example of this is Bultmann's conclusion that the Gnostic Christians forced Paul to depict Jesus' resurrection as a visible fact in history (I Corinthians 15: 5-8, see above) which assumes a split between the natural and the supernatural. He rejected any mixing of the transcendent and the immanent not only in the resurrection of Jesus' body (Bultmann, 1952: 294; 1984: 7, 37), but also in other miracles (Bultmann, 1984: 4), in divine intervention in the inner life of persons (Bultmann, 1984: 5) and in the sacraments such as baptism understood not as symbols of supernatural power, but as natural events that put supernatural powers into effect (Bultmann, 1952: 135). These were rejected alongside the view that Jesus descended into hell (Bultmann, 1984: 98) and that spirits move the stars. According to Bultmann, there can only be natural phenomena interpreted as divine action in the world. The resurrection of Christ was not possible because it presupposes supernatural divine action in the natural world. God's action in the world must conform to the naturalistic interpretation of the world.

At the next level, *historical analysis of the context of a Bible text* may clarify or question a particular interpretation. This is different from an analysis of text history in that the context may include other parts of Scripture, information from archeology, from ancient historians, from social–scientific reconstructions of ancient society and thought. The goal is to identify the cultural context into which the concepts of the Old and New Testaments had to be translated in order to be communicated. Paul was exposed to at least four cultural factors related to a view of the person. These were the influence of orthodox Judaism with its characteristic holistic dualism flowing out of the Old Testament tradition, his upbringing in Tarsus which must have exposed him to the dualism of Hellenistic Judaism as well as to the dualism of Gnostic Christianity, and his encounter with the religious materialism of the Sadducees. The story of Paul's manipulation of the Sadducees and Pharisees on the question of the resurrection of the body shows how well informed he was about the Hellenistic dualism of the Pharisees and the religious materialism of the Sadducees.

An example of historical analysis of Pauline texts concerns the dating of Gnostic sources such as the Mandaean writings. Bultmann held that Gnosticism (i) is a non-Christian religion rather than a Christian heresy, (ii) existed during early Christianity, (iii) is illuminated by the sacred books of the so-called Mandaean religion, (iv) provided Paul with the concepts he needed for some of his theology, (v) was opposed by Paul (e.g. the world is the creation of God and not of demonic powers), and (vi) had a cosmology that is interpreted existentially by Paul. The Gnostic hypothesis assumes that Gnosticism predates Christianity. If it had emerged from Christianity it would have been too late to be an influence on Paul. Contemporaries of Bultmann did not believe that the Mandaean writings were independent of and chronologically prior to the

New Testament writings.[4] Thus, Bultmann adopted the Gnostic hypothesis from his pupil Hans Jonas (Bultmann, 1984: 15) without sufficient historical warrant. Recently, the Gnostic hypothesis has been rejected (Yamauchi, 1994).

The assumption underlying Bultmann's interpretation of Pauline texts on the activity of supernatural forces in nature and the human body was that in Paul the traditions of the Old Testament and of Gnosticism merged. This mixture of frameworks of interpretation suggested to Bultmann that Paul's depiction of the relation between nature and supernature would be fluctuating inconsistently between an Old Testament monism and a Gnostic dualism. The facts were different. In the majority of texts, Paul uses dualistic' terms to refer to the whole person.

Bultmann acknowledged the role of orthodox Judaism in Paul's usual view of the person as a unity of body and soul, but he interpreted the view of the person of orthodox Judaism as a form of monism rather than holistic dualism. "Man does not consist of two parts, much less of three; nor are *psyche* and *pneuma* special faculties or principles (within the *soma*) of a mental life higher than his animal life. Rather, man is a living unity." (Bultmann, 1952: 209). This monism was identified as characteristic not only for the majority of Paul's writings, but as flowing out of Paul's knowledge of the Old Testament where soul, life, self and spirit are synonyms (Bultmann, 1952: 203-205). The influence of Hellenistic dualism on the other hand was seen in the dualistic Pauline texts. Bultmann interpreted Paul as attempting to express a holistic view of the person using the dualistic terminology of Hellenistic Gnosticism, and getting trapped occasionally in the content of dualistic thought.

The next level is that of *ideological criticism of the author*. This is based on the description at the preceding level of historical contextual influences emanating from the cultural and social location' of the author. It involves an evaluation of the effect of such local circumstances as gender, class, race, political or sexual orientation on the interpretation of the Bible text (Wolters, 2000). Related circumstances include upbringing and education seen as factors contributing to the worldview of an author which may affect interpretation. Wolters (2000) locates both ideological criticism of authors and ideological criticism of commentators at this level. In contrast, I locate the latter at a separate higher level because the worldview context of a commentator can affect that commentator's ideological criticism of an author.

---

4. In "Church and Gnosis." Burkitt interprets the Gnostics as Christians who attempted to adjust the OT cosmology to what was at that time modern science and the result was Gnosticism. This requires Gnosticism to post-date early Christianity (Henderson, 1966: 26).

Operating on the level of ideological criticism of the author, Bultmann was concerned with the meaning of the Pauline texts about bodily resurrection for Paul's audience. He was careful to indicate that texts with traces of Gnosticism are exceptions to the rule of a definitive contrast between Christianity and Gnosticism. It would be a mistake, Bultmann wrote, to interpret the soma-concept that is characteristic of Paul on the basis of such exceptions.[5] In that light, Bultmann applied ideological criticism to Paul's dualistic texts. For instance, the assumption that Paul is arguing against the Gnostics led Bultmann to the conclusion that Paul had initially mistaken his opponents in attributing to them the view that with death everything ends. Bultmann read this in I Cor. 15: 19: "If for this life only we have hoped in Christ, we are of all men most to be pitied." and in I Cor. 15: 32: "If the dead are not raised,   Let us eat and drink, for tomorrow we die.'" Since the Gnostics believed that the real self continues its existence through death, Bultmann took Paul to have failed to inform himself about this aspect of Gnostic beliefs.

Bultmann (1952: 230) did express one misgiving with the Gnostic hypothesis. He wrote that "The historical observation, correct as far as it goes, that Old Testament tradition and Gnostic tradition have flowed together here, does not sufficiently explain the facts." These   facts' refer to Paul 's depiction of the creation as the theatre both of divine blessing for humanity and of the activity of evil powers restricted by the will of God. The Gnostic hypothesis, however, predicted that Pauline texts on creation should reveal a mix of occasional cosmic dualism with predominant monism similar to the case of the body. This they did not reveal. The Pauline texts on creation did not leave room for the Gnostic view in which the creation was fallen under the control of evil powers.

Moving to the eighth level, *redemptive-historical analysis* "looks at a Bible passage from the standpoint of its place in the grand narrative of the Christian canon." (Wolters, 2000). This approach presupposes that the New Testament is a continuation of the history of the Old Testament. But, according to Bultmann, the history of Israel *as history* has no relevance in the life of Christians today. The *history* of Israel could be accepted as salvation history only on condition of pre-existing faith because objective historical analysis cannot   see' salvation (Bultmann, 1984: 115). Bultmann's separation of objective history and existential interpretation made it impossible to understand the New Testament as the fulfilment in history of the Old Testament because existential exegesis required

---

5. For instance, while developing his monistic interpretations of N. T. texts about body and soul, Bultmann consistently refers to O. T. interpretations either to reveal differences or to show consistency such as in the fact that *soma* can denote both the body and the whole man, the person (Bultmann, 1952: 196). This applies also to *psyche, pneuma* (204), *nous* (211).

an understanding of the New Testament in its relevance for the existence of contemporary believers. The New Testament could not be relevant for us because we do not live in a New Testament culture. It is easy to misunderstand Bultmann in this respect. "That God is not visible outside of faith does not mean that God is not real outside of faith. [ ] To claim that faith could be proved would imply that God could be known and established outside of faith and thus put God on the same level as the available world that can be disposed of by an objectifying view." (Bultmann, 1984: 114-115). Faith is an answer to the proclaimed word of God's grace, not as a compendium of doctrines nor as a document containing the faith of others, but only as a response of the contemporary believer to the proclamation.

Answers given at the preceding level influence what people take God to be saying to them and what this means for them personally and for the community of Christians. "As a distinct level of interpretation, *confessional discernment* focuses on what God has to say to his people. [ ] In academic discourse it is usually referred to as theological' interpretation, as discerning the message' or kerygma.'" (Wolters, 2000). "It is necessary," Wolters (2000) explains, "to distinguish between what a text meant for its original audience and what it means for believers today." For Bultmann, this distinction is the one between the mythological frame of reference of the New Testament and the scientific worldview of today. His main concern was with the meaning of the Gospel for modern believers.

For instance, the salvation-occurrence' as he called it is not a cosmic-natural occurrence as depicted in the Gnostic myth, but a genuine occurrence in man's actual life. It did not occur in the past on a cross, but it occurs whenever the word is proclaimed (Bultmann, 1952: 302). "The meaning of Jesus' resurrection was not that He is translated into the beyond, but that He is exalted to the status of Lord ...." (Bultmann, 1952: 306). For us, the resurrection of Jesus body means that we should understand ourselves as crucified with Christ and thereby also risen with him (1984: 40). Likewise, when Paul writes of the battle of the spirit powers against Christ or of Christ's battle against them, he and his audience understood this as a conflict between the powers of a transcendent supernatural world which could affect the immanent world inhabited by humans. "In reality," Bultmann wrote, "he is thereby only expressing a certain understanding of existence: The spirit powers represent the reality into which man is placed as one full of conflicts and struggle, a reality which threatens and tempts." The message of this myth for people today was that they are not in control of their life (Bultmann, 1952: 259). In sum, in classical Christianity the meaning of the Gospel is rooted both in God's action in nature and history and in its meaning for human existence. For Bultmann it was rooted only in its ability to address existential concerns. Its roots in God's action in nature and history had disappeared under the pressure of the scientific world view.

Bultmann's program of demythologizing meant that the meaning of New Testament myths was to emerge out of an existential interpretation of the myths.

Finally, the *worldview level* includes an analysis of the reading of the biblical text by later commentators in terms of their worldview. Interpretations of texts and their authors also depends on assumptions which themselves may be ideological (Wolters, 2000). I include it as the highest level of interpretation rather than as part of the ideological criticism of the author because the ideology of the commentator can shape a commentator's understanding of the message at the level of confessional discernment. Bultmann recognized this himself when he wrote that "a particular understanding of the subject matter of the text, grounded in a life relation to it, is always presupposed by exegesis; and to this extent no exegesis is without presuppositions." (Bultmann, 1984:149). However, the exegesis of a text cannot be justified by its connection with presuppositions because this is a historical rather than a material link (Bultmann, 1984: 25). Bultmann's relation to the text was shaped by his concern to make the Bible intelligible for contemporary believers. He developed an existentialist interpretation of Pauline texts based on Heidegger (Bultmann, 23, 25, 82) and Jonas (Bultmann, 1984: 15). In the process he ended up using some of the main features of 20th century Western culture such as objectivism and naturalism as criteria for intelligibility. Accordingly, ideological criticism of Bultmann has focussed on the role of existentialism, naturalism and objectivism.

Bultmann criticised Paul for what he perceives as a concern with objective knowledge that is misplaced because it is about Jesus who cannot be known objectively. In I Cor. 15: 5-8, Paul lists witnesses who have seen the risen Jesus. Bultmann (1952: 295) interpreted Paul as being deceived into thinking that he can guarantee the resurrection of Christ as an objective fact by listing witnesses. Further, he took the expression "there is no God but one" in I Cor. 8: 4-6 to mean "That God's existence is not an objectively perceptible, mere existing like that of a thing. [ ] If God were being spoken of as only a cosmic Thing, the statement, "there is no God but one," would not be right at all" according to Bultmann. "For in this sense of is,' other gods' and lords' are'" whereas God is unique in that He exists for us and can be understood only as such (Bultmann, 1952: 229). In both texts, Bultmann read Paul anachronistically as if he was concerned with contemporary questions about objective scientific knowledge and subjective personal knowledge while in fact these were Bultmann's concerns. He also imposed upon the text a dilemma between an objective and an existential meaning. This ruled out the possibility that a fact with existential meaning such as the Resurrection had been observed. In sum, reading Pauline texts as if he was concerned about objective knowledge is a distortion informed by Bultmann's ideology of objectivism.

Bultmann adopted the Gnostic hypothesis from his pupil Hans Jonas (Bultmann, 1984: 15) without sufficient chronological warrant. Such an uncritical attitude could be a reason for ideological criticism of Bultmann if there were evidence for this in his work. Bultmann provides such evidence by identifying Jonas' existentialist interpretation of Gnostic myths as his model for the interpretation of Gnostic mythology in the New Testament (Bultmann, 1984: 15). That is, his research tradition was informed by the concern to make the Gospel relevant for the existence of 20th century Western believers. This required a reinterpretation of New Testament myths according to the criteria of naturalism and objectivism.

Bultmann's interpretation of Pauline texts in which there is activity of supernatural forces in the natural world reveals the presence of a religious naturalism. He rejected divine and demonic action both in the human body and in the cosmos as incredible in the light of the natural sciences. I offer three reasons for the presence of naturalism. First, the majority of texts both in the Old Testament and the New Testament reveal a view of the person known as holistic dualism (Cooper, 1989). However, Bultmann interprets them as monistic consistent with a religious naturalism. Thus Bultmann's critique of Paul's body-soul dualism is warranted by his religious naturalism, not by other parts of Scripture. For instance, in I Cor. 15: 5-8, Bultmann (1952: 295) took Paul to be arguing against the Gnostic teaching that the supernatural can enter the natural in the form of a divine spark in a material body. This made the resurrection of the body superfluous because the spiritual bearers of the heavenly spark would travel to heaven on their own strength. Paul was thought to have adopted Gnostic body-soul dualism to make the point that there is a bodily resurrection. However, there would have been no dualism to be explained by Bultmann's Gnostic hypothesis if he had assumed that Paul combined the unity and separability of body and soul as in holistic dualism. Clearly, Bultmann was presupposing that the holistic view of the person in the Bible is not of the dualistic, but of the monistic kind. This made Paul's distinction between body and soul look like a dualistic separation that could be explained in terms of Gnosticism. Both the problem and its explanation are unnecessary if Paul is understood as a holistic dualist in line with the rest of the Bible.

My second argument for the presence of naturalism in Bultmann's interpretation of Paul is that he ignored religious naturalists as possible opponents of Paul instead of Gnostic dualists. This concerns his criticism that Paul erroneously attributed to his Gnostic opponents the view that existence ends with death (I Cor. 15 : 12-32). One might raise the objection that this putative mistake disappears if Paul is assumed to have been arguing against religious naturalists who did believe that with death everything ends. They could have been Sadducees, a Jewish movement of religious materialists. In that case Paul did not misunderstand the Gnostic teachings, and his second letter to the Corinthians was not a correction of this mistake. Bultmann did not justify why he preferred the Gnostic theory over others.

Thirdly, Bultmann failed to provide internal evidence for the presence of traces of Gnosticism that is independent of his working hypothesis. This occurred despite his ideal that the criterion for the elimination of New Testament myths "must not be derived from the modern worldview but from the understanding of existence of the New Testament itself." (Bultmann, 1984: 12). The reason for his failure, I suggest, is his stated view that "What is at issue is the truth of this understanding, and the faith that affirms its truth is not to be bound to the New Testament's world of representations." (Bultmann, 1984: 10). This view appears to contradict his ideal. There is, however, no contradiction when one considers that according to Bultmann Paul usually considers the body and the soul to be a unity in accordance with most of the Bible. Bultmann interpreted this unity as a monism in terms of which Paul's dualistic slippers have to be interpreted. Thus the third reason for a presence of religious naturalism in Bultmann is that his naturalistic interpretation of the texts on body and soul allowed him to claim that his critique of the dualistic worldview of New Testament Christianity was "not derived from the modern worldview but from the understanding of existence of the New Testament itself." (Bultmann, 1984: 12). In sum, Bultmann's criticism of the body-soul dualism of New Testament Christians was not based on an understanding of existence of the New Testament. I conclude that the ideological nature of Bultmann's criticism of Paul's dualism was based on a religious naturalism, not on a presumed monism in the Old and New Testaments. In this, Bultmann failed to honour his own ideal that the criterion for the elimination of New Testament myths "must not be derived from the modern world view but from the understanding of existence of the New Testament itself." (Bultmann, 1984: 12). His research was informed by the desire to make the Gospel relevant for the existence of 20th century Western believers through a reinterpretation of New Testament myths in accordance with the demands of naturalism and objectivism.

Effects of Bultmann's worldview across the levels of interpretation of Scripture

In Bultmann the interpretation of nature and Scripture was connected at the level of his worldview. At this level the focus is not on how the meaning of Pauline texts is shaped by the context in which Paul was educated and worked, but on the context interpreters of Paul bring to the meaning of his texts. Bultmann distinguished clearly between what the text meant for Paul's audience and what it means for us. He did not question the content of the objectifying representations of the New Testament, but he questioned the world view of which they were a manifestation. "What is at issue is the truth of this understanding, and the faith that affirms its truth is not to be bound to the New

Testament's world of representations" (Bultmann, 1984: 10). His principal strategy was to establish the meaning of a text for its original audience, to identify the world view behind it and to subject the latter to his own ideological criticism. This led to top down effects.

One top down effect occurred when Paul lists persons who have seen Jesus in the body after his death. Bultmann took the text to mean that Paul was concerned (mistakenly) with establishing the resurrection objectively as a supernatural event in the natural world. Since supernatural events reported in the Scriptures cannot be established objectively as events in the natural world, texts about the insertion of transcendent into natural causes are myths. Ideological criticism of the commentator shaped synchronic literary analysis.

Further, such texts must be re-interpreted accordingly for a contemporary audience such that its existential meaning is not rooted in natural or cosmological meaning. Bultmann argued that salvation by Jesus demands a previous faith "For the resurrection, of course, simply cannot be a visible fact in the realm of human history." (Bultmann, 1952: 295). One might think that supernatural events occurring in nature could be known subjectively so that existential value could arise out of natural fact, but this is not possible according to Bultmann. On the other hand, the fact that the bodily resurrection of Jesus cannot be known objectively did not lead Bultmann to say that it cannot occur. He wrote: "We find incredible a theory of satisfaction that describes God's act as a cultic or juristic act and a Christ occurrence that cannot be understood as having to do with our own personal existence." (Bultmann, 1984: 97). The resurrection of the body of Jesus is not a miraculous event due to the power of God, but "is nothing other than the emergence of faith in the risen one in which the proclamation has its origin." (Bultmann, 1984: 39). The naturalistic presuppositions of Bultmann called for a change in the message of resurrection texts. Bultmann's claim that religious naturalism characterized the Old Testament as well as most of Paul's texts is questionable in light of the fact that orthodox Judaism holds a wholistic dualism (Cooper, 1989). Therefore, this is a top down effect in which ideological critique by the commentator shaped confessional discernment of the message of the text for people today.

This raises the question of the meaning of texts referring to the resurrection of the human body. Bultmann took expressions such as the earthly tent', the building from God, an eternal house' and the heavenly dwelling' as having had a dualistic meaning for Paul's audience. Thus his naturalism had no top-down effect at the lexicographical level. But he also took Paul's dualistic expressions as part of a context that must be considered outdated in the light of science. Therefore, there could be no resurrection of the human body for Bultmann. As in Jesus' resurrection, the existential value of the resurrection of his followers was not rooted in their bodily resurrection from the dead, but in the fact that their figurative death, i.e., their conversion gave new meaning to their life. Here ideological criticism in the light of science affected confessional discernment of what the text means for people living in a scientific culture. By removing the natural meaning of such texts, Bultmann hoped to immunize religion against science.

A second implication of his naturalism concerns body-soul dualism. Most passages in both the Old and New Testaments referring to the body, the soul etc., can be interpreted as referring to the unity of the person. This is an interpretation in the tradition of orthodox Judaism with its characteristic holistic dualism. Philosophically this allows for three interpretations known as monism, dualism and holistic dualism. Bultmann interpreted Paul's thought as shaped by the combined effects of Old Testament monism and the body-soul dualism of Hellenistic Judaism in Tarsus where he grew up (Bultmann, 1952: 202). Projecting his own interpretative categories onto Paul, he contrasted Paul's dualistic texts with what he saw as Old Testament monism. Given this choice, Bultmann described his task as "To set forth connectedly the extent to which the understanding of the Christian message in Hellenistic Christianity was unfolded by means of Gnostic terminology." This is a research tradition shaped by Bultmann's presuppositions. Bultmann did not justify his monistic interpretation of Old Testament texts referring to body, soul, etc. However, given the availability of a legitimate alternative, viz., holistic dualism, and considering his scientism, it is reasonable to infer that his preference for monistic exegesis was mandated by a naturalistic interpretation of science. This implies that Paul's so-called dualistic texts need to be seen as concessions to or acceptance of Gnostic or Hellenistic dualism. However, Paul's dualistic texts can also be interpreted as forms of holistic dualism and so can the Old Testament texts so that there is consistency within the Scriptures (Cooper, 1989). In sum, scientific naturalism drove Bultmann's monistic interpretation of the majority of texts on the body.

In conclusion, the fundamental concern that operated in Bultmann's ideological criticism of the worldview of Paul's audience was to make the Gospel relevant for the existence of 20th century Western believers. His strategy consisted of the reinterpretation of New Testament myths according to the criteria of naturalism and objectivism. That is, Bultmann's research tradition was informed by the ideologies of existentialism, naturalism and objectivism. Naturalism meant that supernatural events cannot occur in the natural world. At the lower level of synchronic literary analysis this presupposition constituted his conception of myth as a report of the action of supernatural powers in natural events. Since such events are not possible, the real intention of myth must be "to talk about human existence as grounded in and limited by a transcendent, unworldly power, which is not visible to objectifying thinking." (Bultmann, 1984: 95, 98, 99). He meant that there can only be natural phenomena interpreted as divine action in the world. Natural phenomena cannot testify to supernatural power by being miraculous. This presupposition also constituted Bultmann's research tradition of demythologization. Demythologization takes a naturalistic interpretation of nature based on the natural sciences as the standard for the kind of events that are possible and interprets myths accordingly. From the perspective of ideological criticism of the commentator, however, naturalism itself is an interpretation of the natural sciences and not implied by them. It is a philosophy of life or world view. Since it is a world view that is antithetical to that of the Scriptures it is not suitable as a framework for its interpretation. Bultmann's willingness to critique the truth of the New Testament world view is an instance of this objectivism. Therefore, while there is a bridge between the interpretation of Scripture and the interpretation of nature in science, the natural sciences serve as a source of cultural authority for naturalism. One result was that Bultmann's existential religion is a naturalistic religion. Another conclusion is, therefore, that the interpretation of the Pauline texts has lost its connection with internal criteria of meaning. The irony is that Bultmann himself stipulated and claimed that the interpretation of Scripture must use internal criteria only. If Gnosticism and dualism are seen to provide external criteria of meaning that need to be removed, so must naturalism. At his point, the interpretation of Scripture has lost its integrity. In sum, the effect originates at the level of Bultmann's worldview and reaches down via Bultmann's ideological criticism of the author Paul to Bultmann's characterization of texts as myth at the level of synchronic literary analysis.

THE INTEGRITY OF SCIENCE AND SCRIPTURE

There are effects of science down the levels of interpretation of Scripture as well as effects of religious beliefs based on Scriptural exegesis down the levels of interpretation of nature in science. How can the interpretation of each remain true to what is being interpreted? I propose *a model in which their engagement is mutual and respects the integrity of both*. In this model the interpretation of both Scripture and nature would proceed through a hierarchy of levels as described in the two case studies, with each lower level being a prerequisite for the existence of the next higher level. The levels can be distinguished, but not separated. This notion receives support from the history of interpretation of both Scripture and nature which reveal effects both up and down the levels of interpretation.

An important feature of this model is that mutual engagement between the interpretation of nature and Scripture occurs at the highest level in the interpretative hierarchy, the worldview level. For interpretation to remain true to what is being interpreted, one could picture the engagement between the interpretation of nature and Scripture in terms of a trigger. The mechanism of a gun is designed so that the trigger sets in motion a predetermined chain of causes and effects resulting in the firing of a bullet. In just the same way a scientific consideration could trigger a series of interpretative moves the dynamics of which reflect the requirements of good exegesis. For instance, in the past dualistic interpretations of Bible passages were in fashion, but in the last few decades there has been a switch to monistic interpretation (e.g., Brown, Murphy and Malony, 1998). This switch was triggered by neuropsychology. The integrity of exegesis would be respected if its content was informed not by neuropsychology, but by the Bible. The metaphor of the trigger means that the relation of worldview to scientific theory and exegesis is causal, not logical. This allows an interpretation of nature and Scripture according to their own methods. Each has respect for the integrity of the other and is open for contributions from the other.

Respecting the integrity of interpretations of Scripture and nature means that interaction between the interpretative hierarchies at levels below that of the worldview must be prohibited. The intent of this hermeneutical procedure is to include a critical assessment of ideological interpretations at the worldview level as well as to exclude Biblicism. For instance, substantial engagement between interpretation of nature and Scripture occurred at the level of Bultmann's worldview. In that case, the integrity of Biblical hermeneutics can be respected by requiring a critical assessment of Bultmann's ideological' interpretations of nature and history. Augustine urged that knowledge of nature and history be used to help decide between different interpretations of Bible passages. He could take knowledge of nature at face value stipulating only that it should be reasonably established. For us scientific knowledge is far more problematic. Theories and explanations come and go. Also, ideological readings of natural phenomena are possible notwithstanding what I consider the moral duty of scientists to avoid them. Examples include such well-known notions as that of the eternal soul and the temporal body, geocentrism and heliocentrism, and the fixity or variability of biological species. These ideological readings' of nature give rise to top-down relationships. That is, interpretative moves at lower levels depend on those at higher levels. As we have seen, Dobzhansky's religious belief in divine providence in which social progress is paid for by moral evil and suffering has informed the balance theory of evolution in which freedom to adapt is paid for with natural evil of mutation. Religious knowledge about society has been transformed into a specific testable hypothesis in biology with the help of the metaphor of progress. Historical studies indicate that Dobzhansky is not an isolated case of an ideological reading of nature. For instance, the rediscovery of Aristotle in the Middle Ages made available seemingly well-established scientific' findings such as the geocentric world picture (Grant, 1986). Medieval interpretation of the Bible can be shown to have followed Augustine's advice in deferring to science. It thus perpetuated what can now be recognized as the unscientific influence of Aristotle (McGrath, 1998: 119-120). This pattern repeated itself in discussions about the fixity of biological species following Darwin (Ruse, 1996: 114-117). Similar situations may be found in current science. For instance, one could point to the confusion of is' and ought' in the assumption that human altruism might be explained as a case of kin selection in social insects or in the conclusion that homosexuality in humans is natural because it appears to be natural in animals. Likewise, the fundamental shift in the message of Jesus' resurrection in the hands of Bultmann warrants a critical assessment of his scientific naturalism as the interpretative context of choice over dualism. In sum, ideological readings of nature indicate that the interpretation of the Bible needs to make room for a critical assessment of interpretations of nature and history before it is decided that there is a question for biblical exegesis. In this way biblical hermeneutics can be open to its cultural context while maintaining its integrity. This is the main reason why I believe that interaction between Bible and science must be restricted to their interpretation at the worldview level where such assessment can take place.

At lower levels, integrity in the interpretation of both nature and Scripture can be maintained via the worldview level. Bultmann followed this procedure when he stated his goal not to allow his scientific naturalism to determine the meaning of words at the lexicographical level. For instance, he determined that Old Testament words referring to the body all mean to express the unity of the person (Bultmann, 1952) thereby leaving open how this unity is to be interpreted. Elsewhere, Bultmann interpreted it monistically in the tradition of naturalism rather than in the orthodox Judaic tradition of holistic dualism as in Cooper (1989). Locating the interaction between Bible and science at the worldview level in this way makes the need for an assessment of ideologies transparent. On the other hand, Bultmann's designation of stories about the supernatural action of God in the natural world as inadequate God-talk (myth) exemplifies a failure to respect exegetical integrity at the synchronic literary level by the use of an external naturalistic criterion for adequacy.

At the lowest level of textual criticism, questions about the interpretation of a text are not likely to be raised by science since the establishment of textual reliability precedes engagement with science on issues of interpretation and belongs to the study of the history of its transmission. This level is analogous with the level at which in science questions may be raised about the reliability of measurements and observations. At this level, interpretation shapes how data are obtained experimentally. Engagement is also unlikely because the technical issues related to the collection of data experimentally are too different from those involved in establishing the reliability of a text. Such engagement could arise, however, if textual criticism or analysis of the history of a text were inconsistent with radiocarbon dating of ancient documents containing the original Bible texts. Likewise, at the level of theories about texts on the one hand and about population genetics on the other, there is no occasion for engagement directly between these lower levels because the theories are about mutually unrelated objects: texts and natural phenomena. What if the texts are about natural phenomena? Scriptural geology and Scriptural biology exemplify attempts at linking the lower level directly. They failed because Bible texts do not provide information about natural phenomena that satisfies the criteria of the natural sciences. However, such texts can give rise to a general view of reality at the worldview level that could become a specific testable theory in science. The indirect causal link between this theory and the text means that rejection or acceptance of the theory can have implications for the exegesis of the text only indirectly as a cause for more exegetical work. Since the relation between theory and text is mediated by worldview, it is not a relation of entailment. What if science is about the subject matter of a text, for instance the resurrection texts? Again, Bultmann does not allow a reinterpretation of these texts on the ground that we do not experience resurrections. Instead, he rejects the worldview of New Testament Christians on this ground and allows his naturalism to inform his existential exegesis. Hence, the resurrection of Jesus is interpreted as a symbol for the transition of his followers from spiritual death to spiritual life both of which occur in this life. Again, Bultmann's view of Jesus' resurrection is not entailed by naturalism because it requires the additional belief that naturalism applies generally. Other interpretations are possible. They could start with an acknowledgement that Bultmann has captured only part of the meaning of Jesus' resurrection, but only part of it. By leaving out the resurrection of the physical body, Bultmann leaves out the guarantee for the physical resurrection of Jesus' followers on a newly created physical earth. As Nancey Murphy observes: "If theological meanings are not grounded in theological facts — facts about the character and acts of God, in particular, then they are mere fairy tales, however comforting they may be." (Murphy, 1996: 153).

CONCLUSION

It has become evident that the understanding of nature both in and outside of science as well as the understanding of Scripture in theology each involves levels of interpretation. Each takes place according to its own procedures that are different because they seek to do justice to different objects. Further, worldview can have effects down the levels in each hierarchy of interpretation. What I have not shown is that worldview connects the two hierarchies in one person. That would require a case study of a person who was involved to the same degree in the scientific interpretation of both nature and Scripture. Due to the specialization of professions such cases cannot be found among contemporaries. Dobzhansky's interpretation of Scripture did not have the same depth as his interpretation of nature. Likewise, Bultmann was not a professional interpreter of nature. One might have to turn to Isaac Newton, Johannes Kepler or John Philoponos to find equal involvement with both nature and Scripture.

Therefore, what I have shown is that Dobzhansky's religiously formed world-view influenced his explanation of population genetics, and that Bultmann's scientifically shaped worldview affected his interpretation of New Testament texts about the resurrection. However, no Christian is without a pre-scientific interpretation of nature and Scripture. Therefore, what I have shown is that pre-scientifically worldview connects the two hierarchies in one person

Direct interaction between the hierarchies is possible at any level. However, this often creates problems such as, for instance, a neglect of differences in subject matter and in context. Interaction at the worldview level would avoid these problems because at that level the hierarchies of interpretation share the subject matter, namely nature seen as divine creation. There are at least two benefits of restricting direct interaction to the worldview level. First, it opens up worldview to critique. A critique of worldview can often proceed independent of the different scientific theories or exegeses presented under its umbrella because their link with world view is not logical, but causal and indirect. Second, ideas originating at the worldview level can be specified and become hypotheses whose testing can proceed according to criteria internal to science and exegesis. In this way the integrity of both is respected. "[R]eligion can purify science from idolatry and false absolutes." (Pope John Paul II, 1988: M13). For instance, Bultmann's understanding of science can be purified of the false absolutes of naturalism and its accompanying scientism by religion. But it can do so only from a position of integrity. This means that the story of creation, Fall, and redemption cannot be retold naturalistically. Further, biblicism in science can be avoided while different scientific concepts and explanations of nature can be introduced. Likewise, "Science can purify religion from error and superstition; ...." (Pope John Paul II: 1988: M13). That is, science can purify religion from the error of telling its story in the terms of a false world picture. Celebrated examples include the correction of the geocentric interpretation of texts about the earth and of the static-Platonic interpretation of texts about 'kinds' of animals and plants. In such cases science can help correct exegesis and scientism in exegesis can be avoided because mutual purification presupposes that the integrity of both science and exegesis is respected. This can be achieved if science finds cause in theology to reconsider its knowledge and *vice versa*. To a Liberal theologian this may seem like biblicism while to a Fundamentalist this may seem like Liberal Theology. It is neither.

Acknowledgments

George Vandervelde and Al Wolters graciously allowed me to benefit from their expert knowledge in systematic theology and biblical studies by commenting on a previous draft of this paper. Any remaining infelicities are on my account.

Bibliography

Anderson, R.S. (1998) "On Being Human: The Spiritual Saga of a Creaturely Soul." In: *Whatever Happened to the Human Soul? Scientific and Theological Portraits of Human Nature.* Eds. W.S. Brown, N. Murphy, H. Newton Maloney. Fortress Press. Minneapolis. pp. 175-194.

Brooke, John H. (1985) "The relations between Darwin's science and his religion." In: John Durant, editor. *Darwinism and Divinity: Essays on Evolution and Religious Belief.* Basil Blackwell. Oxford.

Brooke, John H. (1996) "Religious Belief and the Natural Sciences: Mapping the Historical Landscape." In: *Facets of Faith and Science.* Vol. 1. *Historiography and Modes of Interaction.* Ed. Jitse M. van der Meer. The Pascal Centre/The University Press of America. Lanham. pp. 1-26.

Brooke, John H., Osler Margaret J., and van der Meer, Jitse M. editors (2001) *Science in Theistic Contexts.* Osiris 16 (forthcoming).

Brown, W.S. "Conclusion: Reconciling Scientific and Biblical Portraits of Human Nature." In: *Whatever Happened to the Human Soul? Scientific and Theological Portraits of Human Nature.* Eds. W.S. Brown, N. Murphy, H. Newton Maloney. Fortress Press. Minneapolis. pp. 213-228.

Brown, Warren S., Murphy Nancey and Malony H. Newton. Editors (1998) *Whatever Happened to the Human Soul? Scientific and Theological Portraits of Human Nature.* Fortress Press. Minneapolis.

Bultmann, Rudolf (1968) "Ethical and Mystical religion in Primitive Christianity." In: Robinson, James M. (ed.) *The Beginnings of Dialectical Theology.* John Knox Press. Richmond. VA.

Bultmann, Rudolf (1933) *Glauben und Verstehen*, Band I. J. C. B. Mohr (Paul Siebeck). Tübingen.

Bultmann, Rudolf (1952) *Theology of the New Testament.* Vol. 1. Tr. Kendrick Gobel. SCM Press. London.

Bultmann, Rudolf (1976) *Der zweite Brief and die Korinther.* Vandenhoeck & Ruprecht. Göttingen.

Bultmann, Rudolf (1984) *New Testament and Mythology and other Basic Writings.* Ed. Ogden, Schubert M. Fortress Press. Philadelphia.

Cooper, John W. (1989) *Body, Soul & Life Everlasting. Biblical Anthropology and the Monism-Dualism Debate.* Eerdmans. Grand Rapids.

Dobzhansky Papers: Theodosius Dobzhansky Papers, American Philosophical Society,

Philadelphia.

Dobzhansky, Theodosius (1937) *Genetics and the Origin of Species*. Columbia University Press. New York.

Dobzhansky, Theodosius (1967) *The Biology of Ultimate Concern*. New American Library. New York.

Eger, Martin (1999) "Language and the Double Hermeneutic in Natural Science." In: (M. Fehér, O. Kiss, L. Ropolyi eds.) *Hermeneutics and Science: Proceedings of the International Society for Hermeneutics and Science*. Kluwer Academic Publishers. Dordrecht, Boston. Pp. 265-280.

Grant, Edward (1986) "Science and Theology in the Middle Ages." In: Lindberg David C., Numbers, Ronald L. (eds.) *God and Nature: Historical Essays on the Encounter between Christianity and Science*. Pp. 49-75. University of California Press. Berkeley. 1986.

Green, Joel B. (1998) " Bodies — That is, Human Lives': A Re-Examination of Human Nature in the Bible." In: *Whatever Happened to the Human Soul? Scientific and Theological Portraits of Human Nature*. Eds. W.S. Brown, N. Murphy, H. Newton Maloney. Fortress Press. Minneapolis. pp. 149-173.

Gregersen, Niels H. (2002) "Beyond the Balance: Theology in a World of Autopoietic Systems." In: Gregersen, N. and Gorman, U. (eds.) *Design and Disorder*. T & T Clark. Edinborough. Wm. B. Eerdmans. Grand Rapids.

Henderson, Ian (1966) *Rudolf Bultmann*. John Knox Press. Richmond, Virginia.

John Paul II, Pope (1988) "Message of His Holiness Pope John Paul II." In: Robert John Russell, William Stoeger, S.J. and George V. Coyne, S.J. (Eds.) *Physics, Philosophy and Theology: A common Quest for Understanding*. Vatican Observatory. Vatican City State.

Johnson, Roger A. (1987) *Rudolf Bultmann: Interpreting Faith for the Modern Era*. Collins. London.

Laudan, Larry (1977) *Progress and its Problems: Towards a Theory of Scientific Growth*. University of California Press. Berkeley.

McGrath, Alister E. (1998) *The Foundations of Dialogue in Science and Religion*. Blackwell Publishers. Oxford.

Murphy, Nancey (1996) "On the nature of theology" In: *Religion and Science: History, Method, Dialogue*, eds. W.M. Richardson, W.J. Wildman. Routledge. New York, NY.

Murphy, Nancey (1998) "Human Nature: Historical, Scientific, and Religious Issues." In: *Whatever Happened to the Human Soul? Scientific and Theological Portraits of Human Nature*. Eds. W.S. Brown, N. Murphy, H. Newton Maloney. Fortress Press. Minneapolis. pp. 1-29.

Polkinghorne, John C. (1989) *Science and Providence.* SPCK/New Science Library. London.

Polkinghorne, John C. (1994) *Science and Christian Belief: Theological Reflections of a Bottom-Up Thinker.* SPCK. London.

Poythress, Verne S. (1988) *Science and Hermeneutics: Implications of Scientific Method for Biblical Interpretation.* Zondervan. Grand Rapids.

Ramm, Bernard (1954) *The Christian View of Science and Scripture.* Eerdmans. Grand Rapids.

Ruse, Michael (1996) *Monad to Man: The Concept of Progress in Evolutionary Biology.* Harvard University Press. Cambridge, MA.

Soskice, Janet (1985) *Metaphor and Religious Language.* Clarendon Press. Oxford.

Van der Meer, Jitse M. Editor. (1996) *Facets of Faith and Science.* 4 Vols. University Press of America/The Pascal Centre. Lanham.

Van der Meer, Jitse M. (1999a) "The Role of Metaphysical & Religious Beliefs in Science." In: *Studies in Science and Theology 5:* 247-256 (1997). (Eds. N.H. Gregersen, M.W. Parsons). Labor et Fides. Geneva.

Van der Meer, J.M. (1999b) "The Engagement of Religion and Biology: A Case Study in the Mediating Role of Metaphor in the Sociobiology of Lumsden and Wilson." *Biology and Philosophy* (Forthcoming).

Wykstra, Stephen J. (1996) "Should Worldviews Shape Science? Toward a Integrationist Approach of Scientific Theorizing." In: *Facets of Faith and Science. The Role of Beliefs in Mathematics and the Natural Sciences: An Augustinian Perspective.* Vol. 2, ed. J.M. van der Meer. Lanham: University Press of America/The Pascal Centre. Pages 123-171.

Wolters, Albert (2000) "Confessional Criticism and the Night Visions of Zecheriah." In: C. Bartholomew, C. Green and K. Möller (eds.) *Renewing Biblical Interpretation.* The Scripture and Hermeneutics Series, Volume 1: pp. 90-117. Paternoster Press, Carlisle, U.K. and Zondervan, Grand Rapids, U.S.A. 2000.

Yamauchi, Edwin M. (1994) "Gnosticism and Early Christianity." In: Wendy E. Helleman, ed. *Hellenization Revisited: Shaping a Christian Response within the Greco-Roman World.* University Press of America. Lanham. Pp. 29-61.

Toward a Theology of the Human Body

Father Earl Muller, S.J., Professor of Theology, Sacred Heart Major Seminary in Detroit, has taught many courses in theology both on the graduate and undergraduate level. He earned his PhD in 1987 from Marquette University where he taught theology from 1987-1995. His dissertation: *Trinity and Marriage in Paul: Theological Shape as Ground for a Scriptural Warrant for a Communitarian Analogy of the Trinity*, was subsequently published by Peter Lang Publishers in New York in 1990.

He served as Visiting Professor of Theology at the Pontifical Gregorian University in Rome from 1995-1999 and also wrote a number of articles among which are: "Real Relations and the Divine: Issues in Thomas's Understanding of God's Relation to the World," *Theological Studies* (1995) and "The Trinity and the Kingdom," *Studia Missionalia* (1997). He has also delivered many lectures.

Introduction

What follows are primarily sketches of some issues relevant for a complete theology of the body. The largest section which follows, on transcendence, is actually a prolegomenon addressing the question whether a theology of the body is at all possible. It also aims at identifying several pitfalls for such an endeavor. The much shorter final section is a series of brief reflections exploring various aspects of a theology of the body.

One's instinctive tendency is to understand the human body in terms of the biochemical system that constitutes the individual human person. The term 'body' has a wider use to include social realities as in the expression 'the body politic' but this is generally taken to be a metaphorical use. One reason for this is the shift in the mode of unity that defines a given body. On the large scale it is gravity which provides the mode of unity for celestial bodies, whether it be the universe as a whole or smaller bodies such as galaxies, stars, or planets. On a smaller scale bodies are constituted by the electromagnetic force and it is to this category that the biochemical system of the individual human body belongs. Nuclear bodies are defined in terms of strong and weak forces. Social forces that form the basis for communal bodies do not fit readily into any of these physically based definitions for a body; hence, the tendency to distinguish the individual's body sharply from the social body in terms of the literal and the metaphorical.

This, however, runs the risk of overlooking or misprizing important aspects of the individual's body that have primary importance in terms of functioning within the human community. It is the species that has materially evolved and the materiality of that species must be considered in all its aspects if an accurate appreciation of even the individual's body is to be achieved. This is simply one manifestation of a relational metaphysics which would locate the reality, meaning, and value of beings in terms of their relations to others. Such a relational metaphysics has its ultimate foundation in the Christian doctrine of God who is Himself understood in terms of subsistent relationality.[1]

Human reality exists in three distinct, if inseparable, modes - the individual, the communal, the interactional.[2] The primary mode is that of the individual in that the other two modes presuppose the existence of individuals. The interactional likewise presupposes the communal mode since all human interaction takes place in a communal context. This may seem counter-intuitional if, for instance, community is understood primarily as a nexus of human interactions. Human interactions, however, never occur in a vacuum. Something that is established only on the level of the communal is always operative in these interactions even if it is only the bare recognition that the other is human. Having said this it is also true that the three modes of human existence mutually imply one another. Thus, the individual comes into existence and grows only in the context of the human community, only in the context of concrete human interactions. The following presentation must, accordingly proceed in such a way as to take this complex way of human existing into consideration. Each of the three modes will be considered separately for the sake of clear exposition but there will need to be a constant referencing to the other modes.

The theological character of the following remarks presuppose, of course, a further relational dimension to human reality, one that leads in a transcendent direction. Transcendence has traditionally been understood to be twofold — a relative personal one usually identified as the rational soul, also often identified with the personhood of the individual (not to be confused with personality) and an absolute divine transcendence which is of another order of being. Some account of the (atheistic) humanist denial of transcendence characteristic of modernity needs to be considered and this for three reasons.[3] First, humanists have laid claim to science. If their claim is valid then it would follow that theology can have nothing valid to say about the human body. Second, precision needs to be provided to the relation of the human body to the transcendent dimension. For this purpose several false versions of this, part and parcel of the humanist critique of theology, need to be cleared away. Third, science has progressed beyond the data and paradigms which had driven the humanist critique to date. Some account needs to be made of this if the present discussion is to be properly situated. Since the validity of any theology of the body depends on these issues being addressed this paper will begin here.

Transcendence, Science, and Humanistic Culture

Popular culture associated with science is a curious beast in that it finds itself closely associated also with fantasy and even with spiritualism. The late night commercials for mediums and tarot readings which accompany science fiction offerings provide their own eloquent testimony to this. There are important reasons for this alliance between science and fantasy in the popular mind which have some bearing on the present topic.

"Most good 'fairy-stories'," wrote J. R. Tolkien, "are about the *adventures* of men in the Perilous Realm or upon its shadowy marches."[4] He argues a genuine fairy-story should be presented as true.[5] The story-maker "makes a Secondary World which your mind can enter. Inside it, what he relates is 'true': it accords with the laws of that world. You therefore believe it, while you are, as it were, inside."[6] The skill of the story-maker is in being able to evoke such a world. There is no suspension of belief, according to Tolkien, "no special 'wish to believe'" or conviction "that such things could happen, or had happened, in 'real life.' Fairy-stories were plainly not primarily concerned with possibility, but with desirability. If they awakened *desire*, satisfying it while often whetting it unbearably, they succeeded."[7]

He distinguishes "Faerie" from Magic, even while acknowledging their similarity. The former "is magic of a peculiar mood and power, at the furthest pole from the vulgar devices of the laborious, scientific, magician."[8] Later he spells this out. It is enchantment which "produces a Secondary World into which both designer and spectator can enter, to the satisfaction of their senses while they are inside; but in its purity it is artistic in desire and purpose." Magic, on the other hand, "produces, or pretends to produce, an alteration in the Primary World. It does not matter by whom it is said to be practised, fay or mortal, it remains distinct from the other two; it is not an art but a technique; its desire is *power* in this world, domination of things and wills."[9]

The Primary World and the Secondary World of fairy-stories are not totally diverse. "Fantasy is made out of the Primary World, but a good craftsman loves his material, and has a knowledge and feeling for clay, stone and wood which only the art of making can give .... fairy-stories deal largely, or (the better ones) mainly, with simple or fundamental things, untouched by Fantasy, but these simplicities are made all the more luminous by their setting."[10] He expands on this thought in his epilogue: "Probably every writer making a secondary world, a fantasy, every sub-creator, wishes in some measure to be a real maker, or hopes that he is drawing on reality: hopes that the peculiar quality of this secondary world (if not all the details) are derived from Reality, or are flowing into it."

Much the same sort of things could be said of science-fiction and Tolkien is explicit on the point. Benedict Ashley is convinced that "the literary genre which has been most characteristic of Humanism . . . has been the novel which has also formed the basis of much that appears in the cinema and television." He goes on to provide a somewhat piquant view of recent science fiction:

> we find ourselves in a world that transcends the space and time of earth and enters a world of light and darkness where the form of the human body takes on protean shapes and the distinction between nature and machines vanishes. The objective world seems totally absorbed into the subjectivity of the human inventor and yet that subjectivity gives birth to nothing but robots engaged in star wars.[11]

As a fan of the genre I tend to be more optimistic about its potentialities. Still, Ashley is not wrong about the cultural truisms that frequently show up in this literature. Whether it is Hal of the *2001* series of films or the character Data of *Star Trek* or Asimov's robots or any of a multitude of other examples, machines in the popular culture have been endowed with personhood which has the converse implication of a denial of any human transcendence. These are surely literary creations with no counterpart in the 'real' world. Still, they are believed in by many people in this world. There are scientists engaged in artificial intelligence work, attempting to create a Turing device (one which can mimic human responses beyond detection) who believe this.

In the *Wizard of Oz* Dorothy is transported to a world where inanimate objects (the scarecrow and the tin man) and animals (the cowardly lion) talk. Science fiction has its robots and aliens. There are scientists engaged in building up language skills in gorillas and chimpanzees and who claim that their 'success' undercuts the human claim to uniqueness. The SETI project is specifically aimed at finding talking animals in the universe besides ourselves because "surely we are not unique." The laws of chance practically dictate that if an intelligent species, humanity, can arise once from the process of biological evolution it can arise more than once, indeed, many times given the vastness of the universe.

The reductionism of these visions proceeds from two similar sources. Occam's Razor, that "entities should not be multiplied unnecessarily," which is to say, "that the simplest of competing theories be preferred to the more complex or that explanations of unknown phenomena be sought first in terms of known quantities," is appealed as well as its correlate, the pragmatic principle.[12]

> The pragmatic method is primarily a method of settling metaphysical disputes that otherwise might be interminable. Is the world one or many? — fated or free? — material or spiritual? — here are notions either of which may or may not hold good of the world; and disputes over such notions are unending. The pragmatic method in such cases is to try to interpret each notion by tracing its respective practical consequences. What difference would it practically make to any one if this notion rather than that notion were true? If no practical difference whatever can be traced, then the alternatives mean practically the same thing, and all dispute is idle. Whenever a dispute is serious, we ought to be able to show some practical difference that must follow from one side or the other's being right.[13]

There is, on one level, no particular difficulty religiously with these postulates. Whether or not one has an eternal destiny dependent on the existence of a munificent God who has sent His Son for human salvation is certainly an eminently pragmatic question. Judeo-Christian faith has certainly exercised something similar to Occam's Razor in calling into question the need for a multiplicity of gods and goddesses to explain the origins of the world or the human experience of redemption. The humanist, however, presses these principles to argue that there is no need for any transcendent dimension to explain empirical reality. Of course, Christians point out any number of empirical events that challenge such a reductionism: the resurrection of Christ as attested to by a number of witnesses or various miracles down to the present day for which competent scientists have no demonstrable explanation to mention two. There are phenomena that support a religious (and thus, theological) interpretation. Tolkien concluded his essay on an explicitly theological note:

> I would venture to say that approaching the Christian Story from this direction,[14] it has long been my feeling (a joyous feeling) that God redeemed the corrupt making-creatures, men, in a way fitting to this aspect, as to others of their strange nature. The Gospels contain a fairy-story, or a story of a larger kind which embraces all the essence of fairy-stories. They contain many marvels — peculiarly artistic, beautiful, and moving: "mythical" in their perfect, self-contained significance; and among the marvels is the greatest and most complete conceivable eucatastrophe. But this story has entered History and the primary world; the desire and aspiration of sub-creation has been raised to the fulfilment of Creation. The Birth of Christ is the eucatastrophe of Man's history. The Resurrection is the eucatastrophe of the story of the Incarnation. This story begins and ends in joy. It has pre-eminently the "inner consistency of reality." There is no tale ever told that men would rather find was true, and none which so many sceptical men have accepted as true on its own merits. For the Art of it has the supremely convincing tone of Primary Art, that is, of Creation. To reject it leads either to sadness or to Wrath.[15]

That humanists can proffer explanations such as hallucination, chicanery, or physical principles as yet unknown does not change this. This diversity of explanatory schemes does, however, underscore the fact that all such systems, Christian or humanist, are imaginative renderings of the human mind. They are synthetic grasps of human experience, either the messy day to day experience of life or the controlled experience of scientists. The ability to generalize and abstract, to synthesize and explore new possibilities underlies scientific methodology, cultural syntheses, and good story-telling alike.[16] The question will be whether and to what extent the most recent advances in science provide support to these two competing visions. In what follows I will set out some of the reasons why humanists have arrived at the view of man they have and address the question whether the most recent discoveries continue to support the reasons originally adduced by humanists for their position.

A. *Shifting paradigms*

The humanist view of man arose out of several converging lines of thought, some of which were related to advances in science. Some have tried to see this simply in the rise of modern science itself. This is simplistic. "The chief seventeenth century founders of modern science. . . were Christians who were convinced their scientific discoveries would bolster the Christian faith, not undermine it."[17] Others have looked to the renaissance of Greek learning in the period leading up to the Reformation but this was simply an extension of the medieval assimilation of Greek philosophy. Still others have looked to the rising of the middle-class rebelling against the narrowness of a prior theology and far more inclined to a skeptical, critical attitude. The Protestant Reformation is seen as an instance of this. Still, this skepticism tended not to be anti-Christian as such but anti-intellectual and the rise of critical methodology was as much the work of Christians as of those who rejected Christianity.[18] Ashley is inclined to agree with Arnold Toynbee that the root of secularist humanism lies in the religious wars of the sixteenth and seventeenth centuries which concretely called into question Christianity's claim to be a redemptive religion. That modern science was developing at the same time provided for such people an attractive focal point for an alternative world-view.

The sort of impact that the development of science has had on the anthropology of humanist culture was captured by J. L. Blau's expression: "With Freud, man lost his Godlike mind; with Darwin his exalted place among the creatures on earth; with Copernicus man had lost his privileged position in the universe."[19] These shifts and the reasons for them need to be considered briefly before moving on to a consideration of the human body proper.

The displacement of man was not the initial problem raised by Copernicus's *De Revolutionibus*. More immediate was the felt challenge to the regnant Aristotelian (and Ptolemaic) cosmology which left even many contemporary scientists cool to the "Copernican revolution" and to the inerrancy of Scripture which seemed, in passages such as Jos. 10:12-13; Ps. 93:1, 104:19; Eccl. 1:4-5, to imply a geocentric universe.[20] Copernicus was rather cautious and avoided any condemnation in his own lifetime. That came some seventy years later in the context of the controversy that erupted over Galileo who made himself the champion of Copernicus's system. Neither Copernicus nor Galileo had any challenge to man's place in the universe in mind but

> by challenging the traditional view of the universe, Galileo upset the psychological security that derived from the neatly ordered inter-related hierarchies of astronomy, philosophy and theology. His opponents were afraid that if the geocentric concept fell, the whole construct of cosmology, the truth of the Scriptures and the anthropocentrism of creation would have to fall with it.[21]

Copernicus's system also led to another short-term development that was to have a profound effect on the humanist imagination and this was his solution to the problem of parallax. One would expect to see relative movement among the stars if and as the earth progressed around the sun in its orbit. This was not observable and the only explanation that Copernicus could offer was that the stars were very, very far away.[22] By the time of Galileo Giordano Bruno was arguing that the universe was infinite, with an infinite number of planets circling an infinite number of suns.[23] Bruno thought this befitted an infinite Creator; by the time of the Enlightenment this was no longer taken for granted even if the notion of an infinite universe attracted considerable support.[24] By then also the heliocentric view itself was being reconsidered. The Milky Way as a galaxy was being discovered. The sun was understood to be simply one star among many circling the galactic center.[25] By the early twentieth century even the centrality of our own galaxy was shaken by the discovery of other island universes by Edwin Hubble in 1924 who measured the distance to the Andromeda Galaxy and demonstrated that it was the same size as the Milky Way.[26] Humanity had been thoroughly decentered from the universe, "tucked away in some forgotten corner of the Cosmos."[27]

The second shift was rooted in the emerging understanding of the human body itself. From the time of Massacio naturalism in art reigned, certainly in the Florentine school.[28] Figures were painted "in the round, and not merely as flat things on the canvas .... the pictures showed off a knowledge of muscles or virtuosity in the handling of problems of perspective."[29] The older anatomy of Galen and Aristotle was being challenged already in the time of Copernicus. Vesalius published his *De Fabrica* the same year that the *De Revolutionibus* appeared. This led to William Harvey's discovery of the circulation of the blood in the time of Galileo. Harvey described "the heart as 'a piece of machinery in which though one wheel gives motion to another, yet all the wheels seem to move simultaneously'."[30] There was throughout this time a growing "interest in the operation of pure mechanism."

> One thing is clear: not only was there in some of the intellectual leaders a great aspiration to demonstrate that the universe ran like a piece of clockwork, but this was itself initially a religious aspiration. It was felt that there would be something defective in Creation itself — something not quite worthy of God — unless the whole system of the universe could be shown to be interlocking, so that it carried the pattern of reasonableness and orderliness.[31]

This interest in explaining "everything in the physical universe by mechanical processes had important effects upon the biological sciences, upon which it tended to imprint its own peculiar character."[32]

It took some thirty to fifty years for Harvey's work to be widely accepted.[33] René Descartes, a contemporary, while disagreeing with (and not understanding) Harvey on various points[34] nonetheless accepted the notion of the body as a complex mechanism. That notion has long survived his system "and came to dominate the whole development of modern science."[35] Descartes was convinced "that every natural structure . . . had been brought about by natural processes." These process were able "to build the most complicated living structures because they were regulated very precisely by the laws of motion instituted by God."[36] This thought eventually leads in two directions within humanistic culture — the dispensability of the soul and the theory of evolution.

The notion of a watchmaker God, characteristic of Deism, who wound up the universe and let it run without interference was easily extended also to the human body and its soul. And as the one was quickly judged to be superfluous so was the other. Thomas Hobbes, a contemporary of Descartes was already arguing that

> the notion of an incorporeal substance is incoherent . . . Persons are not some combination of matter and spirit, but are wholly corporeal begins .... Thoughts and sensations are really the internal effects of external stimuli operating upon the body's sense organs and from them on the brain and heart. Psychological states and events are produced in us by the motion of the body's complex machinery.[37]

A century later Julien Offray de La Mettrie was arguing that "humans are *nothing but machines*, that is, that mechanical processes are the key to understanding human activity, including reason.[38] The nineteenth century saw

> the development of brain physiology, experimental psychology, and scientific psychiatry.
>
> Brain physiologists and psychiatrists noticed the direct causal influence of cerebral functioning on states of consciousness. Mental capacities such as thought, memory, understanding, and even the use of the senses were found to be correlated with specific area of the brain . . . Consciousness, mental capacities, and personality characteristics are rooted in the brain and the organism, not in some immaterial substance or unobserved entity called the soul or mind ....
>
> Similar positions were emerging in experimental psychology. Whereas classical psychology had always claimed the soul and its faculties as its proper object of study, pioneers of the new scientific psychology such as William James and Wilhelm Wundt preferred to speak of consciousness and its functions. Psychologists no longer took themselves to be dealing with the operations of a distinct entity, but a dimension of the organism closely tied to the brain.[39]

More recently behaviorism has developed this tendency.

Butterfield analyzed the problems in terms of the strictness of the separatio Descartes made "between thought and matter, soul and body" that resiste being bridged "with anything sort of a miracle that defeated imagination."

> Animals had a purely corporeal, unconscious kind of sensation, but no consciousness, no mental agony, no real ability to feel pain. God, the human soul and the whole realm of spiritual things, however, escaped imprisonment the process of mechanisation, and were superadded presences, flitting vaporously amongst the cog-wheels, the pulleys, the steel castings of a relentless world-machine. It was very difficult to show how these two planes of existence could ever have come to intersect, or at what point mind or soul could ever join up with matter.[40]

The metaphor that Butterfield alludes to can be traced back to Gilbert Ry| who, after setting forth the "official doctrine" that emanated largely fro Descartes, went on to describe his own attitude toward this view: "I shall ofte speak of it, with deliberate abusiveness, as 'the dogma of the Ghost in the ma chine'. I hope to prove that it is entirely false, and false not in detail but i principle."[41] To that end Ryle tries "to show that the official theories (consciousness and introspection are logical muddles."[42]

Not everyone agreed with Descartes "that every natural structure . . . had bee brought about by natural processes." Robert Boyle a generation later was pro nouncing incredulous "that either these *Cartesian laws of Motion*, or the *Ep curean casual concourse* of Atoms could bring meer Matter into so orderly an well contriv'd a Fabrick as this World." Not only was a divine Architect neede at the beginning but he was of the opinion that it was "utterly improbable tha *brute and unguided*, though *moving*, Matter should ever convene into suc admirable structures, as the bodies of perfect Animals."[43] Boyle's position wa momentarily supported by the experiments of Francesco Redi which dispose of the notion of spontaneous generation of living creatures in nature. Regula generation proved more difficult with its transformation of seemingl homogeneous material into complex living structures but this was resolved b recourse to the Stoic-like notion of minute seeds or germs created at th beginning of the world by God.[44]

If the seventeenth century was comfortable with the notion of a Nature passiv before the creative activity of God, the eighteenth century was not. Under tha view one was required to posit the generation of monsters and other abnorm beings to the divine will. Furthermore, in the generation after Boyle scientis were making discoveries that undermined the idea of pre-existing germ Polyps and hydras were seen to regenerate after being cut into several piece muscle tissue, even when disconnected from the nervous system, were seen to contract when pricked. More and more eighteenth-century philosophers "agreed that nature should be studied directly without reference to a divine Being whose existence could not be ascertained and whose intervention into natural phenomena put a limit, so to speak, on the power of human understanding."[45] By 1747 de La Mettrie, in *L'homme machine*, was concluding that "if nature is spontaneously active . . . there is no need of God. As for the order that obviously reigns over the living world . . . it, too, could be explained without recourse to God."[46]

Be that as it may eighteenth century scientists were still reluctant to see the emergence and development of life as a matter of blind chance. Thus Comte de Buffon argued for the existence of "living matter" made of "organic molecules."

But by insisting that Nature is perpetually active, by emphasizing natural processes rather than natural structures, Buffon's thought tended to eliminate God, replacing Him with Nature and history. By combining the active power of Nature with natural mechanism acting through the course of history, Buffon was able to allow for significant alterations of natural structures. Limited as it is, Buffon's theory of evolution introduced a new historical dimension into biological thought, a dimension that increased the explanatory power of biological mechanism at the expense of the traditional idea of creation.[47]

Still others went beyond Buffon in the eighteenth century, not being satisfied with the presumption of psychic qualities and other sorts of life-oriented forces, and insisted on a "vital principle" in nature to explain things like embryonic development.

The first complete theory of evolution was proposed by Jean Baptiste Lamarck early in the nineteenth century. Lamarck was no vitalist and proposed a mechanical view of the causes of life but still, he did distinguish between the "within" of things and a "without" and proposed an evolutionary process that was not reducible to chance.[48] His descriptions of the physical processes which underlie biological mechanisms, at points fanciful, have not stood the test of time but "his reduction of all biological phenomena to physical processes provided a model that had a far-reaching, though somewhat delayed, influence."[49]

Vitalism influenced European physiology until the middle of the nineteenth century when they were edged out by a new breed who shared the reductionist perspective of La Mettrie and Lamarck. The more radical espoused an openly materialist philosophy. This was fostered by the first synthesis of organic compounds at the end of the first third of the century. It also converged with other developments, the most notable being Charles Darwin's theory of natural selection.

Many naturalists of the nineteenth century were clergymen. Darwin was simultaneously oriented toward a missionary life and toward the observation of nature by his father, an Anglican clergyman. It was in this context that the young Charles was on the Beagle and made the observations that led him to doubt that species persisted unaltered.

> From 1837 he shaped his scientific work as an argument for the proposition that species of organisms arose from other species. To explain the changes that gave rise to new species, he developed the concept of natural selection, by which he meant that in changed conditions of life some organisms will be better adapted than others because of random variations, and they will leave more offspring in the next generation.[50]

Other lines of inquiry converged to provide support for Darwin's position. As early as the seventeenth century Niels Stensen was interpreting rock strata in Tuscany in terms of a temporal sequence of events.[51] Descartes himself had proposed an infinite universe in which the earth and any number of similar bodies could originate by physical processes. A century later Pierre Simon de Laplace was proposing his nebular theory for the origin of the solar system. The eighteenth century saw a proliferation of theories of the origin of the earth in which geological strata and the presence of fossils played various roles. The most significant development during this period was the "separation of the origin of the earth from the origin of mankind." "It created a new kind of history, a history without human documents, which required new conceptual tools."[52]

Biblical cosmology had closely tied the creation of the universe to the creation of humanity. Creation was centered on humanity. The sun, moon, and stars in Gen. 1:14, for instance, were created for signs and for seasons. Ultimately creation was centered on Christ. The geocentrism that was the staple of the pre-Copernican world was part and parcel with this. So too was the centralization of Christ in time. There were four periods of time: the antediluvial from the origins of the earth and humankind to the Flood, the period of the Old Covenant, Christ at the center, the period of the New Covenant, and then the post-parousial millennium to the end of the world.[53] But even as the growing knowledge of the size of the universe had shoved the earth off its pedestal and consigned it to some "forgotten corner of the Cosmos," so the growing knowledge of geological processes decentered humanity from the history of the earth itself. A vaster and vaster time period before the emergence of humankind was discovered and paralleled the ever enlarging universe around us.

Fossils were known in the seventeenth century but the general presupposition was that they were contemporaneous with early humans (and thus compatible with the biblical account). Empirical studies of the earth, often motivated by interest in mineral resources, began to take off in the eighteenth century. It became evident that there was a long prehuman "history" extending for at least hundreds of thousands of years. By the early nineteenth century the shifts in the types and morphology of fossils between the various geological strata were being detailed. The science of geology was coming into its own.

Geologists generally avoided committing to a definite time scale but by Darwin's time the consensus had extended it to something on the order of a hundred million years. Darwin needed yet a longer period of time for his mechanism to work and was attacked on this point. Still, the way had been prepared before him by the new science of geology which provided fossil evidence for the developmental shifts that could take place in the animal population of the earth and for the long periods of time available in earth prehuman existence for a mechanism of development. Subsequent studies have made it clear that the age of the earth is on the order of several billions of years, more than enough time for a process of evolution to produce the human genome.

If previous developments in geology prepared the ground for Darwin the nascent science of genetics provided detail on how a process of natural selection could function. Darwin published his *Origin of Species* in 1859. Seven years later Gregor Mendel was postulating the existence of "units of hereditary transmission" based on his studies of selective breeding. The vulnerability of genes and chromosomes to change provides the explanation of randomness which Darwin's theory required.

Christians impressed with this convergence of evidence consistently sought to reconcile an evolutionary understanding of the origins of the human species with the Christian faith, first with a variety of schemes to reconcile the long geological eras with the framework provided by the Scriptural account but also with arguments that natural selection was one more evidence of the providence of God. The emerging humanistic culture rallied around the agnosticism of a Thomas Huxley and concluded that the processes of evolution did not require even the services of a watchmaker God.

By the first half of the twentieth century the fossil evidence was leading a number of paleontologists to conclude not only that the human species had evolved from animal precursors but that this had happened a number of different times. Humanity was no longer seen to be unique, even on its own home planet. It required little in the way of a leap of the imagination to suppose, given the vastness and age of the universe, that a similar evolution had occurred on any number of different worlds.

The dethroning and reduction of humanity to machine status was complete in the minds of at least some in the secular culture. Thought itself was reduced to processes in the human body and that body was now seen to have derived from purely natural processes. Transcendence was needed neither for the one nor the other; both the ghost in the machine and the watchmaker God were banished from the humanist imagination.

B. *The Present Context*

Humanistic culture did not emerge all at once. It was the result of a number of converging factors ranging from the disarray of Christianity in the wake of the religious wars of the sixteenth century to the shifting paradigms of the emerging sciences. What the above survey also makes clear is that that culture on a number of points crystallized around the science of the nineteenth and early twentieth century. Science, however, has not remained static. In what follows I will examine very briefly some of the changed factors. These will make clear that a number of presuppositions of humanistic culture are not valid; they also pose a number of challenges to a Christian theology of the human body.

Considerable progress has been made in elucidating the cosmic processes needed for the production of the human body. A range of heavier elements are required in large enough concentrations and in a stable enough environment for life to emerge and develop. These elements, in considerable measure, were produced in stellar furnaces and then spewed out in cataclysmic explosions. They were further mixed with primordial gas clouds through galactic collisions that transformed the Milky Way from a small galaxy to its present large spiral form. Dynamics of solar genesis cleared out sufficient lighter elements to allow the formation of the inner rocky planets of our solar system.

What is clear, even in this cursory description, is that the emergence of the human body required a fair amount of cosmic turbulence. It also required a placement of the human species close enough to the turbulence to benefit from it and yet far enough away to avoid being destroyed by it. Both the solar system and the Milky Way have centers that are violent. If our earth were too close or too far away from the sun the human body could not form. If our sun were too close to the galactic core or too far away life on earth would not be possible — close proximity to other stars (or the central black hole) would preclude the sort of long-term stability needed for evolution to function adequately; extreme distance from the core would preclude the availability of the heavier elements needed for human evolution. The de-centered character of humanity is necessary given the physical laws governing the production of the heavy elements required for human existence. Still, there is a relative centering of humanity in the universe.

At about the same time that Hubble was discovering the size of the Andromeda Galaxy he and Milton Humason observed that many galaxies exhibited a red shift which indicated that they were receding from us.[54] This was the observation which provided the basis for the current dominant theory of the origins of the universe, the Big Bang. This should have reinstituted the notion of a center to the universe but humanist cosmologists have avoided this conclusion: "astronomers are fond of saying that space is curved, or that there is no center to the Cosmos, or that the universe is finite but unbounded."[55] More accurately, the center of the universe lies in a fifth spatio-temporal dimension, not in the four dimensions of this universe.

This does not, however, in itself, banish a determinate (even if only a shadow of the fifth dimensional) center from the universe. The example adduced is of an expanding fifth dimensional sphere and it is only in this sort of instance, a closed universe, that there would be no definable center within the universe. Such closure, however, is far from obvious since it would, in effect, require imagining the universe as an enormous black hole. There simply is not enough matter in the universe to create such closure.[56] What this means is that, if it appears to us that we are at the center of an expanding universe, this is not mere illusion.

Observations are now approaching the edge of the visible universe. We are seeing objects over twelve billion light years away which is, by most calculations, some ninety percent of the age of the universe. It is true that deep field studies currently cover only a tiny fraction of the entire sky; still, results to date suggest that the universe is more or less symmetrically arranged around us.[57] Humanity, if not in the dead center, is clearly in the central core of the universe.[58] Whatever else one can say, our section of space is hardly a "forgotten corner."

It is not important to turn this observation into a theological statement. To the extent that such an observation is confirmed the believer can say, "How appropriate." Christian faith, however, does not depend on this any more than it depended on the now irretrievable Ptolemaic system. What is important is that the counterclaim made by modern humanistic culture, which depends in large measure on the premise of the unprivileged position of the human race in the universe, no longer has the support it was presumed to have as recently as thirty to fifty years ago. We are, measurably, cosmically close to the center of things — perhaps about as close as is compatible with the production of human bodies. And this, given the vastness of the universe, occasions wonder.

This presumption that the human race is unprivileged in the universe leads to two correlated judgments. The first is a rejection of human transcendence as, for instance, ingredient in any belief in an immortal soul created by God.

Many, as noted above, are willing to dispense with this "ghost in the machine." Of course, this would require that the totality of the human phenomenon be explainable on this-worldly terms. A second judgment follows as a corollary. There is the conviction that evolution, either on our own planet or on other planets, could have produced other intelligent races. If humanity can be adequately explained in terms of evolutionary mechanisms then there is no reason why this sort of thing could not have happened many times over given the vastness of the cosmos: "Why should we, tucked away in some forgotten corner of the Cosmos, be so fortunate? To me, it seems far more likely that the universe is brimming over with life. But we humans do not yet know."[59] The problem with trying to explain the totality of the human phenomenon on this-worldly terms is the magnitude of the phenomenal shift:

> By a tiny 'tangential' increase, the 'radial' was turned back on itself and so to speak took an infinite leap forward. Outwardly, almost nothing in the organs had changed. But in depth, a great revolution had taken place: consciousness was now leaping and boiling in a space of super-sensory relationships and representations; and simultaneously consciousness was capable of perceiving itself in the concentrated simplicity of its faculties.[60]

Teilhard appealed to the notion of thresholds to describe this transition. Increase in a certain parameter produces no spectacular result until a transition point is reached at which point a small increase in the measured parameter produces large shifts in the observed effects. This, however, is not an explanation; it is a phenomenal description as Teilhard makes clear the footnote to the above citation — "it is only, it seems, *under the appearances* of a critical point that we can grasp experimentally the 'hominising' (spiritualising) step to reflection." This is without prejudice to the question whether the transition observed is understood to be naturally caused or caused by the creation of an immortal soul by God.

What counts as an explanation for a transition point? Physicists, through mathematical models, can demonstrate that transitions between solids, liquids, and gases are a function of the physical properties of the substance under consideration. It is a demonstration that can be made repeatedly with different substances. The transition to human intelligence is not so neatly explainable. The key issue is whether human civilization is sufficiently explained in terms of the development of a complex enough brain and that this large qualitative difference can be triggered by the sort of minimal increase in complexity which distinguishes the human brain from other primate brains. Clearly brain complexity is a sine qua non but is it enough?

The problem is that there is only a single instance available to us of such a small gain in complexity coinciding with the sort of enormous gain in intelligence and high culture which characterizes humanity. Methodologically science is not very comfortable with single instances of a phenomenon because all experimentation or testing of hypotheses is by that fact closed out. One can, in effect, propose whatever causality one desires with no danger of being contradicted by additional data. This will be as true of religious as of atheistic affirmations.

One possible way around this methodological awkwardness is to postulate a polygenetic or multiregional evolution. The data to date is ambiguous. Earlier in the twentieth century, as the number and variety of primate fossils multiplied, the view that modern humanity emerged more or less simultaneously in different parts of the world achieved a certain dominance. This earlier view, however, was largely based on fossil morphology. By the 1980's geneticists were concluding, based on mitochondrial, X-chromosome and other studies, that humanity emerged from Africa from a vanishingly small population. The dates for this convergence vary widely with some predating *homo sapiens* by a couple of hundred millennia. The problem is that these genetic studies may also be consistent with a multiregional emergence for humanity with subsequent interbreeding which has established the characteristics of the current unified species.[61] But this, to a certain extent, begs the question. If interbreeding was possible between these disparate primate groups they were already, in the single most important category, a single species. In any event, a polygenetic view no longer holds the field as it had earlier.

There is the further problem of correlating a specifically human rationality with any of these early hominid groups, especially with those which predate *homo sapiens* proper. This rationality is associated in part with the appearance of art and activity that seems to be cultic rather than simply with the use of tools. The reason for this is that art and cultic activity strongly suggest self-reflective activity in a way that the latter does not. After all, even modern non-human primates make use of and, in some measure, fashion tools. Still, the absence of art does not have to mean the absence of self-reflective consciousness. We simply have no clear means of ascertaining its presence earlier. All we can say with certainty is that currently the unity of the human species coincides with self-reflective rationality of a high order and that this is true as far back as we can reliably trace either phenomenon.[62]

Does Catholic theology require adherence to an "out of Africa" (and implicitly monogenetic) viewpoint? Polygenism is certainly problematic for Catholic theology but it may not be intractable. Pius XII, in his encyclical *Humanae Generis,* set out the relevant issues:

the faithful cannot embrace that opinion which maintains that either after Adam there existed on this earth true men who did not take their origin through natural generation from him as from the first parent of all, or that Adam represents a certain number of first parents. Now it is no way apparent how such an opinion can be reconciled with that which the sources of revealed truth and the documents of the Teaching Authority of the Church propose with regard to original sin, which proceeds from a sin actually committed by an individual Adam and which, through generation, is passed on to all and is in everyone as his own.[63]

There are a number of issues operating in the background of this statement ranging from the necessity of baptism for human salvation to the nature of human sinfulness to the centrality of Christ to salvation. One preliminary observation would be that the pope did not positively exclude a polygenetic view of evolution. He simply pointed out the obvious — it is not apparent how it can be reconciled with the faith of the Church. The concerns of that faith need to be briefly explored before one can decide whether there are polygenetic scenarios that would be compatible. Both the account in Genesis of the Fall and subsequent Christian reflection on it are a theological retrospective reflection — an analysis of humanity's current situation and the retrojection of the structure of that situation back to human origins. In a nature vs. nurture view of human sinfulness Christian faith has consistently held that it cannot be reduced to the latter — human sinfulness is not merely a matter of imitation, even though that is surely involved.[64] Human nature itself is flawed. But in insisting that the problem lies in human nature the Church rejected the Gnostic analysis which judged embodiment itself to be an evil. Human embodiment, as created by God, is good. The current sinful condition of humanity does not take its origin in any properties of matter, in any properties of the animal nature out of which we evolved. It was moral; it was self-inflicted.[65] There is the further claim that the whole of humanity is involved. Judaism had identified itself over and against "Gentile sinners" (cf. Gal. 2:15). But Israel itself had continually rebelled against God down to and including the rejection of His Son. There is no human group that has been preserved unfallen. All have fallen short (Rom. 3:23). Judeo-Christian faith has also made the judgment that this is not a novelty within human history. There has been no golden era, when some human group was preserved from sin. Finally, the insistence on the individuality of Adam is due to the nature of sin — only individuals can sin in the proper sense of the term.

At some point some primate was endowed with an immortal soul. One need not argue that the first true human, in the sense understood by Pius XII, was a *homo sapiens*. "Adam" need not have been morphologically or genetically fully formed. All that is required is that he possessed an immortal soul. It is not even required that he have possessed this soul before he was fully grown. Nor is it required that other members of Adam's immediate species be similarly endowed. The soul was and is a direct creation by God. Coordinate with this would be the possession of intelligent self-awareness which is the prerequisite for the possibility of sin. His siblings would be as they were — hominids but not true humans, possessed of some form of intelligence, but incapable of sin in the proper sense of the word. This first true human chose perversely. The Genesis account actually envisions a second truly human primate, "Eve," but this is not really required. For that matter it is not really necessary that "Adam" be male. His line, however modified by interbreeding in and outside of his (and/or her) primate group, bred true (both with regard to the intellectual soul and to corruption) and came to dominate, came to be the present human species. This, of course, leaves open the possibility that this line of true humans formed liaisons with primates not truly human and that such liaisons were formative for the final shape of the human species, but this is not theologically significant.[66]

Is this the way it had to happen? There will never be sufficient data to decide this on a scientific basis.[67] The point is there is at least one scenario in which a Christian understanding of these matters is compatible with even a polygenetic evolutionary model. There may well be other scenarios possible; there is no need to explore them here. It may well be that the "out of Africa" theory of human origins will triumph. In any event, the humanist's alternative and atheistic vision is not forced by the data.

Another way around the methodological problem posed by the uniqueness of the human phenomenon would be to discover alien civilizations. Indeed, the presumption that humanity is unprivileged in the universe practically demands the existence of other intelligent races on other planets. The discovery of planets around nearby stars (and disks around others) would confirm the commonness of the mechanisms which led to the formation of our own solar system. None of the systems discovered so far would have supported the sort of four billion year planetary stability required for an evolutionary process to produce a species capable of high culture though this result is at present an artifact of the search methodology which relies on stellar wobble. The stars with the greatest wobble will be those with very large planets in close proximity, a configuration which precludes stable earth-type planets. Still, as methods and observations are refined it might be expected that there would be at least a few systems in the near vicinity that roughly correspond to the life-favoring configuration of our own. What is clear even at this point, however, is that the sort of extended stability enjoyed by our own system is other than the norm.

The discovery of other solar systems, by itself, does not resolve the methodological problem posed by human evolution. What is needed is the discovery of other intelligent species. Given the extreme time and energy required to travel to another stellar system (Voyager is estimated to require some 10,000 years) the only practical way that discovery can take place is through radio (or the equivalent) contact. To this end there has been a concerted effort to assay the signals from likely stellar neighbors. The SETI project, dedicated to this endeavor, has been operative for some thirty or forty years now with uniformly negative results. Their latest, more detailed survey, is perhaps a quarter complete, again with negative results.

All of these considerations leave the prospect more and more likely that, even supposing that there is another civilization out there somewhere, in the practical order we will never know about it. Our data set for the emergence of high intelligence consists of only a single clear instance and is not likely to expand. Like the central positioning of humanity in the universe this is a cause for wonder.

In itself the proposal that there are other intelligent races in the universe is not theologically problematic. Christians, for instance, have long been convinced of the existence of angels, which is to say, extraterrestrial intelligences. The Christian imagination has also countenanced the existence of other embodied intelligent races but it does insist on the privileged status of humanity because of the Incarnation. C. S. Lewis's space trilogy would be a case in point.

The view of physical matter itself has been radically rethought in the twentieth century. Newtonian physics and the optimism that everything in the universe could be explained in terms of various mechanisms was, to a certain extent, dependent on a particle understanding of matter. What was discovered in this past century was that matter displays quite a few wave properties and that it, accordingly, keeps slipping out of one's hands. Matter was discovered to be equivalent to energy. Atoms were discovered to be composed of protons, electrons, and neutrons and then rediscovered to be composed of an expanding array of even more elementary particles all of which at times behave as waves rather than particles. Determinate solutions to Newtonian equations have ceded ground to statistical solutions to quantum mechanical ones. Chaos theory is symptomatic of the shift from a search for mechanically determined systems to a search for recurring patterns.

At the same time science was discovering numerous self-limitations. Gödel demonstrated the essential openness of any logical system, which is to say, the inability of any logical system to be completely self-enclosed, ungrounded on any principle outside itself. Heisenberg set out the limits of observation in his uncertainty principle. The universe was discovered through Einstein's relativity and gravitational analyses to be finite in mass and through Hubble's observation of universal expansion to be finite in time.

There have been practical limits as well. Some equations are unsolvable by any but approximative methods. This is exacerbated by the ever increasing number of variables relevant to any concrete dynamic system. Computers have made continued progress possible but there are intractable limitations to what they can do. In important ways the scientific enterprise has become far "fuzzier" than was envisioned in the eighteenth and nineteenth centuries.

One might summarize the considerations of this section by noting that the sort of imaginative synthesis proposed by humanistic culture has lost significant elements of its grounding in more recent scientific advances. A Christian imaginative synthesis has, in contrast, gained ground.

Toward a Theology of the Human Body

The Deist objection to miracles or any special revelation of God was based, at least in part, on the presumption that the universe was a perfectly made clockwork mechanism. Of course, the exclusion of a transcendent God from the universe also had the effect of excluding any transcendent human personhood. If God cannot intervene in nature then, logically, neither can a transcendent human person. Later behaviorist interpretations of that personhood were already presaged by Hume's reduction of the "I" to a bundle of perceptions. But one can come at the question of transcendent personhood, divine or human, from the opposite direction. What sort of universe would God have to create to be compatible with transcendent freedom, where action by God or by a transcendent human person would not be a violation of nature but rather a fulfillment of the potentialities of the universe? It would certainly not be a clockwork mechanism. The irreducible "fuzziness" of the material universe which has been discovered in the last century is precisely the sort of thing one might expect.

The lack of a completely determinate physical mechanism leaves matter, and in particular the human body, available for or open to providing physical expression for a transcendent dimension. This "disponibility" of matter to transcendence lies at the heart of a theology of the body. It is available to God to express Himself as He chooses; it is available to the individual human person to express him or herself similarly. This expression is not, as such, part of the intrinsic intelligibility of matter, as if human personhood or divine activity were merely a working out of the intrinsic dynamics of matter.[68]

Matter is disponible to God and individual humans in different ways. Our power to affect material reality is exercised through our bodies. God is able to affect material reality without the mediation of a body; He also has a human body — that belonging to the Son. Nor does this explanation exhaust the modes of disponibility. As disponible to self-expression, then, the body provides the means for communication among humans and grounds the possibility of human community. The scholastic adage regarding matter captured this: that which separates unites.

This disponibility of matter ought not to be thought of as manipulation of matter at the quantum level. This simply provides a God or soul "of the gaps." Matter is disponible to God, to human persons on the macroscopic level because there is "play" on the quantum level. Methodologically science seeks to reduce all empirical observation to "mathematizable" patterns.[69] Recourse to alternate sorts of explanation (e.g. religious) amount to an abandonment of the method. Science rightly resists abandonment of its proper methodology. It ill behooves theology to pursue a strategy such as that represented by the expression "God of the gaps." An understanding of the human soul as "filling the gaps" in scientific explanation is likewise counterindicated. Either related strategy has the effect of transforming God or the human soul into a physical cause and this is ultimately counterproductive.

The Christological Starting Point

If the disponibility of matter to transcendence lies at the heart of a theology of the body the starting point, indeed, in some ways, the sum total of that theology is centered on Jesus Christ, the Word become flesh. There are two key moments — the Incarnation itself and the resurrection of Jesus. The former validated the fundamental goodness of the body in a radical way. The docetists and their Gnostic descendants, convinced of the divinity of Christ in at least some measure, were equally convinced that that divinity could not truly join to a material body. The body of Jesus was, accordingly, a mere illusion. The Greek Church was equally convinced that Jesus had truly come in the flesh, had truly bridged the gap between a sinful humanity and a just God. The resurrection took that validation one step further. The milder dualism of Plato would look to a discarding of the body (not really considered to be evil) after this life for a purely spiritual existence. It was why Paul's speech in the Areopagus proclaiming the resurrection provoked laughter (Acts 17:32). Jesus did not discard His body but rather transformed it, making it clear that it remains enduringly important and not merely an instrument of passing usefulness.

Christian tradition forces us to a broader consideration of bodiliness because Christ's taking on of flesh is understood in terms of the three modes of being human touched on in the introduction above. Paul's treatment of bodies is instructive.[70] He, of course, knows of the individual body and identifies the Christian's individual body with the temple of the Holy Spirit (I Cor. 6:19). Earlier, though, the body in question is the community itself: "Are you not aware that you (plural) are the temple of God, and that the Spirit of God dwells in you" (I Cor. 3 :16). This is underscored by the extended treatment of the communal body of Christ in chapter twelve: "You, then, are the body of Christ. Every one of you is a member of it" (I Cor. 12:27). Finally, Paul develops a marital understanding of the body as well: "Can you not see that the man who is joined to a prostitute becomes one body with her? Scripture says, 'The two shall become one flesh.' But whoever is joined to the Lord becomes one spirit with him." This marital understanding of the body of Christ, with the same reference to Gen. 2:24, is further expanded in Eph. 5:22-33: "the husband is head of his wife just as Christ is head of his body the Church, as well as its savior . . . Husbands, love your wives, as Christ loved the Church . . . no one ever hates his own flesh; no, he nourishes it and takes care of it as Christ cares for the Church — for we are members of his body."

Augustine and Thomas bear witness to this convergence of bodily modes in Christ as well. Augustine, commenting on the text "As a bridegroom coming forth out of His chamber, He rejoiced as a giant to run His course; He hath set His tabernacle in the sun," makes the following observations:

> as a bridegroom when the Word was made flesh, He found a bridal chamber in the Virgin's womb; and thence coming out as from a closet of surpassing purity, joined to the nature of man, humble in His mercy below all, strong in His majesty above all... The self-same bridegroom then Who did all this, *He set in the sun,* that is, in the open sight of all men, *His tabernacle,* that is, His holy Church.[71]

For Augustine, the wedding of the eternal Son to humanity involves simultaneously the taking on of an individualized humanity and the human community that is His Church. Thomas, for his part, understands Christ's unity with His Church both on the model of an organic body and of a marital union on the basis of the two Pauline texts, I Cor. 12 and Eph. 5.[72]

B. The Individual

In an earlier work I suggested that the traditional understanding of personhood needed to be reworked.[73] Boethius had defined a person as an individual substance of a rational nature and this was largely taken over by the tradition with minor modification. Boethius's definition is awkwardly applied to the divine substance since, given that the Triune God is a single substance, singleness of person is implied. An alternate understanding of personhood was forced by the Arian controversy — the Cappadocians in the East and Augustine in the West proposed a relational understanding of divine personhood. This was eventually codified by Thomas in the notion of subsistent relations.

For humans this subsistent relationality, at least among ourselves, is bodily based — biological generation from our parents. It is this which establishes Christ's solidarity with humanity and why the early Church was so insistent on the genealogies of the Gospels. Through His real relationship with Mary He is in a real relationship with all her ancestors and in principle with all collateral lines, which is to say, with all of humanity.[74]

Christian tradition has insisted on a soul that was distinct from the body in being spiritual, rational, and immortal. And yet, there has been an equally authoritative insistence that the soul is the form of the body.[75] What this latter implies is that concrete human rationality is inseparable from the body. The crucial issue, as noted above, is whether cerebral complexity itself, produced through biological evolution, is sufficient to explain the manifest rationality of the human race in comparison to other primate species. The affirmation of direct creation by God of the spiritual, rational, immortal soul of the individual would imply a negative answer to this question.

Still studies of brain functioning in the past century make it clear that some sort of reassessment is needed. Augustine rejected bodily analogies of the Trinity for a variety of reasons, chief of which was his Platonic presuppositions. In point of fact the sorts of phenomena he describes in the *De Trinitate*, detailing his psychological analogy, can be replicated in terms of states, structures, and dynamics of the brain. Memory, for instance, is perhaps completely a function of the brain. One could argue that this is sufficient grounds for dismissing Augustine's psychological analogy as theologically useful. Alternately, and the position taken here, one could argue that many, if not all, of the criteria Augustine used in judging a useful analogy (perichoresis, equality, commensurability, etc.) can be duplicated in physical structures as they are understood in the modern world.[76] One should be able to construct body based analogies of the Trinity.

What is the "surplus" provided by the soul and by human personhood that is not already ingredient in the intrinsic properties of the human body in its materiality? At root there is the relationality to God Himself. What is claimed by Christian faith is that God has taken an interest in humankind that far exceeds His interest in any other animal species on earth and that this interest is traceable to God Himself who created the human race "in our image, after our likeness" (Gen. 1:26). Karl Barth pointed out the context of this affirmation in the creation of the man and the woman and argued that creation in the image of God was oriented toward the creation of a covenantal partner for God — "deep calls upon deep" (Ps. 42:7).[77] This is in addition to the question whether the phenomena of human rationality manifest in observable human culture is attributable to brain function alone or whether it requires a transcendent vector in human reality which is expressed in a material context that is disponible to such expression. But such a transcendent vector is surely the sine qua non for a relationship to a transcendent God who is "personed."

One needs to distinguish this transcendent vector from personhood as such. The reasons are Christological. The conviction of the Church from early on has been that Christ was and is fully human. The controversies of the third and fourth century of the Christian era turned as much on the underlying anthropological presuppositions of the disputants as on matters of actual faith. Much of the terminology for dealing with person and nature that has dominated Western culture for almost two millennia was fashioned in the crucible of the Trinitarian and Christological disputes of these early centuries. Theologians with Monophysitic tendencies wanted to see a substitution of the higher elements of the human composite by the divine Word. The Antiochean theologians, of whom Nestorius is the most notorious, insisted on the fullness of the humanity of Christ but had not sufficiently worked out the unity of the Christ in the person of the Word. Thomas, faced with the Nestorian tendencies of his own Aristotelian base, could do no more than to affirm that the reason why the body-soul composite of Christ's humanity, which for every other human provides the complete hypostasis for the human person, does not involve a human person in the Christ distinct from the divine Word was because the body-soul-Word composite of the Christ was "more complete" than the body-soul composite of ordinary humans.[78] There is more philosophical and theological work to be done on these questions. For our purposes it suffices to be forewarned against simplistic identifications of human personhood.

Still, personhood, as distinct from personality (which would be an aspect of brain functioning), would belong to this transcendent realm especially insofar as this is understood in terms of a capacity for entering into covenant with the transcendent God. In the last analysis we are enabled to enter into the divine life because God has entered into human life. Our solidarity with God, paradoxically, is grounded in His Son's bodily solidarity with us. But then Paul said as much — "Take note, the spiritual was not first; first came the natural (ψυχικόν) and after that the spiritual" (I Cor. 15:46).

To say that human beings are capable of entering into covenant is to say that they have the structure of love (Augustine's psychological analogy is at its root a love analogy — the structure of love in the individual requires that the object of love is made present to the lover, is comprehended in its lovableness, and actually loved — all of these have a physical basis in various states of the brain). This, certainly in the Augustinian discussion, presupposes a rational soul, i.e., one possessed of memory, understanding, and will. But the love finds its bodily expression as well as spiritual expression which, again, suggests the possibility of a bodily imaging of the Trinity.

A further question is whether this transcendent vector, the immortal soul, in its "surplus" beyond being the form of the body, possesses a memory, an understanding, and a will. This does not really require parallel structures between the soul and the brain. The soul, in being the form of the body, is the form of the brain. Augustine understood the memory in its functioning as making all things present to the mind. But, memory, as Augustine understood it, is surely a function of the brain. The "surplus" provided by the soul is the ability to make even God present to the mind in some fashion and that capacity of the human composite can only be a direct creation by God because such grasping of God is beyond the intrinsic dynamics of matter as such even if matter is open to such a gift.[79] The divine action in the human composite makes it possible for the individual to see God as He sees Himself. This, too, is a surplus since God cannot be seen with bodily senses, though the vision of God will surely have a tangible impact on the body.

The Community

In *Trinity and Marriage in Paul* I developed a communitarian analogy of the Trinity based on the criteria that Augustine set out in the development of his psychological analogy. Augustine had turned away from the possibility of a communitarian analogy in part because he was convinced that bodies (and he understood the community to be a body) could not image the Trinity, even if they were vestiges of the Trinity. Only that which was closest to God in the created order, the intellectual soul, could image Him. I argued there that the human community, particularly as seen in the Church, was a spiritual reality and as such could provide an image-analogy of the Trinity. There terms of the analogy I developed — commonality, structure, valuative dynamics — are as true of the bodily dimension of community as the spiritual. The two dimensions, in point of fact, are inseparable.

Of course, the only true communal body is the Church since it is the only collectivity of bodies that is united by a transcendent intrinsic principle. This principle is the Spirit of Christ. This echoes Augustine's conviction that the only true commonwealth is the City of God.[80] This also makes clear that human community itself has the structure of love, and in the case of the Church, of transcendent love.

The Church, however, is not the body of the Spirit — its disponibility is primarily toward Christ; it receives the Spirit from Him; it is His body. It is not the body of Christ in the same sense that His individual body is. The members of this latter body are not persons; the members of the former are. Thomas, as noted above, expresses this difference by the simultaneous employment of I Cor. 12 as grounding the notion of an organic union with Christ and Eph. 5 as grounding the notion of a nuptial union with Christ. In both cases the union is bodily.

Because the Church is the body of Christ in some real sense, it shares in Christ's bodily resurrection and does so primarily in the same sense that the Church is primarily the covenantal Bride of Christ and individual members of the Church only secondarily members of that covenant by virtue of their membership in the Church. Our personal resurrection depends on the unity in diversity of the individual body of Christ, the communal body that is the Church, and the nuptial body that is the New Covenant in Christ's blood with His Church.

Human Interaction

It is the twin relatedness of individuals, Jesus Christ and the individual believer, to the community that is the Church that grounds our participation in the resurrection of Christ. Jesus, as a subsistent human relation, is correlated with His Church which has its origin in Him. By our insertion into this Church we are brought into correlation with Christ. This relatedness of the individual to the community is mediated by the body. That which separates unites. The very bodies that mark us off as autonomous individuals provide the means for the communication which unites us. We are indeed one spirit with Christ but this is not independently of the body but as mediated by the body.

The root human interaction is that of marriage. There are several reasons for this. The division of humanity into two sexes provides an apt imaging (more apt than mere friendship) of the unity and diversity of the divine persons insofar as we have an instance of individuals who are simultaneously utterly diverse and yet both totally human. Friendship is a partial realization, and only a partial realization, of this reality.[81] Following the imagery of Genesis the man obtains children (the human community) through his wife who gives birth to it. This corresponds well with what one knows of the sexes through science — this interaction is the sine qua non of the survival of the species. This root interaction is itself a trinitarian image of God and is also bodily in structure. It has the structure of love.

Postscript

These all too brief comments will have to suffice. The three modes of human existence, themselves rooted in the body, are correlated into a composite imaging of the Trinity. This is grounded in their articulation of the concrete structure of human loving, manifested in terms of self-love and the love of the neighbor as oneself which itself takes the dual form of a common love which establishes the true commonwealth and the love of one's spouse as one's own flesh.

The choice between the synthetic visions, the fairy tales offered by humanist culture and by Christianity, is between an understanding of a purely materialistic, mechanistic universe, fundamentally indifferent to anything, including humanity, and an understanding of a universe fundamentally structured by love and of a humanity created near the heart of that universe to be loved by Him who is Love. Humanist culture is clearly not "eucatastrophic." Given its rootedness in an, in part, outmoded science which gave us persons as machines and machines as persons, it does not even make good science fiction.

Endnotes

1. The philosophy of Alfred North Whitehead could also be described as a relational metaphysics even if he describes it rather as a process philosophy. His approach is of interest in the present context since he is intent on fashioning a scientifically based philosophy. This is accomplished by recourse to field theory. Fields, however, are fundamentally relational.
2. I develop this more extensively in *Trinity and Marriage in Paul: The Establishment of a Communitarian Analogy of the Trinity Grounded in the Theological Shape of Pauline Thought* (New York: Peter Lang, 1990), pp. 348-61.
3. I will be primarily relying on the account of humanism provided by Benedict M. Ashley, O.P. in *Theologies of the Body: Humanist and Christian* (Braintree, Massachusetts: The Pope John XXIII Medical-Moral Research and Education Center, 1985). Cf. esp. ch. 3: "Humanist Theologies of the Body (1700-2000)."
4. He wrote this in "On Fairy-Stories," originally a lecture at the University of St. Andrews in 1938 and later published in the festschrift for Charles Williams (Oxford: The University Press, 1947) and later in the book, *Tree and Leaf* (London?: George Allen and Unwin, 1964). This last was included in *The Tolkien Reader* (New York: Ballantine, 1966) which preserves the earlier pagination; the quote in the text is from p. 9. My own comments are based in part on Lin Carter's treatment in *Tolkien: A Look Behind the Lord of the Rings* (New York: Ballantine Books, 1969), pp. 87-95. Carter himself is predominantly a writer of science fiction.
5. *Tree and Leaf*, p. 14.
6. *Tree and Leaf*, p. 37.
7. *Ibid.*, p. 40.
8. *Ibid.*, p. 10.
9. *Ibid.* pp. 52-53. John Steinbeck penned a similar thought when he described Morgan La Fay: "she studied necromancy and became proficient in the dark and destructive magic which is the weapon of the jealous. She joyed in bending and warping men to her will through beauty and enchantment, and when these failed she used the blacker arts of treason and murder." *The Acts of King Arthur and His Noble Knights* (New York: Farrar, Straus and Giroux, 1976).
10. *Ibid.*, p. 59.
11. *Theologies of the Body*, pp. 80-81.
12. The definition is Webster's.
13. William James, "What Pragmatism Means," in *Pragmatism and Other Essays* (New York: Washington Square Press, 1963), p. 23.
14. From the perspective of the "eucatastrophe" which he defines in this fashion: "the

'consolation' of fairy-tales has another aspect than the imaginative satisfaction of ancient desires. Far more important is the Consolation of the Happy Ending. Almost I would venture to assert that all complete fairy-stories must have it. At least I would say that Tragedy is the true form of Drama, its highest function; but the opposite is true of Fairy-story. Since we do not appear to possess a word that expresses this opposite — I call it *Eucatastrophe*." *Tree and Leaf*, p. 68.

15. *Tree and Leaf*, pp. 71-72.

16. Cf. Tolkien, *Tree and Leaf*, p. 22. Carter summarizes Tolkien's argument in this way: "He delves into the connections among fairy stories, mythology, and religion; and, briefly, into the connections between history and mythology, drawing the interesting conclusion that history often resembles myth or legend because both are ultimately formed from the same stuff." *Tolkien*, p. 89. This type of insight goes back to Wilhelm Dilthey who "saw clearly that human creativity must be considered in the interpretation of literature . . . he adopted and developed the idea of a mental structure responsible in part for literary expression. He saw this structure as more than a *model* for understanding literary processes in man; he conceived it as a real biological-psychologi-cal-historical structure in man." Edgar V. McKnight, *Meaning in Texts: The Historical Shaping of a Narrative Hermeneutics* (Philadelphia: Fortress Press, 1978), p. 95. Various forms of structuralism have expanded on this insight particularly from the perspective of linguistics and the work in itself. Many of the early studies were focussed on Russian fairy tales.

17. Ashley, *Theologies of the Body*, p. 59.

18. *Ibid.*, p. 59.

19. "Copernicus, Nicolas" in *The Encyclopedia of Philosophy*, vol. 1 (New York: Macmillan & The Free Press, 1967), p. 222.

20. Robert S. Westman, "The Copernicans and the Churches," in David G. Lindberg and Ronald L. Numbers, ed., *God and Nature: Historical Essays on the Encounter between Christianity and Science* (Berkeley: University of California Press, 1986), p. 90-91. Cf. also Herbert Butterfield, *The Origins of Modern Science 1300-1800* (New York: Macmillan, 1961), pp. 20-24.

21. Jerome J. Langford, *Galileo, Science and the Church*, rev. ed. (Ann Arbor, Michigan: The University of Michigan Press, 1966), p. 161.

22. Butterfield, *Origins*, pp. 58-59; Langford, Galileo, p. 43.

23. Westman, "The Copernicans," pp. 96-97.

24. Stanley L. Jaki, *God and the Cosmologists* (Washington, D.C.: Regnery Gateway, 1989), p. 8

25. Stanley L. Jaki, *The Savior of Science* (Washington, D.C.: Regnery Gateway, 1988), pp. 93-97. This was first seriously proposed by Harlow Shapley in 1915. Cf. Carl Sagan, *Cosmos: The Book* (New York: Ballantine, 1980), p. 158.

26. Sagan, *Cosmos*, p. 159.

27. *Ibid.*, p. 3. Cf. also Jaki, *God and the Cosmologists*, p. 28.

28. Arnold Hauser, *The Social History of Art*, vol. 2: *Renaissance, Mannerism, Baroque* (New York: Vintage Books, 1959), p. 34.

29. Butterfield, *Origins*, pp. 38-39.

30. *Ibid.*, p. 50.

31. Butterfield, *Origins*, p. 119.

32. *Ibid.*, p. 122.

33. *Ibid.*, p. 53.

34. Cf. Butterfield, *Origins*, p. 115.

35. Ashley, *Theologies*, pp. 61-62.

36. Jacques Roger, "The Mechanistic Conception of Life," in *God and Nature*, p. 281.

37. John W. Cooper, *Body, Soul, and Life Everlasting: Biblical Anthropology and the Monism-Dualism Debate* (Grand Rapids, Michigan: William B. Eerdmans, 1989), p. 17. Cf. Thomas Hobbes, *Leviathan*, I, XXXIV.

38. Roger, "The Mechanistic Conception," p. 288.

39. *Ibid.*, pp. 22-24.

40. Butterfield, *Origins*, pp. 124-25.

41. Gilbert Ryle, *The Concept of Mind* (London: Hutchinson, 1949), pp. 15-16. Ashley, *Theologies*, pp. 61-62, seems to attribute this expression to Arthur Koestler, *The Ghost in the Machine (The Danube Edition)* (New York: Random House, 1967). Whatever else he is doing (rather than the crass dualism of Descartes' position he proposes an open-ended hierarchy) Koestler is writing in criticism of the behavioristic tendencies of Ryle. Cf. pp. 202-21. Ryle describes the "official doctrine" in these terms:

> every human being has both a body and a mind .... His body and his mind are ordinarily harnessed together, but after the death of the body his mind may continue to exist and function.

> Human bodies are in space and are subject to the mechanical laws which govern all other bodies in space. Bodily processes and states can be inspected by external observers. So a man's bodily life is as much a public affair as are the lives of animals and reptiles and even as the careers of trees, crystals and planets.

> But minds are not in space, nor are their operations subject to mechanical laws. The workings of one mind are not witnessable by other observers; its career is private. Only I can take direct cognisance of the states and processes of my own mind. A person therefore lives through two collateral histories, one consisting of what happens in and to his body, the other consisting of what happens in and to his mind. The first is public, the second private ....

> It is customary to express this bifurcation of his two lives and of his two worlds by saying that the things and events which belong to the physical world, including his own body, are external, while the workings of his own mind are internal. *Concept*, pp. 11-12.

42. *Ibid.*, p. 155.

43. Robert Boyle, *The Origine of Formes and Qualities (According to the Corpuscular Philosophy)*, 2nd ed. (Oxford: Ric. Davis, 1667), pp. 102-4, cited in Roger, "The Mechanistic Conception," p. 283.

44. Roger, "The Mechanistic Conception," pp. 284-85.

45. *Ibid.*, pp. 286-87.

46. *Ibid.*, p. 288.

47. *Ibid.*, p. 289.

48. Cf. Pierre Teilhard de Chardin's remarks on his own Lamarckian tendencies in this regard in *The Phenomenon of Man* (New York: Harper & Row, 1959), pp. 149-50, n. 1.

49 *Ibid.*, p. 291.

50.	A. Hunter Dupree, "Christianity and the Scientific Community in the Age of Darwin," in *God and Nature* , pp. 352-53.

51.	Martin J. S. Rudwick, "The Shape and Meaning of Earth History," in *God and Nature*, p. 303.

52.	*Ibid.*, p. 308

53.	*Ibid.*, pp. 298-301.

54.	Sagan, *Cosmos*, pp. 159, 209-11.

55.	Sagan, *Cosmos*, p. 217.

56.	*Ibid.*, p. 221. The concept of a closed universe goes back to the 1920's when a pair of spiral galaxies were discovered in the opposite direction from the Andromeda Galaxy. This led some to wonder whether "they were seeing the Milky Way and M31 from the other direction — like seeing the back of your head with the light that has circumnavigated the universe?" The effect depends on the relativistic bending of light in a gravitational field. Jaki, *God and the Cosmologists*, pp. 70-76, has cogent remarks on the embarrassment caused by the inability to find enough matter in the universe to support various theories which presupposed an invariability (an eternity) of the universe from place to place and from epoch to epoch. Many such schemes have as their ulterior motive the desire to dispense with the necessity of a transcendent Creator. This requires that the universe be functionally equivalent to nothing at all since nothingness requires no metaphysical grounding. One device is an appeal to the tunnelling phenomenon: "The core of those claims is nothing less than the spontaneous tunnelling of the entire universe, nay of countless universes, through the infinitely high energy barrier that separates the 'nothing' from what really exists." *Ibid.*, p. 127.

57.	Which is not to say that the universe is symmetrical. Given the explosive nature of the Big Bang perfect symmetry would seem unlikely.

58.	Of course, the center of the universe, insofar as it resides in this universe, may be uninhabitable, the locus of an enormous black hole.

59.	Sagan, *Cosmos*, p. 3.

60.	Teilhard, *Phenomenon*, p. 169.

61.	Cf. Bruce Bower, "DNA's Evolutionary Dilemma," *Science News* 155.6 (February 6, 1999), pp. 88-90.

62.	This is not necessarily compromised by indications of such rationality among Neanderthals. There are also indications that they were close enough to *homo sapiens* to interbreed.

63.	HG 37. He is reliant on the Council of Trent (Conc. Trid., sess, V, can. 1-4) and Rom. 5:12-19.

64.	Conc. Trid., sess, V, can. 3.

65.	There are many mechanisms whereby a moral failure by one generation is passed on to the next in the form of a wounded nature — drug abuse by the mother, to give one fairly clear physical example. The crucial loss for humanity is the broken intimacy with God. Below the notion of the human person as a subsistent relation is developed. Clearly if one term of the relationship is fallen one might expect that the other, except by way of exception, will be as well since subsistent relations are constitutive, and in the case of offspring, causative. Of interest is also the principle omnia agens agit simile sibi.

66.	It would be theologically significant only if generation of truly human offspring required two truly human parents. The Incarnation provides the counter example. Mary was the only truly human parent of Jesus.

67.	I always liked Teilhard's expression in this regard — "the automatic destruction of the peduncle of the phylum" — which roughly translated means "they will never find the bones." Cf. *Phenomenon*, pp. 186-87.

68.   This is one of the dangers of Teilhard's attempt to see a "within" of material reality. Cf. *Phenomenon*, pp. 53-66, et passim.

69.   Immanuel Kant at one point described his philosophical project as one of making room for faith in the face of the empirical methodology that was then taking the field in epistemology. Kant was content to make such room in the realm of practical thought, accepting empiricism's challenge to philosophy (and theology) in the speculative realm. It is not difficult to understand why philosophy might have thought itself challenged by the nascent approach. As a method it collects data and attempts to organize that data into meaningful patterns determinable, at least in desire, with mathematical precision. As a method it encounters none but self-imposed limits — often of a practical nature determined by politics, concrete resources, etc. but also some theoretical limits such as noted in the text — on the collection of data and the attempts to organize that data. As a method it attempts to transcend any present state of knowledge either through the acquisition of new, unforeseen data or by the development of new theory. As a method, then, science will attempt to understand any human event, including claims of divine intervention, in such a manner.

70.   The following comments are based on my treatment in *Trinity and Marriage in Paul*, pp. 64-73.

71.   *Ennarationes in Psalmos* 19.16.

72.   The former text is the basis for his discussion in his *Expositio super epistolam S. Pauli apostoli ad Ephesios* I.viii . 2-3, the latter, obviously, for V.viii-x. The points he makes here are found scattered throughout his works (cf, for instance, *Summa Theologica* III.8., on the headship of Christ). Thomas treats the union of Christ and the Church as sui generis but as similar to both models which are, after all, sanctioned by Scripture.

73.   "Real Relations and the Divine," *Theological Studies* 56 (1995): 673-95; cf. especially pp. 68690.

74.   Thomas denied that Jesus had a real relationship with Mary. I deal with these issues in more detailed fashion in the just named article.

75.   The latter was defined at the Council of Vienne in the first decree. Cf. *DS* 902. The most complete statement of the former is found in a schema prepared for the First Vatican Council but which was never voted on. The Fifth Lateran Council in the eighth session defined the immortality of the soul against Neo-Aristotelians. Cf. *DS* 1440. It reaffirmed the definition of the Council of Vienne.

76.   I set these criteria out in *Trinity and Marriage in Paul, pp.* 218-43.

77.   Karl Barth, *Church Dogmatics*, vol. 3: *The Doctrine of Creation*, pt. 1, ed. G. W. Bromiley and T. F. Torrance, trans. J. W. Edwards, O. Bussey, and Harold Knight (Edinburgh: T. & T. Clark, 1958), pp. 183-206.

78.   Summa Theologica III.2.3.

79.   *Confessiones* X.

80.   *De civitate Dei* XIX.21. 24-27.

81.   Obviously one speaks of the ideal here — husband and wife are friends. But they are also so much more than this.

Bāśār-Nepeš: Sarx-Pneuma; Body-Soul: Death-Resurrection: An Essay in Pauline Anthropology

Father Donald Keefe, S.J. has been Professor of Dogmatic Theology at St. Joseph's Seminary, Dunwoodie, New York since 1994. Prior to his present tenure, he was a theologian for the Denver Archdiocese. Father Keefe has taught dogmatic theology at Canisius College in Buffalo, Saint Louis University and Marquette University. After serving in the U.S. Navy in World War II, Father Keefe earned his J.D. at Georgetown University Law School before entering the Society of Jesus in 1953. He was ordained a priest in 1962. Father Keefe was a member of the Bar of the District of Columbia, of the State of New York and the Supreme Court of the U.S. He has written several books on theology and theological method, notably, *Thomism and the Ontological Theology of Paul Tillich* and the two-volume work, *Covenantal Theology: The Eucharistic Order of History*. This latter volume has been summarized in a one-volume work. Father Keefe is the author of more than thirty articles on dogmatic theology.

Introduction

This anthropological inquiry was prompted by a theological lecture which could find no more than a mimetic significance in personal death, arguing that the radically salvific adequacy of the death and resurrection of the Christ bars discovering any salvific significance in our own personal deaths, except insofar as they may imitate his. This view, which echoes the Reform's historical pessimism, puts in issue the need for the sacrament of baptism by which, according to Paul and with him, the Catholic tradition, we enter, personally, sacramentally and objectively, into the death of Christ the Head, in order that we may enter into his resurrection to life eternal.

For Paul, and for the Catholic tradition for which he speaks, only by entry into the death of Christ are we able to enter into his resurrection and so enter into the "newness of life" which the risen Head mediates to his Body, the Church. Thus for Paul, and for the doctrinal tradition, it is only by our personal entry into the death of Christ that we can enter into his risen life. If the universality of the divine salvific will be given its due, this personal entry into Christ's death must be a gift given all men in all times and places. Only our creation in Christ provides for the necessary radical universality of this historical grace by which alone we have access to the Father.

Creation in Christ

No theological discussion of anthropology can proceed apart from the primary consideration, that we are created in Christ. That we are so created is the explicit teaching of, e.g., Jn 1:3, Eph 1:4-12, and Col 1:16-17; many other passages in the New Testament might be cited to the same effect. Further, the hermeneutical rule proclaimed by the Symbol of Chalcedon, which affirmed seven times that the subject of all Christological affirmation is the "one and the same" Jesus the Christ, the eternal Son of the Father and the historical Son of Mary, forbids the commonplace dehistoricization of such scriptural texts, by which they are made to refer to the divine Son of the Father but not to Jesus, the human Son of our Lady. Nonetheless, it cannot seriously be questioned that what is said of the eternal Son in Scripture, in the liturgy, and in the doctrinal tradition is said of the Son of Mary, Jesus the Christ. Liturgical, scriptural, and doctrinal statements are alike historical statements, for they are entirely dependent upon the historical revelation, and exist only to mediate its Truth.

It is obvious that creation in Jesus Christ our Head is gratuitous and that the gratuity is the grace of Christ, *gratia Christi*. It is equally obvious that this grace is substantial, for creation is said of substance, not of accidents: "in him we live and move and have our being." To be deprived of this foundational grace is simply to cease to exist, while to possess it is to have been created in the Image of God who is Christ, who is our Head, and who is so by his primordial union with the Second Eve, "before the world began."[1] This grace of creation in Christ is given universally to all human beings by the fact of his Headship of all creation: the Mission of the Son from the Father terminates in the creation of those of whom He is the Head by reason of his unity in One Flesh with the Second Eve. Creation is single: everyone for whom Christ died is included within his Body, the Second Eve, who is never apart from him, whether in fallen history or primordially, "in the Beginning,"[2] "before the world was made."[3]

The Universality of Grace

St. Thomas, following St. Augustine, recognized a universal grace, i.e., one given to all men wherever and whenever found, in whatever condition. St. Augustine had labeled this grace the *trahi a Deo*: "to be drawn by God."[4] By it, the Father draws us to the Son, in whom we cannot believe unless we are drawn thereto by the Father. Thus to be drawn to the Truth is quite evidently to be illumined: it is not too much to identify the *trahi a Deo* with Augustinian illumination, the graced intuition by which our minds are freed, able to transcend our fallenness to know the Truth who is the Lord of all creation, not subject to its fallen necessities, but redeeming it from them, making all things new.

In this grace God is present to us the "interior Master," the *Intus Magister* whom Augustine, in his commentary upon the text of the Johannine Gospel, observes is nearer to us than we are to ourselves. To each of us, God is *intimior intimo meo*.[5] Clearly, this 'being drawn' is a reality in us prior to our response to it in faith: it is prior to all ecclesially-mediated grace, and so is prior to faith itself, and to baptism into the Church. In fact, this most radical grace is the condition of possibility of being baptized. In sum, God has loved us first, in order that we might return his love. For this reason only the Father sent his Son to give his Spirit, a gift which terminates in our creation in Christ. Consequently, this substantial grace, the grace of creation itself, is also the condition of possibility of the Fall.

Thomas encountered the problem of the universality of grace by way of his late recognition of the problem posed by the possibility — the 13th century would have put it more strongly — of the sinfulness of pagan infidelity. His solution of it, a universally distributed *trahi a Deo*,[6] given prior to faith as the temporally and causally prior condition of possibility of conversion to the faith, obviously given *ad salutem* and therefore as a grace, represents a departure from substance-accident analysis St. Thomas had until then relied upon. For although he provided for it no metaphysical analysis, the universal distribution of the *trahi a Deo*, a gift *ad salutem* whose rejection is sinful, must be free if it is to be a gift and not a necessity of human nature. That no one is necessarily graced is true simply as a matter of definition. Thomas had the problem thus of accounting for a free universality, not a necessary or "natural" one, and his substance-accident analysis of being into its intrinsically necessary causes was inadequate to the task. Consequently, he could give no metaphysical account of the *trahi a Deo.*

The substance-accident, matter-form analyses of the Thomist metaphysics are identical to those of Aristotelianism, in that they rely upon the same postulated intrinsic necessity of the act-potency causality of substance and accident, of matter and form. This methodologically postulated determinism, when applied to the metaphysical analysis of grace, cannot but suppress or ignore the free intelligibility, and therefore the free efficacy, of the sacramental signs of the Church's worship.

One must conclude that St. Thomas' metaphysical method, in its theological application, fails to reconcile its necessitarian and deterministic, substance-accident analysis of human actions with the intrinsic freedom, graced *ex nihilo*, of Catholic sacramental worship, which is to say, with the intrinsic freedom of historical existence *in ecclesia*, which is the full expression of the free truth of historical reality as such.

In sum, within a Thomist world, supposedly governed by the quest for intrinsically necessary reasons or causes that is the Thomist metaphysical project, there can be no merely natural (ungraced) freedom while, in that same world, the Thomist commitment to the accidental standing of the grace of Christ bars the universal distribution of the grace of being drawn to faith in Christ by the Father, which Thomas himself, toward the end of his short life, had recognized to be actual in the world of fallen man.[7]

The Metaphysics of the *Trahi a Deo*

We have seen that because the redeemed, sacramental order of creation and of history is free, it must be appropriated in freedom, which free appropriation requires and presupposes in its turn that the fallenness of the unbaptized human condition, its lack of substantial unity and freedom, be open nonetheless to the grace of conversion; be capable of a free conversion to the freedom of the sacramental order of creation, our full entry into which is by participation in the worship of the Church. This openness, this inamissable historical freedom, given at the level of creation in Christ, which is to say, of substance, is the Augustinian *trahi a Deo*, the illumination which frees the mind from the darkness of opinion merely and enables man to turn to the light of Christ. The reality and universality of the *trahi a Deo* was affirmed by St. Thomas in a late theological development but he did not provide for it a metaphysical account.

We have seen that the lack of a metaphysical account of the *trahi* is easily remedied. Because the *trahi a Deo* is a gift *ex nihilo* of a universally distributed, graced awareness of the object of faith, it can be given only at the level of substance, i.e., as an inarticulate direct intuition, rather than a reflex, discursive knowledge, a witting, conscious attraction, or being drawn, by God the Father to a salvific knowledge of his Son (Jn 6:44, 65). This intuition is actual in our self-awareness as *simul peccator et justus*, equivalently the Augustinian subjectivity of tension between "two loves," at once *sarx* and *pneuma* in their existential simultaneity and inseparability, which is a freedom to turn to the Christ in a moment of conversion, and so to covenantal fidelity, to responsible existence in history. This graced freedom to be free co-exists with its alternative: freedom to turn away from freedom and so from God. However, one of these decisions is always effective in fallen man: either the love of God that is an ongoing *conversio*, or in the aversion from Him that seeks an ever more complete personal autonomy. In Augustine's words, *amor meus, pondus meum:* "my love is my commitment, my orientation, my fidelity, my firmness, my consistency."[8] There are of course "two loves," two mutually exclusive dynamic tendencies innate in fallen man, which in history are constantly-building "two cities," the city of God and the city of man.[9] In this fallen world, the two cities intersect, as do the two loves which build them, in such wise that we live our fallen lives, private and public, in this intersection or overlap, on the cusp of an always reversible decision, *simul peccator et justus*, at once *sarx* and *pneuma*.

The fact of this universal grace of our creation, which is not overcome by the Fall, means that the sinfulness, the mortality, which afflicts every human person is not a bar to moral freedom: upon maturity, every human being is free at every moment to choose to be free, in the sense of refusing to be locked into the futility of *sarx*, the frozen, deterministic dynamic of personal fragmentation consequent upon Original Sin, whose sign and culmination is death, the inescapable return of all that is physical to the ultimate dissociation and alienation, the atomization that is dust, in the Old Testament and the New,[10] the playingout of the quest for autonomy by which men would "be like God."

The restoration of the universal capacity for the freedom otherwise lost in the Fall is clearly in the order of salvation, and therefore can only be of grace. Its universal distribution, independent of the historical circumstances of the individual beneficiary (e.g., paganism before Abraham was universal, yet this grace was given) is explainable only as a grace given at the level of creation itself, which is to say, at the level of substance, not of accident. St. Thomas' late discovery of this necessity has not entered into the Thomism systematized by the schools. Nonetheless, the experience of being drawn by God, the *intus magister* who is more intimate to each of us than we are to ourselves, *intimior intimo meo* in Augustine's idiom, is proper to historical human consciousness as such, at its most profound and most universal level, the level of substantial rather than accidental *intellectus*, viz., the direct or substantial consciousness, illumined by its creation in Christ, that is causally prior to any reflexive, accidental, inevitably fallen, discursive articulation.

Original Sin and The Fall from Grace

The Original Sin of the first Adam and first Eve is best understood as a rejection of the free, nuptially-ordered covenantal unity[11] which has been restored to us *in sacramento* by the institution of the New Covenant on the Cross and in numerically identical Eucharistic offering, *in persona Christi*, of that redemptive One Sacrifice. Our only access to an understanding of the primordial Original Sin and Fall is by reference to the First Adam-Second Adam parallel, in which the historical recapitulation of all things in Christ, the Second Adam, into the free unity, the One Flesh, by which that primordial tragedy was undone, casts light upon its negative reflex, the sin of Adam which that recapitulation presupposes and remedies. There is no other, independent source of information on Original Sin, and on the Fall which it caused.[12]

This rejection of free, substantial unity issued in the degradation of substantial being that is personal existence in the *sarx-pneuma* composite characterizing fallen humanity. This composition is of being with its negation, with nonbeing. Humanity is the object of the Good Creation, substantially integral, as *pneuma*: it is the nonbeing, the negation of free unity, chosen by original sin, the original and deconstituting refusal to be free, to be nuptially ordered and unified, that it is *sarx*. *Sarx* therefore has no independent reality: it can exist only as an absence of the good that is free unity; it is real only as the destructive determinism imposed upon the Good Creation by the original sin, the original refusal of the goodness of creation, viz., its free unity, by the first Adam who, by accepting that free and nuptial unity with his glory, his body, would have been the head of "the mother of all the living." His refusal and hers did not undo the Good Creation, but destroyed its free integrity, reducing the human community to what a tradition older than Augustine named a *massa damnata*, irrevocably bent upon its own dissolution.

This refusal, the original sin, could not but be effective *eo ipso*, even *ex opere operato*, for even the Creator cannot force free unity upon his creation. Therefore the original refusal was simultaneous with the creation of a broken dichotomous humanity, whose members are at once *pneuma*, by reason of the indefeasible creation in Christ, and *sarx*, fallen human being is to his *pneuma* as the drive toward death, the resistance to life, is to the fullness of life.

If, with Paul and Irenaeus, we may sum up the redemptive work of Jesus, the Second Adam, as "recapitulation," it follows, as has been seen *supra*, that we must assign to the sin of the First Adam the destructive effect of "*un*capitulation" by the Original Sin, humanity was bereft of its birthright, of its free unity as the Body of the Head. It must follow that, as "recapitulation" is achieved in the institution, on the Cross and in the Mass, of the One Flesh of the New Covenant, so the sin of the first Adam can only have been a refusal of his nuptial relation to the first Eve, that of Headship, which was offered him "in the beginning."

Our solidarity in the sin of the first Adam and Eve is simply inexplicable except as the consequence of a refusal by the first Adam of an offered headship, an offer of the office of bestowing free unity upon the body, with the consequently inevitable disintegration of the body, the free community, of which the first Adam was to have been the head. Note that the first Adam's refusal of headship was effective in the loss of free, nuptial unity not only for himself but for us as well, for it is the ineluctable implication of the redemption in Christ that humanity have neither unity nor freedom except insofar as it proceeds from our head. The very term used by Paul in Ephesians to describe the redemptive deed of Christ, "anakephălaióō" in the Greek, literally translated as "recapitulate" in English, supports this necessary inference: it invokes "head," not as the Greeks would have understood it, a source of necessary unity, but as Paul understood it, as a principle or source of free unity, which can only be nuptial — which is to say, covenantal.

If this be accepted, as it would seem it must be accepted simply on the grounds of our solidarity in the sin of Adam, the condition of possibility of his rejection of the free integrity of nuptial headship can only be the pre-existence, or primordiality, of the One Flesh of the New Covenant, whose free and lordly transcendence of and causal priority to the moment of the Fall is that of the Alpha and the Omega, Eucharistically realized, *per modum substantiae*, in the Second Adam's nuptial union with the Second Eve. Their One Flesh, immaculately consummated by the Second Adam and the Second Eve, the "whole Christ," could not be imposed upon the human multitude, but must be offered to the full host of the humanity destined freely to be incorporated in the Body, the Church — those for whom Christ died. Only on this basis is it possible to understand our fallen condition of tending inexorably toward death, our immanently necessary dissolution, the continuing fragmentation of our flesh into the biblical "dust" of the fallen universe from which we came and to which we must return.

The free, substantial, and nuptially-ordered unity of humanity is its imaging of God, a nuptial imaging whose secondary sacramental sign in our fragmented and fallen world is the marriage of one man to one woman. This sign is secondary in that it is utterly dependent upon the prior institution *in sacramento* of the One Flesh of the New Covenant, in which terminates the Son's Mission to give the Holy Spirit. In an unfallen world, the nuptial union of the one Man, the first Adam, and the one Woman, the first Eve, would not be, as it now is, the effective sacramental *sign* of the substantial unity of humanity, but its primordial *realization* — as its refusal must be, and is, the primordial Fall, at the level of our created substance, into the reverse of the free unity of "One Flesh," the aforesaid dust of death.

Thus the Fall was into the necessary and dynamic disunity of flesh merely, i.e., into the actual historical human condition which lacks a principle of unity. Here it must be noted that the flesh that is our fallenness cannot be unified, redeemed, on any necessitarian basis, as all our philosophical striving to recover that lost historical unity has shown. A necessary unity has been shown to be a flat impossibility.[13] Our fallen race encounters historical unity, goodness and truth only on the level of sacramental objectivity. Insofar as our physical experience is concerned, the "world" and the "flesh" are imprisoned in necessity, as Paul has it in Romans 8:19ff, while eagerly awaiting the same liberation as do the sons of man.

The sacramental, radically Eucharistic mediation *in ecclesia* of the free unity of the One Flesh of the New Covenant restores to each of us, *in signo*, the freedom personally to appropriate the same goodness, the same free unity, which was offered, "in the Beginning," to the primordial first Adam and first Eve. It has proposed above that the only way to begin to grasp the reality of the Original Sin is to compare the Eucharistic One Flesh to that which depends upon it utterly, the one flesh of the sacrament of marriage. Sacramental marriage is the personal appropriation of the primordial free unity of the Good Creation, the Beginning in which the Mission of the Son terminates, the One Flesh of the Second Adam and the Second Eve, the full outpouring of the *Spiritus Creator* for which the Son was sent. We were created in solidarity with the first Adam and first Eve in such wise that our free unity is dependent upon their appropriation of that free unity in the primordial moment of its offer to them "in the Beginning" by him who is the "Beginning," One Flesh with the Second Eve. For St. Augustine, this nuptial union the *Christus totus, Christus integer*, "the Whole Christ" whose unity is at once free, primordial and irrevocable.

The first Adam and the first Eve sinned by their refusal of the nuptial unity offered them by the Whole Christ. This free and nuptially-ordered unity, their free imaging of the Triune God, is the plenary goodness of the Beginning, the Good Creation, which was to have been theirs but which could only be freely accepted and appropriated — it could not be imposed upon them. Their refusal of their free nuptial offices of head and body, whose freely responsible exercise issues in the One Flesh which would have been their free appropriation of their creation in the image of God, is the primordial sin, Original Sin.

The Original Sin was identically their entry into the mystery of iniquity and, by reason of our solidarity with them, rooted in our prospective membership in the body whose free unity would have been given it by its head, the Original Sin issued in our loss of the *free unity* which is our birthright. As has been seen, the Fall is the negative reflex, the reverse, of the free unity offered: it is descent into the sole alternative, the *necessary fragmentation* that is existential fallenness, universal throughout creation. So to exist is to be *sarx*, the sole alternative to the *mia sarx*, the One Flesh, of nuptially ordered covenantal existence in free community.

The offer to Adam was of marital headship: his refusal to be the head deprives the body of the free unity by which mankind would have been immortal, without any dynamic of fragmentation: *pneuma* simply. It should be remarked that this understanding of the first Adam as prospective head involves no infinite regress: the first Adam's body or "progeny"[14] would have been free by the grace of Christ, not the grace of Adam. Here we speak of that body or glory which is Eve and her 'progeny', of which Adam was to be the head. The correlative offer to Eve was of the responsibility of being his body and his glory, an office analogous to that of Mary, the second Eve, for the first Eve would have possessed that near-identity with her progeny that Mary has relative to the members of the Church, of whom Vatican II has proclaimed her the mother.[15]

We must remember that the Second Adam and the Second Eve, as fully human, are integral with the Good Creation which fell, in the Beginning, with the first Adam and the first Eve. By the Fall they also fell; they "became flesh," even as we, but their immanence within fallen humanity is that of the primordial Good Creation, the Beginning, and carries with it the promise of an ultimate restoration in grace. Thus the Fathers have always read Gen 3:15 as the "Protoevangelium," the anticipation of the good news of our redemption by the Second Adam.[16]

It appears that this is the only satisfactory interpretation of Original Sin and Fall as these are revealed in the third chapter of Genesis, read in the context of the Church's faith and worship, for this interpretation underwrites the reading of Jn 1:14 and Phil 2:5-12, not as statements whose subject is the pre-Incarnate divine Son, but as statements about Jesus the Christ — the interpretation required by the Chalcedonian "one and the same." For our liberation Jesus, the Alpha and the Omega, was "made sin." He emptied himself of his primordial dignity, that of the Second Adam: He "became flesh," "obedient unto death." Eve, in turning toward the Serpent, turned away from her husband, who acquiesced in her infidelity. From that instant, the free unity of man and woman, with each other, with God and with the Good Creation was lost, and death entered the world as the necessary consequence of that loss, as the ultimate expression of necessary disunity, the disintegration, which is "flesh," *sarx*, *bāśār*, which ends in the dust, the ultimate atomization that is the destiny of "all flesh." That free unity, the goodness of the Good Creation, could be restored from its substantial Fall only by an act of creation, only by the "obedience unto death" by which Jesus the Christ, the eternal Son, fulfilled his mission, to give the fullness of the Spirit to a fallen world. His unconditioned obedience recapitulated all things in and under a new Head, the Man, the Second Adam, who is the eternal Son, the historical Word of the Father.

When the Word became flesh, *sarx*, subject to death, the God-Man took upon himself the full weight of the Fall in all things save sin, including death. His victory over death, his Resurrection, is that of the new Head, with whom all mankind may again have free solidarity, for their freedom is restored. This restoration was implicit in the Mission of the Son to give the Spirit: even the sinful disobedience which refused the goodness of their creation and ours could not defeat his Mission, although that disobedience changed it into one of redemption as well as creation. The institution of the One Flesh of the New Covenant, the New Creation, on the Cross, was quite simply the restoration to "all flesh" of the free and nuptial unity and fullness of life which was offered, and refused, "in the Beginning."

The Sacramental Mediation of Grace in Fallen History

The risen Christ is present in the world as the Lord of history; his presence in history makes history to be salvific. His presence is his Lordship, his sac-rificial-Eucharistic institution of the Church, the mediatrix of all grace to all the fallen creation. His omnipotence, primordially effective in his gift of the Spirit to the Church by which the Second Adam and the Second Eve are united in One Flesh, is exercised in history through the infallible efficacy of the sacramental signs which Jesus instituted. Through these, He causes the Church to exist in fallen history, in the free, nuptial, sacramentally-signed unity of One Flesh with him, and brings into the free unity of his ecclesial Body those who enter into the worship whose ultimate historical expression is the celebration of the Eucharist. By the same outpouring of the Holy Spirit whom He was sent to give, Christ the Head renews the fallen creation through the restoration to it, in sacrament, of the free and nuptially-ordered unity that is proper to the Beginning, the Good Creation as such. Apart from the Second Adam's outpouring of his Spirit on the second Eve, the history of the fallen universe would be mere entropy, the unwinding of the world, and the physical creation would be merely the world and the flesh, the realm of inexorable disintegration and death, without freedom and so without significance. However, the Christ could not abandon the Good Creation by reason of its Fall, for He cannot abandon his Mission from the Father; thus his outpouring of the Spirit bars the final dissolution upon which world and flesh are intent.

The sacramentally-signed unity of his One Flesh prevails over all creation, as its Alpha and Omega, its originating and its final cause. The longing for liberation which Paul attributes to the entirety of the fallen creation bears witness to the presence of the *Spiritus Creator* in the world, "interceding with sighs too deep for words." But we must remember, with Augustine, that the Spirit, proceeding from the Father, is given only by the Son: "The Holy Spirit indeed does these things, but far be it from Him that He do them without the Son."[17] To forget this is to forget the order of the Trinitarian Processions, and thereby to depart from the Nicene Creed.

The sacramental worship of the Church has as its goal the personal appropriation of that fullness by those who are called to worship in the Church, there to be fed with the Bread of Life and the Cup of Everlasting Salvation. The first of the seven sacraments which the Christian encounters is of course baptism, by whose reception the Christian becomes a member of the Church, the glory who proceeds from the Head, the Second Adam, by which procession Christ is the Head, the Image of the Father.[18] It must be understood at the outset that the Church is primordial, at one with her Head in the Beginning, and thus is prior in being to all those who are her members. It is thus that she is sinless, uncontaminated by the world and the flesh. Baptism does not cause the Church. It causes membership in the Church. The cause of the Church is Jesus the Christ's sacrificial institution of the New Covenant, which does not recede into an ever more remote and less attainable past because it is Eucharistically represented in a manner, *per modum substantiae*, by which it transcends the determinism of fallen space and time.

Excursus: Christ's Eucharistic Lordship: The Salvific Order of History

It must be remembered that we can understand the fatal impact of the disobedience of the first Adam only by reference to ecclesial tradition, liturgical and Eucharistic before it is scriptural, of the redemptive consequences of the obedience of the Second Adam: there is no other access to the effects of the Fall.

The lack of any other *point d'appui* for the theology of the Fall than is given in the Eucharistic Christ cannot be overemphasized. Apart from the Eucharistic immanence of the risen Christ, there could be no Lordship of history, no "recapitulation of all things in Christ," for the event of the Cross would then be submitted to the immanent necessities of *sarx* and, as submitted to them, could not redeem them.[19] The One Flesh of the Second Adam and the Second Eve, the free union of Head and Body that is the Beginning, the Good Creation in its fullness and its totality, given "before the world began," carries within itself the possibility of the Fall, for the free unity it offers must be freely accepted. It is a free consequence of the Trinitarian Missions, for it is grace simply. However, the transcendent immanence or primordiality of the One Flesh, the

Whole Christ, within the Good Creation is not undone by the Fall, for with the Fall, "the Word became flesh" to initiate that economy of salvation by which alone can the Spirit be given a fallen humanity in a fallen world. With the Fall, the Word, Jesus the Man, could not but become flesh, could not but suffer and, in obedience to his Mission, could not but re-institute the New Covenant on the Cross and on the altar, which is the outpouring of the Spirit upon all creation, the universal liberation of which Paul wrote in Rom 8:19-26. The Lukan Gospel affirms the necessity "that the Christ should suffer and so enter into his glory." (Lk 24:26)

It is thus that our fallen history is salvific: viz., by the Eucharistic immanence of the Second Adam, One Flesh with his Bridal Church, the Second Eve. The offer of free unity, rejected by the first Adam, is returned to us *in sacramento* by the Second Adam, in the worship of the Church. This is the nuptial unity of the *Christus integer*, the One Flesh of Christ and his Church, the New Covenant by whose institution we may freely enter into the sacramental worship of the Church, whose sacramentality is her historicity, and ours, when we worship there. For there is no other free unity open to us than that which is sacramentally mediated by the Eucharistic representation of the One Flesh. In that One Sacrifice the Head continually pours out upon his bridal Church that Spirit by which we may approach his Father as co-heirs of the Kingdom, destined for freedom in our Father's house.

Within the necessary dynamic toward yet further fragmentation that is proper to *sarx*, a dynamic whose final goal is universal death, that final end of dissolution or entropy which the Bible refers to as the dust from which our flesh arises and to which it must return, there is no remedy other than the pagan flight from history which intends to be a flight from the fatality, futility, fragmentation and anguish of historical existence. This pagan quest for salvation has turned out to be only a nihilism, a quest for nothingness, for annihilation. No soteriological quest alternative to this is within the range of fallen man: without grace he can do, and does, only Nothing. The past century bears an irrefutable witness to the utter futility of all his salvific devices.

Baptism

Inasmuch as baptism is the sacramental anticipation and realization of personal entry into the death and resurrection of Christ, our dying can hardly be thought insignificant, for it is only by dying into the death of Jesus the Lord — whether sacramentally or physically — that we can enter into life.

We must remember that the same salvation in Jesus Christ, who died for all men, is mediated to non-Catholics and non-Christians as well as to Christians. Not only the unbaptized Christian infant but the unbaptized generally, including Jews, Moslems, and the "pagan saints" such as Melchizedek and Balaam, are all within the scope of salvation history simply because they are included, with all the other human beings living or dead, in the number of those for whom the Christ died. This universal and effective historical mediation of redemption in Christ to the unbaptized would appear to be by means of the sole historical universality with the baptized which they possess, precisely the event of physical death into the death of Christ, whether sacramentally anticipated or the actual separation of their flesh and spirit at the end of their earthly lives.[20]

For the death of Christ has changed physical death utterly and has done so "from the beginning:" it is as the Lamb who was slain that He is the Alpha and the Omega, the Lord of history. Were it otherwise, our baptism into his death would be futile. His victory over death transcends all death, not merely the death of human beings, as Paul insists in Romans 8:19-23:

> For the creation waits with eager longing for the revealing of the sons of God; for the creation was subjected to futility, not of its own will but by the will of him who subjected it in hope; because the creation itself will be set free from its bondage to decay and obtain the glorious liberty of the children of God. We know that the whole creation has been groaning in travail together until now; and not only the creation, but we ourselves, who have the first fruits of the Spirit, groan inwardly as we wait for adoption as sons, the redemption of our bodies. (RSV)

It is then reasonable to propose that the uniquely salvific death of Jesus the Christ, the Servant, the Lamb of God, has made all death to be an entry into Christ's death which, according to Rom 8:19ff, is effective for the restoration of the free unity of the universe: "Behold, I make all things new." In Rom 8, Paul sees the whole of creation eagerly awaiting the liberation of humanity, a liberation which Paul insists is given Christians by their baptismal entry into the death of Christ, but whose mediation is to the whole of creation, and quite clearly is not limited to the baptized. The whole of creation, all mankind, has been imprisoned by death, and the whole of it is liberated from that imprisonment by the death of Christ.

The advantage of the Christian's objective entry into Christ's death by baptism is of course that during his baptized life, only the Christian is able, through the permanent *character* given him definitively at baptism, to enter into Eucharistic Communion with the risen Christ. This union not available to the unbaptized short of their physical death which, for all who die — that is, for everyone without exception and, if Romans be taken at the letter, for every living thing, not merely for humanity — is entry into the death of Christ, the Head of all creation, and thereby into his life.

These considerations raise the problem of the nature of the baptismal *character*, i.e., the problem of the *res et sacramentum* of baptism, the infallible and permanent effect of the reception of that sacrament in the person baptized. However, as has been seen, that problem, in turn, presupposes our having recognized and provided for the radical condition of possibility of receiving baptism at all: i.e., in adults, this amounts to the condition of possibility of conversion and, in infants, to the condition of possibility of the reception of baptismal grace, and so of the baptismal *character*.

We have indicated that this radical possibility is the *trahi a Deo:* for Augustine and for St. Thomas, the prior reality of this universally-distributed freedom to convert is the *sine qua non* of entry into the sacramental worship of the Church, and thus the *sine qua non* of baptism. We have seen that the *trahi a Deo* is intelligible only as a grace given at the level of substance, which is to say, at the level of creation: this can only be the grace of creation in Christ. It is evident that the resolution of these questions cannot fail to be anthropological: we are investigating the human condition in salvation history, and are concerned for human nature in the sense taught by Pope John Paul's great encyclical, *Veritatis Splendor*, in which man's nature, the criterion of the moral good, is that which is created good "in the Beginning," which fell with the First Adam, was redeemed by the second, and in him, raised to the right hand of the Father.[21]

This creation "in the Beginning" (who is the Christ) is "primordial" human nature, that which all men have in Christ, "the Beginning" in whom they are created and only by union with whom are they redeemed. We must now further pursue this anthropological inquiry by investigating the baptismal *character*, the permanent gift infallibly received in sacramental baptism. We will do so in the context of what has already been established, the rooting of the *trahi a Deo*, the radical *gratia Christi, gratia Capitis*, in our creation in Christ. That we are created in Christ is a clear datum of the Catholic tradition, long obscured by the resolutely cosmological preoccupation of classic theology with upholding Greek metaphysical postulates fundamentally at odds with that tradition.

The Baptismal *Character*

St. Thomas held the baptismal *character*, like the *character* given in confirmation, and the *character* given in orders, to be an accident at the level of intellect, given as a principle of worship." This is traditional doctrine: it is even self-evident that a sacramental *character*, whether that of baptism, confirmation, or orders, is given as a principle of worship.[22] This is particularly obvious in baptism, for without baptism, our Eucharistic Communion with the risen Christ, the historical *telos* (goal or final object) of all participation in the Church's sacramental worship wherein Christ's salvific Lordship of history is actual and efficacious in the personal history of everyone who worships there, would be impossible. However, a number of problems are immediately posed by St. Thomas' definition of the sacramental *character* as a metaphysical accident in the order of intellect.[23]

The Baptismal *Character* as a Substantial Grace

In the first place, it appears that the effect worked in us by the outpouring of the *Spiritus Creator* upon us at baptism, as in our creation, and also in confirmation and ordination, effects in us entirely too radical, too complete a transformation, to be accounted for at the metaphysical level of accidental change, as St. Thomas would do. Further, St. Thomas' relegation of all grace to that same level, that of an accidental change effected in a natural substance, generates other, and fatal systematic-theological, (metaphysical) dilemmas which his substance-accident analysis of the sacramental mediation of grace simply cannot resolve.

We have already seen that notable among these dilemmas is the universal distribution of grace. This universality is explainable, within the Thomist metaphysical analysis, only insofar as understood to be a necessary accident — this by the same necessity by which, e.g., a man has an intellect and a will as accidents proper to his substance — proper, therefore, in the sense of immanently necessary, indispensable to his human existence. This level of universality is substantial in the sense that human nature, the human substance, is inconceivable except as intellectual. However, the universality of grace is by definition free: grace does not and cannot enter into the definition of man as man, for it is a gift and therefore not reducible to a necessary implication of human existence. Consequently, it cannot be reduced to an immanent necessity of man, although it is given wherever man is found. We can only conclude that because the universality of grace must be substantial, it can be so only in terms of the freedom of his graced creation,[24] which is to say, by creation in Christ. We shall see that the baptismal *character* is a similarly substantial grace, dependent upon the creative outpouring upon the baptizand of the *Spiritus Creator*, by whom the Christ creates and re-creates, renewing the fallen world.

The Baptismal *Character* as the Graced Restoration of Personal Integrity

The theological dilemmas raised by the Thomist postulate that all grace is accidental are resolved and Thomas' fundamental insight into the universality of the *trahi a Deo* is saved when one regards the baptismal *character* as *the graced restoration in signo* — viz., sacramentally, not empirically — *of the personal integrity, the free personal unity, the undivided heart, which was lost by Original Sin*. It must be emphasized that this objective restoration of integrity *in signo* is actual under the conditions of obscurity, or veiling, which are proper to fallen existence.

The recovery of personal integrity can only be substantial, that is, it can only be an effect of the divine creative omnipotence — the Father's sending of the Son to give the Spirit — for it is simply the objective, historical restoration, *in sacramento*, of the baptized person's unfallen condition as "in the Beginning." The baptismal *character* must then be the sacramental restoration (the *spiritualis regeneratio*, as St. Thomas has taken it from the patristic and monastic tradition), of the goodness proper to his creation, i.e., the nuptial]y-ordered personal unity which the first Adam and the first Eve possessed by reason of their creation in Christ, and which they lost in the Fall, for themselves and their "progeny."

The baptismal recovery of free unity is a personal participation in the free integrity of the Beginning, the Good Creation, which can only be on the level of substance. This free personal unity is objectively but not empirically restored *in sacramento* to those human beings who, fallen from the substantial unity of their creation in Christ, have within their fallen history been sacramentally re-created in Christ by baptism into his death, and so into his risen life. The objectivity of this personal participation in the resurrection of Christ is that of the New Creation.[25] The baptismal liturgy is insistent upon this theme of the New Creation, and theology cannot ignore it. However, its implications pose considerable difficulties.

The graced restoration of personal integrity or free unity — a restoration given *ex nihilo*, for it has no antecedent possibility — can occur only at the level of creation: i.e., of substance, not at the level of mere alteration, of accident. Otherwise, ungraced or "natural" human substance, as a simple matter of definition, would be the antecedent possibility of grace; as substance must account for the prior possibility of every accidental modification of an historical reality. Were the baptismal character understood to be thus dependent upon a prior substantial cause, it would cease to be as it is, *ex nihilo sui et subjecti*, and baptismal grace would cease to be grace.[26]

The baptismal character, understood as the restoration of personal integrity *in sacramento*, requires in turn that the substantially restored order of the Beginning, the One Flesh of the Good Creation — that is, its free nuptial unity — be sacramentally objective in history: not as empirically manifest but nonetheless as objectively and actually given in history. This is required by the historical objectivity of our baptismal participation in it. The fullness of the New Creation is historically objective in and by the Event of the efficacious sacramental representation of the Eucharistic Sacrifice, a sign infallibly effective *ex opere operato*.

Baptism has no other purpose than to enable personal participation in this Eucharistic representation and celebration of the plenary outpouring of the

Spirit by the Son instituting the Good Creation, whose historical reality must be temporally as well as metaphysically prior to baptism. The institution of the Church, into whose nuptial unity one is baptized, is an immediate effect *ex opere operato* of the Eucharistic celebration: where the Second Adam is, there always is the Second Eve, One Flesh with her Lord. The baptismal *character*, the infallible effect, given *ex opere operato*, of the sacramental sign of baptism, places the person baptized within the dynamic interchange of that free communion. Membership in the Church is not static, for it is free and thereby active. The actual and unfailing exercise of personal freedom is therefore the immediate implication of that membership, which is the immediate effect of the baptismal *character*, the gift of re-stored integrity which is irrevocable — not as a static state but in a concretely historical exercise of freedom. This exercise requires a choice between "two loves": either *pneumatic* or sarkic, *conversio* or *aversio*: there is no neutral use of freedom. However, baptism's restoration of personal integrity has its infallible effect only at the level of substance, of creation, not of activity or choice, for baptism does not remove one from the fallenness of historical existence.

Therefore the understanding of the *immediate effect of baptism* as membership in the Body of Christ does not require that there be no sinners in the Church. Penance (reconciliation) is after all one of the seven sacraments, and thus a constitutive element of Catholic worship. Rather, its implication would seem to be that the baptized, insofar as they fall into sin, do so with full personal responsibility: they do not act under the burden of Original Sin, but are free. In such baptized sinners, restored to personal integrity, the *trahi a Deo* requires but does not force a permanent conversion to the Truth who is Jesus the Christ, for that conversion must be free. When made by the baptized person, the *conversio* to the Truth who is Jesus the Christ is permanent, for it proceeds from an integrated person, "clothed" with *sarx*, as Paul has it in II Cor 5 but no longer submitted to it.[27] It must be stressed that in the sinner this inamissable faith, uninformed by charity, is the sort termed "dead faith," or *fides informis*: this is the faith by which the demons tremble and believe.

The Meaning of "Soul": *Nepeš-Pneuma-Spirit*

The Catholic tradition refers to the soul as the principle of this universal, substantially graced, concretely historical, *personal ability to pass from the initial aversio a Deo, in which we are born, to a salvific conversio ad Deum. It is particularly to this personal openness to recreatio*[28] — man's concrete, historical openness therefore to the sacramentally-recreated, substantially restored level of personal existence, that the word "soul" refers. Very simply, the soul is man as the subject of redemption, as the immortal person for whom Christ died.

The soul is then that within each of us which is preserved from the full destructive and annihilating impact of Original Sin by the fact of our creation in Christ, which no human act can undo. We remain *pneuma* despite the death worked upon us by our necessary solidarity with the sin of Adam, despite therefore our sarkic mortality, our "flesh." If sin could not destroy the *pneuma* in each of us that is ours by our creation in Christ, it is evident that death, which is no more than the sign of sin, can not do so: our *pneuma*, our "soul" or, better, our "spirit," survives death.

Personal Immortality

The understanding of "soul" as the *pneuma*tic principle underlying our personal freedom to convert does not invoke the immateriality according to which the word "soul" is ordinarily understood when spoken of as the "form of the body," viz., the sense in which in fact it was understood by St. Thomas.[29] Rather, *pneuma* is "soul" in the concretely historical, biblical sense of *nepeš*, and is better translated as "spirit." Because the Thomist reading of "soul" is so universally accepted in contemporary theological writing, the distinction between the Thomist understanding and that understanding of "soul" which corresponds to the Old Testament's *nepeš* and the New Testament's *pneuma* — both of which are more properly translated as "spirit" — must be developed.

The time-honored metaphysical equation of immateriality with immortality is finally Platonic. Its roots are neither biblical nor Catholic; rather, they are found in the pagan soteriology which seeks surcease from the unhappy self by flight from historical, i.e., material, existence as a self — a goal neither Jewish nor Christian.

The Christian belief in personal immortality is identical to belief in the resurrection of the flesh, whereas the philosophical/theological notion of a "natural immortality" is inferred from a supposedly "natural" or ungraced creation for which there is no support in the liturgical/doctrinal tradition. It is important further to note that there is no liturgical or doctrinal ground for the widespread impression that the soul, as understood in Scripture and in tradition, is immaterial and consequently indestructible: i.e., that the soul, as the necessary implication or immanent necessity of its immateriality, viz., as a "natural" or necessary attribute, some form of immaterial survival after death. The Thomist/Aristotelian theological interpretation of the dogmatic definition of the soul as the "form of the body" has popularized that impression,[30] but it is not part of the teaching of the Church.

The conventional supposition of the immateriality of the human soul rests upon habits of thought imposed on Western theology by a Platonic-derived metaphysical postulate, which supposes that, within history, immaterial form exists in a debated polarity with matter.[31] This pagan interpretation of the fallen human condition arises out of a mimetic liturgical tradition whose philosophical expression is a metaphysical dualism which has nothing in common with the *nepeš-bāśār*, or *pneuma-sarx*, or soul-body, polarity of the Jewish and Christian liturgical, doctrinal, and spiritual tradition.[32] While it is defined doctrine that the "soul is the form of the body,"[33] this doctrinal affirmation is not to be read as though it were a theological statement. As doctrinal, it transcends — and challenges — all theological interpretation. *An adequate theological interpretation of the dogmatic meaning, of "form of the body" requires that the theological anthropology underlying that interpretation rest upon the Judaeo-Christian liturgical experience rather than that of Greek paganism.*

Continuing to speak theologically, and therefore hypothetically, as a matter open to correction, rather than doctrinally, as of a matter integral to the Church's faith, there is ample reason to conclude that the Catholic Church's soul-body doctrine is not saved by the Thomist/Aristotelian reading of "soul" as the immaterial form of the body,[34] while it *is* saved by understanding "soul" as the historically objective principle of the freedom of the human person who is graced at the level of his substantial and concrete actuality in such wise as to be drawn by the Father to faith in Christ our Lord. We have identified this radical and substantial grace as the human person's creation in Christ, in the Image of God. As unfallen or integral, the human person is created in the risen Christ who, as Paul says, is "a life-giving spirit" sent by the Father in order that we may have life "more abundantly," as John's Gospel has it. This increase can only be substantial, the gift of the Spirit: its fullness is participation in the resurrection of the Head.

Thus the "soul" of every human being is the sacramentally objective, physically concrete and historical human person, created in the Second Adam, in him whom Pope John Paul II has named "the Beginning," fallen in the first Adam, but redeemed by the One Sacrifice of the Second Adam and, in him possessed of a humanity which has been raised to the right hand of the Father. Of each human being it must be said that his integrity has been lost in the first Adam and that he is therefore also *sarx* but further that, as fallen, he is freed from the fully destructive impact of the sin of Adam by the substantial grace of Christ, i.e., by the creative gift of the *Spiritus Creator* bestowed from "the Beginning" upon the bridal Church.

By this gift, inherent in his creation in Christ, the human person remains capable, under grace, of freely entering into the redemptive death of the Second Adam, whether by his own physical death in the case of the non-Christian or, in the case of the Christian, by sacramental baptism in which the personal integrity of his *pneumatic* existence is objectively restored, but *in signo*, in sacrament.

The Christian, in the here and now of salvation history, having been restored by baptism to the free unity of personal integrity, is objectively — sacramentally — freed from sin and death, and enabled freely to enter into the full measure of historical freedom; the Church's Eucharistic worship, the "medicine of immortality, the antidote that we should not die, but live forever in Jesus Christ."[35]

It follows that the Eucharist is utterly crucial to an understanding of the soul-body, *pneuma-sarx* composite that is historical man. Here Augustine's witness is crucial, so much so that it is foundational for St. Thomas' *Summa Theologiae*, as indeed for the entire doctrinal tradition concerning the Eucharist. St. Thomas opens the exposition of Eucharistic realism in the *Summa Theologiae III*, q.75, which contains eight articles. The first of these raises the radical challenge to Eucharistic realism as it had been posed since the ninth century by Ratramnus of Corbie as against his abbot, Paschasius, and against Hincmar of Rheims: viz., the issue of "symbolism" versus realism. Thomas cites Augustine's admonition, *spiritualiter intellige,* in the context of what may be called the spatial or the transportation problem to which St. Augustine had responded by the invocation of the Pauline *pneuma-sarx* polarity:[36] the risen Christ, *qua* risen, as *pneuma*, is not empirically present, and the objectivity of his presence on the altar of the Eucharistic Sacrifice is thus in need of being shown to be not an absurdity; to this end, Augustine had rebuked a Capharnaitic empiricism.

In fact, St. Thomas might have gone further, for Augustine's language of "spiritualiter intellige" invoked the Pauline anthropology and its corresponding epistemology of a freed and converted *pneumatic* understanding of the Eucharistic mystery which the "fleshly" or sarkic mind cannot grasp, locked as it is within a pragmatic determinism impervious to the truth of a mystery that its immanently necessary logic cannot control. Augustine's *spiritualiter intellige* refers not only to the Johannine "Verba quae locutus sum vobis, spiritus est, et vita," but equally to Paul's identification, in I Cor 15:45, of the risen Christ, the last Adam, victorious over death, as "a life-giving spirit." Christ is risen as the Head of the Body in the irrevocable unity of One Flesh, from which He is never separated. It is as the source of the free unity of the *Christus totus, Christus integer*, the Head and the Body, the New Covenant — in fine, as the redeemed and renewed Good Creation, the Whole Christ — that Christ is risen. This explains the significance of the Assumption of our Lady who, by her Assumption, is the risen second Eve and the Queen of the Church triumphant, in that "spiritual" or immortal unity with her Lord which the sacramental One Flesh of the Eucharistic Sacrifice, "Una Caro," represents in our fallen history.

In the light cast by Catholic sacramental realism, "spiritual" always refers to the

Christ's concrete transcendence over death that is communicated to the baptized by their sacramental immersion in the death of their Head, the Christ, and thereby into the triumph of his Resurrection into eternal life as the Head of his Body, the bridal Church. Whether as baptized into his death, and so into Body or as unbaptized, by our mortal dying into his death, and thereby into his Body, this "spirit" is our sacramentally objective personal reality, manifest not empirically but as signed and caused by baptism, as affirmed in and sustained by the Eucharistic worship of the Church. This "spirit" is the work of the *Spiritus Creator* in us: it is to be contrasted with our "flesh," which is given over to death: see Rom 8:10-11, 1 Pet 3:18-22.

All biblical and dogmatic reference to soul and body should be thus understood: viz., in the context of the liturgical, apostolic, and Scriptural tradition, not of Platonic or Aristotelian metaphysics. Within the Catholic tradition, "Spirit" takes its meaning from the Resurrection of the Christ, and has nothing to do with immateriality. That false connotation is due to an unreflective acceptance, already visible in some patristic writing under Neoplatonic influence, and all too evident in medieval theology, of the Greek argumentation for the reservation of immortality to the nonhistorical and immaterial One. Within Christianity, the ultimate ground of our "spiritual" immortality is the Father, whose gift of life through his sending of the Son to give the Spirit and thus, through the sacrificial life, death, and Resurrection of the Head, is our divinization, our sharing in the divine life through baptism.

It follows that the late scholastic preoccupation with a natural or ungraced immortality has no basis in the Catholic liturgical and doctrinal tradition, for it is not written into the dogmatic meaning of "soul," despite the usual supposition that the soul's immateriality is included within the dogmatic definition of the soul as the form of the body.[37]

However, under the influence of St. Thomas' Aristotelian anthropology, "Soul" in its ordinary "soul-body" usage has retained, *contra* the Augustinian anthropology, an unfortunately abstract and passive connotation. "Soul" is generally understood structurally, or statically, as "the form of the body," rather than dynamically and historically, as its vitality. In fact, the soul, when understood historically, as *pneuma*, is never static, never awaiting a "concursus" in order to move from potency to act.[38] It is always in act, as the "first act" of the acting human person, whether his acting be the exercise of his baptismally-restored integrity, or the rejection of free unity and thus an *aversio a Deo*, a conversion to his own immanent and fatal necessities, to the imaging of an idol. "Soul" is therefore not commonly understood as it should be, as *pneuma*, as graced in its creation, as freed *in sacramento*, which is to say, in history, from the immanent determinism of *sarx* and, in every moment of personal existence, in a situation of having either freely entered upon the *conversio ad Deum* or *amor*

Dei which builds the City of God in history, or upon the *aversio a Deo* that is sarkic man intent upon his own annihilation, his immanently necessary reduction to the dust of death.

The Thomistic failure to recognize the historicity of the soul precisely misses the Pauline meaning of soul as *pneuma* in its concretely graced historical relation to *sarx*, to flesh. When the "soul" freely refuses to engage in the graced, personal appropriation of salvation history, Paul refers to it as *psyche*: for him, "psychic" man and "sarkic" man are the same: i.e., autonomous man, unconverted man, man deliberately turned toward his own immanently necessary disintegration, oriented toward the ultimate disunity that is dust in the Old Testament as well as in the New: in sum, man as *Sein zum Tode*, man doomed to die: man as dynamically conformed to death rather than to life.

Excursus on the "immortality of the soul."

The immortality of the soul is beyond question: the doctrinal tradition is clear. Every human soul is created immortal. The basis of this immortality has become confused in the minds of many Catholics by reason of the Thomist doctrine of the ungraced or natural character of creation: as we have seen, Thomas insists upon "nature" as the object of creation, and grace as an accidental modification of nature. This stance requires that the immortality of the soul — which is the object of creation — be natural, in the sense of independent of the economy of salvation and of the victory of Christ on the Cross. But "natural" goes further in this reasoning: the term implies an immanently necessary intelligibility; whatever is "natural" is accounted for, explainable, in terms of intrinsically necessary causes. Thus, the immateriality of the soul is relied upon to prove its immortality, arguing that, as immaterial, the soul has no principle of corruption; lacking the material potentiality for intrinsic divisibility, it is immune to death.

We have earlier referred to the pagan foundation of this reasoning and need not dwell upon it here. The Thomist tradition is itself uncomfortable with the inferences to be drawn from it: Thomas for example is forced to suppose that Paul's stress upon sin as the cause of death is to be understood "spiritually," in the sense that sin is not the cause of the physical death which Paul so evidently has in view, but only of that "second death" which is damnation. For Thomas, death is natural in the sense of immanently necessary. Adam in Paradise had been preserved from it by a grace which lifted him above the necessities of nature: thus, the Fall consequent upon Adam's sin was a fall back to a naturally necessary state of mortality.

There is a sense in which this argument can be accepted, for in fact the Fall was from a condition of offered integrity, of existing as *pneuma* simply, to that of *sarx*, the fallenness whose sign is death. *Sarx* can be rationalized, and its fallenness reduced to an immanent necessity: it is then assimilable to the Aristotelian/Thomist "nature," which knows no moral freedom and for which the dissolution of death is an immanent necessity.

However, this analysis ignores the reality of the Fall, reducing it to a mere loss of habitual grace, whereas it is comprehensible only as a fall from an offered and refused integrity. For we learn from Protoevangelium of Gen 3:15 that the Fall was not absolute: its remedy is there foreseen as already provided for. Thus to regard fallen man as mere immanence, locked into a necessary dissolution, is to ignore the existential condition of fallen man who although fallen from the integrity of *pneuma* is yet graced by the grace of the risen Christ in whom we are created, as Paul teaches in Col 1:16. The Fall has not undone the Beginning, Good Creation, whose goodness is restored, *in sacramento*, by the institution, on the Cross, of the One Flesh that is the New Covenant, the New Creation.

By this redemptive gift, fallen man exists in his historical fallenness in that riven state which is marked, as Augustine taught, by the two loves that divide him and leave him restless until he rests in Christ. These two loves correspond to his composite condition: historical man is at once *sarx* and *pneuma*, and throughout his life must choose to live in the Christ, as *pneuma* or choosing *sarx* as the norm of his existence, he may live toward death, freely choosing the dissolution which is damnation. This graced capacity to choose is his dignity: he is not forced to be free, but freedom in Christ is continually offered to him, for as long as he lives. At bottom, this is the freedom to worship, to image God. *Contra* the Reform, man retains a moral freedom which he cannot abdicate: he chooses responsibly, under the intrinsic grace of Christ, and his free choice will be honored, finally ratified. Jesus has promised that He will turn away no one who comes to him; at the same time, He cannot deny himself by denying man the freedom to reject him who is the way, the truth, and the life.

Solidarity in *Pneuma*

Passive Solidarity

Our passive solidarity in *pneuma* is simply our participation in the Good Creation which is good only as in the Whole Christ, "in the Beginning": otherwise put, it is to have Christ as our Head, whether we recognize him so to be or not. The creation of humanity — and all things — in Christ carries no implication of fallenness. Further, it cannot but freely entail free membership in his Body, the Church, whether this membership be fallen or unfallen. In our fallen world, our merely passive solidarity in *pneuma*, our creation in Christ, demands a baptism into the Church. We enter the Church freely, by a personal choice, but can do so only through the dead and risen Christ, who by his obedience in a fallen world became the gate, the way, the truth, the life, by which we have access to the Father through our entry into his redemptive death.

We have seen that this baptism into his death may be sacramental, as it is for Christians; for non-Christians it must be by way of personal entry into physical death, for Christ's victory over death has made the physical death of the unbaptized to be their gateway, their means of access to the active solidarity in *pneuma* which is membership in the Kingdom of God. Passive solidarity then amounts to being among those for whom Christ died, and thus to have received involuntarily, by our creation, that *gratia Capitis*, the *trahi a Deo* which, as the beginning of salvation, looks to and draws us toward its achievement.

Active solidarity

Our active solidarity or community in *pneuma* cannot but be freely chosen by a personal choice that is entry into the concrete exercise of covenantal, nuptially ordered fidelity; it is entry in the history of salvation. This personal, salvific historicity, this membership in the Church, is the consequence of a free conversion from an existence normed by the determinism of the fallen physical universe to an existence normed by the freedom that is covenantal fidelity. This free community is the Church in its full sacramental historicity: as *sacramentum tantum* (the Old Covenant), as *res sacramenti* (the New Covenant), and as *res tantum* (the Kingdom of God). This decision is to enter into a covenantally or nuptially ordered sacramental/historical existence in the Church in her broadest extension. We have seen that this decision is possible to everyone at every stage of fallen existence in history. That is, the salvific faith was and is possible for those people who live in a paganism comparable to that which was universal in the Near East prior to Abraham, i.e., without knowledge of the historical revelation. It is possible for the people living in the context of the Old Covenant, who do not acknowledge Jesus as the Christ but who accept the historical revelation of Jahweh to his people. Finally, it is possible for those of the New Covenant who live in the era of the fullness of the revelation who is Jesus the Christ.

All of those for whom Christ died were and are substantially graced: all are drawn by the Father to faith in the Son, sent to give the Spirit; this is to say that all are created in Christ, and so cannot but be included within the people for whom He died, for his Mission is single. Insofar as they respond to that grace — which is to say, insofar as they depart from the personal irresponsibility that is idolatry to enter into a free personal quest for Truth, they enter into the solidarity of the Church's worship, whether at the historical level of the *sacramentum tantum* proper to the Old Covenant, and to the pagans such as Balaam whose presence in the Old Testament witnesses to the reality of the Old Covenant as the pathway from paganism to Christianity,[39] or at the level of the *res et sacramentum* of salvation history, which recognizes the fullness of revelation in the event of Jesus the Christ. Solidarity in *pneuma* amounts to solidarity in the sacramentally unified, free history and free community of salvation that is made to be salvific by the transcendently free and redemptive Eucharistic immanence of the Lord of History, Jesus the Christ.[40]

The Meaning of "Body": *Bāśār, Sarx (Soma), Caro*

The "flesh" or "body" whose "form" is the soul, is understood by the Catholic tradition to be the polar correlative of the soul — the correlative which the Hebrew of the Old Testament names *bāśār*, and which the Greek of the New Testament refers to as *sarx*, sometimes as *soma* which latter term the Latin translates as *corpus*, but which, when held in polarity with "spirit," has the connotation of "flesh" in the sense of *sarx*.

The same body-soul polarity which the Hebrew of the Old Testament affirms to exist between *nepeš* (or *ruach*) and *bāśār*, the Greek of the New Testament affirms to exist between *pneuma* and *sarx*.[41] "Soul," as to be understood in its sacramental objectivity as the graced capacity for baptism and thereby for the restoration of the person's free unity or integrity, viz., the baptismal *character*. Thus soul, or *pneuma*, is properly contrasted to, or held in correlation with 'body', only when the latter is also understood at once dynamically and sacramentally, i.e., in the sense of *bāśār* or sarx. In Scripture these terms designate not man's corporeality, but his fallen historicity, and particularly his subjection to death by reason of the Original Sin of the first Adam and the first Eve, but at the same time designating his capacity for the restoration of the personal free unity given in Baptism, an irrevocable personal participation in the *mia sarx, una caro*, the free unity or substantial integrity of the "One Flesh" of Christ and his Church. Personal participation in this nuptial union, and in its fidelity, is *sola gratia*, given in a moment of graced conversion and of freedom from the immanently necessary dynamism of flesh toward the ultimate dissolution of death, the biblical return to dust.

The correlation of *pneuma-sarx*, phenomenologically considered, is that of Augustine's "two loves which built two cities." In any given concrete personal situation, one of them is dominant: hence Augustine's apothegm, *"Amor meus, pondus meum,"* with *"pondus"* understood not in the sense of weight or momentum, but rather of steadfastness and fidelity; its alternative "love" is fleshly: the choice of death over life.

"Body," or *sarx*, is more difficult to identify than is man's *pneuma* or spirit, for while *sarx* also designates the reality of the fallen human person, it does so negatively, with particular reference to his mortality. *Sarx* is what is ephemeral in man, by reason of which he must die, must return to the dust from which he was made. In this sense, "dust" or "ashes" is the alpha and the omega of the body: *sarx* begins from and ends in absolute fragmentation. The immanence of that principle of disintegration in fallen man, its reality in and even as his body, is the incorporation of the inexorable process of *dis*-integration, the on-going corruption inseparable from flesh. *Sarx* is then man's subjection to the necessity of fragmentation and final physical dissolution; about this he can do nothing. Only the *Spiritus Creator* can restore what has been lost by sin.

Fleshly or sarkic man is therefore man as devoted to death. *Sarx* designates man as necessarily atomized within and without, for it must be remembered that we have to do not with a merely material condition: *sarx* refers to the totality of the person, touching his soul as well as his physical being. Left to his own devices, i.e., considered as sarkic merely, he is bent upon yet further disintegration, still further alienation. Furthermore, fallen man exists as a *pneuma-sarx* polarity: within history we cannot isolate our *sarx* from our *pneuma*, our flesh from our spirit. These are given together in each fallen human being, and their rationalization, their ideal isolation or abstraction each from each, would be their falsification.[42] Historical man, fragmented by reason of the Fall, lacks the free unity or integrity he should possess, but he is not annulled by the Fall for he is freed by Christ's gift of the Spirit, and thus freed is made capable of being drawn by the Father to the Son.

Apart from this gift, sarkic man has only that "love" which builds the enslaved "city of man": it is only as freed by Christ that wherever found, he lives out a tension of choosing between "two loves," a choice which has eternal consequences. He can choose death or life. In this life, his choice is made in those circumstances which Paul has named obscurity and ambiguity: only God can read his heart.

Thus historically and sacramentally understood, *sarx* exists in a free, i.e., graced, and yet paradoxical historical relation to *pneuma*, which is to say, *sarx* exists as flesh, *bāśār*, to soul, *nepeš*, in the freed unity of the historical person, who is at once just and sinful by reason of the immanence within him of the two mutually exclusive "loves" which are inseparable from his conscious subjectivity: for as long as he is just, he is tempted to sin; for as long as he sins, he is tempted to conversion.

The *sarx-pneuma* relation exists and is the realm of freedom, of our deciding between "two loves," only by reason of the free immanence of the Second Adam in history. We are created in Christ who "for freedom has made us free," whose at once primordial and eschatological immanence in and transcendence over fallen history as its Alpha and Omega is finally and radically Eucharistic[43] — *per modum substantiae*[44] and therefore is ecclesial, or liturgical. The Augustinian and radically Pauline anthropology of *simul justus et peccator*, the existential "two loves" which Augustine saw to specify our fallen consciousness — these bespeak a phenomenology of existence in the Church, of existence not only as graced, but as at once worshiping and under judgment. Only within this ecclesial existence *in Christo* is the human dilemma comprehensible, for only within that worship do we recognize in Jesus the Christ who is the Lord of history by his Eucharistic transcendence and Lordship of history. The Eucharistic immanence of the Lord of history, the Alpha and the Omega, bestows upon history the free sacramental significance of salvation in the Kingdom of God for all who freely enter into the historical order of that free worship, whether remotely as pagans, proximately and prospectively as Jews, or fully, as Christians in actual Eucharistic communion with the risen Christ.

In this view, wherein the historicity of our existence, and that of the whole of creation, is objective and concrete only at the sacramental level, it is only on this level of sacramental freedom that we image the Triune God, in the nuptially-ordered unity (One Flesh) of the Church's Eucharistic worship. This is the only possible basis for understanding that already-cited passage in Rom 8:19-23 which makes creation depend, for restoration to its primordial free unity and thus to its primordial beauty or glory, upon the prior restoration in Christ of the lost freedom of "the sons of men." Thus, the recapitulation worked by Christ (Eph 1:10) is to be understood as the restoration by the Second Adam, the Head, of the free (nuptially-ordered!) unity by which the Good Creation, even as fallen, is primordially good and very good (Gen 1:31; 2:24). The loss of this free unity by reason of the Original Sin of the first Adam, is that by which the Good Creation, as fallen into necessity and disunity, became *sarx*, whose alienation, fragmentation, unfreedom and consequent mortality is the secular, neo-pagan alternative to the free and now sacramental re-appropriation of the nuptial unity, the One Flesh (*mia sarx*) restored to us by the One Sacrifice in which Christ instituted the New Covenant: see Col 1:15ff. That the salvific alternative to despair is available to us, that freedom to be free in Christ is universally offered us, is the work of the Spirit poured out by the Eucharistic Christ upon his Church and, through her sacramental-historical worship, upon all humanity. *Pneuma* in us is this free awareness of moral freedom; *sarx* in us is that *indole*, the spiritual inertia or sloth, the burden of our sins, which fears freedom because freedom connotes the undertaking of covenantal responsibility and, ultimately, participation in the worship of the Lord of history, by whose gift alone are we able to enter into the history of salvation, the history of covenantal fidelity, freedom and responsibility that the *sarx* in each of us dreads.

It is therefore precisely because we are redeemed that the paradox of the soul-body, *sarx-pneuma* relation is intrinsic to every human being existing in fallen history. The Pauline tradition has insisted on this intrinsic tension, a tension which the Augustinian tradition especially has explored, via Augustine's description of it between "two loves which built two cities" or, more succinctly, as the awareness of being *simul justus et peccator* that is proper to every human being.

This paradox cannot be rationalized: attempts to do so, as in theories of pre-destination, inevitably exclude one or another of its logically incompatible limbs. The same rationalist and ultimately dehistoricizing ambition haunted the unresolved medieval controversy between competing theories of the soul — the Christian Platonism which exalted the soul to the level of a quasi-independent substance, as opposed to the effectively Thomist anthropology, which so stressed the role of the soul as the Aristotelian 'form of the body' as to render it impersonal upon separation from the body at death. These debates, whether over predestination or over the multiplicity of substantial form, represent dead ends, for they respond to questions posed abstractly, nonhistorically, *sub specie aeternitatis*. An authentically theological treatment of the soul-body relation con-stituting the standing paradox of human existence in history must itself be his-torical. Abstraction from the paradox is always a begging of the question. How-ever, neither is it adequate to relegate the paradox to a merely historical dia-lectic, for that imports a soteriological flight from history: Tillich's account of the Christological resolution of existential alienation provides a sufficient illus-tration of this propensity.[45] It illustrates the gnostic dehistoricizing tendency in contemporary Christology to which Cardinal Ratzinger has recently drawn at-tention.[46] Such systematic dehistoricizing is merely the academic version of sarkic rationality, a normalization of the flight from historical responsibility by the provision of a rational justification for it as an immanent necessity of thought. But historical reason has no immanent necessities except those which are personally chosen, self-imposed: we are free in history to choose freedom: our *pneuma-sarx* composite is not doomed but, as composite, is redeemed, *pace* the pagans.

Our freedom, sacramentally restored by our baptismal participation in the death which is Christ's institution of the One Flesh of the New Covenant, is freely appropriated by fallen, "sarkic" men, but only through the mediation of that freedom in the Eucharistic worship of the Church. The Catholic fullness of this worship is remotely anticipated by the pagan worship (hence their in-clusion in the Old Testament), and has its sacramental antetype in the sacri-fices of the Old Testament. Both anticipations take place within a history whose free unity is sacramental, effectively signed by the Eucharistic Presence of the "Lamb who was slain," the sacrificed Christ, the Eucharistic Lord of his-tory, who by his Presence in history *per modum substantiae* transcends history from within history, and through that transcendent Lordship makes it to be the history of salvation.

The free unity of salvation history, which is to say, of sacramentally significant history, of history whose unity is Eucharistically grounded, is the free unity, the integration given *ex nihilo*, of the Old Covenant, the New Covenant, and the Kingdom of God. This unity is the consequence of the free immanence within time of the sacramental signing — *sacramentum tantum, res et sacramentum, res tantum* — of the Eucharistic sacrifice which institutes the New Covenant, wherein all things are restored, now in sign, but manifestly at the *Parousia*. This Eucharistic signing of the One Sacrifice is the free integration, *in signo* of an otherwise merely "sarkic" time: time as merely empirical, quantified, tied to fragmentation and to necessity — time as fatality. This implies the sacramental unity and significance of history: it is salvific by reason of the Eucharistic integration of its past, its present, and its future, i.e., the Old Covenant, the New Covenant, the Kingdom of God.

As baptized, we can enter into the fullness of that Eucharistic worship — the only worship there is — and into the sacramentally-signed freedom of salvation history, by Eucharistic Communion with the risen Christ, an entry is made possible by his baptismal restoration to us of our integrity, for nothing unclean can enter Heaven. The unbaptized infant, the pagan, the Jew, belong to that same salvation history, at *sacramentum tantum* level of sacramental signification that is preliminary to the New Covenant, and so is objectively part of the single salvific history of the universe, the temporality whose past, present and future are freely integrated by Jesus the Christ's Event-immanence in time, which thereby is the salvific history which effectively symbolizes, *ex opere operato*, the fulfilled Kingdom of God — the only inherent significance that history has.[47]

Here, it may be suggested, is the only legitimate role for the notion of the fundamental option, which supposes that each person at the moment of death must choose between the Kingdom of God and the kingdom of Satan. This cannot be true of the Christian who has lived in and by the Catholic confession that Jesus is the Lord, or for the Jew who has lived in covenantal fidelity, but it would appear to be the implication, for those unbaptized who have lived at an unreflective level, of the universal efficacy of Jesus' salvific death, of which they are the free beneficiaries at their death, in a moment of radical choice, made in that moment which is their personal judgment because it is their vision of the risen Christ. Augustine has taught that the same vision of the risen Lord is at once salvific and damnific: no one is saved or damned except by a personal choice, made here or hereafter.

This consideration raises the final question of the theological interpretation of the traditional description of death as the separation of soul and body. We have pointed to a basic inconsistency in the classic Thomist interpretation of this separation, with its notion of an immaterial "separated soul." It is necessary to set out the alternative interpretation here proposed, viz., death as the separation of *pneuma* from *sarx*.

Solidarity in *Sarx*

Passive Solidarity

Passive solidarity in *sarx* is universal in man: it is equivalently our participation in the Fall, as the consequence of our solidarity in the fallen Adam, and so also in his sin; it is Original Sin in us, passively viewed. It is entirely involuntary: we are members of that fallen humanity which fell in Adam when he refused the responsibility of headship offered him in that climactic event which is his Original Sin. The first Adam's failure to accept his headship is his failure to provide the free unity to the body, the humanity, which it was his office, as head, to provide. The consequence is the sarkic humanity, lacking both freedom and unity, of which we are members. Further, because the first Adam was to be the head of creation also, all of creation is locked into that same disunity, into that same fatality or subjection to necessity. This we know by reference to the Head, the Second Adam, whom Paul in Col 1:16 affirms to be the Head of all creation.

Active Solidarity

The active meaning of solidarity in *sarx* is equivalently to choose damnation over free participation in salvation history under the lordship of the Christ. It is freely to affirm the normative character of the flesh in one's personal life, and freely to live out the implications of that affirmation. Man's graced freedom is innate, the radical grace of his creation in Christ, which no choice of his can undo. Throughout his life he lives on the edge of choice: if a sinner, he is tempted despite himself by the intuitive knowledge that he may reform his life and return to fulfilling the image according to which he was made; if he is living a life normed by the Spirit of Christ, there is always present to him temptation, the "impossible possibility" of sin,[48] of turning toward death instead of life, of imaging a false god, of that idolatry of the self which is pride.

Until fallen history closes with the *Parousia*, the restoration of all things in Christ which Paul describes in I Cor 15:20-28 and again in Eph 1:10, we live in a world whose immanent dynamism is toward death. To conform to this dynamism, to accept its implacably destructive logic as the governing principle of one's life, is to live according to the flesh, which profits nothing. So to live is a standing denial of the unity, truth, and goodness in a history which even as fallen is imbued with the glory of God.

The price of this choice is, quite simply, personal damnation. In rejecting the nuptial fidelity of the Covenant, and the personal responsibility which that normative fidelity requires, one must deny oneself, and one must also continually distract oneself from the "unhappy consciousness" that, in rejecting the covenantal foundation of the peace and freedom of all free society, one has chosen the isolation of an impersonal atom in an impersonal and atomized world whose only unity is coerced. This radical alienation from the covenantal order, the salvific historicity of the Good Creation, this dehistoricization of the self, embarks one upon a quest for the personal possession of the unconditioned power by which alone one's chosen isolation from the free historical unity of the Good Creation may be secured, in order that one thereby may reign unconditionally sovereign in the personal void which can recognize no reality save one's autonomous self. This quest for the feral autonomy that is freedom from all responsibility amounts to a personal apotheosis, the devout pursuit of a personal ambition "to be like God" by which one may think to distract oneself from the immanent anxiety, the substantial, existential tension, that is inseparable from a deliberate alienation from Christ, the *Intus Magister*, and from his substantial illumination and freeing of one's mind. One has chosen the finally intolerable contradiction between one's creation in Christ and one's rejection of that grace in favor of Nothingness. Active, chosen solidarity in *sarx* is finally Satanic: as you see him, so you have him.

The Meaning of Death: Separation of Soul and Body

The doctrinal tradition is clear: death is the separation of the soul from the body, the separation of that which is immortal from that which is mortal, but with the proviso that the separation, death itself, pertains to the composite, the person who is soul as well as the body: it is the total human person who died, soul and body, and this death as the result of Original Sin.[49]

The doctrine of the immortality of the soul, understood in the biblical sense of *pneuma* or *nepeš* (*ruach*), is equally clear.[50] It is this personal human reality that is vindicated in the resurrection of the flesh. The resurrection is the transformation of the necessary fragmentation and mortality of fallen, sarkic, humanity into the risen Body of Christ and so into the One Flesh (*mia sarx*), the nuptial unity of the risen Church with the risen Christ who, by his resurrection, "became a life-giving spirit (*pneuma*)" who, *semper interpellans*, pours out his Spirit upon his bridal Church, making it to be One Flesh with Him. To die in Christ is to enter into that *sancta societas*, the One Flesh of Christ and his Church, as it is fulfilled in the Kingdom of God. The doctrine of the resurrection of the flesh looks to this final end, in which the defeat of death by Jesus on the Cross is manifest in eternal life.

Sarx in Death

That which is *sarx in man* is mortal; it has no future other than the dissolution that is dust, unless it be vivified, clothed, by *pneuma* in the resurrection of the flesh which is fullness of life in Christ, full personal participation in the plenary Gift of Christ's Spirit to the Church by which it is the Kingdom of God.

With death, we leave behind us, all that is sarkic, all that is fleshly, all that is corporeal in the sense of bound to the insignificance of the fragmented and deterministic time and space which comprise the fallen universe. Specifically: we leave behind us that from which Paul sought deliverance: "Who will deliver me from this body of death?" Once again, one need look for no metaphysical dualism in Paul's anthropology, by which corporeality as such would be the cause of sin and death. We are delivered from "this body of death" not by a flight from it, but by the resurrection of our Head, wherein "all things are made new."

Because it is our material component, our fallen body, our "flesh," that is subject to the immanent dynamism of fragmentation, to the intrinsically neces- sary loss of free unity which marks fallen history, it is in our bodies that we move inexorably toward the ultimate physical dissolution of death. As has been said, this led pagan philosophy to the now-commonplace supposition that death is proper to the body, and does not touch the soul which, as immaterial, was supposed by the pagan speculation to be immortal.

But the Fall is not, as the pagans supposed, from immateriality into corpore- ality; rather it is from an offered personal integrity or free unity: therefore *sarx* in us touches the personal self, *psyche* as well as *soma*, for the fallen person also has lost his free psychic unity, to become the subject to two laws, according to Paul,[51] or to the two loves of man as *simul peccator et justus* which, in Augus- tine's rendition of the Pauline analysis of historical existence, build two cities, of man and of God. Phenomenology and existentialism have explored the di- chotomous experience of our fallen historical ambivalence in quest of a remedy for the presumed irrationality of that experience, but the rigorously determin- ist and voluntarist resolutions offered by contemporary speculation have left the human situation as enigmatic as they found it. Husserl's construction of phenomenology as a *strengwissenschaft* denied that enigma a priori, but could not resolve it, while the exploitation of Nietzsche's defiance of absurdity, and his assertion of the absolute autonomy of the self, has ended in the sullenness of deconstructionist nihilisms.

The fallen and thereby riven human self, the self as fragmented and autono- mous, the immanent self, is locked into its own fragmentation, its own atomis- tic isolation, by necessities as fatal as those which fragment the physical universe. "*Sarx*", or "flesh," describes the whole of fallen man, neither his body nor his consciousness in isolation, but their fragile and tormented union from which the enormous resources of a scientific age offers distraction but no escape.

It is then evident that the universality of the human dilemma is not free: we cannot avoid our solidarity in it, viz., in *sarx*, and, within fallen history, no exit from it is possible: the history of humanistic speculation establishes that if little else. However, death is the departure from fallen history for each of us. We speak here not of "natural death," as if death were a more or less secular reality, untouched by the grace of Christ. For Catholic theology, the meaning of death is set by the death of the Head. Consequently; death is a strictly theological category: like history, it has no secular meaning. Whatever lives, lives in Christ; whatever dies, does so in Christ. Life and death are in him, and have no other significance, no other intelligibility, than is given them by the Head.

Until the *Parousia* nonetheless, death signs the sinfulness of our fallen historicity; it is the radical expression of the disintegration to which all flesh must come, the return to the radical disunity of dust, the *terminus ad nihil* of sin. At the same time, the triumph of sin and death — of fallenness — over the flesh, its utter destruction, is the dehistoricization of the soul: separation from *sarx* is identically the separation of the *pneuma* from historicity, from the fallenness of the world, of time and of space as we know them. From this "existence unto death" we are delivered by the victory of Christ over death by his death upon the Cross. As has been seen, participation in this deliverance can only be free: it may be refused, in favor of what the liturgical, scriptural and doctrinal tradition has seen as eternal death.

Pneuma in Death

Here we must recall a Pauline theme, our twin solidarities, in *sarx*, and in *pneuma*. Solidarity in *sarx* is our unfree solidarity in the unfreedom of the fallen first Adam: our coincident and correlative solidarity in *pneuma* is our free solidarity in the freedom won for us by the risen Christ. The former solidarity is in sin and in death; the latter is a solidarity in the historical worship of the Church, and so a solidarity in life. The former is implicit in the headship of the fallen Adam; the latter is explicit in the Headship of the Christ.

We have seen in our solidarity in *sarx* the summary of the immanent condition of fallen man, whose fallenness is not free, and from which he is not free to escape. Were this the whole of the human condition, those philosophical anthropologies would be warranted in seeking to dismiss our fallenness by normalizing it, thereby nullifying the significance of historical existence by reducing it to the immanent necessities of *sarx*, although the intellectual *eros*

which drives such reductionism would remain inexplicable for, ideally or ra-
tionalistically, "natural man" does not seek to escape or transcend his nature
by comprehending it any more than a goldfish longs to be dry. The similar
Thomist effort to rationalize the fallen human condition as "nature" is self-de-
feating: *pace* Karl Rahner,[52] "natural" humanity does not exist nor can it:
insofar as the term points to the immanently necessary causes of concrete human existence, "human nature" lacks the substantial potentiality which its creation presupposes.

It is only insofar as he is *pneuma*, as freely unified, that man possesses life, and
longs to possess it "more abundantly." This longing is as innate in the human
condition as is the melancholy recognition, with maturity, that the goal he
seeks is radically beyond his grasp, outside the range of his immanent possibilities. He cannot, by taking thought, remedy his fallenness.

Then it is that he recognizes in himself a personal dichotomy: he is *simul justus
et peccator*, imbued with a longing for an unattainable goal, for unconditioned
and unqualified life, life without end, life eternal, beyond all limit, beyond
death. This longing is identically his longing for freedom, for life is not other
than existence in freedom and unity, in quest of an ever greater union with
a free unity beyond all division. The Unity with whom he seeks union is yet
free, as he will learn finally only from revelation, because it is Triune, the God
in whose image he is made, from which image he is fallen, and to which
image, the plenitude of freedom and life, he longs to be restored. The "god
of the philosophers," whose unity is absolute, cannot support the freedom by
which man seeks the human *telos*. As all the learned paganisms have discovered, under that awful aegis man can seek only his own nullification — the
abolition of man that is the implication of every idolatry.

The restoration of man's integrity, of his free unity, can only be by gift, for
freedom freely must be received by one who of himself has no freedom, as he
has no unity, for he is in search of both, while they elude him utterly. Therefore the very freedom by which he seeks his freedom and his unity is itself a
gift, a prospective deliverance from the immanent necessities of *sarx*. This de-
livery, this hope of freedom and of life, is innate, even as fallen: as doomed
to die, man is yet able to transcend his fate: his quest for deliverance from dissolution and death signs that he is more than *sarx*: he is also *pneuma*, and is
so by gift, which is to say, *gratia Christi*, by the grace of Christ.

The first moment of the reception of the grace of Christ is simply one's creation, but this is a complex event. As Pope John Paul has taught, human "nature" was created in its fullness, its integrity, "in the Beginning;" this is the
primordial Good Creation, which is so as only in Christ, as Paul in Col 1:16
teaches. The Good Creation is realized as unfallen in principal (*in Principio, in*

Capite), in the integrity of the One Flesh, *Christus integer*, of the primordial or pre-existent Second Adam and Second Eve. This, "the Beginning" which Pope John Paul II has identified in *Veritatis Splendor*[53] simply with the Christ, the "whole Christ," is the full outpouring by Christ of the Spirit, upon his bridal Church. Upon this plenitude of grace, the creation of humanity in the *pneumatic* integrity or the free unity of the One Flesh, depends all else in creation, the entirety of the universe, whose free unity is in Christ alone.

This primordial creation is of man as *pneuma* simply. But that creation fell in the first Adam and first Eve, to whom the free unity of their marital One Flesh was offered, and by whom it was refused. This primordial refusal of free unity of the Good Creation issued, as has been seen, in the sarkic condition of fallen humanity, man's subjection to necessary dissolution, to death.

However, this mortal, sarkic condition is also complex, for it is not absolute. Our creation is single, and it is in Christ; therefore our creation — which is to say, the personal, substantial existence of each of us — is graced. Therefore man is not *sarx* merely, but *sarx-pneuma*: human sin could not and cannot undo the primordial Good Creation, nor is the free and covenantal unity of its One Flesh annulled by humanity's universal solidarity in the primordial first Adam's refusal of a free participation in its nuptial order, in the One Flesh by which it is good. That primordial free unity, the integrity of the One Flesh of the Good Creation, the New Covenant, does not cease to be real, for it continues objectively to exist in our fallen world, in our fallen humanity. This is the message of Gen 3:15, the Protoevangelium which, immediately upon the punishment of the now-fallen Adam and Eve, announces their future redemption. But this objectivity is not manifest, not evident in the world darkened by sin: only the revelation of the Truth, the Event of the Christ, the Good News, informs us of it, albeit in the enigma and obscurity of faith.

Nonetheless, that intuitive outreach to what transcends us absolutely is not defeated by the fleshly fatality in which we are immersed: we know that we should be free, that we should be at one with ourselves and all humanity, and that death cannot be the goal of living. The *non omnis moriar* of late paganism corresponds to that irrefragable conviction; it is given more fully in the Psalmist's faith-assertion that his redeemer lives, that finally in his own humanity he shall see him, for which vision he is filled with longing. The Christian confirmation of that witness is summed up in Augustine's "Our hearts are restless, until they rest in Thee."

Our *pneumatic* existence, equivalently our freedom in Christ, is not empirical, not a subject of pragmatic experience. Rather it is most radically and universally encountered as an absence of that integrity of whose reality we have a dim and inarticulate intuitive knowledge, *intimior intimo meo*, as Augustine puts it —

for we live in enigma and obscurity, as Paul has taught —: an awareness of our poverty, our indigence, our failure to be what we should be, and a correlative hope and longing, as has been said, to recover the fullness of life which we have in some manner lost but which yet belongs to us. If this personal desolation is universal in historical existence, yet its correlative is as universal: an indefeasible hope whose object, revealed over the long history of salvation, is the Kingdom whose King is Christ the Lord, the Head whose victory over sin and death is our heritage, the restoration of our integrity.

This situation of fallen ambivalence is the arena of historical existence: it requires of us a choice, whether to remain in fallen futility, or to use that freedom which is ours as created in the Trinitarian Image, in the *Christus integer, Christus totus*, the primordial One Flesh, to return to that imaging from which we are fallen, but to which we are continually tempted to return. This situation of two competing loves, as has been remarked, is ended only by death. Until then, there is before us the choice between participation in and nourishment by the sacramental objectivity of our heritage in Christ, and the re-affirmation of our solidarity with the irresponsibility of the fallen Adam who would be "like God" and was the first idolater, whose idolatry is ours, apart from the grace of Christ.

We read in Rom 8: 19ff that this universe, as fallen and thus enslaved to necessities which it cannot transcend, longs — and until the *Parousia*, will long — for the liberation of the sons of men. In this fallen world, only the *pneumatic* component of man — *pneuma* — can enter into life. If, under grace, the individual has entered freely into the sacramental historicity that is salvific — the only history there is —, if he has been nourished sacramentally, whether remotely, by the *sacramentum tantum* of salvation history (the Old Covenant), or proximately, by the *res et sacramentum*, the plenitude of the New Covenant that is Eucharistic Communion, being fed by the Bread of Life which Ignatius Martyr famously named "the medicine of immortality, the antidote that we should not die, but live forever in Jesus Christ," and thus dies with his sins forgiven, he will enter into that fullness of life which Christ died that we might have, and more abundantly. This immortality was purchased at a great price: it is not "natural," but the greatest of gifts: *gratia Christi*. It cannot be earned, but under the primordial grace of our creation in Christ, it can freely be chosen and accepted, as a longed-for gift is accepted, to become one's own, forever.

Those who have lived otherwise, who have chosen the way of the flesh as their own and who die in that determination, do so in ratifying the contradiction which they have lived. By Christ's entry into death, all death is changed: all flesh dies in Christ, and in death is given that vision of the risen Christ, which Augustine teaches us is for everyone either damnific or salvific: "as we see him, so we have him."

That this judgment occurs immediately upon death, upon separation from fallen historicity, which is to say, from *sarx*, has been settled doctrine since the 14th century. The supposedly immaterial "separated soul," as Thomas knew, could not be a person as a matter of definition. Therefore, inasmuch as a personal judgment awaits each of us immediately (*mox*) after death, it must be inferred that our death cannot be understood, without annulling the immediacy of that judgment, as that separation of the soul from the body which would transform us into "separated souls" in that impersonal Thomist sense commonly taken for granted.

The doctrine of the resurrection of the flesh achieves its full significance in its intimate linkage to the Resurrection of Christ — and to the Assumption of the second Eve. Our personal resurrection — which is to say, our entry into immortality — is entirely dependent upon the prior resurrection of the Christ who, primordially, from "the beginning," is One Flesh with the second Eve, whether as the Church or as Mary, as type or as antetype. Where the Groom is, there also is the Bride.

Until the *Parousia*, the Bridal Church is the Church militant and the Church suffering as well as the Church triumphant: in it, we make up the sufferings which are lacking to those of Christ for the redemption of the world. Until the full eschatological restoration of the Church as the Kingdom of God, our dead bodies are locked into the fragmentation and determinism of all things earthly: only in the fullness of the *Parousia* is the full unity of the Kingdom manifest, in the resurrection of the flesh, when all things are made new and all that is of the old man, all that is sarkic, is restored to *pneumatic* life.

Until then, the Assumption of the *Theotokos*, the antetypal second Eve, is the pledge of the eschatologically-realized Assumption of the Bridal Church, no longer the sacramental consort of the Body of the Eucharistic Christ, but the glorious Kingdom of the Risen Christ, the Bride who exists no longer in the obscurity of salvation history, but in the manifest splendor of the New Creation.

The resurrection of the flesh, which is to the condition of *pneuma* simply, free of all association with the fallenness of *sarx*, concludes and closes the sacramental order: no longer is there given the distinctions of *sacramentum tantum*, *res et sacramentum*, *res tantum* which have ordered the brokenness of time into the obscurity and enigma, the veiled freedom and unity, of salvation history. In that final outpouring of the Spirit, our buried flesh, as risen, will have become "like Him, for we shall see Him as He is." No longer dichotomized by the Fall, we shall live in the free unity of the Kingdom of God which the

Eucharist signed, in our nuptially-ordered substantial reality, wherein our free unity is finally manifest and, with ours, that of the whole creation. Faith will have ceded to vision, sign to glory, image to reality, hope to fruition.

Endnotes

1. This primordiality is affirmed in II Tim 1:9, among many other places in the New Testament. The primordial imaging of God is nuptially ordered, a free communal imaging of the free Community that is the Trinity which, in history, is revealed in the Father's sending of the Son to give the Spirit. Pope John Paul has explored the nuptial imaging of God in his "theology of the body"; see esp. his LETTER TO FAMILIES, §6, quoted *infra* in note 8.

2. John Paul II, in VERITATIS SPLENDOR, has underlined the anthropological significance of "the Beginning," who is finally the Christ, Alpha and Omega, the Lord of history, in whom we live and move and have our being. E.g.:

> To call into question the permanent structural elements of man which are connected with his own bodily dimension would not only conflict with common experience, but would render meaningless *Jesus' reference to the "beginning,"* precisely where the social and cultural context of the time had distorted the primordial meaning and the role of certain moral norms (cf. *Mt* 19:1-9). This is the reason why "the Church affirms that underlying so many changes there are some things which do not change and are *ultimately founded upon Christ,* who is the same yesterday and today and for ever."[97] Christ is the "Beginning" who, having taken on human nature, definitively illumines it in its constitutive elements and in its dynamism of charity towards God and neighbour.[98]

> 97.   Cf Second Vatican Ecumenical Council, Pastoral Constitution on the Church in the Modern World *Gaudium et Spes,* 10.
> 98.   Cf Saint Thomas Aquinas, *Summa Theologiae I-II,* q. 108, a. 1. St. Thomas bases the fact that moral norms, even in the context of the New Law, are not merely formal in character but have a determined content, upon the assumption of human nature by the Word.

VERITATIS SPLENDOR, §53., pp. 83-5 of the *Libreria Editrice Vaticana* edition.

3. "Before the world was made" is a reference to the primordial goodness of creation, antecedent to the Fall by which it became "world" and "flesh." These biblical terms are both deprecatory references to fallenness, both invoking the loss of the free, nuptially-ordered unity by which, as Gen 2 informs us, the creation was "very good." Recent exegesis is beginning to move in this direction, acknowledging that "the beginning" in the Johannine Prologue is a reference to the opening phrase of the Book of Genesis, and therefore has a primordial rather than an eternal, nonhistorical connotation: see Pheme Perkins' commentary, "The Gospel According to John," NEW JEROME BIBLICAL COMMENTARY §60:22 which at 951 expressly refers the Johannine "In the beginning" to Genesis, *contra* Bultmann. Reginald Fuller, reviewing Raymond Brown's THE BIRTH OF THE MESSIAH, has understood Brown to hold a similar position, vis-a-vis the communication of idioms: see CATHOLIC BIBLICAL QUARTERLY 40 (1978) 118. F.-X. Durwell has made the same point; see "Eucharist and *Parousia,*" LUMEN FIDEI 26 (June, 1971) 295, n. 45.

4. "*Trahi a Deo*" is an Augustinian coinage, first deployed in Augustine's commentary on the Eucharistic passages in Jn 6; see IN TRACT. JO. 26, 4 (CCHR.SL 36:261-262); a translation of this passage is provided by James O'Connor in THE HIDDEN MANNA: A Theology of the Eucharist (San Francisco: Ignatius Press, 1988), at 2. In the following

sections of IN TRACT. JO. 26, Augustine links the "*trahi*" to the divine "*intus Magister*" ,whose presence, "*intimior intimo meo*," is in turn difficult to distinguish from illumination and inspiration; see CCHR.SL 36: 262-263.

5. CONFESSIONS, 3, 6, 11.

6. Roger Aubert, LE PROBLÈME DE L'ACTE DE FOI: Données traditionnelles et controverses récentes, 3e Edition (Louvain: E. Warny, 1958) 43-71, esp. 65ff. Aubert's discussion refers to ST ii^a ii^{ae}, q. 2, a. 9, ad 3; q. 5, a. l; q. 8, a.4, ad 3; q. 10, a. 1, ad 1; COMM. IN IOANN. v, 6, 8-9; xv, 5, 4 and QUODL. ii, a. 6, ad 1 & ad 3. The *trahi* is also the subject of Max Seckler's doctoral dissertation, INSTINKT UND GLAUBENS-WILLE NACH THOMAS VON AQUIN, which concludes by avoiding the question of whether the *trahi a Deo* is grace or nature. Edward Schillebeeckx favorably reviewed this work in an early article, and approved Seckler's refusal of this crucial issue: see REVELATION AND THEOLOGY, II (New York: Sheed and Ward, 1968), at 32-54. To admit the obviously gratuitous character of the *trahi a deo* is to overthrow St. Thomas' early insistence on the accidental nature of grace, which was the implication of his commitment to the ungraced condition of creation as such. Implicit in St. Thomas' view of the historical creation as ungraced ("natural") is a rejection of the historicity of grace as such, which St. Thomas neither developed or accepted.

7. It cannot be objected that St. Thomas esse-essence analysis of creation provides for freedom on the level of substance, for the relation of *essentia* to *esse* which he understood to obtain in composite created substances is not historical and covenantly free but abstract, and therefore contingent: freedom is a historical category. The contingent is the merely unnecessary, as opposed to the necessity of the relations between the correlative intrinsic causes of substance, matter-form and substance-accident. Abstract non-necessity bespeaks randomness, not freedom. Gilson's early recognition of the abstract quality of the creation-Creator relation led him at that time to reduce it to a merely logical standing insofar as the physical sciences are concerned: he considered that they ask no questions bearing on existence, being concerned only with the intrinsically necessary intelligibility of essence: see his BEING AND SOME PHILOSO-PHERS, second edition, corrected and enlarged (Toronto: Pontifical Institute of Medieval Studies, 1952) 161ff. eight years later, in LE PHILOSOPHE ET LA THÉOLOGIE (Paris: Fayard, 1960), at 60, he wrote, "La nature thomiste n'est pas la nature aristotélienne" but he failed to provide an act-potency account of their difference, which could only remain nominal. However, he recognized then and thereafter the theological foundation of philosophical speculation: e.g., at 88.

8. CONFESSIONS, xiii, 9, 10 (CCHR.SL 27:246-247; cf. ENCHIRIDION THEOLOG-ICUM SANCTI AUGUSTINI, ed. Francisus Moriones (Madrid: BAC, 1961) at 521, §1789: ET of text and context by Vernon Bourke:

> Love lifts us up to it and Thy Good Spirit lifts up our lowliness 'from the gates of death.' Peace for us lies in good will. The body inclines by its weight toward its own place. A weight is not necessarily an inclination toward the lowest level, but to its proper place. Fire inclines upward; a stone, downward. They are moved by their weights; they seek their places. Oil poured out below water rises above the water; water poured on oil sinks beneath the oil. They are moved by their weights; they seek their own places. My weight is my love; by it I am carried wherever I am carried. By thy Gift we are inflamed and are carried upward; we are set on fire and we go. We ascend the 'steps of the heart' and sing a canticle of the steps. By Thy Fire, by Thy Good fire, we are sent on fire and we go; for we go upward to the 'peace of Jerusalem' for 'I rejoiced at those who said to me: we shall go into the house of the Lord.' There shall good will give us our place, so that we desire nothing more than 'to abide their (sic) forever.

St. Augustine, CONFESSIONS, tr. by Vernon J. Bourke. Ser. Fathers of the Church, 21 (New York: Fathers of the Church, Inc., 1953), at 416.

9. For extensive discussions of the interrelation of Augustine's "two loves" and the "two cities" which they build, see Gerhard Ladner's classic study of the Augustinian theology of history, THE IDEA OF REFORM: Its Impact on Christian Thought and Practice in the Age of the Fathers (New York: Harper and Row, 1967[1959]), 238-283, and A. Lauras & H. Rondet, "Le thème de deux cités dans l'oeuvre de saint Augustin," H. Rondet et al., ETUDES AUGUSTINENNES; ser. Theologie 28 (Paris: Aubier; Editions Montaigne, 1953), 99-160.

10.   Toward the end of §19 of his "Letter to Families" (1994), John Paul II writes of the atomization and depersonalization of humanity which results from the dissolution of the free unity of the marital family under the impact of the contemporary rationalism:

> Within a similar anthropological perspective, the human family is facing the challenge of a "new Manichaeanism," in which body and spirit are put in radical opposition: the body does not receive life from the spirit, and the spirit does not give life to the body. Man thus ceases to live as a person and a subject; regardless of all intentions and declarations to the contrary, he becomes merely an object.

Earlier in the same section the Pope had written:

> St. Paul's magnificent synthesis concerning the "great mystery" appears as the compendium or summa, in some sense, of the teaching about God and man which was brought to fulfillment by Christ. Unfortunately, Western thought, with the development of modern rationalism, has been gradually moving away from this teaching. The philosopher who formulated the principle of "Cogito, ergo sum," "I think, therefore I am," also gave the modern concept of man its distinctive dualistic character. It is typical of rationalism to make a radical contrast between spirit and body, between body and spirit. But man is a person in the unity of his body and his spirit.[46] The body can never be reduced to mere matter; it is a spiritualized body, just as man's spirit is so closely united to the body that he can be described as an embodied spirit. The richest source for knowledge of the body is the Word made flesh. Christ reveals man to himself.[47] In a certain sense, this statement of the Second Vatican Council is the reply, so long awaited, which the Church has given to modern rationalism.
>
> [46]"Corpore et anima unus," as the Council so clearly and felicitously stated: Gaudium et Spes, §14.
> [47] Gaudium et Spes., 22.
>   "Letter to Families," §19. In the same section the Pope's describes as a "New Manichae-ism" the modern dualistic expression of this rationalism.

In VERITATIS SPLENDOR §48, dealing with the same modern denial of the significance of the body, the Pope had also quoted the "felicitous" "Corpore at anima unus," from the Second Vatican Ecumenical Council's Pastoral Constitution on The Church in The Modern World, GAUDIUM ET SPES, §14. He later addressed the same theme in THE LETTER TO FAMILIES:

> The divine "We" is the eternal pattern of the human "we," especially of that "we" formed by the man and the woman created in the divine image and likeness. (§6)

11.   In private correspondence, Prof. Joyce A. Little of the University of St. Thomas in Houston, has developed on this basis a theology of Original Sin which sees Original Sin as a primordial refusal of nuptial fidelity, and so of the freedom of nuptial unity. This primordial infidelity is actual in Eve's turning away from Adam, her head, to the serpent, with the acquiescence of Adam. Gen 3 details the disintegration of their free unity in terms of their consequent alienation, from each other, from Jahweh, and finally from a creation which by their defection from free nuptial unity is itself no longer good,

no longer informed by the free unity of their "One Flesh" by which alone creation is good and very good precisely by the free unity realized in the imaging the Triune Creator by the Head.

12. The reader is referred to my COVENANTAL THEOLOGY: The Eucharistic Order of History. Revised edition, with an Appendix; two volumes in one (Novato, CA: Presidio, 1996) for an extensive treatment and development of the theology of history as Eucharistically ordered and thereby salvific. The second and third chapters deal with the theology of Original Sin and the Fall. It must suffice here to observe that a theology of the Fall can be of Catholic interest only when its foundation is the New Covenant instituted by the One Sacrifice of the Christ for his bridal Church. The Christ's transcendence of history is Eucharistic, for it is only as Eucharistically represented that He is the Redeemer, the Lord of history, the Alpha and the Omega. Apart from his Eucharistic transcendence of the determinism of fallen time and space, He does not exercise the transcendent Lordship, as Head, by whose recapitulation of all things we are redeemed, but instead, *per impossibile*, would be thus submitted to historical fallenness as to be an event moving inexorably and finally irretrievably into the past.

13. In 1931 Kurt Gödel's incompleteness theorems established the incapacity of the mind to frame clear and logically coherent comprehensions on any serious level; see Ernest Nagel and James R. Newman, GÖDEL'S PROOF (New York: New York University Press, 1958). In pointing to the logical "incompleteness" of our knowledge, Gödel said no more than Aristotle had said in describing all historical knowledge as the ongoing actualization of an always potential intellect which as such is incapable of transcending its own potentiality.

12. DS §§'1512-'1513. The Council of Trent, in decreeing that our solidarity in the Original Sin of Adam is by propagation and not imitation" *(propagatione non imitatione)* was commonly understood to have taught our hereditary unity in sin as understood by the patristic tradition. However, in the years just before Vatican II, theologians under the influence of Teilhard's evolutionary anthropology began to view this unity on the level of genetics and within the framework of evolution in such wise that the patristic understanding of the primordial character of Original Sin and the Fall gave way to a rather unreflective supposition that it was an intrahistorical event, in some way to be correlated with if not assimilated to the evolutionary dogmatics of contemporary paleontology. This posed the question which Pius XII, in HUMANI GENERIS (DS #3875-#3899), attempted to resolve, the genetic unity of humanity, which the Pope understood to be implied by our unity in the sin of Adam. For an overview of the subsequent controversy, see the quite disparate positions taken upon it by Karl Rahner in successive articles written over more than a dozen years: "Theological Reflections on Monogenism," THEOLOGICAL INVESTIGATIONS I, 229-296, "The Sin of Adam," *ibid*, 247-262, and "Monogenism," SACRAMENTUM MUNDI: An Encyclopedia of Theology I-VI: IV, 105-107, all of which assume the theological necessity of bringing the doctrine of sin and Fall into agreement with the generally accepted postulate of the evolution of man, over a period of some millions of years, from lower orders of life. However, the event of Original Sin and Fall, as historical and objective, is not thereby to be understood to be within the fallen order of time: rather, Original Sin is the primordial principle, the a priori cause, of the fallenness of the historical order, as of the fall of the entirety of the Good Creation. Therefore it cannot be rendered theologically intelligible by its submission to the immanent necessities governing the fallen universe of space and time, whether or not these be adequately articulated in a

146

theory of evolution. Further, evolutionary theory cannot provide for the unity of man, in the first place because no such comprehensive theory can escape its own intrinsic "incompleteness," to use Gödel's term and, secondly, because even were such a unified, rationally coherent theory possible, it would proceed according to the canons of logical coherence, which presuppose necessary causes, whereas the unity of man is free — else he could not put it in issue.

Whatever be the unity of the "progeny" of the first Adam and the first Eve, meaning those in solidarity with their sin, and so with its consequence of fallenness, of "sarkic" existence, of "being unto death," this cannot be found in the sin and the Fall; these provide only a necessary disunity. The only possible source of the solidarity of man in the first Adam is his solidarity in the Second Adam, which at bottom is his creation in Christ. As has already been stressed (pp. 3ff., *supra*) our sole positive solidarity is our recapitulation in Christ, apart from which we can understand nothing of a solidarity with the fallen first Adam.

15.   Mary, the Second Eve, is the mother of a "progeny," the members of the Church whose head is the Second Adam, while the first Eve is the mother of the "progeny" of which the first Adam was to have been the head. Thus the negative analogy between the first and the Second Eve holds, as it does between the first and Second Adam.

(Mary) is "clearly the mother of the members of Christ...since she has by her charity joined in bringing about the birth of believers in the Church, who are members of its head."[3] Wherefore she is hailed as a pre-eminent and wholly unique member of the Church, and as its type and outstanding model in faith and charity. The Catholic Church, taught by the Holy Spirit, honors her with filial affection and devotion as a most beloved mother.

    [3] Cfr. S. Irenaeus, *adv. Haer*, 111 24, 1: PG 7, 966 B; Harvey 2, 131, ed. Sagnard, Sources Chr., p 398. LUMEN GENTIUM, §53, Vatican Council II; The Conciliar and Post Conciliar Documents Study Edition. General Editor, Austin Flannery, O.P. (Newport, N.Y., Costello Publishing Co., 1987[1975]) at 414; cf. 416, n 6.

16.   See Andrd Feuillet, "Les épousailles du Messie: La Mère de Jésu et l'Église dans le Quatrième Évangile," REVUE THOMISTE 86 (1986) 357-391 and *ibid.* 87 (1987) 537-575, esp. 548ff., on the exegesis of the "Protoevangelium" in Gen. 3:15.

17.   An approximate translation of Augustine's "Facit haec quidem Spiritus Sanctus, sed absit ut sine Filio facit." (CONTRA SERM. ARR. 32 (PL 42:704-705), at 705.

18.   That a "head" is such by reason of a glory which proceeds from the head is a basic Pauline tradition: see I Cor 11:2ff.; in the fallen world, the glory of the head is obscured, but not undone.

19.   This was the crucial point of agreement between Cyril of Alexandria and John of Antioch; by 433 it permitted them to transcend their school differences in the Formula of Union. Cyril had no investment in a non-historical reading of the Alexandrine *Logos-Sarx* Christology, as John had none in a comparably non-historical reading of the Antiochene *Logos-Anthropos*.

20.   We prescind here from the end-time situation described by Paul in I Thess 4:13-17, insofar as it concerns those living at the time of the *Parousia* of the risen Christ.

21.   Cf. note 2, *supra*.

22.   ST iii[a] 63, a. 1-5; q. 69, a. 10. Here St. Thomas teaches that sacramental *character in genere* is an instrumental spiritual power (*potentia*), a permanent participation in the priesthood of Christ, by way of an imaging of the Trinity, conferred or imprinted on the intellectual soul by valid baptism, to perfect it in things pertaining to divine worship. In this, St. Thomas witnesses to the patristic-monastic tradition: his statement is not so much theological as doctrinal. It is his understanding of this *potentia* as a metaphysical

accidens (ST. iii³ 63, a. 4, ad 1) that is problematic. His theological interpretation of the doctrinal tradition is yet clearer in ST iii³, q. 69, a. 10, c. where, after asserting that "baptismus est quaedam spiritualis regeneratio," he goes on to develop his metaphysical--theological analysis of this traditional understanding of *character* as an accident. However, *accidens* is hardly up to the dogmatic weight of *spiritualis regeneratio*.

23 St. Thomas holds that the baptismal *character* is a *potentia*, or power, rather than a *passio* or passivity, and that the power is an accident in the order of quality; see ST, Q.63 , a.2, c.

24.   It must be remembered that St. Thomas considered creation to be "natural" in the sense of ungraced: it is difficult to avoid the conclusion that he had in view the Aristotelian universe as the object of that creative deed, which for him was not Christocentric, not a consequence of the Father sending the Son to give the Spirit.

25.   II Cor 5:16-17.

26.   Karl Rahner has frequently been criticized for this mistake: see Walter Kasper, JESUS THE CHRIST, tr. V. Green (London: Burns and Oates; New York, Ramsey, NJ, Toronto: The Paulist Press, 1976), Ch: 2, for a pertinent critique of Rahner's Christology. Rahner builds on the "supernatural existential" and "anonymous Christian" themes of his theological anthropology to discover in man, merely as man, an openness to God whose complete and final expression is the Incarnation. The notion that the Incarnation is a possibility inherent in the human condition as human is reminiscent of the *"mediante anima"* Christology stemming from Origen, as well as of Teilhard's notion of Christogenesis as the culmination of a Spirit-driven evolution. This now common error is criticized with vigor by H. U. von Balthasar in his CORDULA ODER DER ERNSTFALL, mit einem Nachwort zur zweiten Aufl. (Einsiedeln: Johannes Verlag, 1967), ET: THE MOMENT OF CHRISTIAN WITNESS; tr. Richard Beckley (Glen Rock, NJ: The Newman Press, 1969) The same criticism of Rahner's Christology has been taken up by F. Ocariz et al., THE MYSTERY OF JESUS CHRIST (Dublin: Four Courts Press, 1994) 127-129, and by Jean Galot, S. J., WHO IS CHRIST: THEOLOGY OF THE INCARNATION (Chicago, Franciscan Herald Press 1981), 31-34, 279-80. The latter two citations I owe to Eamonn Keane of Sydney, Australia.

27.   The pertinent text is vv. 1-5:

> For we know that if the earthly tent we live in is destroyed, we have a building from God, a house not made with hands, eternal in the heavens. Here indeed we groan, and long to put on our heavenly dwelling, so that by putting it on we may not be found naked. For while we are still in this tent, we sigh with anxiety, not that we would be unclothed, but that we would be further clothed, so that what is mortal may be swallowed up by life. He who has prepared us for this very thing is God, who has given us his Spirit as a guarantee. (RSV)

28.   St. Thomas cites the GLOSSA ORDINARIA, a theological summary from the early 12th century, probably the work of Anselm of Laon, in support of his theology of the image of God:

> GLOSSA ORDINARIA distinguit triplicem imaginem: scilicet creationis et recreationis et similitudinis. Prima ergo imago invenitur in omnibus hominibus; secunda in justis tantum; tertia vero solum in beatis.
>
> ST i³, q. 93, a. 4

It must be kept in view that the tradition upon which St. Thomas relies understands the baptismal *character* as a permanent participation in the priesthood of Christ, by way of an imaging of the Trinity, conferred or imprinted on the intellectual soul by valid baptism. The *character* is then indissociable from the personal imaging of God. Given at creation, this imaging of God, whose operation is assimilable to worship, is lost or disabled by Original Sin, for it is only by the spiritual regeneration which St. Thomas, following the tradition, identifies with the baptismal *character*, that man, created in the divine image, may enter into the Church's Eucharistic worship.

The *transitus*, recited *supra* in the GLOSSA ORDINARIA, from *creatio to recreatio* to *similitudo*, is the *graced* passage from our initial condition of fallen *aversio a Deo* to that of *conversio ad Deum*, and then from historical *conversio* to eschatological *beatitudo*. Specifically to our point, the monastic tradition summarized in the GLOSSA looks upon the moment of conversion as a *recreatio*, not as a change merely preceding out of possibilities already latent: Paul taught this "New Creation" to be the consequence of baptism into the death and the resurrection of Christ. There is then every reason to identify the image which is *recreatio* with the gift of baptismal *character*: the GLOSSA's affirmation of a "triplicem imaginem" bears the hallmark of the sacramental paradigm — *sacramentum tantum, res et sacramentum, res tantum* — of the patristic tradition, which reached this classic statement in that same School of Laon, at the same time: the early 12th century. For the sources and dating of the GLOSSA, see Beryl Smalley, THE STUDY OF THE BIBLE IN THE MIDDLE AGES (Notre Dame: University of Notre Dame Press, 1951), 56-66; for the final development of the Augustinian-patristic paradigm of sacramental causality *(sacramentum tantum, res et sacramentum, res tantum)* at the School of Laon in the early 12th century, see Pedro Lopez Gonzalez, "Origen de la expresion 'res et sacramentum'" SCRIPTA THEOLOGIA 17 (1985): 73-119, also F. Soria, "La teoria del signo en S. Augustin" CIENCIA TOMISTA 92, 1965, 357-396, and H. M. Féret, "Sacramentum-Res dans la langue théologique de saint Augustin," REVUE DES SCIENCE PHIL. ET THÉOL. 29 (1940) 223ff.

29.   See the articles on "Soul," esp. (in the Bible) and (Human), and on "Spirit (in the Bible)" in the NEW CATHOLIC ENCYCLOPEDIA, vol. 13, s.vv., for an overview of the biblical and patristic data, and theological disputes surrounding the soul and its unity in the 13th and 14th centuries, esp. after the death of St. Thomas, when the controversy stemming from his adoption of Aristotelian psychology for theological purposes had become overt. The speculation of the High Middle Ages is covered in more detail by Anton Pegis' revision of his doctoral dissertation, ST. THOMAS AND THE PROBLEM OF THE SOUL IN THE THIRTEENTH CENTURY (Toronto: St. Michael's College Press, 1934). See also Claude Tresmontant, LE PROBLEME DE L'ÂME (Paris: Editions de Seuil, 1971), and especially his small masterpiece, A STUDY OF HEBREW THOUGHT (New York, Paris: Desclée, 1960), of which Part Two is particularly relevant to the problem here under examination.

30.   The 14th century definition of the soul as the form of the body (DS §*902; cf. §§*900, *1440, *2828) must be read as a dogmatic statement, not a theological one. Its interpretation therefore is as independent of Thomist presuppositions and methodology as it is of those of any other theological tradition. Rather, all theological affirmations rely upon the prior truth of the doctrinal tradition with which this definition is integral.

31.   The tension is as real within the Aristotelianism and the classical Thomist anthropology as within the Platonic. Neither the Aristotelians nor the Thomists have been able to account for or to dispense with the reality of the human species, the intellectual community within which immanent activity of human persons, i.e., intelligent intraspecific communication, must take place. In short, in those anthropologies, there can be no historical human communion because there is no objectively actual or historical, specific form — i.e., *intellectus* understood as a *concretely historical* universal — in which the members of the Aristotelian or Thomist species might commonly

participate. On the other hand, an ideal or specific form — i.e., a nonhistorical abstraction (second substance), by reason of its merely abstract standing, cannot ground such an immanently interactive human community. Consequently, there is an ancient and rationally insoluble debate over the location of the Aristotelian agent intellect, which would be that specific form, to which all members of the species would be in potency by reason of their participation in it. It is not possible to account for the potentiality of the human intellect apart from its participation in such a concrete specific form. This problem has no rational solution. We may then suppose it to have been falsely posed by the Thomist postulate of a *natural* creation, one intelligible in terms of intrinsic necessity.

32.   See Claude Tresmontant, A STUDY OF HEBREW THOUGHT, Ch. 2, cited *supra* in n. 26, for a most insightful exposition of the Pauline anthropology of *pneuma-sarx*, itself the Christian development of the OT anthropology of *nepes-basar*.

33.   DS §§*900, *902, *1440. *2828.

34.   An illustration of the difficulties it poses is found in Pope John XXII's EP. "Nequaquam sine dolore" AD ARMENIOS, 21 November, 1321, excerpted in Denziger-Schönmetzer as follows:

> De sorte defunctorum
>
> . . . illorum veto animas, qui post sacramentum baptismatis susceptum nulllam omnino peccati maculam incurrerunt, illas etiam, quae post contracti peccati maculam vel in suis manentes corporibus vel eisdem exutae et purgatae, in *caleum mox recepi* — Illorum autem animas, qui in mortali peccato vel cum solo original decedunt, mox in infernum descendere, poenis tamen ac locis disparibus puniendas.
>
> DS §*925-6; cf. §*857-8, from the "Professio Fidei" made by Emperor Michael VIII Palaeologus to Pope Gregory X; it is included in the documents of the Second Council of Lyons as an element of the proposed reconciliation with the Greek Church which was among the major and unrealized goals of that council. See Jedin, HANDBOOK OF CHURCH HISTORY IV, 203-07. Emphasis added.

The "mox," or immediacy after death, of the personal judgment, by which one enters into salvation or damnation, is in serious conflict with the Thomist doctrine concerning the impersonality of the "separated soul," which, understood by St. Thomas as an immaterial "part" of the soul-body composite constituting the human person, lacks the incommunicability proper to the totality that is indispensable to a person as such, and therefore can scarcely be considered to be the subject of a personal judgment.

35.   Ignatius Martyr, EPHES. 5.20.2; tr. Kirsopp Lake, APOSTOLIC FATHERS I; ser. Loeb Classical Library (Cambridge: Harvard University Press; London: William Heinemann Ltd., 1975), at 195.

36.   The pivotal Augustinian text reads as follows:

> *Spiritus est qui vivificat; caro autem nihil prodest: verba quae locutus sum vobis, spiritus est et vita* (Io 6:63) Spiritualiter intellige quae locutus sum. Non hoc corpus quod videtis manducaturi estis et bibituri ilium sanguinem, quem fusuri sunt qui me crucifigent. Sacramentum aliquod vobis commendavi. Spiritualiter intellectum vivificabit nos.
>
> Augustine, ENARR. IN Ps. 98, 9 (CCHR.SL 39:1385-6) at 1386; see Franciscus Moriones, O.R.S.A., S.T.L., ENCHIRIDION THEOLOGICUM SANCTI AUGUSTINI (Matriti, B.A.C., 1961), p. 601, §2075.

In translation:

> "It is the Spirit who gives life; the flesh is of no avail; the words that I have spoken to you are spirit and life." (Jn 6:63) Understand spiritually what I have said. It is not this body that you see which you will have eaten, nor will you have drunk the blood which those who crucified me will have shed. I have entrusted a certain mystery to you: Spiritually understood, it will

give you life.

This language has become a *crux interpretum*, especially since the Reformation, but St. Thomas met its difficulties first by denying its presumed presupposition of a *substantial* **local** presence of Christ in the Eucharist, and explaining first that the substantial Real Presence is **local** only *per accidens*, by way of the sacramental species or *sacramentum tantum*, and then by showing that Augustine was not so crass as to think a Platonic dualism adequate to the theology of the Eucharist (see ST III^a, q. 75, a. 1, ad 1).

37.   This preoccupation was normalized by Cajetan, whose late medieval interpretation of St. Thomas developed a rationalism only latent in St. Thomas' thought. Nonetheless this latency, officially promulgated in such documents as the "Twenty-four Theses," (AAS 6 [1914] at 383-386) became the Thomism of the schools, from which de Lubac departed, and after him a host of former Thomists: among them we may instance Lonergan's phenomenological reading of Thomist metaphysics in METHOD IN THEOLOGY, Teilhard's rejection of the Suarezian Thomism taught him at the Jesuit scholasticate in Jersey in favor of a Neoplatonizing evolutionary approach to Christology, Karl Rahner's adaptation of the Heideggerian "turn to the subject," and Hans Urs von Balthasar's rejection of systematic theology as such.

38.   The baroque Thomist notion that such a divine "concursus" is necessary for the passage of a creature from potency to act presumes that the divine creative act terminates in an immobile universe. This supposition is implicit in Cajetan's rationalization of St. Thomas' metaphysics.

39.   This interpretation of the history of the Old Covenant, otherwise warranted by the sacramental historicity of the Church, is developed by H. U. von Balthasar in THE GLORY OF THE LORD. A THEOLOGICAL AESTHETICS I: SEEING THE FORM; tr. Erasmo Leiva-Merikakis; eds. Joseph Fessio, S.J. and John Riches (San Francisco: Ignatius Press; New York: Crossroad Publications, 1982), 634ff.; he describes Judaism as the passage from paganism to Christianity at 647.

40.   See note 12, *supra*.

41.   See the extended discussions by J. L. McKenzie in DICTIONARY OF THE BIBLE (Milwaukee: Bruce, 1965), sv. 'Flesh' and 'Soul' and 'Spirit;' cf. DICTIONARY OF THE BIBLE, ed. James Hastings, revised ed. by Frederick C. Grant and H.H. Rowley (New York: Scribners, 1963) s.v. "flesh," "soul", and esp. the extended discussion of "holy spirit;" see also J. Fitzmyer, PAULINE THEOLOGY: A Brief Sketch (Englewood Cliffs, NJ.: Prentice-Hall, 1967). The Pauline understanding of *sarx-pneuma*, as set out by Tresmontant (*supra*, note 29) and Fitzmyer, is clearly a free development of the Old Testament usage of *nepes-basar* , freely continuous with it, not its necessary implication.

42.   This is the "self-salvation" which Tillich scorned. Its classic expression is predestination, whether, as with Origen, to salvation or, with Augustine, to an eternal destiny known but to God. In another guise, it entered late medieval speculation as "pure nature" in the rationalized Thomism of Cajetan. Under the influence of Descartes and later, Rousseau, its realization became the project of the Enlightenment.

43.   It must suffice to observe here that it is only as Eucharistic, as present in history *per modum substantiae* — i.e., integrally: no longer *sarx*, but "a life-giving spirit," present as *pneuma* simply by reason of his victory over death — that Christ is the Lord of history, thereby is the source, in his One-Flesh union with the second Eve, of its restored sacramental unity and salvific significance. This *pneumatic* immanence of the risen Lord is sacramental. Integrity can exist within history on no other basis, for on

the empirical level, our physical existence in history remains sarkic: at that level, one encounters in the "flesh" only fragmentation, hence the perennial and insoluble problem of the quest for the immanent unity in history. There is no empirical unity discoverable in history, nor can there be: the unity sought is forever ideal, for the most exhaustive empirical scrutiny discovers only multiplicity. A theological exposition of history as Eucharistically integrated and thereby freely intelligible as sacramentally significant is presented in my COVENANTAL THEOLOGY: see note 12, *supra*.

44.   The term appears to have been anticipated by Alger of Liege who, in the early 12th century, described the Real Presence as "substantial" in order to account for the immunity of the Eucharistic Lord to accidents of space and time. The same term had been used a few years earlier by Guitmund of Averso to describe the conversion of the Eucharistic elements. In this he had followed Faustus of Riez who, at the end of the fifth century, had spoken of a Eucharistic "conversion of substance." Alger's Eucharistic theology is summarized in his DE SACRAMENTO CORPORIS ET SANGUINIS DOMINICI (PL 180:739-860): cf. J. de Ghellinck, "Eucharistie au xiiᵉ siècle en occident," DICTIONNAIRE DE THÉOLOGIE CATHOLIQUE II, 1234-1302, at 1236. St. Thomas' explanation of his variant of Alger's phrase, i.e., a presence "per modum substantiae," (ST iiiᵃ, q. 76, a. 1, ad 3) fails to explore the Eucharistic transcendence of history which it imports: he uses the Eucharistic presence *per modum substantiae* only to account for the immunity of the physical presence of Christ in the Eucharist to the accidents of space and time. The later nominalist explanation of this immunity, as due to Christ's Eucharistic presence *diffinitive*, will "spiritualize" the Real Presence, by denying it the accident of quantity, thus rendering the Eucharistic presence effectively immaterial and thereby in effect denying its historical objectivity.

45.   Paul Tillich, SYSTEMATIC THEOLOGY, II: EXISTENCE AND THE CHRIST (Chicago: University of Chicago Press, 1955). Tillich's explanation of the non-estrangement of the Christ as Essential God-Manhood, vis-a-vis the estrangement of existential human persons, having assigned the achievement of personal uniqueness to separation from the divine Center and consequent estrangement, must identify salvation from that estrangement with depersonalization: viz.: with absorption into the mono-Personal unity of Essential God-Manhood: this finally reduces to the pagan soteriology which eliminates the unhappy self by its absorption into the One. Within Tillich's systematic theology, as with the Orphic eternal return, an integral or non-estranged human person would be divine by definition.

46.   Cardinal Ratzinger concluded a theological conference on "Christocentrism in Contemporary Theological Reflection. Problems and Prospects" held in Rome from April 12-13, with an address which the "Daily Dispatch" for April 17, 2000, of the international news agency, *Zenit,* reported as follows:

> Love and obedience to God's revelation is what makes of Christianity not just one more theory of a Gnostic character, but a salvation event. This was, in essence, Cardinal Joseph Ratzinger's contribution to the International Congress on "Christocentrism in Contemporary Theology," which was held at the Pontifical Athenaeum "Regina Apostolorum" in Rome.
>
> In commenting on Jesus' words, "Truly, truly, I say to you, if anyone keeps my word, he will never see death" (John 8, 51), the Cardinal explained that "merely academic or intellectual knowledge is not real knowledge of the Word. The Word must be lived and obeyed and not just known."
>
> The Cardinal explained that the word "keep" can be translated from the Greek as "accepted." Whoever "accepts" the Word obeys, like Christ.
>
> "Obedience characterizes Christianity. Obedience is what distinguishes Christianity, for

example, from Gnosticism, a religious and philosophical doctrine stating that it is possible to obtain salvation through the sole avenue of knowledge. Today we have many Christianities that become a kind of Gnosticism, because they are satisfied with academic knowledge, and want nothing to do with obedience," the Cardinal pointed out.

The Cardinal also commented on Christ's words, which the Gospel narrates shortly afterward. "Your father Abraham rejoiced that he was to see my day; he saw it and he was glad." He clarified that with this phrase: Christ used an ancient Jewish interpretation, which was very widespread in its time, according to which Abraham had a vision of the fulfillment of the promises God had made to him. All God's promises to Abraham were centered in his son Isaac. In asking him to sacrifice his son Isaac, God's promises seemed to vanish. The lamb caught in the thicket, which he substituted for his son, once again represents the fulfillment of the promises.

"Jesus is the promise; that the lamb in the thicket redeems, he substitutes the son of Abraham, and becomes the sacrifice in his place. The lamb restores life, the promise, everything," continued the Bavarian Cardinal.

The lamb is of decisive importance in John's Gospel. According to this evangelist's chronology, Jesus died on the cross at the very moment of the immolation of the paschal lambs. He is the lamb of God that restores life, hope and future to us, the Cardinal said.

"Every time we celebrate Mass, Jesus is immolated in the thicket, in the thorns of history. For our sake he touches the thorns and becomes a sacrifice for us. In this way, He restores life to us," Cardinal Ratzinger concluded. (ZE00041414)

47.   It may be argued that the language of DS §§*925-6, esp. "Illorum autem animas, qui in mortali peccato vel cum solo originali decedunt, mox in infernum descendere, poenis tamen ac locis disparibus puniendas," should be read as teaching the inevitable damnation of unbaptized infants. However, it is also possible to read this passage as assuming rather than as teaching their damnation, which is to read it as leaving that question open. This article so reads it, subject to a better judgment.

48.   This expression is borrowed from Karl Barth's CHURCH DOGMATICS, II: THE DOCTRINE OF GOD, I. Authorized Edition (Edinburgh, T.& T. Clark), 1957, at 64.

49.   DS §§*222, *223, *371, *400, et *passim.*

50.   DS §*1440.

51.   Rom 7:22; 8:1-3

52   Karl Rahner, "Questions of Controversial Theology on Justification," THEOLOGI-CAL INVESTIGATIONS IV, 210-218, esp. 212ff.

53.   See note 2, *supra.*

DISCUSSION

SESSION 1

BERTRAM　　　　　　　　　It has been a while since we have had an entire workshop devoted solely to theological essays. That is not the usual pattern of these workshops; it is the exception. Since I am a theologian myself, I am not apologizing for that. Those whose first language is not the language of theology may have had difficulty reading theological essays. Let me say, without sounding mean, that it serves you right. Finally theologians are having a chance to fight back. Usually, we are the "lay people" on the team, reading what neuroscientists or astronomers have been writing. I have to grant, though, even for those who are theologically at home, it wasn't racy reading. Take Fr. Keefe's paper. The English in which he writes isn't what we call basic English, but it's worth every moment of reading. I told him earlier that my most pleasurable time this week was reading his endnotes.

As we said in the invitation, this session will first be devoted to a discussion of papers by the essayists. Each of the essayists will have fifteen to discuss his or her paper or comment on the other papers. Then tomorrow we will open the sessions for general discussion. We will begin with Pastor Michael Hoy and proceed through the list alphabetically.

HOY　　　　　　　　　I am the pastor at Holy Trinity Lutheran Church in St. Louis fourth-fifths time and the Dean of the Lutheran School of Theology in Saint Louis. With my two jobs as pastor and dean, I have an occasional opportunity to write papers. I appreciate the opportunity to be present at this conference. This is my first ITEST Workshop. I am excited about the work that ITEST has been doing and I am glad to be a participant in that work at this time.

My primary field of studies has been in theology and ethics. I did my doctoral studies on Juan Luis Segundo, a Latin-American Jesuit priest in Uruguay who died a few years ago. I specifically focused on his understanding of the relationship of faith and works, juxtaposing that with Lutheran understanding and concepts. I'm interested in ecumenical dialogue and this meeting offers an opportunity for ecumenical dialogue on the topic of the theology of the human body.

Who is the dialogue with? I explored this aspect in my paper. I want to pick up on one of the most significant current issues in scientific study today and to look at that from the Lutheran theological perspective. In my paper I looked at the matter of the breaking of the genetic code and the issues of genetic science as fundamental now. I believe they obviously carry some understanding of how we will interpret, analyze and appropriate the human body in the future. How do we stay true to human nature, including the truth inherent in our genes, in our analysis of the understanding of the human body? The question is theologically foundational from a Jewish-Christian perspective, seeking to keep the body connected with nature and not dancing off in some kind of Docetic enterprise.

I recently had the chance to read Daniel Boyarin's book *Carnal Israel*. Interestingly, one of his criticisms of Christianity, from his Jewish perspective, is that too often we separate the body from a part of understanding the Christian life, particularly the body and the soul. He traces this to Paul. I am sure that Father Keefe will comment on that issue. A particularly hard issue for us is to keep the body grounded in the reality of its own nature.

The question that emerges from the sciences for me stems particularly from the language of "leashing," the principal theme that runs all through my paper. It borrows its initial claim from E.O. Wilson's argument that the leash of the genes is long in the human being. The genes comprise our structure, the human body, and also inform, according to Wilson, the nature of our human culture. His position is obviously highly deterministic. Together with the other Darwinians he is perhaps also highly pessimistic in his depiction of the human being. This is especially true if we look at it in Dawkins' and other Neo-Darwinians' understanding of the genes. I find it interesting that a new book by David Loye, *Darwin's Lost Theory of Love* has recently been published. I haven't had the opportunity to read it yet. In that particular book the author argues for a kinder, gentler Darwin and how genes have some degree of self-seeking morality in addition to the quality of selfishness. I'll be interested in checking out this argument more fully.

The argument against the Darwinians is that of the Gifford lecturer, Holmes Rolston, who has argued against the definition of genes as selfish. He has implored descriptors of genes to put a greater emphasis on their creativity and their "seeking" dimensions. Ultimately for Holmes Rolston the leash that genes hold on the human being is broken at the emergence of human culture, though he would also argue that certain biological determinants still apply. For example, he traces to the *anima* what he calls ubiquitous problems. In those cases determinism still tends to reign. This is an engagement with the philosophical issues of determinism and freedom and how we understand the human body in the context of those philosophical issues.

I would like to be more convinced by Rolston's argument over against the argument of the Darwinians. I must confess that Rolston's assessment of the Darwinian position that the natural world is being negatively judged is probably accurate. From the Darwinian perspective there may be more to the issue of who's doing the judging. The Darwinians want to argue that the genes inform the nature of the human body. This informs the nature of culture and holds this very long leash which controls it all. Rolston wants to say that the genes are there and they inform part of the human being and the understanding of the human body. When we get to human culture, there is a significant break and human beings control the nature of their destiny.

From a theological perspective I at least argue that all along God is the one who holds the leash on the reality of the human being. He is not simply a lure as in Rolston's reasoning. God is one who holds the human being accountable. Accountability plays the critical role in Rolston's analysis. I would cite one of the key quotes from my own paper (page 9, second paragraph):

> The Darwinian biologists can only perceive one process at work: that of natural selection, survival of the fittest. The human body, complete with all its genes and culture, finds itself in a competitive environment. This is where Rolston objects that "the natural world is being negatively judged." But maybe Rolston was on to more than he realized, theologically, when he made that claim (that the natural world is being negatively charged). Rolston wants to advocate that God is doing something truly creative in the natural world, but he wants to see that creativity in a positive light — a "lift-up." But Rolston also realizes that "the life epic is lived on in the midst of perpetual perishing, life arriving and struggling through to something higher. Knowing that God is "superintend[ing] the possibilities" behind the created orders — with all its perishing and struggling — may not necessarily leave room for theological comfort. Maybe it is not only the biologists that are seeing to it that "the natural world is being negatively judged." Maybe the way that God is doing God's good creating, keeping it lifted-up and elevated, is by considering it worthy of God's judgment, holding it accountable, criticizing it (human life) into being.

That's a critical theological point but at least it's one of the major emphases that I think this paper needs to lift up for us to consider the issues of accountability, the human body in its accountability before God.

The thrust of the solution, although it is the least developed part of the paper, is the one that is radically Christological. I need to think through the fuller dynamics of how this plays. I appreciate Bob Brungs' comment that we can be long on the diagnosis or the problem part. But in terms of the solution, how do we come to the recognition of how Jesus Christ makes a difference? That reality becomes a critical issue for us. It is necessary for the body to be liberated; it needs to be cruxiformed and connected into Christ's own passion and resurrection. That raises some inherent sacramental and ecclesiastical points for me. Those, perhaps, are not stressed as much as they need be, along with even wider reaching cosmological points. They are definitely not addressed for the liberation of all of creation through the Body of Christ.

158

I at least want to lift something up from J. A. T. Robinson's book on the body, *A Study of Pauline Theology*. An interesting quote in the conclusion of his work should give us some food for thought:

> The mass of human existence, for all its sin, its destructiveness, its determinisms, is still *soma*; it's made for God. Though it may have become conformed to the *sarx* and its end, that is not its true constitution as it has been created and redeemed in Christ. The Church is alone the witness to the world of its true nature and the pledged instrument of its destiny. Those incorporated by God into the body of His Son are to be a kind of first fruits of his creatures. So Paul sees the redemption of the divine body begun in the eschatological community of the Spirit as the hope ultimately not only of all people but of creation itself. The Body of Christ will stand forth not as it is now, a world within a world, but as the one solidarity, the restoration of the original image of creation where there cannot be Greek or Jew, circumcision and non-circumcision, barbarian, Scythian, bondman, free-man, but Christ is all and in all.

There's food for thought in Robinson's argument. It touches the heart of what I argue for when I pun on the "new leash on life in Jesus the Christ," how Jesus the Christ leashes us into his own new ownership and brings about a new kind of being. That continues to be the dynamic cutting edge of how we can develop the Christological, the ecclesiological, the sacramental and the cosmological significance of how Jesus the Christ makes a difference and changes the nature of how we understand and appropriate the human body in the light of the sciences.

That's largely what I wanted to say. I wanted to highlight a Confession that we make weekly in the Lutheran Church where we confess each week: "I am in bondage to sin and cannot free myself." I want to be clear. I don't have a problem with the issues. I know the idea of the leashing aspect implies a kind of determinism. I am not uncomfortable with the issue of theological determinism. I don't believe there is life within that context, even in understanding freedom. But I'm not uncomfortable with the idea of a theological determinism that recognizes that we are never in a situation where we are apart from God and the relationship with God. God controls the dynamic of our being in all of its nature and in all of its re-creation as well.

KEEFE   I teach dogmatic/systematic theology at the Major Seminary in New York. I've been there for six years. Before that, I was at Marquette, St. Louis University and Canisius College in Buffalo. I was also in Denver for some years. I've been working in systematic theology since 1966. The paper I have written is obviously the product of a considerable theological musing on problems which are inherent in Catholic systematic theology — especially as it is traditionally presented generally in a Thomist format. I have found Thomism problematical and in many places quite incoherent, judging it by the content of the Scriptural and Patristic tradition as mediated largely through Augustinian auspices.

A year and a half ago one of my students asked a question that brought me to a consideration of the Pauline anthropology. Much has been written on the Pauline anthropology, most of it, however, written by persons who have been looking at Paul through Thomist lenses. I find that counterproductive. I don't want to appear here in the guise of a Thomist-basher. There are a lot of bashers around. It's a waste of time. The work of theology is not the study of any theologian no matter how normative his thought may have become. The work of theology is what Anselm called it in the beginning of the 11th century: faith seeking an understanding. It is faith that seeks the understanding; it seeks it from the tradition mediated by the Church. There are various ways of looking at that tradition quite evidently. I look at it as a Catholic theologian and I consider that tradition entirely normative for the work of theology. That said, it is always necessary to return to the tradition.

In the past several decades a new appreciation of the necessity of going back to the Fathers has formed. My own personal theological hero, Henri Cardinal de Lubac, is notable in initiating and pushing through a re-examination of that entire tradition. I depend very heavily on what he has done. At the same time I investigate in this paper an area which, insofar as I am aware, he did not particularly turn to, namely, the flesh/spirit relationship that Paul refers to in the Greek *sarx/pneuma* dichotomy in historical man which Paul links to the Fall. That is to say, we are fallen into this fleshly condition, into the condition which, if considered in itself as autonomous, is a process of ongoing disintegration. The Fall then is a fall from that free unity which reflexively we find in the salvation worked by Christ. This is to say that we can understand the Fall of the first Adam only by looking at the resurrection, or at the redemption, given in the Second Adam.

Thus the Fall is a kind of anti-creation event freely entered into. But what was freely entered is a necessary process of disintegration. This ends notoriously in dust; because we have sinned in Adam we return to dust. The "dust" is simply the Old Testament expression for the ultimate disintegration of the human reality. This disintegration has no remedy within itself. It is the misfortune of Catholic systematic theology, and I would imagine systematic theology across the board insofar as I have encountered it, that all speculation is inherited from the Greek, which is to say a pagan, context. It is not too much to say that the pagan wisdom — the pagan philosophy concerning which Paul has made some very negative remarks (pagan wisdom is "foolishness in the eyes of God") — is a rationalization, an effort to normalize the *sarkic* or fleshly condition of man, that process of disintegration.

These philosophies, whether Mediterranean, Chinese, Indian or Persian, all end in a dualism and ultimately in a dehistoricization process which locates reality outside of the physical condition of fallen history. This always ends in a kind of a nihilism. About 50 years ago C. S. Lewis in a famous radio address spoke of the abolition of man as the process in which the modern world is enthusiastically engaged. This is entirely within the Pauline understanding of natural man left to himself. However natural man is not left to himself. But, as left to himself, he has no remedy within himself. The flesh, as we are told authoritatively, profits nothing and that nothing is to be taken seriously. It is the *nada* of Hemingway. He increasingly used it as he moved on toward the suicidal end of his life: *nada, nada, nada*. The utter absence of hope, the futility that marks much of the Greek culture particularly, is found in its great literary works. There are comedies which try to forget and mock the human condition and tragedies which accept it and generally recommend a stoic courage as the remedy, most famously Sophocles' *Oedipus Rex*. The pessimism built into pagan rationalization is one of the most obvious elements of our intellectual heritage. Yet, systematic theology is dependent upon the Aristotelian, and before it, on the Platonic systematization of this pessimism.

Both philosophers (Aristotle and Plato) take for granted that the human condition is locked into a necessity insofar as it is historical. The human mind operates exactly within this context; as fallen it disintegrates, it does not integrate. All the integrity the human mind can find is gratuitous, "novelistic"; insofar as strict reason proceeds it ends up in an analytical inquiry that seeks forever some indivisible reality in history and can find none. This then is the ratification of the condemnation to disintegration which is Paul's insight into the Fall. What can we do about that?

Paul inherits from his Pharisaic tradition a rejection of Greek wisdom. That has been fought out, as I note in passing, with the Hasmonean Sadducees who were very much taken with the Hellenistic culture. The Pharisees resisted; Paul as a Pharisee will have nothing to do with Greek wisdom simply as a part of his Pharisaic heritage. But he knows also that the Pharisaic insistence on the resurrection of the body over against the Sadducees, upon which he pivoted famously, is something that has no satisfactory explanation or justification within that Pharisaic tradition. They look indeed to a day of Jahweh but this really doesn't say much about the resurrection of the body. Nevertheless this is part of his tradition. He converts that tradition by looking to the Christ as the source of life, the source of Spirit, the source, then, of that in man which does not die. That not dying is pure gratuity.

There is nothing in man — *contra* the hellenistic optimism which came up from time to time — that enabled these philosophers to find in man's immaterial reason some non-historical principle of survival corresponding to some non-historical principle of immortality. This has passed into the Thomist tradition as the immortal soul; this is said to be immortal because it has within itself an isolation from the body which precisely isolates it from death. We're back into a dualistic situation, a rationalistic attempt to provide for the survival of the separated soul in Thomas. The separated soul has no support whatever in the doctrinal, scriptural or liturgical tradition. It simply does not work theologically. As an account of some kind of natural immortality I cannot but look upon it as something which has led far too many theologians astray from the proper attempt to understand the Pauline tradition which is most eloquent on this point.

Paul, beyond all the other New Testament authors, is intent on the absolute importance of our survival of death. He goes so far as to say that, if the dead are not risen, then Christ is not risen and we are left in despair. Precisely. But it is necessary to understand more than is ordinarily understood exactly how that is. In the beginning of the 12th century, the sacramental theologians of the monastic schools concluded with an utterly brilliant paradigm dependent on Augustine's discovery of a double causality within the sacramental sign. The paradigm describes the event which is the event of Catholic sacramental realism, but it is the order of history itself. It is the free unity of the past and the present as they point towards, symbolize, the Kingdom of God.

On that level, then, one can look at flesh as simply the sign which of itself has no intelligibility whatsoever. Its sole meaning is that it points to that which it is not, the free unity of the One Flesh of the New Covenant, the union of Christ and the Church. The *One Flesh* then is the gift of unity to man in history which is purely sacramental, not empirical, not in any sense available to the senses in a laboratory or in reflection or cognitional analysis to use Lonergan's term; none of this assures us of immortality. Nonetheless, within the worship of the Church it is understood that we are restored in Christ, within the Church, to this free unity. Here the notions of "body" and "flesh" come together. Paul speaks — he uses the term uniquely of the Church — of the Church as the Body of Christ. In this he understands the Church to be also the glory of Christ as Christ is the glory of the Father proceeding from the Father. So the Church proceeds from Christ, from the wounded side. The Fathers are practically unanimous in speaking of the water and blood from the side of the pierced body of the dead Christ as the emergence of the Second Eve from the sleeping Second Adam.

This insight guides a good deal of the paper that I have written. We can, then, look at the Pauline anthropology not simply as a definition of man but as the description of the event that Pope John Paul II portrays in *Veritatis Splendor* as man created good in the beginning. The "beginning" for the Pope and for the Johannine tradition, is Christ as the *alpha* and the *omega*; He is the beginning. We are created good in Christ. This again is Pauline in Colossians: all creation is in Christ. The same thing is affirmed in the Johannine prologue, but here we are dealing with Paul.

We are created in Christ, in the Second Adam; the goodness of our creation is its nuptial character, which is to say, the freedom of the "One Flesh," the nuptial community grounded in the primordial union, "in the Beginning," of Christ and his bridal Church. It is from this free unity that we are freely fallen by the primordial refusal of Adam and Eve to be free in Christ. By reason of their fall — which sullied but could not defeat the Good Creation — the freedom of the "One Flesh" is now given us sacramentally, primarily in the Eucharistic anamnesis of the Sacrifice which redeemed us by instituting the One Flesh of the New Covenant, and secondarily in the sacrament of marriage. The marital "One Flesh" is grounded in, and itself images, the free unity in One Flesh of Christ and the Church. This free unity, the New Covenant and the New Creation, is the "whole Christ" who is himself "the Beginning" — and also the End: the Alpha and the Omega, the Lord of history who by his presence in history, his Eucharistic union with the Church, makes history to be salvific.

We are given access to that in the worship of the Church. But the worship of the Church is not self-sufficient; it is sacramental. It points to that absolute fulfillment which is the Kingdom of God.

Thus, within the Pauline anthropology, we have a passage from absolute futility, fallen man as he encounters himself without hope; he is given this hope in faith in a living Christ who is a life-giving spirit by reason of his resurrection from the dead by that full gift of the Spirit by which the Father raised him from death. This resurrection is ours because He is raised as the head of the Body He instituted on the cross. The entirety of those for whom He died are in principle raised in Him. His death is that Baptism into which we enter, either by baptism or for those who are in a situation preliminary to the salvation history beginning with the Jews, through this worship of the Church; they stand in the position of the sacramental sign oriented toward heaven, toward the kingdom of God, through the worship of the Church.

I recognize that this is a hyper-Catholic statement which cannot but require emendation by those who stand outside that tradition. Nonetheless, let me continue within it. This seems to me to be the one way in which one can make sense of the human condition, recognize that its unity is gift, that it is free and that it is given only on a sacramental level in this world. But that

sacrament — again in the Catholic tradition — is effective because it was instituted by Christ, not because we are dandy people worshipping in the
Church; we are not. We are a Church of sinners, but it is a Church instituted
by Christ; its worship as sacramental is instituted by Christ in his institution
of the Church on the cross; this is centered upon the Eucharist. In the Eucharistic *One Flesh*, the condition of man as flesh is healed, within history.
Within history, he is enabled to act significantly, to do those things which are
simply labeled covenantal fidelity. This, then, is what my paper is about.

MULLER   I am a Jesuit priest currently teaching at
Sacred Heart Major Seminary. It is the Archdiocesan Seminary for Detroit.
I previously taught at the Gregorian University in Rome, Marquette University in Milwaukee and Spring Hill College in Mobile, Alabama. I began my
life, as it were, as a physicist at Spring Hill many years ago but somewhere
along the way I got shanghaied by theology. I am currently teaching systematic theology. For this Workshop I was asked to replace Msgr. Langsfeld who
is listed as an essayist in the brochure. I say this to explain why my paper is
somewhat disjointed. I simply ran out of time. [*Eds.: A somewhat edited version
of his paper appears in this book.*]

Because my paper is disjointed, I want to provide some of the background
for making some of the moves that I made in writing it. My initial intent was
to explore aspects of the theological anthropology I had developed in my
dissertation, *Trinity and Marriage in Paul*. There I had developed an understanding of humanity as consisting of three distinct modes — as individual,
as a community and in interaction with marriage, the paradigmatic human
interaction. In the dissertation I developed this under categories of the
"spiritual." I studied Augustine's work on the Trinity, pulling out all his
criteria for a useful theological analogy, which he used to develop his psychological analogy. I intended to show that these categories apply also to human
community, and, in particular, to the community which is the Church.

The occasion of writing this paper led me to think that what I had phrased
at that time as spiritual categories when writing my dissertation could be
even better recast as corporeal categories. It was with this in view that I
began this paper by setting out these categories. When I had written my
introduction I decided that there was yet another dimension that needed to
be looked at. I originally thought that the relational dimension which characterizes human reality in terms of our relations with one another, relations in
community, also led in a transcendent direction. I felt then it was necessary
to look first at this notion of the human body as the focal point for transcendence before proceeding to this three-fold anthropology that I had initially planned to develop in my paper.

This topic of transcendence , as it were, took over my paper. Before I knew it, I was looking not so much at the encounter between theology and science but between fairy tales and science fiction. The reason for taking that particular tack was my desire to first set up some of the relevant issues involved in a theology of the human body in particular problem areas. Ideally this would involve a study of the challenges to a theology of the body presented by a scientific culture. I was looking for a quick entry into this notion of a scientific culture and, of course, the quick entry was by way of science fiction.

This led then to a consideration of J. R. R. Tolkien. In his essay on fairy stories, he raises interesting issues on the relation between what he refers to as the primary world — what can also be called the real world — and the secondary world, the world generated or created by the storyteller. Tolkien was convinced that in point of fact there is considerable overlap and even if we discount clearly fictional material — in his case, hobbits, orcs, ents — there is nonetheless a carry-over from one's understanding of the primary world to this secondary world.

I then trace some ways in which we can move from some of the devices used in science fiction to the primary world, giving some instances of scientists who exhibit the types of attitudes we find within science fiction. I then asked the question: where does that view arise in this humanist culture? Then, in the next part of the paper, I look at various developments in the last 500 years that gave rise to the sorts of understanding of the human body that we have within the humanist culture. J. L. Blau in the *Encyclopedia of Philosophy* captured some of the issues involved in this transition. He wrote: "With Freud man lost his Godlike mind; with Darwin his exalted place among the creatures on earth; with Copernicus man had lost his privileged position in the universe." I will basically (and quickly) trace out those transitions to the near modern period.

In the next section, which should have been developed in more detail, I attempted to show the further shifts in the scientific data that have taken place since the more popular humanist culture was formulated. My intent is not to prove anything but simply to point out that the presuppositions that had led to the rise of the humanist culture made machines look like persons or persons like machines. In some measure these presuppositions are no longer operative; science has moved beyond this point. Obviously, some of this material is somewhat tentative. I merely wanted to show some of the reasons why humanist culture arose as it did and to point to the fact that scientifically we no longer think the same way. But the culture has a certain inertia. Thus, we need to distinguish what's going on in the culture and what scientists are actually doing.

Next I started to move toward a theology of the human body. I wanted to focus on the issue of materiality itself since that would be the basis on which we talk about the human body. In this I look upon the shift to relativistic and quantum physics as quite important in breaking up the old mechanistic understanding of material reality in the 18th and 19th centuries. Mechanistic interventions of whatever sort are deemed inappropriate in the new physics. I describe this as *disponability*. Modern physics understands matter in general as far "freer" than it was thought in a more Newtonian understanding. That "freedom" within material reality provides a basis for talking about an ability of matter to be expressive of a transcendent dimension in a way precluded by a more mechanistic understanding.

At this point in my paper I started to list some quick notes in terms of my original intent, namely, the three focal points of human existence: the individual, the community, the interaction or the marital issues. In this regard, modern studies of the brain and how it functions mirror somewhat closely the dynamics that, for instance, Augustine discussed in his work on the Trinity in arguing for a psychological analogy of the Trinity. Augustine was convinced that characteristics — circumincession would be a case in point — precluded a material presence of memory, understanding and will. I think advances in science have suggested a way in which Augustine's judgment need not be taken as definitive. One can then, perhaps, begin to move toward an understanding of bodily imaging of the Trinity in such a way as to be able to use most, if not all, of the criteria that Augustine set out as necessary for a useful theological analogy of the Trinity.

SCHNEIDER   I am in the second year of teaching at Texas Lutheran University in Seguin, Texas. I teach the courses in Church history and the Introduction to Theology class. This latter is a required class so it's large and always a challenge. I also teach a survey course on religions in America. My PhD dissertation at Princeton Theological Seminary was on the connection between Christ and Christians in Athanasius and Luther. Prior to that I worked at Lutheran School of Theology in Chicago on my MDiv where I had Bob Bertram as a teacher. He is my connection to ITEST. He invited me to present this paper.

I understood my task as looking at what is happening in genetics scientifically as raw data and trying to interpret what I saw through the lenses of the traditional theological loci. So I approached the Human Genome Project with such questions in mind as: how does this research impact the meaning of what it is to be created in the image of God? Or, in light of these biological discoveries what are we really saying as Christians when we say that the Word of God became flesh and dwelt among us? Does the scientific discourse about DNA contribute anything to the Christian understanding of what it means to eat the Body of Christ or to be in Christ by faith? What is the resurrection of the body? And so on.

As I approached the topic with these questions in mind, however, I kept bumping up against ethical objections to the applications of genetic research. Many of these objections are from Christians and a disproportionate number are from non-white and non-American or non-European people. I am convinced that the Body of Christ which excludes those people is not the Body of Christ. So I determined to take into account as much as possible the theological reflection of anthropology of what it means to be human made by people from that underside. The result was that I always had to hold together in my work the bodily aspects of humanity and the personal aspects of humanity. Biological determinism is not trusted at all by those who have had to struggle very hard to assert their humanity.

In working through the paper I confined myself to five theological loci. They are: creation of humans; evil; salvation; the Lord's supper and the new creation. I chose those simply because they seemed to correspond best to the material I was reading.

On the topic of creation, I began by thinking about DNA as the internal message that informs our identity both as humans and as individuals. That led me straight back to Athanasius who speaks of the Word of God as the original Form of humanity who has since become enfleshed in Jesus Christ. Then I asked the question: is there any sense in which we can see the image of God in that genetic information with which we are encoded. I saw that this message contains life and the continuity of life as its purpose. Furthermore, the specifically human genome enables us to speak and to be self-transcendent. Humans reflect the Word not only bodily but personally.

Next, I dwelt a while on the concept of person as intrinsic to theology, to being in the image of God. I use Catherine Mowry La Cugna's excellent work analyzing the Trinity and especially focus on the Cappadocian contributions to understanding God as a perichoretic relationship of Persons in love. But here is the catch which brings me to the locus on evil. We see neither life nor love unambiguously in humans. People die and they cause others to die in order that they themselves might live. Humans have created structures that are routinely oppressive on many levels, such as race, class, gender, culture, nation. Because humans are self-transcendent, those who are suffering through these structures do not see what is happening to them as sheer impersonal biological survival of the fittest. They see a conscious agency at work in the things that happen to them.

For those who believe that God is an agent, the oppressive structures of the world raise the question of theodicy: does God really mean for us to live? All of us or just those who have power? For those on the bottom the question becomes: does God really love me, me personally? Or if it's a group, us personally? DNA cannot tell us this. DNA perpetuates a stream of life in general but it doesn't perpetuate any single life in particular. Cells are programmed to divide only a certain number of times. So, what is the salvation I talk about here?

It's in the locus on salvation that I tried to answer these questions that arise. I quote the *Formula of Concord* which says that, because of human weakness, God put our salvation "for safekeeping into the almighty hand of a Savior, Jesus Christ, out of which no one can pluck us." That comes from John 10. He died in the body; He let his own genetic composition get shut down. However, his followers insisted that they saw him alive again after that, but transformed in some way — having gone then beyond the normal limit for human beings. Those thoughts led me to the Lord's Supper because, then, we as the Church say that He gave his body to others to mingle with their own bodies in the Lord's Supper. Science is showing that what it means to be human is malleable and DNA can be transferred from one body to another even from a human body to a non-human substance and back.

Then I asked the question: can Jesus as the Word of God in the Person, in the flesh, be at least as flexible as his image in the rest of us? So, perhaps it is so that we can know that Christ is with us wholly in our dying and in our rising, that He might come to us in bread and in wine that forms our faith and mingles with the chemicals that feed our body, actually becoming part of our physical body.

Heading toward the new creation, I hold up the sentence that Christ himself is the picture of the future for Christians, the picture that they show to the world. If that is so, then the future also includes those who have died and have suffered and who have been on the bottom also because Christ was there before the resurrection.

In my conclusion, I try to raise some points where there may be future conversation between scientists and those who have religious beliefs, particularly Christians. I found a book that puts a parallel column: the attitudes of what the author calls scientific materialists versus believers on certain topics related to genetics and shows where they are in agreement. All approve the work of the Human Genome Project and agree that genetic research should continue to be supervised by the government. All agree that DNA research points to the interrelationships of all organisms and that some of the consequences of this knowledge should be a strong prohibition on the use of genetic information for biological weapons as well as a strong push for equitable access to the use of genetic information for medical advances. As long as there is no discrimination all approve of genetic testing and public screening as well as somatic gene therapy. All disapprove of eugenics and the enhancements of traits. There is a little common ground there for the discussion between those who have a Christian faith specifically and those scientists who do not.

VAN DER MEER   My first language is not theology; I am by training a biologist. Later in life I decided that I should also have some knowledge of the philosophy of science. This comes basically out of an experience I had as an undergrad student. I became interested in the question of faith and science in high school and when I started studying biology I quickly found out that science wasn't going to give me all the answers I wanted. I needed to learn something about how science was done. Pretty much for the rest of my career, even though much of it was devoted to scientific research, I've stayed interested in the philosophy of science to try to understand how, let's say, religious belief can interact with scientific knowledge through philosophical ideas. That's the model I work with and you'll probably recognize that in my paper.

I have decided to give a brief survey of the paper to help you recall it. Basically it's a methodological paper which applies to the topic of this workshop, *A Theology of the Human Body*, but could apply to many other topics as well. My objective is to move away from this long-term interest I've had, the relation of religion and science mediated by philosophy, and to ask: how is the Bible relevant in all of this? I noted in the last decade or so that in studies of religion and science very little mention was made of the role of the source of theological knowledge, which I found surprising. Maybe that surprise was more the surprise of a scientist than a theologian. I don't know. This is my objective and obviously the things I want to avoid is on the one hand, doing theology — developing new theological ideas without any reference to Scripture — and on the other hand being very simplistic about it as in biblicism, scientific creationism and so forth. This I tried to do in the model I proposed in which I use an old metaphor — two pillars and a bridge: one pillar standing for different levels of interpretation in the natural sciences and the other one for different levels of interpretation in theology, in exegesis, I should say. The two are then connected at a high level of abstraction by what is known as worldviews. That's where the bridging occurs.

My claim is then that science can in fact influence the interpretation of Scripture at lower levels of interpretation prior to world view, prior to higher levels. I'll give some examples of that. Likewise religious beliefs can influence interpretation of natural phenomena in that same way. That is why I presented these two case studies in my paper: one by a theologian-geneticist, Theodosius Dobzhansky. I will give a very brief overview of some of his important ideas.

At the worldview level in Theodosius Dobzhansky's ideas we'll find a religious belief in Divine Providence that covers nature as well as society. Specifically — this has to do with his Russian background and the experience of the Russian Revolution — he had to deal with the question of how to deal with the evil people do to each other in the world if this is all happening under God's Providence. The answer he came up with was a very standard one, namely, for humans to have the freedom to do what they want there has to be room for evil. The interesting thing is that in his biology he applied that belief to nature as well. So, as you have in ethics the free will defense of evil, he proposed that there is a free nature defense of natural evil as he called it.

Let me explain what he means by natural evil. He looked at the relationship of an organism in the environment in the same terms as he looked at the relationship of people in society — in terms of conflict. Mainly in terms of natural selection eliminating various genes from groups of organisms, he saw that natural selection in terms of a process that counters progress in nature — the kind of evolutionary progress that you find in the Darwinian theory of evolution. This is why he came to reject the particular scientific theory, namely, the so-called "selection theory" of population genetics. In population genetics, very briefly, the view is that all the genetic information present in a population of animals or plants is subject to natural selection. This is the way in which evolutionary progress comes about according to the "selection theory." He said this is not really possible because natural selection would eliminate all sorts of genetic information and the population will become poorer and less adaptable and therefore less free to adjust itself to new situations in the environment.

It was exactly this idea of freedom and adaptability that had a religious origin in his thinking. This is why he came to prefer a theory known as the "balance theory" of evolution. I'll spare you the genetic details. We look at a population as a storehouse of genetic information, most of it hidden, not subject to natural selection. The population at any time has the freedom to adjust itself to new environmental situations when they happen. I have that case study in here because it's a clear example of how that idea of "natural freedom" — an idea with a religious origin — shaped his choice of theories. That's the point of the example. We can see how his interpretation of biological facts was shaped in a religious framework that penetrated to the content of theories. That's the one pillar.

For the other pillar I took Rudolph Bultmann who is best known as a professional theologian who was influenced by a scientific view of reality. Let me give the same kind of outline of his way of looking at Scripture. In him we find at the worldview level a naturalism that originates in a sort of metaphysical extension of the natural sciences. That is transformed into a religious naturalism. In this view we find, for instance, that God does not act in the natural world. Also, myth is a kind of story in which supernatural events are presented as if they were natural. These kinds of concepts play a very important role in his exegetical work. In my paper I distinguish quite a number of levels of exegesis and I need to acknowledge my colleague Albert Wolters who has developed these things. Remember, theology is not my first language. I have used some of those to try to discern how this religious naturalism in Bultmann has an effect at lower levels of his theological work.

The highest level I want to begin with is the one I've called the level of confessional discernment. I would like to read a very small part of my paper here:

> The majority of Old Testament passages are best interpreted as referring to the unity of the person. Philosophically this allows for two interpretations known as monism and holistic dualism. Bultmann takes the monistic position. He does not provide an explicit justification for his monism. However, given the availability of a legitimate alternative, viz., holistic dualism ... (which was the view among the Hebrews, I understand) ... and considering his scientism, it is reasonable to infer that his preference for monistic exegesis is mandated by the natural sciences. This implies that Paul's so-called dualistic texts ... (which Bultmann did a lot of work on) ... need to be seen as concessions to or acceptance of Gnostic or Hellenistic dualism (rather than an expression of holistic dualism which was apparently quite common among the Hebrews -a view defended by Cooper who says): ... However, (Cooper) Paul's dualistic texts can also be interpreted as forms of holistic dualism and so can the Old Testament texts so that there is consistency within the Scriptures (within the Two Testaments.) (Cooper, 1989). In sum, scientific naturalism drives Bultmann's monistic interpretation of the majority of texts on the body.

So there we have an example of why his scientific worldview affects his theological position of interpretation of texts about the body.

Then I move one level down — that of ideological criticism. Here I'd like to read a small part of my paper again:

> Bultmann develops one implication of his naturalism in the form of a conditional argument. If supernatural events could occur in the natural world, he argues, they could not be known objectively in the manner of science because they cannot be manipulated for experimen-

tal study. Bultmann argues that salvation by Jesus demands a previous faith "For the resurrection, of course, simply cannot be a visible fact in the realm of human history." (Bultmann, 1952: 295). One might think that supernatural events occurring in nature could be known subjectively so that existential value could arise out of natural fact, but this is not what Bultmann means. Bultmann is saying that the bodily resurrection of Jesus cannot be known objectively because it cannot occur. He writes: "We find incredible a theory of satisfaction that describes God's act as a cultic or juristic act and a Christ occurrence that cannot be understood as having to do with our own personal existence." (Bultmann, 1984: 97).

That's a clear example of an effect of scientific naturalism on Bultmann's interpretations in his exegetical work and how that shapes his exegesis.

Finally let me get down to what my colleague Wolters called the synchronic literary analysis. This involves the question of literary form; what kind of literary form does a particular part have in the book I'm talking about, the Letter to the Corinthians. Are certain passages myth or history? It is interesting that Bultmann describes everything that in some way refers to God's action in the natural world as myth. That is his definition of myth. We can see that there is a hermeneutical circle operating here; his particular scientific naturalism shapes his definition of myth, namely, the presentation of supernatural actions as if they are natural. That cannot happen. By definition that would mean that these passages are mythical. Those are some of the levels of interpretation in Bultmann that are shaped by his scientific naturalism.

Then I asked how we can avoid those kinds of things? How can we maintain integrity, not only in the interpretation of Scripture but also in the interpretation of nature? I suggest then a kind of trigger model by which science can provide the reasons for reconsideration of a particular exegesis, but the way that is carried out needs to be faithful to the Scriptures itself. Likewise in the natural sciences, the way we can allow, let's say, biblical insights to shape the interpretation of natural phenomenon also needs to remain faithful to what we actually observe. That in brief is the model.

I'm proposing that on both sides — theology and science — we need to have an attitude that takes things critically. For the theologian, it means not to take science for what it says it is, but to ask the question: is there any ideological payload that comes with the particular theory? There are plenty of examples in the history of science where that has been the case. The most common examples are those of geocentrism and fixity of species that were once long ago presented as scientific fact. We now understand that they were shaped by philosophical positions. The theologian needs to look at that first before he or she can decide if there is a question for exegesis. Likewise, of course, the scientist has to do that. I don't want to say too much about that because that is the standard situation anyway in the natural sciences.

I'll end by highlighting two of the challenges that I've mentioned, one of which has to do with an exegetical principle, that of accommodation. For example, take Dobzhansky's evolutionary progress idea and contrast that with the Genesis story. We can then say, "well, the Genesis story is an accommodation. God has stooped down to our level of understanding, or He has stooped down to a level of understanding of people at all times and in all cultures, and this is how we can deal with the discrepancy." How can we distinguish between accommodative and non-accommodative parts of Scripture? Let me give an example that I mentioned in my paper. Perhaps we would feel comfortable with presenting this as an example of accommodation, but would we feel comfortable with someone who said that looking at God as a person is also a form of accommodation rather than looking at God as a Force as in the expression: "let the Force be with you." That is one challenge I might put on the table: is this exegetical procedure of distinguishing between accommodative texts and non-accommodative texts really very helpful at all.

The other challenge is the distinction between the Bible as a book for morality and religion on the one hand and science on the other hand as the book for the body and nature. This is a standard kind of attitude for people to have. It provides a convenient and quick way of separating the two and having not too many conflicts. Let's say, however, in the last decade, if we look at what neuropsychology has discovered about the unity of the body and the mind, it begins to look as if that separation will be passé very soon. Therefore there are reasons to say that this neat division needs to be reconsidered. That is one of the other challenges I'd like to put on the table. If that is the case, if neuropsychology makes those kinds of suggestions, how can we do justice to a role of the Bible in our understanding of nature, and in particular our understanding of the body of humans.

BERTRAM   Was there some one theme that all the papers had in common, apart from the formal one of theology of the body? Were there common structures in them all? If that had happened, that would have made this, indeed, an atypical meeting of ITEST. I'm not sure that we could have handled such an eventuality. But were there common recurring themes? I had a hypothesis which sounded pretty tenable through the first four papers. It broke down when I got to van der Meer. I will have to apply more thought to this overnight. Now we will close this session. Tomorrow morning we'll hear first from the panelists, then from all of you.

BERTRAM   We decided at the end of the session last evening to hold the next speaker, Frank Andrews, for the this morning's first session. Frank will be speaking about a faith/science group he has begun in Maryland. After Frank's report, we will go back to our regular program.

ANDREWS   At my home parish, St. Mary's Church in Annapolis, we've started a religion/science study group. The motivation came from my own interest in religion/science and my attendance at the more recent ITEST meetings. In a sense, we're a chapter of ITEST but we don't call ourselves that yet; we will eventually I suppose. We have recruited twelve members. Half of them are "regular members" and half are "associates." The difference between the two is that regular members have obligated themselves to do some work; the associate members thought it would be interesting to belong to such a group but they didn't want to do all the work associated with it. Our routine consists in monthly meetings just like ITEST's annual meeting. We have chosen two references: one you'll recognize — it is an ITEST publication, *Transfiguration: Elements of Science and Christian Faith*, 1993. The other is Ian Barbour's book, *Religion and Science*. At the monthly meeting we have one of the regular members present a paper, written beforehand and promulgated through the coordinator, me, by mail or e-mail. Everyone will have had the opportunity to read it over before the meeting — regular members in particular. I will ask one of them to be a commentator on that paper. To get started, as the coordinator I did the first paper, covering Father William Wallace's paper on the history of religion and science. The next paper will be on Chapter 4 of Barbour's book; the one after that on Chapter 5, and so on.

If an individual has some pet topic that he/she wants to talk about, that will be fine as long as it's related to science. For example, one of our members is quite interested in Darwin. He's written a book on Darwin and Darwin's problem. When the paper is finally presented, I'll put a copy of it on our web site for documentation and future reference. We have our own web site hosted out of a high school server. Our high school has quite a computer setup and I have the capability with the passwords to publish the papers. We tell ourselves that our goal is really to enhance our faith through understanding. We are not scholars. We have to get decent references from the scholars to get the material to work with. We have to read and write in order to understand what we're talking about. We hope to keep on this way for some time. That's pretty much it. The final goal is written on our web site.

The address (the URL) is that of the high school. It's quite long. If you'll send me an e-mail (fandrews@annapolis.net) I'll answer it quickly. There will be a hyperlink on the e-mail. All one has to do is punch the hyperlink and he or she will go right to the site.

POSTIGLIONE   We could link you with our ITEST web site. Let us know whether or not you would want to be so linked.

ANDREWS   Our homepage states: "There are two books, the book of religion and the book of science, but there's only one author." We want to understand better how the two books fit together.

BRUNGS   You'll find out that it's a lot more work than you decided to take on. But I commend your efforts to start a process of thought concerning the work of the Church in this area.

ANDREWS   That's one reason that we have carefully defined the regular members. If I had to be the teacher and the coordinator, the group could get to be too much work. On the other hand, the regular members have to do something, they love it; they learn by having to write it down. The key is to write it down.

BERTRAM   There is a reason that the Lord doesn't tell you at the beginning what Father Brungs just revealed. It's just like marriage. He only tells you as much as you need to know to get you through the honeymoon. The rest comes later.

Last evening after the five essayists finished their summary statements I made bold to say that I had been entertaining an hypothesis after the first presentation. It seemed to hold after the first, second, third and fourth presentation. I wasn't so sure when we got to van der Meer at the end whether the same hypothesis would apply. I am speaking about a common thread that holds the beads together. I am not suggesting that this should be an agenda item for the rest of you to refer to, but I thought there was, at least at an abstract level, this common denominator in the first four, possibly in the fifth as well.

In the biological order and in the realm of the bodily, of creation, there seemed to be no disagreement — we wouldn't expect any among Christians — over the fact that that order, as we now encounter the creation, is fallen. But within that biological order there is trouble. For all the integrity that may still have survived the Fall, there is a question. The question is raised within that fallen creation itself. That is Step A. The form that that question takes varied from essayist to essayist. It may be, to use a conventional term, as in the case of Carolyn Schneider's paper, sin, to which the people who suffer the consequences of that sin may be particularly sensitive. Or it may be death, one of the themes of Father Keefe's statement of the problem of the fallen creation. Or it may be the Law of God, God's judgment, prominent as one of the problem factors in Michael Hoy's paper. At any rate, there's immanent in the fallen creation and also in its bodily dimension a question that makes the creation itself questionable.

Step B: There is not within the same order, immanent within that fallen creation, the necessary solution to the question. If there is to be a solution, the solution will have to come from without, from beyond.

Step C: In the standard Christian sequence there is hope, there is prospect of just such a solution. This is not just hope in some transcendent sense, if by that we mean other-worldly. It is precisely in the worldliness, the sheer bodiliness, of the Christian solution there comes a solution that fits like a hand in a glove. I could not help but link that hypothesis to Father Brungs' opening remarks when he said quite tentatively: judging by what we've seen in the papers we know we have questions. What the answers to those questions will be remains to be seen. We certainly have gotten first tastes of what that answer is both from the written essays as well as the oral presentations by the essayists last evening.

I had another thought, although it is not particularly profound nor original. The essayist cannot diagnose the original problem in the fallen creation at Step A, had they not already had some inkling of what the solution was going to be. A theologian on my doctoral committee, a theologian whom I know is appreciated by Father Keefe, Paul Tillich, used to say that the culture raises the question and the message, *kerygma*, of the Christian Church provides the answer. But later on, because that became a kind of shibboleth which was abused by his groupies, he felt he had to nuance that to say, "Yes, as the question is raised by the culture, it is answered by the message, the *kerygma*." But the *kerygma* has a way of transforming the original question and deepening it; and it may well be that we couldn't have even thought to ask the question had we not known the answer beforehand.

As I say, I thought I saw signs, though in quite variegated forms, of that sequence of A), B), C) through the particular essay presentations last evening. I simply offer this for your consideration. You may have nourished some hypotheses of your own as you heard the presentations. Let's give privilege of sequence to our essayists. Now that they've heard one another they may have something to address to one another in the form of questions, commentary, agreements. We don't have to follow the sequence in the roster.

HOY   Mine is partly a comment and a question to Father Keefe. I appreciated your exploration of your paper last evening. It allayed some fears I had when I raised the issue in my own presentation of body/soul dualism. There needs to be a kind of monistic appropriation that

I found in your look at the Pauline literature; there was some recognition and realization of that over against Thomas. I appreciated that dimension.

The question I have is with a Christology that precedes the whole dimension of creation. It's not the first time that I heard that. I heard that, not from a Roman Catholic, but from Karl Barth who also talks about Christ as the First Adam. Could you explore this issue and say some more about this?

KEEFE   Do you mean the transcendent Christology from which the rest of it derives?

HOY   Yes.

KEEFE   The priority of Christ always raises the problem of the tension between a sacramental immanence, which is the Catholic position, and that transcendence by which the Christ can be called the *Alpha* and the *Omega*. In other words, its transcendence to history is from within history as a sacramental, Eucharistic transcendence. I link this in the paper to the presence of Christ *per modum substantiae*. This is simply a medieval Latin way of "solving" a problem. It was anticipated in fifth century Patristic literature, but it received its development largely in the twelfth and thirteenth centuries. Then the problem was how to save the Eucharistic Lord from the indignities incumbent upon his presence as signed by the consecrated bread and wine. Finally, the expression, the presence *per modum substantiae* (presence in the manner of a substance), not in the manner of accidents, was adopted.

If we say Christ's presence is "in the manner of accidents," the incidence of spatial and temporal change is important. Take an absurd example: One holds up the host and turns it over. Have we turned Jesus upside down? Clearly not! To account for this, it was necessary to understand Christ to be present in a fashion which did not subordinate him to what we would today call entropy — in terms of change. The phrase was pretty much left there as a means of accounting for a problem raised in the Middle Ages. It has always seemed to me that this is an inadequate statement of what *per modum substantiae* means. It is really a statement that, as Eucharistically present, Christ is present as the Lord of history, as transcending space and time.

The transcendence of space and time is ordinarily understood as the absence of God from the world. He transcends space and time by remoteness. But within the Eucharistic understanding of the divine transcendence of history, it is that transcendence given by the Father sending the Son to give the Spirit which terminates in the New Covenant. The Eucharist understood as the immanence of the achieved New Covenant would be the immanence then of what Augustine calls the whole Christ, the relationship of the Second Adam to the Second Eve. That relationship is the "One Flesh" of the New Covenant. It is in this relationship, Eucharistically established, then, that Christ is King of the Kingdom. It is in this relationship that the Church is present to Christ in sign, as He is present to the Church in sign. It is in this presence that He orders the past of the Old Covenant to that presence which He achieves on the Cross. The whole of it, all of the past, all of the present, points to that Kingdom in which the sign of the Eucharist is given its manifest fulfillment. All of this means, then, that Christ is the beginning and the end, as the Johannine Gospel has it. The Apocalypse emphasizes this, of course, and we find the anticipation of it in the Johannine prologue. We find it in Paul's letter to the Philippians in the hymn in the second chapter. It's found in various statements in Ephesians and elsewhere.

This is an interpretation given within the Catholic tradition which responds to your question. It explains for an example, what fallenness must mean. Again to beat Thomas about the head and body, he is very unsatisfactory with respect to the Fall because he looks upon it as a fall to nature from an antecedent glorified situation. But I believe I'm correct in saying that he does not link that antecedent creation to Christ. That has its explanation which I can hardly go into here. But it is one which has led a number of Thomists into a neglect of the theology of the Fall amounting, tragically, to a denial of the Fall itself. A young Calvinist theologian named Vandervelde — it was in the 70s — wrote a doctoral dissertation in which he analyzed what the Catholics had done with this tradition and discovered that they had all fallen under the hypnotic influence of Teilhard. Teilhard had made the notion of evolution the tool by which he could analyze Christology, particularly.

In these circumstances very bad things happened. One of them was that he put the Fall within the historical time line. He encouraged theologians to suppose that the Fall had occurred some time between the appearance of Adam and Eve and where we are now. This was thought to be a continuity and it became very difficult to locate exactly when the Fall happened. This got Rahner into a discussion about monogenism and polygenism and all sorts of strange *theologumena* resulted. What had been forgotten was that the whole of creation, all of it, is fallen. We know no unfallen time, no unfallen space. There are no pre-Adamites. It's all fallen. We will perhaps remember the story about the old man/woman who went to a cosmology lecture at Harvard where various astronomers were explaining how it is. She (or he, if you prefer) stood up at the end and said to the main lecturer, a notable physicist, "Sonny, you're all wrong. The world stands on the back of a turtle." The lecturer fell into the spirit of things and said, "But what does the turtle stand on?" She said, "Sonny, you can't fool me. It's turtle all the way down."

There isn't anything we encounter that is not fallen. The principle of integration, then, in this fallen universe has to be given prior to the Fall, in a sense, it has to transcend the Fall. This is the force of Gn 3:15, the so-called proto-Evangelium, in which the opposition is set up between the woman's seed and the seed of the serpent. There is even in the fallen condition of man that by which the Fall is overcome. Not, it must be said by anything given to man but by the prior transcendence of the entire human condition by him in whom it is created, that is created free. But the remedy for the misuse of the freedom is given by anticipation. Thus in the Lucan gospel on the Road to Emmaus we hear our Lord saying,"Was it not necessary?"

Now the necessity is locked within his free obedience, obviously; but given his free obedience, it is the free obedience by which the Son is immanent in a creation which can and did fall. His immanence within that fallen creation is that by which it is integrated. It is that, of course, by which He is born, lives, dies on the cross and is raised again. All of that is a little difficult to put into a single imaginative synthesis. But I think it does work as theology and is, I hope a reasonably brief answer to your question.

SCHNEIDER   I have a question for Dr. van der Meer. I liked your paper. I thought it flowed very smoothly. But I'm trying to find an integrity for each of the two lenses you used — the hermeneutical lenses that operate within science and those that operate within theology. I have a point of conversation as well, a plain factual question. I am struggling to understand what Dobzhansky is trying to do when he attempts to pit adaptation and natural selection against one another. In my mind these things are part of one single whole. So I have difficulty figuring out what difference he sees between them so that he would see them as opposed.

VAN DER MEER   That's a good question. It has to do with Dobzhansky's seeing natural selection as a negative force, which contemporary biologists no longer do. For him, natural selection would eliminate collection genes from the population. The consequence would be that populations would not be as capable as they were before to adapt themselves to new environmental situations, because it would have lost that genetic potential to do so. That's why we can also see the idea of conflict coming through, conflict between the environment and the survival of the population which, I argue, comes straight out of his view of society. He had experience in the Russian revolution where the fate of individual people was subject to the progress of the society as he understood it. That is my explanation of his position.

SCHNEIDER   How does he explain what adaptation is in opposition to that?

VAN DER MEER   There is a specific comment about that in my paper. It has to do with his choosing as his explanation the balance theory of population genetics. Maybe I should explain this a bit more than I did yesterday. I went over the details rather quickly last evening. I may have to introduce a bit of high school genetics to do so. Let me begin with this. Most of us are familiar with the fact that some traits in our families skip a generation or so. Maybe we're glad that they did. For every trait we have there are two genes involved, two things in chromosomes that bring that about. Sometimes one of the two dominates the other so that the other cannot come to expression. We call that a dominant gene as opposed to a recessive gene. The condition of that individual is called heterozygous as opposed to homozygous where we have two of the same genes. Now, the fact is that in such a heterozygote the recessive gene is in hiding, as it were, because its genetic information is not expressed in the individual. The only genetic information expressed in the individual is that coded for in the dominant gene. We may have two genes for eye color, one brown and one blue, but we have blue eyes because that's the dominant one; the other is recessive. Our offspring could have brown eyes, if that brown gene was combined with the brown of the other parent and came to expression in the offspring.

Here is Dobzhansky's idea of how we can have adaptability. In a population submitted to natural selection, only the traits that are expressed that are submitted to natural selection. Those are the ones coded for by the dominant genes. The ones coded for by the recessive genes are not expressed in traits and therefore they are not subject to natural selection. They may be in the population because sometime in the past they conferred an advantage. They came to expression. Over time a population collects many of those recessive genes which are, as it were, a pool that it could use for future occasions when the organism needs to adapt to another kind of situation. What then happens is that natural selection weeds out and removes the unadapted ones but there is enough potential in the population in the form of those recessive genes for those individuals to become offspring and survive the new environment. This keeps the population alive. Does that explain it?

SCHNEIDER   I'm still grappling with that. If someone is killed, he or she is killed with all the genes, the recessive and the dominant.

VAN DER MEER   You may have noticed that I was talking about populations. Biologists here do not pay any attention to individuals.

BERTRAM   Are these the genes you referred to last evening as the hidden genes?

VAN DER MEER   That is an important question. As a matter of fact, this is an example of a physical way of thinking that has been introduced in biology where organisms are not the focus of attention; only the genes that the organisms carry are the focus. Then you can make that point.

I would like to reciprocate, Dr. Schneider. I very much appreciated your paper as well. Perhaps I can make a connection between our two papers to answer the question of our Chair who thought that maybe his hypothesis evanesced by the time he got around to my paper. I would like to suggest that theologians ought to be critical about the scientific knowledge when they are working in the area of the importance of DNA. In your (Schneider) paper there is a very strong focus on DNA. This is not surprising, because this is the focus we find among biologists. One of the strongest expressions of that focus is where you cite Richard Dawkins. It is in the section on evil, in the second paragraph: "When looked at on a purely natural level, pain and suffering are not a problem but a necessary fact. It is accurately stated by Richard Dawkins who points out that the universe operates to preserve DNA." That's a very strong statement: the purpose of the existence of the universe is the preservation of DNA.

On that point it would be good for scientists to hear theologians ask critical questions about the centrality of the DNA molecule. Let me give you some examples. I think that it was also in your (Schneider) paper that I read that, when you compare the chromosomes, let's say, between humans and apes there are only five that have any kind of difference in gene sequence. I remember that of those five it is perhaps only 1% that's different. The only difference is the sequence in the genes, inversions and so forth. That's a fact; we can say that. But here's the point I want to make: if there is so much similarity between the chromosomes of, let's say, chimpanzees and humans, then we must look at the real beings and see how different they are.

For a person like me — I'm a developmental biologist and study the development of embryos — there is an enormous question: how can I explain this difference, if I cannot explain it in terms of DNA? I can speculate about that, but this is not the time to do so. It raises the question of how central DNA is in understanding the human being, the human body alone. I am not talking about the fact that we are also religious beings, and so forth. I'd like to have your comment on that. What do you think about that as a theologian?

SCHNEIDER   When I talked with the biologists on the campus they too were wary of putting too much emphasis on the DNA. They talked about the dangers of relying too much on gene therapy. They said there are many different proteins in the body interacting with genes and we don't know very much about those interactions. They are complex; so many things happen. Let's just say that we can alter a gene and that will result in the kind of expression of characteristics that you want. "It ain't so." It may not interact well because we don't know what's going to happen with all the interactions between the time that that gene is altered and the time that that characteristic has been expressed. The scientists I know personally are also worried by this extreme position that puts so much emphasis on DNA. My impression is that there is not agreement within the scientific community; not everyone in that community operates from the same interpretive stance.

VAN DER MEER   That is an important observation. I would say, for example, Richard Dawkins is known as a materialist or a naturalist. For materialists there is really no other option than to invest the DNA with the capability of bringing about a human being and also explaining what a human being is in terms of DNA. I think the operative term there is interpretation. Your colleagues, Carolyn, are in a Lutheran University; they may already have another view of organisms from which they interpret.

SCHNEIDER   Correct. Both of them are Roman Catholics.

VAN DER MEER   Even so, they may have another view of human beings from which they interpret the importance of DNA, and this is why they were cautioning you about the focussing on DNA. So that would be an example of how hermeneutics plays a role in the interpretation. That's why I appreciated your paper so much for that emphasis.

SCHNEIDER   One of the biologists is an environmentalist and so he deals not with human DNA — not even primarily human DNA — but with plant DNA; that is his focus.

MULLER   I would like to continue this discussion a little bit in terms of the question of the slight difference that we find within the human genetic material in contrast to that of our closest animal correspondents. In mid-century, Teilhard suggested the concept of thresholds. When we reach a certain level of complexity, a small step may take us over the threshold to manifest a very great difference. He used this to explain the step that takes place from the chimpanzee level to the human level. The question that was put to him in effect by the Catholic magisterium was basically: "Nonetheless, is this a sufficient explanation?" This gets back to the point that Dr.van der Meer raised. I want to add to this the problem faced by science that this is a single instance of this mechanism.

It's difficult for science, it seems to me, to work up testable theories and hypotheses when we deal with what is fundamentally a single instance, a singularity. We end up being left with data that may support a number of different hypotheses, some of which are fully compatible, let's say, with Christian faith; others may not be compatible with Christian faith. There will be a number of issues like that which we will have to face where we may never have the data that would allow us to make a distinction here. Yet we have to move ahead and make a decision, because some kind of decision is necessary. How else can we conduct ourselves ethically? Religiously, we also must look at things we decide or do not decide. How are we going to orient ourselves to the world? It seems to me that we always have this question. Someone can always come up with a suggestion for a mechanism why such a little change on the molecular level creates such large changes on the macroscopic level. It's very much like the butterfly effect in chaos theory, as it were.

BERTRAM   Could I interject a follow-up question? At a lay level, I had a question similar to Carolyn Schneider's as I was reading the papers of Earl Muller and Jitse van der Meer. We have the gene — I probably tend to visualize genes as things you can see. We don't have — perhaps even the smartest people who map the genome — the history that that gene is going to have. This may involve the interaction of proteins and so on that we spoke of. But there's no way of knowing what almost infinite possibilities lie in the future until that gene has a chance to play out that history.

I wonder if this isn't a kind of originism: if we can somehow locate the origin of this thing we have implicit in it a way in which we can figure out what will be explicated from it in time to come. But we don't have this implicit way. The game has to be played out. When the Cardinals faced the Atlanta Braves everyone in his right mind said that the Cardinals didn't have a chance. Did we fool them! That's a limping analogy, but I wonder if there isn't a fixation among people like Dawkins, materialists, who concentrate on the source and ignore the complicated possibilities that might ensue. We have no way of observing them until they've happened. Does that make sense?

VAN DER MEER   Yes, it makes a lot of sense. May I give an example of what you just said to make it more concrete? Biologists know that genes have all sorts of influences on animal behavior but we cannot move theoretically from a description of the activity of genes influencing animal behavior to a description of the behavior of the animals. This is becoming more widely accepted among biologists as a form of non-reductionism whereby we can look at organisms at different levels of complexity. I am just mentioning the genetic and behavioral ones. Each level needs its own irreducible language and descriptions, concepts and theories.

This refers directly to what Earl Muller mentioned, namely, that we can't wait for the biologists to solve all their problems on the genetic level because we have to make ethical decisions. If this is the case, as I'm saying now, we can look ahead and make those decisions. We don't have to wait for biologists to figure out all the genetics. We have to consider in some cases what genetic effects are important. This does not determine the content of decisions we have to make. I hope that illustrative of what you said.

BERTRAM   Yes. It helps.

SCHNEIDER   I'd like to ask a question of Earl Muller. It's not really a question; I am asking you to be conversation-partner on some issues that your paper raised for me. In your paper (see page 78) you talk about shifting paradigms. In the last few sentences of the first paragraph you trace the history and look for the roots of secularist-humanism in the religious wars of the sixteenth and seventeenth centuries which concretely called into question Christianity's claim to be a redemptive religion. You also mentioned that modern science was developing at the same time and provided an attractive focal point for an alternative world view.

When I read that I thought of the problem of evil again. It seems what bothered people of that time which led to secularist humanism was evil. It's a pattern that I've seen preparing for this conference and reading science. It comes back to the problem of evil. Here the secularist-humanists will say: "Well, Christianity doesn't help us. It does not solve that problem for us. So we're going to try to solve it scientifically or secularly through other means." I am looking for more reflection on the basic nature of the problem of evil. It comes up in Dawkins; it came up in Darwin's view. He turned to secular humanism, not because of his scientific achievements, but because his daughter died. The concept of the survival of the fittest becomes problematic. The notion of DNA being selfish comes back to the question that there may be evil or sin at work in all of the processes. Does that make sense?

MULLER   It makes a certain amount of sense. It seems that on the felt level the religious wars created an immense problem, because both sides of the dispute, Catholic and Protestant, were claiming a salvific message and were proclaiming a God of love. But that proclamation was not manifest in their actual behavior. This has been a problem for Christianity throughout the centuries. It's the type of response the Jew will give to the Christian who asks: "Why don't you believe in Christ?" They respond: "When Christians believe in Christ, i.e., when Christians begin to live out in their lives what they claim about Christ, we will believe too."

It's an issue for which a solution has been given, but even those to whom it has been given — I'm thinking of the power of the Spirit — are themselves struggling to fully integrate that solution into their lives. Constant scandal is given. The response to the things that the secular humanist tries to find as alternatives is to point out that for all of the religious wars between, say,

Catholics and Protestants, we do not have the utter devastation that was and is perpetrated by the ideologies of modernity. The various Communist regimes would be one instance. A utopian understanding of the world based on non-Christian premises leads naturally to the extermination of all those who do not agree.

SCHNEIDER   Survival of the memes?

MULLER   Yes. This is a constant issue which underscores the need for an apologetics or a proclamation of the Gospel always to be accompanied by a continual renewal within of those doing the proclaiming. When that takes place, there is more fruit. That's not particularly surprising. The solution provided by Christ is attractive to the extent that it is made manifest in the lives of those who proclaim it.

SCHNEIDER   That leads to my second question. In your paper (see page 84) you talk about the age of the earth being formed much earlier than humanity's presence on the earth. In my Introduction to Theology class for freshmen I start with creation and then talk about vocation. I try to tell them that human beings have a vocation as human beings to care for the earth. The shape that vocation takes is different in each person's individual life, but the basic vocation of humanity is the same: to care for this earth. But as I read this, I realized the earth was here for many millions of years before humanity was here and it did just fine. So what are we here for? It leaves me with that question: what are we here for?

MULLER   Let's go back to the Babylonian myths and other myths that provide the historical context for the Genesis narratives. A common theme is that human beings are created for the service of the gods. They take over the jobs that the gods and goddesses got tired of doing. It was an issue of tending the garden or herding the sheep used as sacrifices that provide something for the Pantheon. The Genesis account is very curious in that it strips away that understanding of why humans were created. They are still tending the Garden but the tending of the Garden is finally for themselves because they're the ones who enjoy its fruit. Genesis leaves us there in terms of why humans were created. As we move through the Old Testament it's clear that humans owe a debt of service to the Lord. But it's also clear that the Lord does not need that service. I think we can say the same thing vis-a-vis the earth. The earth does not need our service. As you said it can take care of itself. Our caretaking of the earth is for ourselves. This corresponds to the shape of the Genesis narrative as we have it in its historical context.

Having said that, the question arises: what is the significance of the relationships between the history of the earth, which is long beyond imagining before humans ever appeared on the scene, and humanity itself. There are a number of different imaginative frameworks we can provide for answering this question. Obviously a more atheistic or secular humanist answer would be "well, finally there is no particular significance except for ourselves." We find this in a Carl Sagan who argues that our world is utterly insignificant for the universe; it's only significant for us. This says that significance is something that we ourselves endow on the things important to us.

Another approach we could take — this is the one taken by Teilhard — is to look at the world dynamic and understand the emergence of humankind as its high point. To do this we need a framework in which we can see, rather than sheer randomness, a teleology at work, producing occasionally more complex structures that may catch hold and become self-replicating. This in turn gives us a certain dynamic of self-stability that allows for development. That imaginative framework, or the choice we make in that regard, comes back to the issue: "Gee, we have the single instance; and we're never going to have data to be able to decide which framework is the best fit." The question then becomes: are we going to understand this in terms of the faith perspective or not? Taking a faith perspective, seeing the world process producing Jesus Christ gives the believer confidence that the axis of development for the world process is indeed through humanity and that it has its culmination in Jesus Christ, not simply in humanity. At this point I would be shoulder to shoulder with Teilhard while recognizing the problems of getting any non-believer to accept this teleology within the world process. There is this issue of world views that you (van der Meer) brought out nicely in your paper. It's going to determine what we do here in what kinds of questions we'll be asking.

KEEFE   If I may add a caveat there, one might dispute interminably what Teilhard meant or didn't mean. The question immediately arises: when we look upon Christogenesis as the meaning of evolution, we have the chicken-egg problem — which came first? Is the explanation evolutionary or is the explanation Christological? Does Christ transcend the evolutionary process or does the evolutionary process transcend Christ in such a way as to be the explanation of Christ, in the sense that Christ is somehow an inevitable product of evolution left to itself over a period of four or so billion years? The difference between the two is enormous. In the end it is remedied by Augustine's answer which I cite in my paper: these things indeed happen but they do not happen without the Christ.

The Teilhardian notion of the process of evolution is that it is, of course, Spirit-driven, which it is undoubtedly is. But is the Spirit sent to give the Christ or is Christ sent to give the Spirit? There lies the entire difference between Christianity and its alternatives. If the Spirit is here on some free-flowing basis which is not Christological then obviously we have a non-incarnate, and in some sense non-historical, transcendence of history by which it is driven willy-nilly. If we have the dynamic rest upon the Christ who is immanent in history on a free basis then we have a completely different process which is inherently free. It cannot be the object of scientific curiosity such as drove Teilhard. If he was right, he could not possibly have been curious about what he was right about.

VAN DER MEER   I would like to see if I could add a dimension to the developmental view that you, Earl, suggested, where you see Christ as the outcome of the process of evolution, connecting it with the theme of the workshop, a theology of the human body. Perhaps I could begin by saying "there's the scriptural expression which says that the human body is a temple of the Holy Spirit." One of the things that means for me is that in itself it is a reason to take care of my body. Analogous to that, I look upon taking care of the creation in the same way, namely, perhaps also for my own good, but primarily for the glorification of God who created it all. This is a different, maybe complementary way, to what you suggested. One can have people who are, say, materialists who come to the conclusion that the only reason why one has to take care of the creation is for ourselves. We can answer: this has another purpose, namely, the one I just mentioned. This also takes care of the problem of time that you (Carolyn Schneider) introduced. This includes the idea of the enormous amount of time during which the earth was going quite fine without us. We have that problem not only when we consider geological time; even if we had always been around we would still have the same problem in terms of the immensity of space. There's so much in outer space that we cannot reach and take care of, to put it mildly, we would have the same problem. But humans can be seen as created simply for the sake of wondering about it all and giving glory to its creator.

BERTRAM   I will begin with a reflection on what was said thus far. This reflection is not comprehensive. It doesn't comprehend the whole of what was said before, but a single line of thought bears highlighting. The problem of evil has been mentioned by several of the essayists. Darwin was mentioned in the same connection. From what I know of early post-Darwin history, little was made of that in the Victorian Age. It has been mentioned more as research about Darwin continues. I'll formulate the question as a theologian coming out of that post-Darwin history: can a design that is not benign still be divine? The classical formulation of the so-called problem of evil is a problem of God. It was formulated by Epicurus in the form of a logical trilemma with God as the target.

If God is neither able nor willing to prevent evil (that was his fourth proposition) why do we call him God? That was Epicurus' way out. His choice was the choice of atheism. I have a hypothesis about Darwin and, if anybody wants to address it later on, that's fine. It was pointed out that Darwin lost his daughter. He himself was not well most of his life. Whether that has anything to do with this biographically I don't know. As I understand Darwin, he's not opposed to design anymore than Dawkins is. Darwinism is a teleology. In fact I am amazed that evolutionists use natural selection almost as a substitute for the Creator; they use it grammatically as the subject of the sentence: natural selection does this; natural selection does that! I know they'd be nominalist enough to say that's just a way of speaking, but natural selection seems to be imputed with agency — it does things. It's like sociologists who speak about society doing this; society doing that."

I was trying during the coffee hour to recall the subtitle of *The Origin of Species*. I think that after the colon it read: *By Means of Natural Selection Or the Preservation of Favoured Races in the Struggle for Life*. It sounds a lot like a secular version of the debate between the Arminians and the Calvinist Orthodox at the Synod of Dort, the "favored races." Since the Enlightenment at least, if I am correct, the opposite of benign is evil, but evil has come to take on a particular profile as well, characteristic of modernity. Evil is not just the opposite of good, but evil is partiality, evil is inequity, inequality. It's not that there is no design, it's that the design does not favor all races, or, within a single race, all people. Carolyn Schneider alluded to that last evening. Whatever is in charge of the universe does not seem to favor even all human beings equally. There is design but it seems to be prejudiced. I think that, especially when we're dealing with the question of the bodily, as laypersons standing on the sidelines watching folks who are interested in gene therapy and so on, we are, if nothing else, interested in "leveling the playing field." That is a pragmatic response to the problem of evil so defined.

ANDREWS   I would like to take advantage of a note that
I got from Carolyn Schneider. I want to make a comment in the hopes that
somebody will respond to it. At the first meeting I came to Bob Bertram was
moderator, as he is now. I'll never forget his statement: "Well, there's a lot
of speculation in theology." Father Brungs, at the beginning of this meeting,
said that from the papers it seems as if we're getting good at stating the
problem but we don't have *the* solution. The theme of this Workshop is *A
Theology of the Human Body*. As an amateur in this business, I would like to
see something that I read about in the textbooks on religion and science. I
would like a kind of a model that tries to put "the body" and the brain together with one's spirit or one's soul together with the Holy Spirit. A flow
diagram or a kind of tabulated list would be helpful to me.

The model that impresses me and helps me in my thinking is Avery Dulles'
book, *Models of the Church*. Only the second, Fr. Keefe, is the Body-of-Christ
model. The last two models he gives are things I am beginning to see in Ian
Barbour's book on the latest thinking on models of God and nature. His
latest model is the Church-as-Servant model, the Pilgrim People model. We
are a Pilgrim People marching towards some end. What end we are seeking
is clearly something called Teilhard's Omega Point. By the way, while I'm
thinking of that word, I would like to have one of the essayists explain to me
what they think Teilhard's Omega Point is.

I also picked up a book by a Father O'Grady in which he speaks about six
models of Christ. He lists them as the Incarnation of the Second Person of
the Blessed Trinity, the mythological Christ, Jesus the liberator, a man for
others, Lord and Savior, the Human Face of God. It doesn't remind me so
much that there's speculation in theology, but that there's an evolving or
developing notion of what we really ought to cling to. For example, there
was the notion that we belong the Body of Christ model. There was an earlier notion in medieval days — it extends now into some circles — that we are
part of God who is a Ruler in a Ruler-Kingdom. We are beholden to Him.
It's like the Jewish-God, a Person who makes it hard for us. If we do the
right thing, fine; if we don't we're going to suffer.

I hope that some model will surface. I know enough about research papers
physicists and theologians publish. They are sophisticated because they're
written for those in the same profession. There comes a time, however, when
these papers are made accessible to the "laity." I'm talking about people who
want to understand it. Eventually some priest or minister has to preach that
this is the way one ought to think. It ought not to be something that is so
old that it is obsolete; there's new thinking going on.

In my own personal life I've studied the Creed and asked: "Do I believe this?" I have no problem with the first point: I believe in God, etc. When I get to "I believe in Jesus Christ, the Son of God," I say, "Look, that's difficult because it's a biological interpretation." The word "son" has a biological meaning for me. God's a spiritual being. "Son" implies a biological relationship. I then say: "don't worry about it. Go on and think of other things." Then I got a book by Karl Rahner in which he mentioned the same problem. This recognized theologian had the same problem. He didn't say the words "Son of God" were wrong. He merely said that it didn't make him happy to think about it. If people want to think about the Son of God, fine, but I have another one. I see that Christ, the Messiah, is the final, unsurpassable Word of God's self-promise to humankind. For me, that says it all. That tells the whole story; that tells me about a Christ-driven evolution. If someone here, having thought about the problem of the notion of the human body and of the spirit, has a quick model they're thinking about, I'd like to hear it.

FORD   I'd like to direct a question to Michael Hoy. On the penultimate page of your paper, Jesus Christ appears for the first time. You mention a "new creation." There's no reference that I could find in your paper to creation, only to new creation. Let me pose a related but perhaps second question. You mention creation in the word "creationist." You commend evolutionary sociobiologists for perceiving what is at the root of the creationist argument. This isn't apparent to me. You commend them for dismissing the creationist argument, but I don't see "creation" in your paper.

HOY   Thanks for raising the issue because it is central to much of my argumentation. It corresponds in part to Fr. Keefe's paper and it gives me an opportunity to respond to Frank Andrews. First, beyond some of the creationist argument there is a concern for a look at the minutia of creation. Let me highlight what is the heart of your question. Is the creation good? Do I articulate that anywhere in the paper? Yes, but in only one place. It's not in the place where you picked up on the creationist issue. I said: "To be sure, there may a worthwhile argument that would not simply be splitting theological hairs (or biological chromosomes) on whether human beings are sinful in their 'nature and essence' or whether their nature reflects a 'horrible, deep-seated, and indescribable corruption' through sin. Perhaps that is what lies behind Rolston's complaint that "the natural world is being negatively judged," — remember that's his criticism of the Darwinians whom he doesn't see as having any kind of view of life that is beyond negativity. In my estimation that doesn't seem to be the real thrust of Rolston's argument. I continue: "Rolston, as we will see, is more interested in placing the *Homo sapiens* on a pedestal of evolutionary achievement different from what one might encounter in the rest of nature." I am taking *Homo sapiens* off the pedestal theologically.

The whole discussion here reflects a serious dispute within the Lutheran camp itself in the *Formula of Concord* between the Gnesio-Lutherans and the Philipists who argued over the reality of creation itself, specifically, the doctrine of sin. Is it sinful to be a human being? The Gnesio-Lutherans said "yes" and the Philipists said "no." The *Formula of Concord* came down heavily on the side of the Philipists, saying, "no, the creation of God is good in essence, in nature and essence. But it has become corrupted by the Fall." In the larger picture, my whole paper, in essence, talks about creation. I think it talks more about creation than Christology per se. The first article in the Creed focuses on: how does the Creator, God, who brought all things into being, continue his creation? My answer: is through the creative process of accountability. That's where I embrace in essence the Darwinian biologists who at least want to talk more about the idea of not being unleashed in total freedom. God continues to hold his creation accountable. That gets to the heart of my comment last night. I want to support and clarify, when I talk about theological determinism, that no part of creation, no part of reality, is apart from the dynamic of God being involved in that process.

Let me refer to Father Keefe's paper. I don't have a Christological base that speaks to the idea of creation through Christ. I'm content to leave creation in the first article of the Creed to God the Creator almighty. Are all things created through Christ? That's a tough issue for Lutheran theology. I see Christ as the solution to the problem of accountability. It keeps the emphasis in Christ's coming through his own birth. This brings me to what I want to raise with Frank Andrews: Christ is the only "part" of the deity that was born into this world. The work of Christ in the New Testament, as I see it, focuses on the aspect of Christ who has come as a response to the problem of a fallen humanity that needs to find a way to be raised out of its accountability into having Christ be the response for that accountability.

Frank Andrews talked about not liking "the Son of God" because it's biological. I like the title "Son of God" precisely because it is biological, because it identifies Jesus the Christ with the truth of our biology. He becomes part, He becomes "flesh," one flesh with human beings in his birth: *Sarx egeneto* in John! He shares the dimensions of that one flesh and sees to it that that flesh is put to death so that we may through him be raised to new life. That's why I gravitate in that direction. That is an issue of some disagreement. I don't view Christology as necessarily having preceded creation. If it does precede creation, all that becomes evident for Christ — as Father Keefe raises in his Second Adam — is more of an unveiling or revealing of what has been all along. I don't see having things revealed as something we need. We need to be redeemed from our problem. Perhaps Father Keefe might respond to this.

KUHL   I didn't hear the introductions to the papers so maybe this has already been addressed. First I want to comment on a previous discussion about the vocation of humankind. I have a question for Father Muller. The human genome work demonstrates how all bodies — all of living creation — is interconnected. We can talk about the distinctions within the genome and with other creature's genes, but we can also talk about the connectedness. That might be an important ingredient to consider in a discussion of vocation. Humankind exists not as independent from the whole of creation, but more as a representative or advocate of the creation before God. I am thinking particularly of Romans 8. That chapter in Paul presents the idea of humankind being created in the image of God, the *imago Dei*. Somehow mankind has this representative quality, character, for the whole creation. It calls for an understanding of bodies as always connected, not isolated, one from another. Can the notion of the human genome be thought of as a reality or a discovery that shows how we are connected, not just how we're separate or different — even though these distinctions need to be raised and identified. That means that human beings become the point at which the whole creation is held accountable to God. This is a theme in Michael Hoy's paper. Accountability becomes an ingredient in the nature of the creation itself because of human beings' contribution, role, place within the created world. It contains that whole idea of interconnectedness.

Related to this is a question to Father Muller on "disponibility." That's a new term for me, one with which I am not familiar. Could you explain what that term means? You talk about it relative to the human as an individual. Then you consider the human community as an essential ingredient of bodiedness too. What is disponibility? Will you explain more about that concept?

GREENLEY   When we think of DNA — an in-phrase right now — we find that DNA is nothing but a xerox machine. It prints things. It depends on what those copied things do, namely, the enzymes and other proteins that makes us different from a monkey. Not all DNA produces enzymes even though it has the same sequence in an animal as it does in man. There is a big difference there.

A rather disconnected idea is this: if we had the ultimate telescope could we see creation going on in the universe because it has so long for the light to get here? That would be a neat to see. Carolyn Schneider listed all the things that make humans different. I learned about forty years in first philosophy class that risibility was something unique to humans. Since we're made in the image of God, thank goodness that we can laugh. That means that God must have a sense of humor. If He didn't we wouldn't be here.

MULLER   I will try to do a number of things: first, I want to respond to Frank Andrews. As others were speaking, I saw a way to tie various things together. Let me begin with one of the responses Michael Hoy made to Frank Andrews in terms of the title "Son of God." In the Old Testament this is tied to the use of "Fatherhood of God," which is far more metaphorical. There are different titles that are given to God, a number of types of metaphors. In some ways the title "Father" is not the most important one. It takes on importance in the Davidic dynasty in the prophecy that has Yahweh saying "he will be my son." It has, again, a metaphorical meaning.

In the Christian era, however, the term takes on a very definitive status precisely because of a biological event. Jesus is conceived of Mary and the very natural question arises — it's a very literal, biological, question — who is the Father? This natural biological question receives a very surprising answer: God is the Father of Jesus Christ. Within the Christian dispensation the title of God as Father or Jesus as Son is very much biologically based. We get a sense of this in Thomas' discussion of the missions of the Son and the Spirit. We get it as well in Thomas' understanding of the relationship of the mission, in this case the Incarnation, with respect to the processions which determine the eternal reality of the Persons of the Trinity. Curiously, he identifies the moment. The Incarnation is the procession of the Son from the Father, but with a temporal term. It is at it were an addendum that specifies this as Incarnation rather than simply as eternal procession. In Thomas' presentation they coincide. That's the first point.

The second point is that this is a model for spirit and body. I don't have an exact solution or a tidy model for this, but it leads into my responses to questions addressed to me. In light of the growth in our understanding of how the brain functions, activities that we previously assigned to an immaterial soul can be understood in terms of the processes of the brain. Is there any remainder for what in previous centuries had been referred to as the soul?

At least a beginning answer to this would be in defining the human individual in terms of the relationship with God. In God we have something in a transcendent direction. We say that there is a dimension to the human individual that corresponds to that transcendent dimension which moves toward God. Obviously many things have to be re-thought in terms of, say, the Augustinian or Thomistic understanding of the immaterial soul: memory, understanding, will and so on. Nonetheless we have to speak in terms of this transcendent dimension of the human which makes it possible for the human to be present to God or rather for God to be present to the human being, to enter into covenant with the individual on an appropriate level.

What's required for this transcendent dimension? Let's briefly explore the structure involved in this transcendence. What sort of interface does this have then with brain processes or the processes of the body in general? There's a sense in the modern period that we have to go back and redo that explanation which led to an immaterial soul. I am not going to attempt this re-thinking now. Let me comment on a question that was not addressed specifically to me. Let's look at the notion of the human as the representative of the rest of creation — a constant theme within Christian tradition. We can find roots within the pagan philosophy that preceded Christianity of the notion of the human as the microcosm.

We can find an example of this in Thomas' *Summa*. There he talks about angels first, then about pure matter and, out of pure matter, bodies. Finally he joins the spirit together with body and talks about humanity. It is clear that humanity is his primary interest in the *Summa*. That's the way he has set up the discussion. He uses an Aristotelian framework. We have, then, humanity summing up all of creation both in its spiritual and in its material aspect. This lends itself easily to the notion of humanity as representative of the whole of creation and as bringing creation into the worship of the Lord. Evolution, which talks of the dynamic of the world process leading up to the emergence of humankind, can similarly make a point that creation comes to voice in humankind, a voice that gives praise to the Creator.

What do I mean by disponibility? Availability might be used as a synonym, but it doesn't carry quite the same nuance. At one point Michael Hoy talked about computers and the difference between hardware and software. It suddenly dawned on me that this may provide an apt image of what I mean by disponibility. Let's say that we have a physical system. It's composed of silicon which has certain electrical properties. Yet what we see being done on computers are manifestations of high culture (or a very low culture). This is clearly not something that is going to happen spontaneously. Nonetheless, computers are available; they lend themselves to a manifestation of something. We can say that the physical potentialities present within matter allow for any number of manifestations. There is a certain freedom involved here.

I very much liked Father Keefe's treatment at a prior ITEST meeting, of the discovery of freedom even in the most basic units of matter. It's precisely this play, this characteristic of matter, which lends itself to a transcendent dimension. This, I think, is the first and primary characteristic that goes into building a foundation for a theology of the body. An older metaphysics refers to the body as an instrument of the soul. That's a way of speaking of this reality. Recognizing the freedom of matter, its availability for expressing something else within itself that it itself would not produce if it were left to its own devices, is something we must cope with.

BERTRAM   Could I ask another layman's question? When I read that I was taken by the metaphor which words like "disponible" are.

To settle my own mind on what it meant — at least temporarily — I thought it was like disposable income. The salary check comes in and one spouse says we don't have money for that because that's already budgeted. That's designated income. That's going to the utility company and so on. Finally, if God is gracious, there is some left over and we say that's disposable. We have some freedom, some play. Would that analogy fit?

MULLER   That's all I mean by "disponible." I think the analogy fits. All sorts of things are causally determined. Gravity means that if we step off a cliff we fall down. That's not disposable. Though actually quantum mechanics allows for a disposability even in that case because it is statistically possible, even if astronomically unlikely, that all of the atoms of our body would be simultaneously moving in a single direction, in which case we float. Jesus' walking on the water would be such a case. Quantum mechanics can handle that. There is that play available within material reality to allow for that kind of event. Still, there are physical realities involved there that establish frameworks in which this play, this freedom, operates.

SCHNEIDER   I want to address to Dr. van der Meer. The title of your paper is *The Body and the Bible* [this was the original title]. When I saw the title, my first question was what is the body in the Bible? Is there only one way of looking at the body in the Bible or many ways; is there a development of the "theology" of the body in the Bible? You speak of a holistic dualism as a way of describing the body in the Bible. I next thought: is there a *body* in science or many different ways of viewing the body? Is there a development of ways of looking at the body in science? You are building two pillars and trying to bridge them. What are the pillars with respect to the definition of the body. Are we people in the science world or people in the biblical world, because that was a different culture from the one we have now. Which pillar are we near, or are we somewhere on the bridge?

VAN DER MEER   That's a difficult question. I am sure that if you look at the history of thought about the body you would see a development not only in science but in general as well. It may be that the model with the two pillars separates the thinking about the body too much. It is just a metaphor to try to think easily about what I am attempting. When we think about the human body, we see that it's a totality in itself. We might talk about different ways of looking at the human body that might hold things together better. One way looks at the body simply as a material entity. But there are a number of other dimensions. The obvious one would be a religious dimension. There is also an aesthetic aspect and an expressive aspect to the human body. Interestingly, only one biologist that I know of has ever addressed that aspect, a German biologist named Adolf Portmann. He studies the role of facial expressions, not only in humans but also in animals.

I suppose we could say that those two pillars really reflect only two dimensions — maybe not even two dimensions. One pillar refers to a revealed source of knowledge about the human body. The other represents what we know scientifically about it. Biologists or physicists look at the human body usually from only one point of view. We'd have to go, say, to a psychologist or someone else to get the other dimensions. In that sense I think you are right. It's a very limited approach. I would agree with that. I guess, however, that we have to keep in mind the problem that I set myself in my paper, that is, to see how the two kinds of knowledge — the one we get from revelation and the one we get from science — can somehow be related. More specifically I was asking: how is the religious knowledge we have about ourselves relevant as a guide in understanding the natural knowledge of the human body? Does that answer your question?

SCHNEIDER   It begins to. Behind my question is the realization that the people who wrote the Bible, when speaking about the body, are speaking out of their own way of viewing the natural world. I have a difficult time thinking of everything that's in the body as part of the revelation of God in a direct sense. We don't live in that same culture as they did. Yet on the other hand we say that faith has something to say about the human body even if we look at the human body from a current scientific perspective.

VAN DER MEER   I see what you are asking. This is one of the challenges that I want to put on the floor. What kind of authority does this knowledge possess? Does it have any authority to support it? This relates to a comment made by Frank Andrews about whether or not the expression the Son of God is meaningful or not. We can say that it's a metaphor." That is what it is. But metaphors refer to real knowledge. This raises the question: are we free to use any kind of metaphor to describe the reality of the human body, let's say, or are we bound to use the kind of metaphors that we find in the Bible? I don't have an answer to that. I want to put that on the table here as a challenge. After all the Bible claims to be a guide to life, in the moral and religious sense.

Since we are beginning to understand better the unity of natural life, I don't think we can avoid having to address the question of what revelation means for the more natural understanding of the human body. We have to deal directly with the question of these people living in a particular culture and looking at the body in a particular way. Why should that be authoritative for us or why should that guide us?

BERTRAM   One aspect of your question, as I understand it, is this: when biblical people of whatever age were referring to something like the body, that need not be *toto caelo* an altogether different avenue of knowledge. That was their equivalent of what scientists do; they were responding to data. It does not mean that it may not have been inspired. That would, if true, make it one eligible candidate among "scientific" views of the body. Did you mean that in your question?   (SCHNEIDER: Yes.)

EVERETT   Having mulled over Frank Andrews' question asking for models for proper thinking about the body, I think that in science we need models. We use models to order our data and interpret them. Science studies things that are here and now. Theology concerns itself — whether we are speaking of the body or whatever — with things that are not necessarily here and now. Father Keefe's paper suggests that for much of what went on, let's say, at the Fall, we weren't really present and have no data. Any thinking that we do theologically, whether it is about what brought us to a present fallen state or what the Omega point will be, is going to be strictly metaphorical and analogical thinking. There is no way of checking on whether our model, analogy, is starting to limp. Unfortunately the human habit of thinking comes out of trying to interpret the here and now and out of our habit of model building in the present. We build a theological model and consider it cut and dried with no way of checking whether it's right. We end up with graven images that lead to religious wars and misery.

The only way of checking out a theological model or theological thinking about the body in the relationship of humankind to God is waiting one or two hundred years to see what comes out of the practical application of that theological construct. It may be faster now. This is especially true in pastoral caring and in the way people live. It is true also of the development of culture under the influence of that theological construct. God forbid that anybody should tell me from the pulpit how I should think.

KEEFE   I want to reply to some considerations that Earl Muller drew. Then I'll return to some of the points Frank Andrews raised. There is a certain need for caution in looking to any physical basis for freedom. Father Muller cited a paper in which there is a question of the physical and biological basis of freedom. Maybe it was something Dobzhansky wrote. It has been supposed since the time of Heisenberg's development of the uncertainty principle, on the basis of quantum mechanics and the Copenhagen interpretation, that somehow or other the indeterminacy, the impossibility of discovering the simultaneous speed and position of a particle, is the basis of talking about freedom. Freedom, as it's used within the Christian religious tradition, speaks of a purposive direction towards a goal. Freedom involves a decision, one which is not simply a choice between oranges and apples. Nonetheless freedom rests on a commitment, the ultimate commitment which is freedom in the Kingdom of God. It is a commitment which is absolutely exhaustive of the person and therefore irrevocable.

We see this imaged within the sacramental realm of Catholicism and the irrevocability of commitment to marriage, Orders and so on. That has little to do with the statistical contingency upon which quantum mechanics rests. It is entirely true that whether innately, as the Copenhagen interpretation supposes, or merely by the conditions under which observations must take place if it is to take place at all, we cannot determine the simultaneous speed and location of a sub-atomic particle. That says nothing about freedom; it says something about the contingency of things as they are. We either like the Copenhagen system, which reduces finally to a Buddhist sort of universe, or we can simply say that insofar as we try to investigate anything we cannot avoid disturbing it. This does not mean not that reality is random, as Niels Bohr and the Heisenberg school supposed, but that there are limitations to our ability to measure. That doesn't mean that reality is itself random. This matter, however, can be debated indefinitely.

In any case we're dealing with a notion which is capable of statistical analysis and quantum mechanics is adequate so that it was possible to enter into wave mechanics a few generations ago. I don't know what they're doing now. We can look upon a particle as a wave function; we can refract it, diffract it, treat it simply as a wave. Newton knew that and we have been building on it ever since. It does not all give us any intimation of what freedom may be.

We are not committing ourselves to a notion that the atom or sub-atomic particle is a person capable of love or hate, or anything of the sort. To suppose that this is suggested, in some sense a combination of such orientations and such commitments, is something against which we must guard. This is true particularly insofar as contemporary physics, despite Gödels incompleteness discoveries, still thinks in the eighteenth century models of necessary truths. We may slowly be moving out of this now but nonetheless the ordinary physicist, the ordinary scientist, looks upon truth as something which is innately necessary. If it weren't necessary, it would not be true.

Can we find a model to think about the body or to think about the various things in the field of speculative theology? Frank Andrews mentioned Father Dulles. Thirty years ago or so he wrote his book on models of the Church. From within the context in which he wrote, which is the Catholic tradition of a sacramentally visible Church, it is an unfortunate idea because a visible Church is visible as one. It's not visible in terms of the immediately suggested simile of the seven wise men and the elephant. Each examined a different part of the elephant and announced his findings. The elephant remained an elephant despite one of them examining the leg and thinking it was a tree; others examined the tail, the trunk, and arrived at different conclusions. Indeed it was part of the elephant, but when they got it all together and added up all that they had described, they didn't come up with the elephant.

The models, when added together, do not come up with the Church. This is something from which Dulles has recently moved away but many of his disciples have not. Models suggest that what we are trying to understand is not capable of being grasped in its totality. This is true at least if we're referring to models in the sense in which the term has come to be used. "Model" does not really cut it. In reply to the quandaries which Frank Andrews raises, I think, to discover what body means, for example, we have best go to where this term occurs in Scripture and see what it means within the tradition and the meditation upon that meaning which has been handed down to us through the Fathers of the Church, the Councils and so on.

This is a reliable basis upon which to rest one's speculation. Otherwise we're likely to be reading each other's books as you suggest, talking to each other, but not talking about the reality. The reality is the tradition, the revelation which comes to us over the course of history. We have to rely upon that history at some point; we have to suppose that the revelation indeed is given, although I believe that people such as Elizabeth Johnson at Fordham have put the very idea of revelation in question — where I suppose God can be named anything because no name fits him. If this were the case we would indeed have a problem, as Frank Andrews suggested there is, about the word "Son." There has been a great deal of investigation of the meaning of that term within the Christian tradition. For instance Arius notoriously decided that God could not have a son because God is incapable of genetics, replication and so on. Yet the tradition insists that Christ referred to his Father, referred to him as God, referred to himself as the Son. I am not going to get into the exegetics of this; it's beyond me and in any event I'd rather deal with the tradition itself as it's mediated within the worship of the Church.

Let me speak to that business of "Son" and the problems that, say, Rahner has with it. This takes me back to the great difficulty of letting one's theology rule ones doctrinal position. Rahner was guilty of that in his great work, a rather small book on the Trinity. He argued — and he is not the first to do so and undoubtedly will not be the last — that God has one substance and must therefore be one person. We get this position from Boethius back in the fifth or sixth century. He was killed by an Ostrogothic king for reasons that are obscure. But before he passed on to a better world, he summarized pretty much the metaphysical tradition down to his time. This included the notion that the person is an intellectual substance. In later theology, after the doctrinal definitions, we'd say subsistence.

This raises Rahner's problem: can there be real attribution of Person to God which would not make God mono-personal? The pagan gods, insofar as they claim to be absolute, — in the myths none of them really are — are absolute as mono-personal. As Genghis Khan used to remark while raiding most of

Asia, "There is one God; therefore there should be one Khan." Rule is mono-personal. But the Lord has said: "It should not be like that among you." The model for the exercise of authority always being divine, pagan authority, is always monarchic, one rule. This means that authority is engaged in the sup-pression of the authority of everybody else, since there can only be one boss. There's a notorious TV program now whose theme is "There can only be one" (*Survivor*). If that's the case, we can drop Christianity.

We have the revelation that Jesus is the Son. What does that mean? For a long time it wasn't grasped, but there is a relation between the Father and the Son that is mutually implicatory. The notion of God the Father was read in somewhat Old Testament terms to mean that God is in charge of all that is. The reference was patriarchal, still monarchical. But with Origen in the first half of the 3rd century, it became clear that the Father is eternally Father because eternally He generates a Son. The Cappadocians built on that and did what they could to distinguish what it would be to be a Person with-in a triune God. The doctrine of the Trinity was long in place.

From the first century we were baptized in the name of the Father, the Son and the Holy Spirit. This, however, had not been intellectually absorbed. What's happening is the intellectual conversion that follows religious conver-sion. We believe that Jesus is the Lord. We have had to spend the next 2000 years figuring out what that means because we believe it. Questions emerge from belief. They don't ask: Is this true? Assuming it's true, then the questions emerge. We don't answer them by denying the basis on which they stand. Not and do theology! We're confronted with three names that are personal, Father, Son and Spirit, because the Spirit had been declared the subject of equal glorification and equal adoration with the Father and the Son by the Council of Constantinople in 381. The Spirit is also a personal name, because we adore Persons. The interrelation between them was finally worked out with some clarity by Augustine who hit upon then-brilliant idea in conversations with Arians that God, the Person, is relational.

On that basis, Augustine proposed his Trinitarian model in which that in man images God — this is obscure and I will turn it over to Earl Muller to argue further. He and I argue about one. The model he proposes is one which is achieved in worship in which the Father corresponds to the human memory, the Son to human intelligence and the Spirit to the human capacity for love — the will, if you like. This was worked out by Augustine and it firmly distinguishes at once the unity of the mind and (maybe) the unity of God. Yet it is clear that memory is not will and neither of them are intellect. The notion of a reality which is Trinitarian is present to the consciousnesses of each of us. But not on some intellectual basis, only in worship! This is a phenomenological insight and Augustine was quite obviously a phenomenological thinker, one who relied on experience to understand. But this is experience in the Church, which is to say the experience of worship.

I have added a coda which may or may not be legitimate but I'm fond of it because it is mine, namely, that the imaging is fulfilled in covenantal fidelity. That covenantal fidelity is fundamentally Eucharistic worship. Secondarily it is worship which is marriage. In either case, that which images the triune God is the nuptial unity of the human. God is a triune substance. Man is a triune substance whose triunity is actual only on a sacramental basis as sacramentally signed. This takes us into other directions which we don't have the time, nor I the skill, to pursue. Nonetheless, this does seem to me what is meant by saying "male and female He made them, in the image of God He created them." In other words this is a parallelism in the Semitic idiom. It means the same thing; to be male and female is to be in a unit which is the image of God. Now if we want a model, there's a model. It isn't theological; it's doctrinal and scriptural.

In this we understand what it means to be a person. The human exercise of personal responsibility in marriage is an instance of the man, the woman and the covenant they form by their free exercise of authority with respect to each other. It is a unit in which the man has the full authority of humanity as man; the woman has the full authority of the human substance as woman; the covenant has the full authority of human substance but without competing with the full authority of the man and the woman. They do not compete with each other as the members of the Trinity do not compete with each other. We have now a Trinitarian notion of authority, a Trinitarian notion of dignity, a Trinitarian notion of freedom and responsibility.

This, it seems to me, is the doctrine which the Pope is promoting, suggesting, proposing in documents such as *Veritatis Splendor* in which he says that the criterion of morality is man as "in the beginning." He identifies that beginning as Jesus the Christ, but Jesus the Christ revealed to us on the Cross in the institution of the New Covenant which is the "One Flesh" of Christ and the Church. He says in another place that it is community in man which images the community in God. Therefore, I'm not just blaming on the Pope what I have proposed here. It seems to me that this is the pattern for which you are looking. It is a mystery which we image obscurely in a fallen world. Nonetheless, the fidelity of worship is that by which we image God. This is a worship in truth in which we understand that which we worship in participating in the worship, which is instituted not by our feeble fancy but by God himself, by the Father sending the Son to give the Spirit.

ANDREWS   You got me on your side when you started to explain Heisenberg's uncertainty principle so well. I wish I had your words in writing.

MCLEOD   The question was raised about what metaphors we could have for the body. I always thought that the "Body of Christ" was a metaphor until I was told by scripture scholars that that was not true. So I started to research this. Paul says that Christ takes on more than an organic body. We take on a body as a physical body. We take it as we form a body here at this present moment. But Paul is taking body in a corporeal sense, an organic kind of a body. It's hard for us to assimilate what he's saying. We know that we were told to be living members of this body to such an extent that if someone is hurting, like our foot is hurting, the whole body hurts. We apply that to the way we deal with one another. If we find that a member of the body of Christ is hurting, we have an obligation to try to help him or her. It is an obligation of love.

This raises a further issue: if we take this as an organic kind of body, we have to deal with a living form or a living principle. Where do the two come together? Where is the contact between the vital principle and the body? We're still struggling to try to come close to saying what that is. What's the potential of the body? One of the images from Paul that I like is that of the seed and the flowering plant. All we can see at this moment, in this life, is the seed. We're told to take care of that seed. We have to water it, nurture it. The body flowers after death. It's very hard, Paul says, for our human ability to be able to conceive of what that would be. The mystics use another image which I think is very appropriate, speaking about the relationship between the caterpillar and the butterfly, how that caterpillar is suddenly going to be transformed. I'd be curious to find out what the scientists say about the DNA of this caterpillar — what it has within it that it can transform itself.

Can theology speak to science? Science deals with the body and all that the scientists can say is that the body is going to die. It's going to corrupt. Where does it lead? We're trying to say in theology that we have that sense of the risen Christ. He's pointing in that direction, that this is the future and that the body can be transformed. It has that potential. What can cause that potential to be actualized is the power of God that vivifies us in a totally new creation. Our minds are simply befuddled to try to imagine what it is like.

MULLER   Let me return to the issue of Augustine's analogy. It leads in to the real question I had. The revelation that God is love is the starting point for Augustine in his work on the Trinity. The problematic of the *De Trinitate* is: how do we know God? We obviously have to begin examining a love that is accessible to us. The love of God is accessible to us, but we don't recognize it. We have to begin with a love that we do recognize. This love is love of neighbor.

There are a variety of reasons why Augustine turns away from this love of neighbor as the basis for his analogy. Part of the reason has to be the problem of externality involved in the love of the neighbor. The neighbor is external to myself and for this reason does not appropriately image the oneness and spirituality of God for Augustine. However, scripture itself provides an identification that allows us to reformulate the question. The equation is love your neighbor as you love yourself. For Augustine, Scripture itself then establishes an equivalence. On this basis then he turns the analysis to one of the love of self. In examining in that context the structure of self-love, he develops the notion of memory in which the mind makes itself present to itself, understanding in which the mind grasps itself and then the will in which the mind loves itself. Augustine operates from, basically, a structure of self-love.

I'd like to consider an issue which has surfaced several times, most recently with Fred McLeod. It's the issue of the various metaphors that are used. Let me mention a minor point, first. In Paul — certainly in the authentic letters — we have intimations that Paul has a marital understanding of body. 1 Corinthians 6 would be a location where he is comparing the relationship of the individual Christian to Christ with the relationship of a Christian to a prostitute. There he talks in terms of one spirit and one body. location. Another location in the generally agreed upon letters is 2 Corinthians 11:2 where he describes the Corinthian Church as Eve which he, Paul, has presented to Adam who is Christ. These are marital images. That was a side point.

Another issue has come up several times. Armgard Everett asked how we check out a theological model? Jitse van der Meer asked if we are free to use any metaphor? We might also look at page 5 in Michael Hoy's paper. In the second full paragraph he says: "Let us try to teach generosity and altruism." He's quoting Dawkins. "Let us understand what our selfish genes are up to; we may have the chance to upset their designs, something that no other species has ever aspired to." But that does not change nature as we have it in our genes with their orientation toward selfishness and desire. Obviously the point here is the use of an analogy comparing what's happening on the genetic level with what's happening on the moral level. There's some connectivity going on here. There's also a modeling occurring on that level.

We can raise the same issues that Father Keefe raised about seeing human freedom in terms of quantum play. What criteria are being used to control these analogies between different levels. This is why I began with the Augustinian material. Maybe we can judge what genes are doing, not so much in terms of selfish intent but in terms of a self-love. It is a self-love that is appropriate but a self love which is understood as being interchangeable with, but also flowing out of, love of neighbor. What controls our metaphor here? This gets back to what Theodosius Dobzhansky did in terms of conflict, in terms of governing his model. It seems we can work with the model of self-love just as well. That's clearly not what's happening on the moral level. What are the criteria? That's a question you might address, Michael.

HOY   There are several things to say in response. I am not sure we have an answer for understanding the *imago Dei* and its appropriateness. How we do that is critical. Appropriate self-love and good qualities take place in that context. Survival, the aspect of surviving absolutely, is one of them. There are some good creational things that go on. It's a part of human life and it's a part we should embrace and see as part of the creative process. I am probably raising against Dawkins the point that Rolston particularly wants to stress. If our genes are different by nature, selfish, how do we go about the process of teaching ourselves something different? In essence, I simply wanted to highlight that we cannot change the way things are directly if it's a part of the natural reality — the fallen state.

We can't change that reality. But are there things that go on in the nature of that fallen state, like survival? Even if it's part of the genetic reality, is it something to be embraced and to be seen positively? Absolutely. Survival is not necessarily a bad word. Dawkins describes us as survival machines, the phrase he uses to depict us. It's not necessarily a bad word. A degree of self-love can be embraced. I don't know if that answers your question but at least it gets to the aspect that you mentioned — the appropriateness of self-love.

How we understand the *imago Dei* or how we are created in the image of God is an issue. We may want to look at that later. How do we understand the human being? I see the *imago Dei* more as a relational reality between us and God. God has established us in the context of relationship and the nature of that relationship is to a large degree built on the parameters of responsibility, our responsibility to our God. We might explore this as well.

Bob Bertram raised an issue which came out strongly in Carolyn Schneider's paper. When we talk about "whose body," what body are we talking about? Do we take into consideration the larger dynamic of the people who are among the oppressed, who are not lifted up in the context of our discussion? I did my doctoral work in liberation theology, but we would not know it from reading my paper. I think that aspect is a significant component of what we're doing on the body.

BERTRAM   May I pick up on Michael's last sentences: whose body is it? We've been reminded, yesterday and today, that there's another possessor as well: we are the Temple of Holy Spirit; we are not our own. What does that do to whole issue of self-love and other love?

CROSS   We are discussing a theology of the human body. There are similar themes at most ITEST meetings. One of the values in having a session, which focuses only on theology instead of a variety of disciplines, is that theology forces us to take an overview. I felt pressured to try to put things in some kind of order in a larger picture. I am willing to bet everyone here has a scheme of things similar, at least superficially, to the one I have worked out. The unique thing about being a human being is that each of us has our individual, idiosyncratic views. To try to make sense out of the papers and the discussion I am suggesting a hierarchy of disciplines or sciences. [See the chart on the next page] Although I am trained as a psychologist, I still accept the notion that theology is the queen of the sciences. It supervenes all the sciences below in addition to all that they have; and it has one other source of data that these other sciences lack. It has revelation. We think of revelation in terms of Scripture or tradition or an institution which provides interpretation of both Scripture and tradition. It's unique among the sciences, science in the sense of a systematic body of knowledge. Below it is philosophy, the king of the sciences which doesn't have revelation. It has reason. Below that are the empirical sciences; they have empirical data and that's where I'm trained and where I live.

This morning we discussed some models of the Trinity. In our discussion today, it seems that understanding the nature of the divine is a key concept to understanding the deity and essential to understanding where in the divine scheme of things the human body fits. I was struck by a number of these theological models which I see as trinitarian or trichotomous, rather that dichotomous. That comes from some of my own work at this level. I am suggesting here that in fact, if the Godhead is Trinitarian then throughout the orders of nature, in the various perspectives on it, we should see reflections of the Trinitarian involvement. At the level of neurophysiology there is a logical progression, I would argue, from body to mind to spirit. This parallels Father, Son and Spirit. In fact, all of these are parallel [See chart] and all of them represent a logical progression to which Father Keefe was pointing in his paper, the traditional understanding of the progression of the divine Persons. In my own work in cognitive psychology the logical priority is knowing, valuing and choosing. We cannot love what we do not know; we cannot choose what we do not love — an old philosophical dictum that suggests a logical priority. This is the same logical priority that seems to exist in other orders of nature and these other perspectives. So, we can't have mind without body; we can't have spirit without mind.

In the study of the unconscious — a level higher than neurophysiology —

THEOLOGY OF THE HUMAN BODY

THESIS: THE TRUTH OF THREE PERSONS IN GOD IS REFLECTED PERVASIVELY BUT IMPERFECTLY IN CREATION

THEOLOGY	DIVINE PERSON	FATHER	SON	SPIRIT
Observation-Reason-Revelation	Divine Role (Salvation History)	Creator	Redeemer	Preserver
	Mystical Body (New Covenant)	Christ	Church	Saving Love
	Human Relations:	Husband	Wife	Marital Love
	Church Role	Scripture	Tradition	Magisterium
	Theological Virtues	Faith	Hope	Charity
	Sacramental Progression	Conception	Baptism	Eucharist
	Old Covenant	Nature	Mankind	Stewardship

PHILOSOPHY	SUB-DISCIPLINES	EPISTEMOLOGY	AESTHETICS	ETHICS
Observation-Reasoned Speculation	Hegel	Thesis	Antithesis	Synthesis
	Metaphysics	Potency	Act	Freedom
	Philosophical Anthropology	Knowledge	Valuation	Choosing
	Aristotle	Cognitive	Appetitive	Conative
	Faculties	Intellect	Appetite	Will

EMPIRICAL SCIENCE	SUB-DISCIPLINES	FATHER	SON	SPIRIT
Observation - Reason	Social Psychology	Self	Self Concept (The word)	Ideal Self
	Psychoanalysis	Id	Ego	Super Ego
	Evolution of Consciousness	Unconscious	Conscious	Reflective Consciousness
	Hominoid Evolution	Body	Mind	Spirit
	Biological Evolution	Vegetative	Animal	Human
	Psychology of Learning	Instinct	Conditioning	Insight
	Psychology of Motivation	Tropism	Emotion	Sentiment
	Psychology of Decision	Homeostasis	Conflict Resol. Mechanisms	Free Deliberation
	Cognitive Psychology	Sensation	Perception	Higher Cognition
	Physical Psychology	Matter (primordial)	Energy (Big Bang)	Cosmos (evolving)

PROGRESSION(PROCESSION) ----->

Sigmund Freud sees an id, an ego and a superego. The id is a primitive, un-differentiated aspect of the unconscious which then develops an identity, an ego, which in turn develops a superego. At the level of conscious life I have myself; I think about myself and have a self concept. For me, this is the way, as an individual, I reflect the divine nature. God contemplates himself; his idea of himself is a perfect copy of himself. He himself is perfect. His self-concept is the Word, the Son, the basis of all creation, the ideal self. The ideal self for me is the perfection of my nature. The ideal self for the God-head is a recognition of the Godhead's perfection and the love that exists between the Father and the Son. Parallel in philosophy are the major subdis-ciplines of epistemology, aesthetics and ethics — knowing, loving and choosing.

At the theological level I see these parallels between Father, Son and Spirit, between husband, wife and marital love; between Christ, the Church and sal-vific love; between faith, hope and charity; between conception, baptism and the Eucharist; between creator, redeemer and preserver. So my question to professional theologians: do I have these things ordered properly? Do they belong there at all? The amateur wonders a lot.

I'd like to make one other comment about the spirit and about the problem of evil. This has come up in many of our ITEST meetings. I believe it is an effective way of thinking about evil to see it as the absence of good. Maybe Mary Baker Eddy carried that to an extreme but, just as coldness is the ab-sence of heat, I think we can argue that matter has a negative definition, that is the absence of unlimited time and unlimited space. Matter is in fact spirit which is limited. So, the apparent dichotomy and dualism between matter and spirit — there is some possibility of resolving that mystery in terms of a progression. Is there an evolutionary progression by which matter gradu-ally seems to overcome temporal and spatial limitation and to approach the eternal? This is evident in human nature. We are personal life histories based in part on what we do as long as we're intact and integral. This is much truer than it could be for lower orders of biological nature, physical nature. The strong distinction between matter and spirit, which causes so much trou-ble in dualistic models, I think can be overcome by thinking about the onto-logical nature of matter, limited in space and time. It could become less restricted as part of an ongoing process. This helps me to consider the na-ture of the problem of evil.

FORD   I'd like to question Carolyn Schneider about the very last sentence in your paper. There you have a sentence: "As long as there is no discrimination, all approve of genetic testing, public screening as well as somatic gene therapy. All disapprove of eugenics and enhancement of traits." What do these three things mean?

SCHNEIDER   Genetic testing would be the removal of cells and actually testing them to see what the genes are in those cells and whether there are defects and mutations or something amiss with those genes. That's genetic testing.

FORD   To what purpose?

SCHNEIDER   To heal the anomaly. Then public screening is doing that with whole populations where there is a tendency for certain characteristics to show up and where there is a tendency for certain diseases in those populations — also for the purpose of healing.

FORD   For healing the individual, not the descendants?

SCHNEIDER   Yes; that's somatic gene therapy. It does not deal with the cells that are involved in reproduction, only with the other cells of the body. Any healing then would be only for that person and would not be what one could call a disguised form of eugenics. They all disapprove of eugenics. There is a ban on germ-cell therapy which is why all the scientific materialists and the believers believe that genetic research should continue to be supervised by the government. The supervision by the government is seen as good precisely because it can ban certain forms of research or the application of research.

BRUNGS   I have trouble with the word "all" in a statement like that because not all the scientific materialists find eugenics questionable and not all the "questioning believers" would object to eugenics either. It's overstating the situation. Certainly Dr. Richard Seed would have no trouble with eugenics or enhancement of traits or the use of reproductive cells. I question the government's involvement in this for the reason that they will not in the long run hold to these restrictions. They'll find loopholes and they'll find reasons to relax the restrictions — after all restrictions might mean that this country will not be first in some area of research. It seems to be true that not all somatic genetic therapy is confined to the individual. If at a certain point in his or her life a person is cured of a genetic disease, he or she could very well pass the cure on to any future descendants. We're dealing with moving targets. Specific therapies may very well overlap.

SCHNEIDER   I took this information from a chart in a book by J. Robert Nelson. It is obviously a general statement.

BRUNGS   He is clearly overstating the situation and radically simplifying it. Whenever we see "all", or "ever", or "never" in such a statement, we simply should not believe it.

BERTRAM   You may recall that in Michael Hoy's paper he referred to the book by Lewotin, *It Ain't Necessarily So*; the subtitle is *The Dream of the Human Genome and Other Illusions*. I can circulate this short notice that appeared in the *New York Times Book Review*, but let me read one sentence about him. "He cuts a deep swathe through the promise of an end to genetically caused human illness, describing just how tangential this goal is to the sequencing of the human genome." He calls this "fetishizing" the DNA; he's coined the term "genomania." That might be another side of the story.

SIMONI   My question is two-fold. We were talking about creation in general, and man specifically, as the *imago Dei*, in the image and likeness of God. What does it mean then that God became man, specifically became a human embryo, and experienced all the stages of development, nine months in the womb? How does that help us better understand the theology of the body? *Gaudium et Spes*, no. 22, states: "Christ reveals men to themselves." The idea that God became man and went through all those phases should illuminate a better understanding of the human person. What does it mean that Christ became a human embryo? How does this help us develop a theology of the human body?

My other question is related though it may seem a little far-fetched; it relates to our veneration of relics and icons. They're no longer living matter; relics are not living matter, yet we venerate them. There's something that makes icons different from an ordinary piece of wood. How is that relevant to a theology of the body?

ANDREWS   John Cross' intervention was helpful to me and I would like to use his chart for my study group. That's the beauty of a model. We try to abstract from a whole pack of information the characteristics, the attributes, of a thing or a system. Then we try to put this into one easily graspable entity. This allows for an enormous amount of discussion, because now the terms have been defined. The one thing missing is that, as we go up the ladder, we can't use mathematics as we can down at the lower part of the ladder. We can still have relationships; we can still talk about order and things like that. But is there another element to the right of John Cross' listing. That element would contain the connection between individuals in a community, a family or a nation. There is the contribution of the work of the mind in Teilhard's Noosphere. I am confused on this point. Specifically, how would we relate Teilhard's Noosphere, which is a storehouse of knowledge for centuries and will remain constant over time, to evolution? Will it evolve? It's an entity that has a powerful implication for our thinking.

CROSS   It would be in the formulation of ego. No
human being would exist, could exist, in isolation from other human beings.
The particular influence, say, in a Freudian theory of society, comes in the
formation of the super ego, the prohibitory censor that comes from society.
In social psychology the self-concept shows a collective, social influence. We
form our self-concept, according to social psychologists, by comparing ourselves with others. It's a comparative process. Then we compare ourselves
with ideal others to develop our ideal self. Some of these models are focused
on the individual, but some of the models are Christ, the Church and salvific
love. This is certainly a social, collective concept. A husband and wife are the
primary pair of all social life. Theologians can help in stating the Redeemer
relationship, i.e., the extent to which we are redeemed by Christ as individuals and the extent to which we are redeemed as the mystical body. It is
a mystery; I don't understand it very well, but it's related to your question.

STREETER   John Cross suggested that the theologians respond to what he has proposed. He asked if there was anything to this chart?
Was something missing in it? Also, I want to address Fiorella Simoni's
questions on relics, icons, and the embryo who is Christ. As we look at
questions of the human body, we need to ask how the human, in its embodied totality, is revelatory? How is it a form of disclosure? I am asking a
revelation question because the Incarnate Word proposes to reveal the Godhead to us through the human. So the human — this goes back to the question of the embryo — and all the elements of the periodic table are, as it
were, taken in immense love by the divine and configured in such a way as
to be revelatory. We say in the Pauline passage that Jesus is the image of the
invisible God. So, in Christ's embodiment we have to ask what revelatory
message is being shown to us. What is being disclosed. Then, we have to
move to ourselves and ask how the embodiment that we are, male and female, is revelatory or disclosive?

I want to return to John Cross's triad at the bottom of the chart and look at
the anthropology. We must begin to ask if we have an adequate Christian anthropology to talk of body, mind, spirit. This is the typical psychological
three-dimensional designation we see in all the popular literature. Is not
mind and spirit somehow redundant? Where are human emotions in this
triad? I suggest we flesh out (please excuse the pun) the triad a bit to
expand it. We need more room for psycho-somatic reality — organism plus
psyche. "Organism" we all know. The word represents the systems of the
body, lymphatic, digestive and so on. But "psychic" is an energy field within
us. The psychologists and psychiatrists among us would have to speak to that.
It would include the emotional motors, the deliberate and the spontaneous,
and our image making capacity, the dream, as the psychic energy field. That
has to be taken into account because it draws from our embodiment and also

bridges into what we might call the more spiritual functioning of the human being. Under spiritual functioning I would list such things as — what we call in faculty psychology intelligence and will — the intelligent functioning and the value judgments that produce action or decision.

We can, then, begin to use a different triad, and that triad, I suggest is not three things; it's a triple composite. Then we would have psycho-somatic and psycho-spiritual as the continuum which we have called body and soul; then we have to deal with organism, psyche and spirit. Under spirit, we have intelligence and choice; under psyche we have emotions and image: under organism, we have all the systems of the body. That is a different way I would deal with the triad. I would stretch it out; I would make it more complete.

Let us look at relics, icons and the embryo who is Christ. If we're speaking about matter as revelatory, it would seem that God is trying to say something in assuming all the stages of embryonic development, that all of it is like play. It is pure delight! It is revealing that the human is somehow a microcosm of the entire created universe where, within those stages of embryonic development, we have a manifestation of all the levels of life, peaked by consciousness which we share with the angels. We have the whole revelatory play. In relics and icons we have the human or matter being used as a window. We look through this matter or this thing and we see into the realm that it is revealing to us. That's iconic, where the icon becomes a window into the divine. We stand on this side looking on that other side. And so we have this golden glow coming through.

BERTRAM   Father Muller this morning spoke of one way of conceiving the human being in a larger world view — not identified as a part of the Christian tradition — seeing the human being as a microcosm of the whole cosmos. I don't know, Earl, if you're ready to include that in the remarks you are about to make, but I wanted to make that connection.

MULLER   I can bring it in somewhat. Let me consider the various interventions which have raised points that I think may be pertinent to our discussion. There are some themes that may tie all of this together. John Cross' chart is reminiscent of triads that we find in Augustine. Augustine will make the distinction between the Trinity itself, the image of the Trinity that is found within the individual person and "traces of the Trinity" which he sees as being pervasive throughout all nature, including all of material reality. Augustine would be nervous looking at a triad like body, mind, spirit and trying to see this somehow as an image of the Trinity. His objections would be numerous: he would be reluctant to see any imaging in the body as such. His Platonism led him to see only "traces of Trinity" in the body. He would understand the combination that we are involved in — body and mind — as crossing from one level to another. He would be reluctant to see reflections of the Trinity in tying together various levels.

There may be ways to do this, but certainly Augustine himself did not go in this direction. It's appropriate at this point to say that in my discussion of such themes I was criticized by my dissertation director (Father Keefe) who was more than a little nervous about seeing images of the Trinity in something like a psychological analogy. Here we are looking at ontological structures, necessitarian structures, and the God who is freedom itself cannot be imaged in necessitarian structures. This is why Father Keefe moves in the direction of centering his theology on a structure that is free, and specifically the free relationship between a man and a woman. I think there are ways around the objection that Father Keefe raises. Augustine's understanding of the psychological analogy is a structure of love. This is another way of saying this is the structure of freedom as it is found in a single individual.

Within the tradition, theologians in the past have seen traces of the Trinity even in material reality. One reason for this is the principle of causality: a cause causes according as it caused; a cause causes in a way similar to itself. There is the expectation that in all of the things that God has caused, one will see some similarity no matter how distant the cause is to that reality. Thomas argues that from created things we can only know the oneness of God. God, in acting outside of himself, acts as a single principle; nonetheless, in his discussion of creation, of the single act of creation on the part of the one God, Thomas says that the Father creates insofar as He is Father, the Son creates insofar as He is Son, likewise the Spirit. Even in Thomas we find some basis for talking about traces of the Trinity even in material reality.

With regard to Jesus as embryo, I was reminded of the discussions we find in Mercia Eliade's various works: how things are given significance. He was looking particularly at mythological structures. Things are given significance insofar as some god in the past or some hero has performed an action. All subsequent actions of this sort are understood as an imitation of this primordial action. In the Incarnation, we have God, not performing a single action that is imitated, but God doing everything that we ourselves have done. He has been a zygote; He has developed in the womb; He has walked the earth; He has eaten; He has slept. All these then are the actions of divinity, which, if we follow the thought pattern that Eliade suggests, would imply that, within the Christian understanding, everything that a human does has value because it has been done by God himself.

For the veneration of icons, it is important to know what was behind the prohibition of imaging in the Old Testament. Let's look at the older account in Genesis 2. We see that in the act of creating the man and the woman, Jahweh God performs two actions: He shapes earth and then He breathes life into it. Adam is characterized as a farmer, as one who tills the ground, as one who shapes the earth; Eve on the other hand is portrayed as the mother of all the living. When we look at the polemic against the idols in the Old Testament, we are looking at prohibitions of idols: they have eyes but they cannot see; they have ears but cannot hear, etc. They are shaped earth but not alive. For this reason they cannot appropriately image the living God.

The Old Testament which has this prohibition against images describes the human as in the image of God — male and female He created them. There is a tradition that leads from the older account to the more recent account in Genesis 1 in terms of the understanding of the image of God. With the icons we have another step in the development of a notion that things can refer beyond themselves; it's a sacramental understanding. Here we have, even in Old Testament times, the idea that a statue of the king represents the king and that desecration of that "sacrament" is a personal affront to the one thus represented. This carries over into the Christian era. Aquinas will talk of this referring characteristic as undergirding why we venerate the cross, why we venerate objects that in their ultimate reference refer to the Lord himself. In the veneration of the saints, pictures, etc, it's the issue of referencing the person who is honored in this way.

Returning to my original point, I am completely in accord with these triads one discovers. I'm taken with Carla Mae Streeter's insistence on the defini-tion of terms. One of the problems — this is one of the critiques one could make of John Cross' chart — is that almost invariably these triads are formu-lated with a specific agenda in mind. Augustine, in separating memory, un-derstanding and will is, to a certain extent, deliberately looking for triads. We get this in spades in Bonaventure who will take, for example, the seven gifts of wisdom and demonstrate how, within these seven gifts, there is a triadic structure. Yet sometimes we can overlook parts of a reality while looking for and finding some patterning. A typical one, often overlooked, is the realm of emotions in seeing traces of the Trinity. There is no easy way around this problem. In my own patterning, I self-consciously use a Trinitarian-like patterning to ask whether I am overlooking something. Sometimes when we come up with dyads, we might ask ourselves if there is a third thing around. That is simply a device to ask if we're overlooking something in a dyadic structure.

Finally let me explore the question of making the redemption of Christ effec-tive. I make use of the understanding of the modes of humanness; this in-cludes something Father Keefe said earlier about our involvement individual-ly in Christ as guaranteeing our inclusion in the resurrection. What happens in Christ is that all the modes of human existence are taken up into him, modes of the human as individual, as community, as marital. It is exactly their convergence which grounds our involvement in Christ and his resurrection. That's probably all very murky and I'll leave it there.

KUHL   I want to reflect as well on John Cross' chart. I am concerned with the way we think of the goal, the end, or the way we think of salvation. On the chart we have spirit and revelation as the goal to which we are proceeding. In speaking about the human body we may want to re-think that. Might not theology itself have as its end re-embodiment, not revelation, not re-seeing things we overlooked? Revelation might see the necessity of a new embodiment, a new creation, that needs to happen. When Christians begin to speak about God, theology and salvation, it is about how re-embodiment, how re-creation, how new creation emerges. That's why we use the language of incorporation into the Kingdom of God or incorporation into Christ.

The previous incorporation of Christ or God being incarnated into our world means that we must envision the whole of reality we're talking about through the image of bodies themselves, being embodied. We can affirm that whatever else we are, we are our bodies. As Christians we can't speak of ourselves apart from embodiment. By virtue of Christ's coming into this world and taking human form himself we who are incorporated into him are re-embodied in a new and different way. If we think in these terms we avoid a tendency to gnosticize, if you will, what our goal is. What Christianity — what our lives as Christians are about — is the process of being incorporated, embodied, in this new reality. Thinking of that image of "embodied" as an all-encompassing framework, we can think about what resurrection consists in and how central it is in our Christian understanding of things. I want to stress that.

VAN DER MEER   I want to address the meaning of Christ becoming an embryo. Though theology is not my first language, I speak it now and hope that I don't speak foolishness. I want to caution us about trying to see value in created things via the Incarnation for the simple reason we can say: "well, if Christ has assumed the form of an embryo it must be valuable." There are many things Christ hasn't assumed, like marriage. The other side of the coin is not one that we want to follow. It's not so much of a problem because perhaps seeing value in created things would simply be on the basis that they have been created by the Creator rather than to see it specifically in connection with the doctrine of Incarnation. That's a note of caution.

On the other hand, we have to face the problem of evil, because things were not meant to be the way they are, because they weren't created that way. So, what one sees in the creation one has to approach with caution, because it may not have been intended that way. I would like ask: how can we value the creation in the face of this question of evil? Should we perhaps take into consideration more the notion of the need for creation to be redeemed in its entirety? There is a passage in the New Testament where the creation is described as groaning in travail waiting for the appearance of the sons of God. That's another side of this whole problem. That's a question I would like to ask the theologians: if creation needs to be redeemed how can we take it as something that has a value because it has been created?

SCHNEIDER   I am also addressing the question about Jesus *in utero*. It seems to me this ties into what Steve Kuhl said about how Jesus was really embodied because we are really embodied. If he's going to be human He has to be deeply in the flesh, which He literally is *in utero*. That means He has DNA. He has cells. He shares Mary's body with her then. He is completely dependent on her body; He is completely limited. If something had happened to her He would have died too. Later on He does die. He's that limited, like the rest of us. In order for us to be redeemed or re-embodied, to use Steve Kuhl's terminology, God first came to be embodied in us as we are in the "old" body, that being the body of the weakest of us, of the most dependent — an embryo. That means that He had a body with DNA like the rest of us. When we're thinking of genetics that means that He is linked to the rest of creation because DNA is an connecting thing. It's a connection not only with human creatures but also with all other creatures.

BERTRAM   I thought the last comment from Carolyn Schneider was going to contain one more sentence. Since it didn't, let me add it. It's a rhetorical question which may be answered later if anyone is so inclined. A distinction was made in some of the papers for this workshop that has hardly come up in the discussion. We've been speaking of body. We've said almost nothing about a term that almost certainly does not mean the same thing, certainly not in New Testament Greek. That's the word *flesh*. The reason I thought Carolyn was going to mention that just now is that when the Fourth Gospel talks about the Incarnation it says that the *Logos* became not *soma*, body, but *sarx*, flesh. I wonder whether there's some Freudian reason why we're steering clear of that.

KEEFE   To pursue that same question: the Pauline theme that responds to the puzzlement is that of *recapitulation* in the Letter to the Ephesians. The recapitulation has to do precisely with the *flesh* to which you refer. Flesh is flesh by reason of the Original Sin. If we refer to the redemption to understand what the sin is — this is the only way we can proceed — it can only have been the reflex of recapitulation. In my essay [see page 111] I have referred to the sin of Adam as *un*-capitulation, the refusal to be head by which the free unity which is the "One Flesh" is lost. As a result the physical humanity of Adam and Eve simply becomes flesh subject to necessity, physical causality and so on. The recapitulation, then, is that by which the flesh is overcome finally in the death of Christ.

The resurrection is simply resurrection into that pneumatic existence to which the flesh points, but which it does not itself possess. Thus, the recapitulation covers the entirety of the fallen condition, not simply the human, but insofar as headship refers to the entire creation, the starry universe — all of it, whether we're dealing with galaxies or DNA — has its free unity restored. It's no longer subject to the disintegration which is flesh. It is given life instead of being oriented toward death.

The final significance of *flesh* is simply that it is a sign only in the context of the redemptive work of Christ. It points to that which it is in Christ, the Spirit which has been given life through Christs' gift of the Holy Spirit. Recapitulation is the term Paul uses. Irenaeus makes a great deal of this in the *Adversus Haereses*. It's a way of looking at Christ's relation to all of creation. It includes particularly his Incarnation, which in Greek is *ensarkikos*, following up on what you said about the context of flesh being different from that of body. By becoming flesh, He entered into this broken, dying situation, overcame it as the Creator immanent in the fallen creation, which immanence can only be that of a recapitulation, a restoration of all things in Christ.

This is one of the problems of talking about man as microcosm. It forgets that man is the head of the universe; he is not a reflex of it. The latter gets it backwards. The universe is the reflex of man as restored in Christ. I won't go into some of the other matters that Father Muller has covered at least as well as I could. The Trinitarian models are a problem inasmuch as we tend to use Trinitarian models which are not free, whereas the Trinity (God is love) — speaking here of the triune God — is freedom itself. In Thomas' version of the psychological analogy, we have the Father's knowledge of himself issuing in that Word which is the Son and the relation between him and his Word is that love which is the Spirit.

The problem is the starting point. If we look upon the Father as pure spirit, as *ipsum esse subsistens*, intellect or mind at its uttermost, then mind cannot but know fear treading dangerously close into God's necessary knowledge of himself issuing necessarily in the Son. But this is precisely not the generation of the Son by the Father, or so it would seem to me. I prefer the Augustinian memory, intellect and will, because here Augustine is dealing with explaining how it is that memory, intellect and will are one. He starts out phenomenologically with their experienced unity and pivots on that, which is a far more satisfactory procedure.

FORD   I always find Father Keefe's writings and talking both provocative and difficult to understand. I think I understood something well enough to perhaps disagree with it, or at least ask a question about it. You said, "so that the sin of the First Adam can only have been a refusal of his nuptial relationship to the First Eve, that of headship." My only comment is that the theologian I've studied — a well-known 20th century Lutheran named Bonhoeffer — I don't know if I can say bases his theology on the Fall — but he certainly elaborates it. The Fall as he conceives it would be described differently. The Fall is the disunion of man from God.

KEEFE   It is certainly that.

FORD   He describes it almost entirely in those terms. For example, he has a rather subtle discussion about shame and remorse. One can say we're arguing about words but remorse is what we feel when we've done something wrong. Shame is something we feel when we are disunited from God. He argues that shame is a necessary part of our fallen creation. It has nothing directly to do with the individual acts we've done or experienced. I'm bringing this up because you, in a sense, related the solution to what must have been the original act and so does Bonhoeffer. How would you would respond to the idea that Bonhoeffer sees as the fallen condition. He talks about our stolen likeness with God; eating the fruit of the tree of knowledge is to have the knowledge of good and evil that God alone has.

KEEFE   I have no argument with Bonhoeffer in this at all, as Dr. Ford describes it. While I am only casually familiar with his work, the reality of sin as separation from God is classic. *Aversio a Deo* is the basis of all sin; there can be no doubt of this. But are we going to make the Original Sin simply a matter of flat disobedience in the sense that Original Sin becomes juridical? This has been the catechetical way it has been presented in Catholic catechesis when I encountered it a long time ago. It has certainly has the advantage of simplicity. I never got the impression from my reading of Bonhoeffer that he was simplistic at any level. The difficulty of simply describing Original Sin as separation from God is highlighted by Paul Tillich. I did some work on Tillich. I've been saying negative things about St. Thomas. I'll turn around and say negative things about a great Lutheran theologian.

Let me point out that Tillich explains the integrity of Jesus the Christ in the second volume of his *Systematics and Christology*. I'm speaking from a memory which is not as recent as it should be. Tillich distinguishes between our condition of estrangement — that is how he describes fallenness — and the non-fallenness or the integrity of the Christ. Jesus was never separated from that divine center which is God. His humanity then is totally personal with his divinity. All of that is orthodox. Then he contrasts that with us who have been separated from the divine center by having "person" distinct from God. That, he believes, to be the source of our fallenness; it is by the mere fact that we are personally distinct from the Persons that are the Father, Son, and Spirit. That has the implication that to be a created human person, the human being has to be fallen. I don't think that Bonhoeffer would have said that. Since it not something I believe any Lutheran would be likely to follow, I feel free to criticize Tillich on that point.

If that is not the point, then what is the basis of our alienation from God? A bad answer has been proposed, what is the good answer? I have a gifted student, Joyce Little who teaches at the University of St. Thomas. A few years ago she proposed a development of the notion of the Fall that I consider to be scriptural and remarkably insightful. She looks at the temptation and sin in Genesis 3 as the woman's being seduced from her proper headship to an autonomy. The "you will be like gods" is exactly a temptation toward auton- omy. It is a temptation away from that proper free unity which belongs to human beings. They are free only in their committed relationship to each other, whose sign is nuptial. Thus she proposes — I believe correctly — that the Original Sin is the loss of that free unity proper to humanity. It is im- mediately a fall into an unfree and necessary disunity at once from each other, from God and from the world.

Thus, the world is alien from Adam; he has to work in it. Eve must bear his children in pain and suffering. They are ashamed before God with whom they used to converse at length in the cool of the evening. This seems to me to be a way of explaining alienation from God. This is at once destructive of the reality which is alienated. So we move away from a merely juridical un- derstanding of the punishment to a more metaphysical one in which the fall into an unfree disunity of flesh is precisely the name of the alienation from unity and from the source of unity that is God. It is an alienation from life and the source of life that is God, from love and the source of love which is God. In this I am not disagreeing with Bonhoeffer or the Lutheran tradition in general. This seems to be very near to obvious once we look at it.

Karl Barth, maybe the first of the modern theologians, may have been the first theologian to directly assert that our imaging of God involves a relation between man and woman. His commentary on Genesis 2 is almost angry. He says "this relationship is right there in front of them and they never saw it because they are hypnotized by oneness." I think this is true. The Pope has made it a theme of his anthropology. A theology of the body is really the theology of the "one flesh." That's the short answer to your question.

HOY   I like Father Keefe's position on this particular point. It is quite insightful on how we understand the nature of any kind of triadic perception of the human being. In essence, I believe that still needs to be transcended. One must move beyond that element. In our Lutheran confessional tradition, Article Two of the Augsburg Confession on Original Sin, would say no matter how many models we might add to the reality of the human body, it doesn't seem to get to the heart of the theological issue which is, regardless of where that is, still on the way to Hell in a handbasket. How we can address that reality and somehow raise the human body into something to be treasured and to be restored to fullness must be at the heart of how we seek to address the issue in theology. However much we want to put into the depiction of a Christian anthropology, we must take the Fall into consideration. No matter how well we define the human being, its fallenness must be addressed and overcome. That comes through the reality of Jesus the Christ. To express the reality of Christ has made a difference. I am affirming what Father Keefe said though in different terms.

BERTRAM   Would you give me leave to put to rest the disagreement about Bonhoeffer. I think I can pull several comments together. From the discussion, the one thing I have missed so far, which would characterize a Bonhoeffer/Lutheran's view of the Fall, is the following element. There are probably many others as well. This morning, from time to time, as we strove to describe the human, the question was raised whether the human can be described in her solitariness as an individual or whether the least that is needed beyond that is to describe her relationally with others, the creation, the Creator and so on. Let's get back to the Bonhoeffer/-Lutheran view of the Fall which, thank God, is not original with the Lutherans. The element that might be missing in our discussion so far about describing that fall — several hinted at it — is that the fall is not just evident in looking at the fallen one. The fall of the human one is reciprocated by the fallen human being's Creator. This is a relational fall. Here I return to things that Father Keefe said in his paper. The term in New Testament Greek for this reciprocation from the Creator is called the Wrath of God, *hay orge tou theou*. There is I suppose an almost instinctive tendency on the part of western Christians nowadays to think that you describe the fall of man simply by describing man in his loneliness. Even if the initiative for the fall of man was taken by humankind, it is nevertheless acquiesced in, to put it mildly, by the Creator. There is judgment; the marks of mortality, of biodegradability, of terminality in the flesh that are the marks of the judgment of God. Bonhoeffer would say that; that is certainly in my tradition. But it's first of all in the biblical tradition and certainly in the best Augustinian Roman Catholic tradition as well. That's my intervention.

KEILHOLZ   We talked about Jesus as an embryo and the beginning of life. I am going to shift this to the end of human life. I have a problem with body-mind-spirit analogy, because, if any one of us sitting here were to have a brain injury sometime, our ability to do whatever was governed by that part of the brain would be severely affected, as it is in people who have strokes, develop Alzheimer's disease, have trauma to the brain. I am not too sure how those things fit together, but, if something happens to specifically that part of the body, we're in a lot of trouble. I want also to comment on something [see page 11] in Michael Hoy's paper. He mentions the actor, Robin Williams, in *Bicentennial Man*. I think that was based on Azimov's and Silverberg's *Positronic Man*. This is a bicentennial man not because he was born in the Bicentennial Year, but because he's 200 years old. Over the course of time, all the human members of the family to which he had been assigned as a robot are born, grow, develop and die. He eventually has no relationship left to the family to which he was originally given. I didn't see the movie so I don't know if this fact was played on there. But in the book it is a very touching experience the robot goes through as one by one he gets every human organ placed into the robotic body. He finally asks for one more surgery so that he will be able to experience what the human members of the family to which he belonged experienced, i.e., death.

Death is an amazing thing. The way in which we are human gives me pause when I think that what it means to be human is that our lives will end. This flesh, this body, will go back to its original elements. Having had the opportunity recently to be present near the time of death, and in one case at the death of the person, it is truly an amazing reality to be one minute in the presence of a living body and in the next minute to be present to a body which is no longer living. It's a pretty astounding reality to me that God in the person of Jesus Christ would chose to enter into this kind of existence and offer us such a great hope that the end of this physical body is not the end of the story.

BERTRAM   What if you were in the presence of someone who one minute was dead and the next minute were alive? You who are privileged to receive the Eucharist will be celebrating both moments "on the night in which He was betrayed" of the Lord Jesus Christ. He said: "This is my body", which is now his glorified body and "this is my blood."

SESSION 5

STREETER   There are theologians today trying hard to link the theological discussion of Original Sin with the human sciences, especially sociology and psychology. In doing that they try to work with consciousness and with consciousness analysis, for good or for ill. It's like anything else; it will show its fruitfulness only in the future rather than in their present efforts. One of them working at this is an Australian, a rather young theologian named Neil Ormerod. He has a book called *Grace and Disgrace* in which he deals with this whole question. He follows some of the thought of a Benedictine theologian, Sebastian Moore, who is at Downside Abbey in England and has taught at various places here in the Unite States.

In their approach they go back to the dawn of reflective consciousness as it becomes distinct from the flow of consciousness in the rest of creation. There is no distinction where there is no freedom nor self-reflection, where the created world was simply there — in whatever organism it reacted with all of the environment. They propose that at the moment humans began to be self-reflexive there was a recognition, an awareness, that the mystery surrounding the entire cosmos, themselves included, was other than themselves. So, through self-reflection there is a sense of an-other and me. The moment of choice comes when in that first dawning movement of self-reflection the human beings not only make the distinction but make a separation.

Then the choice is filled with disgrace or shame in that they have set themselves apart by choosing their own autonomous self-operation in conflict with the relationship with this "other" that gave them birth. These theologians are beginning to say that it is by that autonomous dislocation, or that non-relationship — the self-enclosing of the human becoming a law unto itself — that the sin of the world comes. The distinction was natural, the distinction of creature and source was natural. But to make that a separation is a sin. I share that because that's an attempt being made. Whether or not it will be meaningful as we continue to do a theology of Original Sin remains to be seen until the work is more carefully done.

Were there multiple Adams or a single one? There was a period in the 1960s, maybe in the early 70s, when many theologians held a multiple Adam. That position is not firmly held now. We've gone back to the African finding; *homo sapiens* is now traced to a single ancestor in the Rift Valley. There are two schools of thought; I don't think the multiple Adam is a prevailing theological opinion but I may be wrong. My knowledge stops there.

MULLER   It is still debated among anthropologists but the single origin approach has received support from mitochondrial studies. Curiously, some studies trace everything back to a single female ancestress.

Other studies trace everything to a single male ancestor. The dating, however, separates them by thousands of years, 10,000 or 100,000 years.

BRUNGS   In Europe, about 1970, there was a growing movement among theologians and anthropologists to get Pope Paul VI to come down on the side of polygenesis. He didn't do it. It's one case where the slowness of the Papacy may have served us well. These people were pushing hard for a statement on the origins, but the Pope wouldn't make it. We don't know for sure what the empirical answer is. I think we know theologically, but empirically we don't know whether it was one or many. It's better that the Pope not make a pronouncement about something that is scientifically arguable. I was on the periphery of this issue almost thirty years ago, but I was one of those arguing that the Pope not declare that we know scientifically how we came to be.

BERTRAM   Even biblicists have always drawn a blank. If Adam and Eve had children and their daughters married the sons of men, as it was called, where did they come from?

SCHNEIDER   This present discussion leads neatly into the question I had earlier. It's my understanding simply from the Hebrew that the word "Adam" is a collective noun grammatically. It means humanity actually. Whether that's one or many, it doesn't help much in defining how many. But it is collective. I was going to mention before about Adam and Eve and the failure of Adam to exercise leadership over Eve. I have no problem seeing the original unity of the man and the woman in Genesis when I read through the creation story. So the breaking of the unity makes it easy for me to see it as a part of Original Sin. What I don't see as I go through Genesis is any reference to the leadership of the male over the female until I get to Genesis 3. There it is part of God's curse, part of the wrath of God (Genesis 3:16 "In pain you shall bring forth children yet your desire shall be for your husband and he shall rule over you.") As far as I know, that's where it occurs in the context of the Fall, where it is part of God's curse that that should be the way and not part of the original righteousness.

CROSS   How do you know it's a curse?

SCHNEIDER   God had just finished cursing the serpent and He is turning to the woman.

MULLER   I have a couple of points to make. One was addressed earlier. This was the issue of whether the Fall is implicated in the disruption of the couple. In the text, the first effect that we see is this disruption and we can interpret that sequence not so much as a temporal sequence but as an unfolding of the structure of the Fall. These things were discussed earlier.

The second point was raised by Jitse van der Meer. He asked on the one hand about the grounding of the Good Creation — how is this to be done — and on the other hand about the mimetic approach to understanding Christ's taking on humanity. It's true that we don't get the individual Jesus in all his aspects. Doctor van der Meer mentioned one example, marriage. But Christ understood himself as bridegroom. This leads us into the resolution of the other issues. Marital imagery is common among the Fathers of the Church. Augustine has an interesting example in the *Narrations on the Psalms*, in particular Psalm 19, in which he comments on the emergence of the bridegroom from the bridal chamber. He interprets this thus: in the Incarnation Christ weds himself to human flesh, the Word weds himself to human flesh. This is at once understood of his own individual Incarnation but it also includes his nuptial taking of the Church to himself. The minute we start including that, we say that any activity that takes place within the Church is in fact taking place in the Church united to Christ. It shares in this, shall we say, mythological moment — it has its goodness fundamentally grounded.

Given Saint Thomas' understanding that every human is at least in potency a member of the Church, there is then possibility of grounding the totality of human reality in this way. It includes, then, the whole of creation, but with an understanding that the grounding of that goodness is specifically in Christ. That is rather a roundabout way to get this grounding, but we can get it if we understand creation itself as a creation in Christ. Christ's nuptial relationship with his Bride is the basis for the Good Creation. We can talk then about a fall from that state of goodness in terms of emergence of human consciousness. Obviously, in doing this, we have to start working with our concepts of time, because there is a lot of human history prior to the historical moment of Christ. We are going to have to answer or deal with the time issue, if we are going to talk of Christ as the source of all graces.

What about the graces manifested in the Old Testament? We can say that those graces were given proleptically, but trying to use that grace finally severs those graces from the bodily redemption accomplished by Christ on the Cross. If Christ's death on the Cross is to be understood as the efficient cause of the graces of the Old Testament then we must start talking about this human act quite apart from the native potentialities of human nature. In this case it is precisely because of the union with the Word that we are able to have an efficient causality that transcends space and time.

If we accept this, we're able to accept the bridal reality with it as well. God's power is able to work not simply through Christ but through the Church that Christ has united with himself. This is one way around the problem that Doctor van der Meer raised. That problem, though, is real enough. There was another thought about Christ's bodiliness. This goes back to the prior issue about the effectiveness of Christ's redemption. In my prior comment I did not stress sufficiently enough the bodiliness that is required for that redemption. In our fallen condition — Augustine is explicit on this point — there is nothing in common between a just God and a fallen human. The gap is bridged precisely by Christ taking on flesh. This is to say that it is precisely because of the bodily union established through Christ's insertion into the human species that this divide is bridged. This goes back to the assertion of the connectedness of the DNA. It is precisely a bodily connectedness that makes possible the entry into the human species of saving grace.

BERTRAM   Just a quick refrain. The Word is *flesh*, not body; the Word is flesh. There is a difference. Athanasius, when he talks about the Word becoming flesh, then adds "flesh, because death needs that." Death needs flesh; that's why the Incarnate one takes on *carnis, sarx*, flesh; it is terminal, it is mortal. That is the proximate goal of the Incarnation. Flesh, as Father Keefe reminds us, is the body post-fall with its mortality.

FORD   Carla Mae Streeter mentioned this idea of the encounter with the other in effect, as I understood it, being the experience of the Fall itself. I found it compelling. It at least sees the encounter with the other when Adam was given Eve. That's when Adam encounters the other. That's an enormous experience for Adam because before that there was in effect one human only. In effect he knew only his Creator; now he knows another human creature. Bonhoeffer reflects at length on that experience for Adam. The Fall is something else; it is specifically that desire not to be united with God but to know what God knows. It is the desire to be the origin of good and evil, to be able to discern good and evil in the ultimate sense.

The question of marriage is a Lutheran theme and Bonhoeffer reflects this as well. Certainly the Church is the bride of Christ and the nuptial marriage image is appropriate there. I may be skating on thin ice but my understanding would be that marriage first of all pre-dates the Fall and in some sense it predates both Church and state. Even after the Fall marriage is for everybody. A Jew, faithful to his wife, is somehow the beneficiary of the promises placed on marriage. The Turk, faithful to his wife, is likewise a beneficiary — or the atheist or the heretic or whoever. There's something about marriage and the promises attached to it that are not directly related to salvation. A faithful Jew inherits the blessings that are placed in marriage. Those are not related to salvation.

224

BERTRAM I think your initial remark was accurate: you are skating on thin ice.

VAN DER MEER I have a question for Don Keefe. I'll introduce it with a comment about mitochondrial Eve. It was suggested that those observations based on the analysis of mitochondrial DNA indicated that there was one ancestor, but that is not really so. The method only allows us to go back into history until a point when there was what population biologists call a bottleneck in the human population. At that time there may have been such a small population that there was just one mother-figure or one individual who became the mother of all the rest of the population that developed after that bottleneck. That doesn't mean that there weren't many human beings before that bottleneck. The method can say nothing about the time before the bottleneck. So it has no implication in the monogenism/polygenism debate. It does not exclude theories that suggest human evolution started with many individuals in different places.

That leads me to the question about the context of Father Keefe's paper and how I have to understand it. Let me give a few examples where I have some difficulty. Starting on page 113 and in other places, the paragraph that begins "it appears that," you talk about death entering the world. In other places, for instance page 118, you mention the First Adam being redeemed by the Second. My difficulty has to do with the use of theological language and how that relates to what we think might have happened in the history of humankind. There are two possibilities. Are you taking about Paul's position and how he understood that? Paul probably understood that in terms of the first single person called Adam and a single person called Eve. Then I can see what you mean. Is this also your understanding? If so, how do you relate that to what is known about the history of humankind from the study of fossils, etc? How does that relate to the idea, for instance, that the human race emerged from many instead of one.

KEEFE As I remarked earlier in reply to another question, the context in which the monogenism/polygenism debate occurred was Teilhardian; the supposition was that the Fall occurred in some moment of historical time. It is part of the Catholic tradition — I don't know that it isn't part of the tradition across the board — that it is the entirety of creation that is fallen by reason of the fall of him who is to have been its head. That means then that the discussion of polygenism and monogenism insofar as the Fall is concerned is simply besides the point.

VAN DER MEER I understand that. But am I right that you said earlier in the discussion that there never was a time that the creation was not fallen?

KEEFE   We have to speak of that moment which Scripture refers to as "in the beginning." The beginning" is not the beginning of fallen time. We are speaking here of a moment of choice. The Good Creation is good insofar as — the point has been sufficiently discussed if not belabored — the goodness of the Good Creation is obviously a free goodness; therefore, it requires that it be accepted. This acceptance requires simply as its condition of possibility a primordial offer of the Good Creation. This is something that is all too easily controlled by imaginative corruption. It's difficult to discuss it otherwise. Instead of entering into some imaginatively controlled speculation about the nature of the Fall, I believe it's necessary first, with Paul, to deal with the question of the First and Second Adam.

The Second Adam is our source of information about the Fall; we really have no other. To use the expression made famous by the CIA, we need "to track back the cat" from the redemption to that which prompts the need for redemption, the Original Sin. If the redemption is the restoration of a free nuptial unity, as I propose it to be, then the Original Sin is a loss, a free deliberate rejection of free unity which then issues in *sarx*, the destructive dynamic whose result is the dust of death. This moment is the moment in which fallenness and the temporality with which we are concerned begins. I don't mean to match it with the Big Bang or anything like that; I'm simply speaking theologically. Before that point there is no necessity of a fall.

All that is given by the Father sending the Son to give the Spirit is the Good Creation whose goodness is its freedom, and it cannot be imposed; therefore it must be offered. To discuss the offer and the rejection instead of relying on an imaginative entry into "what happened," we have to, I think, look to the Second Adam, to that recapitulation which is the work of redemption. It implies a moment in which that free unity was lost, freely, therefore responsibly, lost. That responsibility refers to an agent. The agent is understood then to be him whose responsibility it was as head to bestow free unity. The absence of that responsible acceptance of headship, by which the starry universe would have been otherwise, is the moment then in the Pauline anthropology as I have tried to understand and develop it. I believe this is basically Augustinian as well, although that's indefinitely discussable. This is all indefinitely discussable obviously.

The moment of the emergence of death, of the emergence of fallenness, the flesh, and so forth, has to be dealt with in entirely biblical terms. They have been clarified and made discussable by Paul's insistence that the resurrection is given in Christ only, that it is presaged by a fall, by the need for redemption, by the redemption and that all of this he compresses into a discussion of the relation of head and body, or head and glory. We find the framework of it largely in the 11th chapter of Corinthians. This seems to me to be the only manner in which one can discuss the Fall, flesh, without becoming embroiled in those Teilhardian quandaries which have so bemused Catholic theology since it was first proposed in the 1950s. One simply has to reject discussions of the mitochondrial Eve because whatever we know about Eve has nothing to do with what we know about paleobiology.

KUHL   Being reminded to talk about flesh, I take it that *sarx*, flesh, is what we are talking about when we talk about the genome. We are classifying what is human flesh. One thing I noticed in the discussion was an interest in what was before what we have now. We can do that. We used to have a wonderful vase in our house. When it got broken by the kids, they used to talk about what it looked like before it was broken. It's one way to avoid the subject, I suppose. At least as I read Paul, in fact the New Testament, the authors don't do a lot of speculating about the nature of the mystery of the breaking. They want to deal with the breakage.

I am looking at Romans 8: especially verse 3 where Paul talks about the flesh as a theological battleground. It is the place in which the reality of sin has lodged. No matter how much our knowledge of the law and sin has been illuminated by the gift of God at Sinai, or however we might want to describe that, what Paul begins to realize is that that great illumination about the truth and reality of what has happened to our life is so embedded in the flesh that, even "though my mind glories in the Law, my flesh is held captive to the reality of sin." That's how Paul describes our reality and what life is now like, regardless of how it got that way. We never do get good explanations about the mess that's on the floor from the kids, but we know we have to deal with it. He goes on to say, "so Christian talk, the talk of Christ, is a talk about what we're going to do about the mess." Paul goes on to say "for God has done in Christ what the Law, weakened by the flesh, could not do by sending his own Son in the likeness of sinful flesh to deal with sin." This is what He did. He condemned sin in the flesh so that the just requirements of the Law that we all know about might be fulfilled in us.

If there's anything as Christians, as theologians, as persons interested in the relationship of theology and science, the body is an important battlefield which we are all called to deal with. It's a battle in which the reality of the judgment of God is manifest as well as is the truth and reality of human sinfulness. The flesh is precisely the place where Paul would have us look to see that battle take place. Let's use a metaphor: Christ is kind of chemotherapy, if you will. He comes to take upon himself human flesh precisely so that He could kill it, but in a way in which through his own divinity — however we describe that — through his resurrection He might resurrect it anew.

There's no saving the flesh, no saving us, without first bringing that flesh to naught, to death, because of the close connection of that reality that Paul calls sin, the Fall. Whenever we begin to deal with understanding the genome — for whatever good reasons we want to be able to heal the flesh — we have to realize that there is something inherent in this fleshly reality that will not be able to be cured. It needs somehow to undergo this death in Christ in order to be reconstituted. That's an inherent truth which the Christian Gospel says needs to be considered if we want to understand what all this entails.

BERTRAM   I don't know if you intended this but, as you spoke about what the flesh being at war within itself manifests, I thought that could be a partial answer to a question Carla Mae Streeter raised before dinner: how is the body revelatory? It may not be what she hoped it would reveal. It reveals a tremendous conflict. If it's a microcosm of anything it's a microcosm of a cosmic conflict. At least as *sarx* it is.

STREETER   I would caution us that it is very dangerous to really equate *sarx* with the body.

BERTRAM   I'm not.

STREETER   We have to be very careful not to do that. If I understand Paul correctly, we're dealing with the recalcitrant, stubborn human being when we're talking *flesh*. If you really go back to the organism, *psyche* and spirit understanding of the anthropology of the human being, it is within the spirit that sin resides, within the will, within choice that the infection spreads. So the body then becomes accomplice or hostage.

BERTRAM   The flesh does.

STREETER   No, the *soma*, the body, does.

BERTRAM   No, no.

STREETER   I am talking about what we call the body as organism, in contrast to *sarx*, as rebellious from God. The body is accomplice to the sin residing in the heart. The source is within the spirit that has become twisted. That's our flesh, our *sarx* condition. That's what I understand.

BERTRAM   I want to interpret. My understanding is that whenever *sarx* has been talked about here this weekend that's exactly what is meant. It is the *soma* in its fallen condition. Exactly.

STREETER   But it's not just the *soma*. It's the spirit of the person.

BERTRAM   In *pneuma*, the term spirit is usually not referred to as part of the flesh. *Psyche*, the psyche is and the *anima*, but that's
part of the flesh. The flesh, as I understand Father Keefe and as he and I
understand the New Testament, the *sarx* is a bodily spirit, an embodied spirit
or a spiritualized body, in its fallen state. (Streeter: I agree with that.) There's
no point in talking about the *soma* unless you are talking about the *soma* in
Jesus Christ. That is the redeemed body. I hope the impression wasn't given,
or I hope that I didn't get the misimpression, that people were saying that
sarx is just another way of speaking of *soma*. *Sarx* is the fallen condition.

Could I add a reflection here that at first may not sound directly pertinent
to this discussion but in the longer reach it might be. It was Frank Andrews
who with unvarnished candor, said that he didn't like the talk about the
Second Person of the Trinity as Son. He wasn't objecting to the maleness of
that term, but he was objecting to the notion at all because it was so biological. I gathered that some of you were saying that's just the point. If we lose
that we lose an awful lot of Incarnation in the process. Starting at that
moment in our discussion and now having it come to bear even more on the
last half hour, may I add another reflection?

The notion of Son, which is unexpungible from the New Testament for
reasons that were given earlier, was pretty clear. Even the most skeptical
Jesus scholars are clear that the language by which Jesus is related to God
the Creator as Son is to Father is probably authentic. If anything goes back
to the original Jesus, this evidently does. We wouldn't have a Lord's Prayer
without it, for example. The scandal of referring to himself as Son or to himself as a child and to God as the Father or the parent, isn't just that it's
biological; the scandal goes farther. It makes the Second Person of the Trinity a dependent; that is a scandal. To use the language of the fourth century
conciliar debates, it makes the Second Person of the Trinity subordinate to
the First Person of the Trinity. No question about it!

The Arians, of course, who wanted to emphasize that the Son was subordinate to the Father made the mistake of changing *subordinateness* to *subordinationism*. They said that, precisely because the Second Person of the Trinity
is the offspring of the Father, therefore the Second Person of the Trinity
could not possibly be God. Then we have no Trinity. For isn't God the one
on whom all things depend? Yes. How could someone Himself depend on
the Creator and yet be God? The early movements by the Nicenes and the
Orthodox, early in the council, were inclined to minimize the Sonship of
Christ just because it seemed to give the palm to the Arians. They knew what
the Arians would do with this: they would say that well, if the Second Person

is subordinate to the Father, the Arians would win the day. There would go the Godhead of the Second Person.

It was only as the credal discussions proceeded that it was the Orthodox who said that, of course, he's subordinate. They turned the tables on the Arians and said: "For that very reason He is no less God but on the contrary that is precisely his Godhead. He is subordinate to the Father in this respect, that his very being depends on the Father's begetting Him. He can't reverse that; the Father is not begotten by the Son." *Homoousios*: we say the Son is of one being (as you proclaimed this afternoon at the Catholic Mass). By the way the Creed I am talking about is not from the Council of Niceae in 325. This is the Nicene-Constantinople Creed with some additions. The Son is of one being with the Father. Never is it said by the Fathers of the Church that the Father is of one being with the Son. The Son is derived from the Father. We can see why it was the Arians at first who would rather resurrect the biblical language of Father/Son and why at first the Orthodox, the Nicenes, preferred less temporal subordinate/superior language like Son/Father and preferred terms like the Word, the Logos, and so on.

We are indebted — I speak as an orthodox Nicene — at least negatively to the Arians for pressing the biblical language of Father/Son. Only if, however, we can make hay out of that. That is exactly what distinguishes the deity of the Second Person of the Trinity. I agree that "in the beginning everything that was made was made by him," as the Prologue in John proclaims. "Without him was not anything made that was made." In that respect He is precisely like the Father. He is the One on whom all things also depend. What is distinctive about him is that He in turn depends as a child depends on a parent for his being. He does the Father's will. He is obedient to the Father. There's no question about that biblically. He turns to the Father for succor.

We shouldn't be embarrassed by that. I suppose it's the Arian streak in all of us that tempts us to say "we'd rather soft-pedal that side." Christians are called to take pride in this. Imagine a God who is a child, a child-God as well as a Father-God. That is one of the things that I think distinguishes Christianity from other world religions — and that quite radically. Pardon that excursus, but it is key to go back to the fourth century conciliar debates on Christology for the very reason. Let's come back to our discussion about a theology of the body. Father/Son language of course is very bodily, and we can say it's a metaphor; of course, it's a metaphor. But is it an apt metaphor, that is, is it true? Does it have elements of fittingness to it? It does.

Is it not important that a Christian theology of the body stress that one of the things about bodiliness is the extreme dependence that bodily creatures have? One of the most vulnerable things about us is that we are bodily. We can be threatened with torture which wouldn't be true if we didn't have a body. We can be made cowards if threatened with a loss of our children. Our bodiliness makes us highly vulnerable. Is it not important that the Incarnate Son of God took on *sarx*, took on body? If the Nicenes were right that even before the Incarnation from all eternity as you said at Mass; "Everlastingly begotten...," there was never a time when the Son was not. There may have been a time when the Man, Jesus was not; there was never a time when the Son was not everlastingly begotten by the Father as a Son. Is it not a key to a Christian theology of the body to recognize that one of the features of bodiliness is its extreme dependence and its vulnerability? If that leaves us with something to bring up if we feel provoked to do that, that's fine. That's been gnawing at me ever since Frank Andrews objected to the biology accent. I thought, "Gosh, that's not nearly the whole of the problem. It's not just biological; "Father" is biological. But "Father" doesn't raise the scandal of dependence that Son does. Yet the Christian believer is the one who can say, "Thank God that God is also a child as well as a parent."

VAN DER MEER   I am still puzzled about the framework of your paper, Father Keefe. I understand what you want to do in connection with the Fall and the first and Second Adam. You want to develop a theological explanation independent of the scientific reconstruction of history. I was led to believe otherwise in a number of passages where you made connections like that. I want to point out two and ask you to resolve my puzzlement. One of them occurs where you say, "The history of the fallen universe would be mere entropy." A scientist would give a very specific meaning to that word, entropy. I don't know if that is what you intended.

KEEFE   Approximately, I do. When I say "unwinding of the world," obviously this is a poesie or something, I'm referring to the unavailability of energy in a progressive fashion.

VAN DER MEER   OK. So you do make that a connection with what happens naturally. This is what led me to believe that you wanted.....

KEEFE   I look upon this as part of the necessary fragmentation, the necessary disunity of the world consequent upon the fall.

VAN DER MEER   OK. Then the second occasion is on page 117 where you say, "for the death of Christ has changed physical death utterly." I guess we should try to clarify what physical death means because it can mean many things. The death of a person as a body, let's say.

KEEFE   I'm referring to the death which we die. I would say this inasmuch as *sarx* is used in the Old Testament in a context wider than mere humanity. One can understand this to be life in its bestowal; wherever we find life, that is to say, all things die. There is a tendency again within the Thomist ambience to suppose that the difference between the fallen and the unfallen state is rather an accidental than a substantial modification. An example I use too often no doubt: Thomas is convinced that it will continue to rain on our picnic whether in a fallen or an unfallen world. He is convinced that when the lion lies down with the lamb, he will get up with the lamb consumed. I think that one must accept — this is to expand beyond where I intended to go — that there is a problem with the salvation of the unbeliever. Thomas recognized it at the end of his life, and, from this point, he turned to Augustine for the *trahi ad Deo* solution which is a universal grace. That grace as universal is directed to the salvation of those for whom Christ died. Lest that be interpreted in the merely juridical fashion, there has to be some linking of the necessity of baptism for salvation with the efficacy of the death of Christ. We are baptized into the death of Christ. He refers to his own death as a baptism for which He longs. It would appear that, if there was an Inuit some 5000 years before Christ, out in his boat spearing whales, whatever, and he had a mischance and died, he died in Christ.

I don't want to enter into the fundamental option squabble; that has been badly used. In the case of the human we can call the good pagan, in that he has done what in him lies, upon his death he leaves behind him all that is mortal, all that is flesh. He confronts the risen Christ then in a moment of revelation and decision. In that sense, then, the death of Christ makes death to be what death was not; He defeats it. He defeats it, as I have stressed, as the Lord of history. Before and after him death becomes a gate and we pass through that gate by death, either sacramental in the case of Baptism or physical death. Paul says that for the baptized Christian there is no death. For those who are not baptized, there is. They die into the death of Christ.

BERTRAM   Can I add a footnote question? Do you link this to the "*descendis ad inferos*," He descended into the depths, into Hades?

KEEFE   As Von Balthasar has stressed, it is not so much the matter of the clearing of hell, as that famous ancient homily that we have in the Office in which Christ says to the fallen Adam, "You are one person with me," implies. It's an unfortunate wording. I think that the death of Christ and his descent into hell is what Paul had in mind when he said "he was made sin for us." He took on himself the full horror of damnation.

BERTRAM   But not preaching to the saints in hell?

KEEFE   That may be Patristic flourish. There may be something in it, but certainly He opened the gates of hell by his death, not

232

by preaching. That obscures the full profundity of Holy Saturday.

BERTRAM   I'm personally grateful to Jitse for raising that question. That plagued me too, as I read your paper.

SIMONI   I want to answer Carolyn Schneider's question about man's dominion over woman. That's the word used after the Fall. I'd like to tie that in to the theology of the body. I use chapter 2 of Genesis, verses 15-25. In verse 15 the Lord said: "the Lord God..." so man is being placed as the steward of creation. "It is not good for man to be alone." This is what God says. Before He presents woman to man He presents all the other creatures. The man names every creature. None of them is a suitable partner for the man. "Then God casts a deep sleep on man." He takes one of his ribs and fashions it into a woman. He gives her to the man. My answer is based on "woman is given" to man first. Man is placed as caretaker of woman and in that receiving of woman he is also giving himself. I tie this into a theology of the body by saying that we must not forget that giving and receiving is innate to the human person. We talked about the relationship between men and women in marriage, but it's also innate to a person himself or herself; we receive life. God has bestowed gifts on us. It's important to include in our discussion, as we develop a theology of the body, a proper understanding of gift and how mankind participates in giving and receiving.

SHEAHEN   This may only be a question about accurate translation. I have been pondering on this from Teilhard de Chardin and maybe a little *Flatland* as well. In any case, the Aramaic word seems to have been translated into contemporary English as "Son." Bob Bertram's discussion of Son/Father ranged over a number of relationships between God the Father and God the Son. We know terms like *Logos* were used that way. When Jesus walked the earth He kept referring to himself as the Son of Man.

I suggest that possibly whatever that Aramaic word meant, a better translation would have been *Descendant* rather than *Son*. The Teilhardian sense is that presumably beyond mankind there are other stages of evolution yet to come. If Jesus is in fact one of those stages of evolution, that is a more advanced creature, a more advanced 'thing' than man, as man is more advanced than earlier primates, then Christ's use of the term "descendant of man" to refer to himself makes a certain amount of sense — in a Teilhardian sense. Furthermore, at this point the relationship of God the Father and the Descendant becomes perfectly reasonable and is no longer constrained to be one of subordination, inferiority or any of that Arian interpretation.

BERTRAM   I never used the word inferiority.

SHEAHEN   Sorry I had it wrong. We can have a situation in which a father has a descendant who is in fact is no way subordinate somewhat downstream — genetically speaking.

BERTRAM   But he's derivative.

SHEAHEN   Perhaps.

BERTRAM   Not perhaps. How else would a descendant descend. He is derivative from the parent. We can never reverse that. The parent is not begotten by the child.

SHEAHEN   In a linear time sequence that would be absolutely correct. If we grant God the ability to do what He likes with time we go back to the "begotten from all eternity" as a way of avoiding that.

BERTRAM   Why would you want to get around it? I appreciate the uneasiness with that. I think that's endemic to *sarx*. I feel it myself. It's scandalous — I use a good New Testament word — it's scandalous of God to do that, to be a child as well as a parent. I can tell that you're thinking of all the honest ways to get around it. There's a lot of controversy, as the other theologians will tell you, about what the Son of Man means, even in the Aramaic. Maybe it means son of Adam. Which Adam are we talking about? There's a pretty good attestation to this. The historical Jesus also referred to him at least to his own circle as Son of God, which complicates your case, Tom.

SHEAHEN   It does.

GREENLEY   I suggested to John Cross that he put in "anthropology" above theology on his chart. It appears that every time there's a new dig, a new theology arises and takes another fork in the road.

God said to an audience: "This is my beloved Son in whom I am well pleased." His audience was two scared-to-death, uneducated, apostles. That may be the only word he could have used to describe Jesus that would make sense to them. It seems we've built a mountain from this simple sentence. They can understand the word Son and whatever it meant at that time.

BERTRAM   It must have meant enough to Jesus that He made it public.

STREETER   I want to take up Tom Sheahen's concern so it's not lost. I would link it with what you tried to clarify for us on the word subordination, Dr. Bertram. We get hung up by injecting our limited human experience of Sonship or subordination onto this mystery. Whenever we talk about the Son being begotten of the Father, it is not a begetting from deficiency as it is with us. We are subordinate from deficiency. We miss something that someone has. That is not true in the case of God. This begetting comes from fullness. That big difference has to be maintained, because we are dealing with a divine mystery here and God is not in our image.

BERTRAM   Our difficulty as human beings comes not in thinking of the Son as subordinate to the Father, but thinking that, because He's subordinate, He is inferior. Not at all! That's his claim to fame.

STREETER   Begotten is in fullness; and the dependency is in fullness. We have no experience of that because our dependence is always from lack. We cannot do such disservice to God as to project our human experience of sonship onto the divine mystery.

I'd like to return to what Fiorella Simoni was getting at with receiving and giving. Again, this is a theological question. In dealing with gender in the question of the divine, we must distance ourselves somewhat from the theologians who are saying, "Well, the Father is male; Jesus is male; the Holy Spirit is definitely female." Now we have two males and a female. The mystery of gender differentiation in creation is not limited just to humans. It has to do with sea horses and frogs, pistil, stamen and flowers.

It's necessary for us to move back to the very nature of God, God as love. We're dealing with a double dynamic in love — neither of which is passive. When we talk about love as Thomas might refer to it, as complacency and concern, or we have this need to offer and the need to accept, one is not passive. Love does both. This is giving and receiving. I don't like the word "receive," because it sounds too passive. I use the example of baby birds in a nest who have their eyes tight shut and they don't have a feather on them. Yet, when the body of the mother lands on the limb with the worm, what happens? The baby bird becomes all mouth, and the trembling! That is acceptance! That is not passive! The two movements that we note in gender differentiation are offer and acceptance, the two dimensions of love. They need one another. We need to go to the nature of God rather than the Persons to get at that gender question.

KEEFE   I want to speak to the reliance on Teilhard and his speculative Christology. It seems to me that Teilhard is doing his best to transcend the concrete revelation in history by some sort of suprahistorical worldview which would be given by an evolutionary vision whose final thrust is dehistorizing. The implication is that, insofar as the revelation is given in history, it's historically conditioned. That which will render the opacity of history translucent will be the theory of evolution. Then we can look to that theory for an examination of what is and isn't possible to God. We have to take the revelation as given. We should always remember in this context that there is One Name by which we can be saved. This is the name of the Son of Our Lady. It isn't Son simply.

The Council of Chalcedon insists seven times that we speak of the Christ always, in every context in which the Church addresses him, as one and the same. That means when we speak of pre-existence we are not speaking of the immanent Son eternally with the Father. The pre-existence of Jesus the Christ for which the Bible is concerned is that which is primordial. This is not to deny his full eternity. He receives from the Father all that the Father has, his fullness of divinity with all that connotes. When we speak of the Christ we speak of him who is the son of Mary at the same time that he, one Person, is the Son of the eternal Father. This is a very radical statement.

It means, among other things, that should we discover a multitude of populated planets, all populated with human beings, whatever their salvation might be, it would travel through that axis which is set by the life, death and resurrection of Christ our Lord who is Jesus the Christ, the eternal Son of the Father, the historical son of Mary. That's a very scandalous statement. It's far more scandalous than simply the fact that Our Lord was conceived, spent nine months in his mother's womb, was born, wore diapers for a while and like other children was a mess at both ends and a noise in the middle. This is a scandal, but the great scandal is the scandal of particularity. Teilhard loves to de-particularize the Christ. We can't do this.

QUINN   Friday evening, when Father Brungs was introducing the program, he said that we're not seeking answers to specific moral questions. Subsequently, Bob Bertram made the observation that this is the first time we've had a single-subject meeting for a long time. We're talking only about theology and we don't have a specific identification of science along with it. While I studied some theology in the context of a formal adult education program, I can't approach the depth of knowledge of probably more than 90% of the people in this room. I came with the objective of acquiring knowledge, not with the objective of participating. I can assure you that that objective has been fulfilled. I want to thank each of you for your contributions. Last night's discussion made the cost of admission worth while. I've had the privilege of being at many ITEST meetings and being involved in many discussions and I thought last night was very good. We're not going to come up with any answers in any specific time frame, but it is certainly a subject that we cannot stop talking about.

BERTRAM   At breakfast we were doing a post-mortem on the weekend and there was not a consensus on whether or not we had addressed the topic of a theology of the body. That train of thought led me to wonder whether I remembered how specifically we had meant to frame the topic. I have to admit, even though I try to check myself, in American English, when I hear "body," I tend to think not just of the soft fleshy parts of the human being. It is not as broad as that. I tend to think of the torso. I remember being caught up short near the end of Earl Muller's first intervention. He referred to the brain. That's right, the cranium is body. Maybe I'm biblically confined in the head/body distinction. Who said "let him who has ears to hear let him hear"? Well, hearing is involved in the body.

If we take the prevalent theme in the New Testament, flesh is not just corporeality. Flesh is a way of thinking. As a matter of fact, if Paul is concerned with flesh as a problem, it's mostly with flesh as a way of thinking or a way of living. There is nothing wrong with flesh *per se*, but, if we live according to the flesh, it is a problem. Then one of the people at the table said "especially if you are male and twenty-one." Fleshly thinking! Even that is not Paul's chief preoccupation. He's thinking about people who think legalistically in their way of salvation, that somehow if you think — this is quite instinctual — that by performing the works of the law you can be justified. For Paul that's *flesh*. That's a fleshly way of thinking. But it's all one continuum with the bodily. It raises the question that, if we were to specify the subject, a theology of the human body, and still be true to what I know is a concern of our ITEST Board — to relate a theology of the body to the recent findings and breakthroughs in the life sciences — is there any conceivable connection between research in the biological sciences and what Paul calls a legalistic way of thinking? Maybe that's too much of a stretch.

VAN DER MEER   This is simply an attempt to help focus on the topic. If I look at the range of meanings of the word *body* that have been making the rounds of discussion, perhaps the best thing for the focus of the workshop would have been "human body" instead of just "body."

POSTIGLIONE   That is precisely what we had on the promotional materials and the program.

VAN DER MEER   I didn't realize that. But I can still make a comment that would help to narrow the focus. In many ways we have used metaphors to talk about the body of Christ. We talk about a social body or a political body. We can also talk about the body of an organism; this brings us into biology. There biologists tend to think about the bodies of animals and plants as something related to what is outside the normal confines of the body. It's relational thinking. If the focus is on the human body one could bring in all the knowledge of biology by way of analogy. The human body is an organic body. Our point of view would have to be not in biology, but somewhere else. Otherwise we end up with reductionistic types of conceptions about the human body.

If we took the purely biological point of view, we would not be able to include studies of the meaning of facial expressions that the body uses to communicate with others. We talk about body language, but it has not been mentioned here. One way of communication is body language, instead of verbally or in writing. Those are the kind of things we would miss out on if we were just taking the biological point of view. So perhaps that's a contribution to the focus. I would want to think that, if one could talk about the theology of the body, our focus seems to be in theology in the first place.

BERTRAM   Let me cross-examine you for a moment on what you've set in motion. When I think of some of the features of the biblical understanding of body or *sarx*, flesh, I can think of a number of additional features. Would this give us a talking point with the life sciences? You mentioned facial expressions, an important aspect in biblical understanding of body. A fundamental theological theme, Old and New Testament, is "glory." Glory is a facial term. It's always a visible term for the Hebraic mind. We couldn't conceive of glory being invisible. A nice way to play on the word "glory" is to spell it "glow-ry"; it's the glow on the face of God. To glorify God doesn't mean just to render praise to God; it means to put a smile on God's face. "The Lord bless you and keep you. The Lord make his face to shine upon you and be gracious unto you." That's the glow-ry of God.

A second feature of bodiliness, especially of flesh, is its mortality. Is that key for a life scientist to say, "By definition, if we're talking about organisms, we're talking about death"? Yesterday Carla Mae Streeter ticked off body, mind, spirit. An Hebraically-minded Jesus would not be inclined to talk of body, mind, spirit. He might say, we should love the Lord our God with all our heart — the emotions — all our soul, the mind, and a big word we've not even talked, strength. Strength is a big word Hebraically and it is brought over into the New Testament. I would imagine — you can correct me — the notion of strength would be an easily transferable theme into the life sciences. I assume it's what gives the body the energy to do anything at all. Terminologically, are these bridge points?

VAN DER MEER   Yes. The easiest one to see is the one in connection with death. I have to make clear what I'm talking about when I talk about death, because biologists mean different things by death. If you think of an organism as something structured in levels of organization, let's say from molecules to cells to tissues to organs, then, when it comes to cell death, the biologists say that is part of what we understand to be the natural situation. That is integral to the way living things function. Most of us have seen pictures of a human fetus. When we look at the hands, we notice that the spaces between the fingers are still closed with tissue. At one point the hand is, as it were, sculpted out with the pieces between the fingers consisting of cells programmed genetically to die off. This is one of the ways embryologists understand how the shape of the human body comes about. Something as beautiful as the shape of the human body involves constructive views of death, but we have to be clear that this is cell death; it is not the death of an entire human being. It has a very different kind of meaning.

In that sense death is integral to organisms. It is integral in another way. We can easily understand it because we do not know how the economy of animals and plants in the environment would work without death of entire organisms. That is not confined to biology, because we do not have a way of thinking about what physical reality would be like without things like the second law of thermodynamics. According to that law everything runs down in terms of transfer of usable energy to unusable energy. This form of death around us are part of natural regularity. These are points of connection.

I was interested in what you (Bertram) said about the meaning of body language according to the Bible I wasn't aware of that. When I commented, I didn't have them in mind. I don't know of a way in which biologists could connect with what you said about "glow-ry" and glow. I don't know how to make a connection with that.

BERTRAM   You had mentioned facial expression.

VAN DER MEER   Yes, I had. This kind of communication, I take it, also occurs between people, people showing a glow on their face because of someone or something they love, for instance. If that is the case, one could think about the human body as being created for that purpose. That's where the biology transcends the material and the physical that biologists normally work with. That can be explained from a different point of view, not from a biological point of view. It is reasonable to say that we can only understand about human facial expressions if we take a spiritual point of view or another point of view. That remark is spur of the moment; there's not much more I can say about that right now.

The notion of strength! You took that, I think, in a physical way. There are plenty of ways to talk about that biologically. The apostle Paul uses some phrase saying that women are weaker than men biologically. He's completely wrong from the biological point of view. Women are much stronger than men biologically. They are structured that way because of child-bearing and other things. They are far more capable of dealing with physical hardship. When you mentioned the word strength you meant it metaphorically too. We can talk about spiritual strength and psychological strength.

BERTRAM   "The strength of sin is the Law." We read that in Paul's Letter to the Romans.

VAN DER MEER   I have difficulty seeing the connection with what biologists say about that. People experience that as their body breaks down; when they grow older, their spirit keeps growing. That seems to be a contradiction. We can understand it if we leave the biological point of view and take a religious point of view. We see that as a preparation for a life after we're finished with the biological body; we live a new existence with a new body.

CROSS   When I was quite a bit younger, I believed in understanding things in the cold light of reason. I had a prejudice against maudlin, popular sentimentality which made me reject what I now take to be probably the most poignant and expressive graphic commentary on the topic of this conference, that is "a theology of the human body." I'm thinking of those pictures of the Sacred Hearts of Jesus and Mary. The resurrected body of Jesus was transparent; the heart with the crown of thorns and the opening from the spear and the facial expression shows suffering, love, the eyes turned to heaven! The same with the accompanying picture of Mary, the Mater Dolorosa, the sword through her heart! This now has meaning for me. It gives me some sense of solidarity with the so-called common people or less educated people, Christians throughout the world, whose homes are adorned with these images that really convey more about the theology of the body than the chart I made yesterday and much that theologians and professionals have to reflect on this topic. I wish we had these pictures right now.

BERTRAM   The cross on the wall has a *corpus*.

KEILHOLZ   Ivan Illich, at our meeting on *Suffering: The Meaning and Management of Pain*, commented that there were no bodies on the crosses at Fordyce House.

BERTRAM   There is a spiritual tradition that would support that the cross refers to the resurrected Christ. I do remember Illich's commenting on that.

ANDREWS   I met Peggy Keilholz on the way into this session. We were talking about a key word which I think is important. She affirmed it from her point of view as a social worker. That's the notion of presence. A purpose of a body is to be present in the life of another body. A purpose of human presence is to be present in Christ. I have a book at home called *The Theology of Presence*. It was written by a lay theologian in the Midwest. He said he was sitting in front of his computer trying to write a paper and all of a sudden it hit him over the head. He says, "The essence of theology is that God has made a covenant to be present with us, and we are obligated to be present in the life of other people." He said, "I sat back and realized that it was the most magnificent thought I ever had." I'll leave it there. Somehow we will have to continue to talk about the details of this structure called the body, but ultimately the key is going to be "presence" in other people's lives and in God. It's the most important thing in the world.

BERTRAM   That is another one, Jitse. Presence is a very bodily thing in the biblical concept. Father Muller mentioned that yesterday when he talked about presence as a feature of personhood.

MULLER   Augustine's understanding of memory is that it makes things present to the mind. The foundation for his Trinitarian analogy is the notion of making things present. I'm listening to this discussion on presence with great interest.

BERTRAM   The Greek word, *parousia*, is used not only when Christ becomes present once more at the end of time. It raises a converse question for theologians. When God is absent, does this not mean lack of presence? But God's absence can be the deliberate withdrawal, which is a form of his wrath. It's not that He forgot to show up.

MATSCHINER   I will add to what we're talking about. I hope it relates. But my oldest son who has had some problems with employment lately, keeps telling me that I told him when he was young that 90 percent of life is "showing up." (BERTRAM: Yes, *parousia*.) The other thing I am going to say may not be relevant. It was simply to add to what Dr. van der Meer said about cell death. It doesn't occur only embryologically. It continues throughout life. There are virtually no cells in our body today that were there when we were born. I don't know much about neurobiology, but the longest lived cells are perhaps neurons. Other than that every tissue has its own "half life." Some of these "half lives" are very fast like the walls of the intestine. Those cells come and go within hours. The half life of cells in the liver is about two days or so. The body is constantly turning over. The cells we function with today are not the cells that we had at any time in the past.

BERTRAM   Is this what we mean by the term mitosis?

MATSCHINER   New cells are formed and old cells die, and are sloughed off, lost.

SCHNEIDER   Mitosis is the division of the cells.

MATSCHINER   .... bringing into existence the new cells. We used to remember it by asking "who ate Isaac Newton."

FORD   I meant to address this to, Pastor Hoy, but he isn't here. I didn't pose it to him because I didn't realize it until now. When I made the comment about creation and Fall not appearing in his paper, the other idea that has now been added to that would be: In the biblical account I believe, it is death that appears at the time of the Fall. Before the Fall there was no death. I wonder how that reality would play out in his or in other scenarios about creation and the Fall. How about death as a consequence of the Fall?

BERTRAM   Since he's not here why don't we ask the people who will speak if they want to include that in their remarks?

STREETER   I'd like to pick up a few threads. When we talk about the body, we're talking about spiritual embodiment or an embodied spirit. It behooves us to keep that integration in mind. I'd like to use that as a starting point. If we have ever been at the bedside of an elderly person just before death, our impression at times is that their skin is almost transparent; they glow. We need to ask is what is coming through? What is happening as that skin becomes transparent? We can almost see the veins and the bones in their body. Something is happening. When they look at us with those sunken eyes, the face glows. What are we seeing in terms of this embodied spirit or the spiritual embodiment?

I suggest that the word "presence" might be the simplest definition of what we call spirituality. There are highly convoluted definitions of spirituality, in contrast to religion. People say: "I have a spirituality and I want to grow spiritually. I want nothing to do with institutionalized religion because of the corruption, foibles, crookedness, bad mouthing I get from my priest or minister, pedophiles, the TV evangelists who are ripping you off." They'll go on and on. Yet they are also talking about a spiritual embodiment, because spirituality which is three feet off the ground is nonsense. When we talk about a human spirituality, we are talking about an embodiment. This means that we have to put up with the vagaries of religion, if we want to hit the ground. Spirituality is not always floating three feet above the ground.

To talk about spirituality as real presence — if that sounds Eucharistic, that's fine — means saying that the person, by means of body, becomes truly present to the situation. He or she is present to the beloved whoever that is, to community or spouse, to the ecclesial community or Church, to the national community or the global community, to the cosmic community, the eco-community. A person's spiritual maturity can be gauged by the quality of presence to people. We cannot forget the presence to the divine which we call prayer. We have the whole gamut of how this integrated organism is somehow communicating through this holistic presence. If a person truncates that presence and decides he or she wants nothing to do with objects, or people, or he or she wants nothing to do with ecological sensitivity, can we say that the spirituality of that person is not sufficiently developed? He or she is refusing presence to a facet of life we all must deal with. If such a person says that he or she wants nothing to do with God, the maturity of that spirituality is deficient at that point. It's a way of looking at the human being as a total, integrated whole, and the body-presence effects that linkage with the rest of reality. We see the body as a revelatory form of communication.

I would like to make a comment on the death question. The Scriptures, in the Book of Revelation, distinguish for us what is known as the first death and the second death. The idea that we don't have a single cell in us that we may have had seven years ago — I don't know that biology well — may lead to transition or change. Perhaps the first death is what we call the birth into this constant transmutation. What we call death is a perceptive cease of the movement. The second death seems to be the encapsulating of the human in evil, as if we had capitulated to evil and a total dissociation from the holy. I understand Revelation saying that we need to be preserved. The first death may be relativized into the transmutation of our presence. I offer that to prod further discussion.

KEEFE   I would like to pivot on some of the questions
that Dr. Bertram brought out in his opening remarks. One of the things that
has characterized the theological discussion of flesh/spirit is the correlative
idea of body in association with head. This is the Pauline/Augustinian contribution to an understanding of community which is basically Trinitarian.
The glory is that which proceeds from a head. The body of the Church then
is the glory that proceeds from the Church's head, who is Christ as the
Second Adam to the Second Eve. This notion of body, then, is not entirely
devoid of that notion of a body having parts. This is the commonplace use
of the term "the body is divisible." But the head is not a part of the body
within this Pauline/Augustinian understanding of the terms. The unity of the
head and body then is not the unity of one person as it is so often misunder-
stood to be. It is the unity of One Flesh.

Here one passes into the imaging between the one flesh as the human substance, the final object of the human creation, the full gift of the Spirit and
that divine substance which is the triune exemplar of the head-body unity,
the free unity of head and body. This immediately moves into the notion of
glory as an expression of the head. That embarrassing passage from Paul,
where he urges women to wear hats in church because of the angels, seems
to embody the idea that glory in this fallen world should be veiled. The
woman's hair is her glory that proceeds from her head. This is perhaps
fanciful on the part of Paul. He doesn't pursue it. But it is at least an
immediate inference from the notion of the glory whether of the Father,
which is the Christ, of the Christ which is the Church, of the man which is
the woman, and glory of the woman suggests itself to Paul as her hair.
Because her hair is her glory, it should be veiled as the glory of Christ is
veiled on the Cross, as Moses veiled his face descending from the Mount, as
Christians turning toward the Christ worship him with unveiled faces in the
sense that they transcend thereby the fallenness which is proper to them as
members of the Church. This is little more than musing, but it has something to do with what we mean theologically by body.

The body is the glory of the Christ and we, insofar as we have bodies, must
understand ourselves in some connection with that head/body union which
is the union of Christ and the Church. We must at the same time keep distinct that understanding of the body which is fundamentally ecclesial and that
understanding of body which Paul sometimes uses as in "who will deliver me
from this body of death." He assimilates it there simply to *sarx* as he sometimes assimilates *psyche* to *sarx*. They are both badges, in some sense, of the
fallenness, the ongoing futility of existence according to the flesh.

That existence according to the flesh has an intellectual component. Today
we would call it not so much juridicalism — in the sense that Paul thought

the reliance simply upon the Law for justification would be thinking according to the flesh — but what today would be called reductionism, the tendency to reduce reality to necessity and by that reduction to end up in a nihilism. That is a threat to all organized logical thought whether theological or scientific. If we look for an interface between religion and science it would be continuing caution on the part of religion, not theology but religion, that there can be no necessary truth even for a scientist. I have suggested elsewhere that we cannot forget the freedom of the historical order which is the subject matter of science. The scientific inquiry is directed to the empirical world. Once that world is understood *a priori* as subject to this reductionist conceptuality it ceases to be of interest because the order of flesh itself is simply without interest.

For Paul its (the order of flesh) dynamism toward death is simply the product of its radical insignificance. In the Johannine idiom: it profits not. It has no significance. Its only meaning is to point toward that which is freely given; its revitalization by association with the One Flesh is the unity of Christ and the Church.

There is a tendency in the sciences to look on what is natural as that which is necessary, the product of an immanently necessary development or proceeding in some way to an immanently necessary end. Insofar as that end is death, the religious tradition out of which we operate always looks upon death as something that involves a separation of the flesh and the spirit. If the flesh is that into which we are fallen by reason of the Fall, it's a diminution in our substantial reality. It's possible to look at it as nothing in itself except insofar as it's a pointer toward that which every human being should be.

BERTRAM   It, meaning flesh?

KEEFE   Yes. In short we have a tendency always simply by virtue of the Platonic component of the western world and of its culture, to think of spirit, whether we will or not, as less substantial than flesh. "This too, too solid flesh" is an expression of this idea. If flesh is a reduction in the full substantial reality of man, as it seems it must be if it is fallen, then the spirit is far more physical, far more solid, far more corporeal in that sense than the flesh/spirit composite which we are. This leads us into paths too difficult to traverse here and now, but death is the resolution of that dichotomy which we inhabit through the death of Christ. We die into Christ, into his death, in one way or another. We are then restored to our full substantial being. That is far removed from the biological notion of death. While the biological notion of death has its value for the scientific community, it does not really contribute other than tangentially to a discussion of death within the theological or religious perspective. These are vagrant observations, things that occurred to me during the discussion.

A final mention has to do with the idea of strength. A prime analogate of strength is the strength which is the Spirit of God, his right arm, that by which He does his wonderful deeds. In that sense, strength is far more a matter of *pneuma* than of the flesh. It is not physical in a sense of being able to move objects in space and time. It has to do with the meaning of freedom; strength is that by which we are free. To be able to do all things in him who strengthens me is to be able to do all things in him who pours out on me and his Church the Spirit by which He is strong. That has pertinence here.

BERTRAM   One vagrant thought that you triggered in me took me back to John Matschiner's remarks about his son who recalled the advice that his father had given him. One time, as I was talking to one of my sons who was coming into his hormonal fullness, he said, "What's so great about having just one woman?" I could tell that that struck him as just the opposite of "free." For many years I have been fond of Fr. Keefe's phrase, "free nuptial unity." To most of the world this sounds like an oxymoron; nuptial unity sounds like the opposite of freedom. I think my son was exploring something like that. I said, "Have you ever thought of the freedom of the one woman man?" That is not the full Keefian depth of what is meant by freedom, but at least a minimal understanding which my son picked up on right away. He said, "Gosh, I never thought of that." Once we lose it, we can never get it back. That's a kind of negative view of freedom as the opposite of necessitarian, necessity, that came to mind. I firmly believe that; I think it's free in much fuller richer dimensions than that.

Then another thought I had which was triggered by Father Keefe's remarks. John Cross mentioned some of the gifts which come with aging in his understanding of what he used to think was sentimental and maudlin. I think I'm right that generally speaking — there are exceptions — in biblical parlance the opposite of old is not young. In the life sciences the opposite of old might be young; but biblically the opposite of old is new. It's possible for people as they become older, if they become older in Christ Jesus, to become newer, not younger. Nobody would claim that; they don't become younger, but they may very well become new. I was taken by Carla Mae Streeter's reference to the transparency of the skin. I've attended a good many dying people where that is quite apparent. At least as a spiritual metaphor you could take that as a sign of the newness that's happening.

KEILHOLZ   I'll start with a personal disclosure. I found in yesterday's sessions the theology I was hearing seemed to be pretty much dis-embodied. I was having a hard time figuring out what this really was all about. Let me start out with a question that has come up for me about the

Fall and its relationship to death. It seems to me that paleontology has told us that death entered the world long before human beings were present. We have fossil evidence of creatures who lived in this part of the country at one time when this was sea. The dinosaurs came and went before human beings showed up. I'm not sure how the notion of death not occurring before this time of the fall fits with that. It may have to do with my understanding of how the book of Genesis was written. It was written as a theological reflection of a people as they observe the human condition. It is one explanation of how things that they saw came to be. If we go to other cultures, we will find different explanations of how things came to be. I want to raise these ideas.

My work witnesses and testifies to the importance of the body. I do a lot of work with people who have been physically and sexually abused. Sometimes, as part of teaching, I ask them why they have this severe reaction to those events. It has to do with the violation of one of our most important boundaries. That is the boundary which is me, the body. When people cross over into it uninvited or in a forceful, abusive way, it does something not only to the body but also to the person's image of himself or herself. It affects how they think about themselves, how they see themselves relative to the world. That can be changed by acts which cross this very significant boundary.

We also see the good that comes when this boundary is flexible enough to receive the hugs and kisses and touch given in love. We have those two kinds of experiences that tell us how important our body is. The body also is subject, of course, to disease and accidents of various kinds. People have to contend with the meaning of those things which happen to them. For me the body is very important. The other thing is that the body is a remarkable unit; it is, for lack of a better word, a thing that shows a tremendous amount of stability in change. We talked about the cells that die over time and how the body changes over the course of a number of years. I look at the parts of my body where there are scars and think, "well these new cells have come but the old scars are still there." How does my body know that's supposed to be in the same place where it occurred when I was eight? Years later it is still in the same place. That is a very remarkable aspect of the body.

I am grateful to be able to talk with Frank Andrews before coming into this session. It has been a matter of concern to me, as one working with people, that it is important for the clients I see to be present to me and I to them. I am present not as someone who has answers or the ability to do away with the bad things that have happened to them but as someone to be with them as they work through the these bad things and try to derive meaning from the events that have happened to them in their lives. I can only do that through my bodily presence with that person and theirs with me. Talking with a person over the phone is a second best. I miss the body language. I am not able to tell over the phone, except from the sound of the voice, how the person might be feeling. I don't see the eyes. I don't see the face or the posture of the body which are things that are available to me when I am face to face with the person. And, of course, they can't see mine either.

We live in a world where the communications are much more through electronic media. E-mails are virtual reality; all of that makes real presence even more important. To me that is very Eucharistic. It's not a matter of what I see going on in some churches at the present time, of being in front of the tabernacle and having adoration in front of the Real Presence of Jesus located in the tabernacle. That's good insofar as it allows me to have this real presence. If it leads to that, that's wonderful. If it's only that relationship with the body of Christ present in the tabernacle, as far as I'm concerned we're done for. It has no meaning to me. We are in an age where it is so important to be present to people, to be present with people in their dying.

Interestingly enough, when I was present with my mother before she died and present with a cousin when she died, I didn't see any of the things Carla Mae Streeter talked about. I was too engrossed in my relationship to these people. Because I was so stunned that I was actually present when my cousin died, I sat down and looked at her and I didn't see Ruth. I saw my Grandmother Keilholz in her face. She looked so much like my grandmother. That memory stays with me. I guess that's part of the other stability in change which comes through the genetics. We can have all these changes, different genetic components brought together, yet at that moment of her passing, I saw in her face my grandmother still somehow present in her and in me and in those of us who are related through that marvelous combination of DNA.

SCHNEIDER   I want to return to the conversation that Jitse van der Meer began about the different words that relate to the body. I haven't had time to develop these thoughts but here are two other words that occurred to me, especially with regard to the face. The word *prosopon* in Greek means face; it has at least two dimensions to its meaning. It's the way the body (the self) is expressed outwardly to others, so that the *prosopon* can be, for instance, a mask. It can be an office or position in society; another part of the *prosopon* is the way that we appear to other people. When the Bible talks about the *prosopon* theologically, it says that God does not regard the *prosopon*; God does not pay attention to the mask. We put that on for others to see. Nor does God pay attention to the positions that we have in society. I'm not sure where to go with that, but that occurred to me in relation to this word "face" — as it appears in the Bible. God does regard the body but not necessarily the "face."

The other word that occurred to me was the word "soul." I believe the Hebrew word for that is *nepeš*. I have never thought about that as mind. When I hear the word *nepeš* I think of "life," the life force itself. It relates to passages in the Torah about the sacrifice of animals and all those regulations on how to prepare food. They say: "Don't eat the blood because the life is in the blood. The *nepeš* is in the blood. We must drain that out and put it in the earth where it came from before we can eat an animal." The New Testament continues that and connects this concept with Christ as the Lamb of God who is sacrificed to take away the sin of the world. The life is in the blood. That comes out Eucharistically: the life is in the blood and we share in that life. I haven't fully developed the thoughts about these two words (*prosopon* and *nepeš*) but these were words that go with your list, Jitse.

BERTRAM   Board members take note! It looks as if we're accumulating themes or sub-themes for another workshop on a *Theology of the Human Body*.

COFFEE BREAK

SCHNEIDER   I was talking about *nepeš* and the life being in the blood; in the New Testament Jesus shed his blood on the cross. The Church takes that up and includes it into the theology of the Eucharist. It brings all back to creation: the body the blood is poured into us, our bodies, which are *adam*, earthlings, red-blooded ones. The blood is put back into the earth whence it came, just like the blood of the animals.

FORD   I want to comment on Bob Bertram's comment on Don Keefe's resonating phrase that I was also pleased to hear — free decision or entering into a free union. I have a philosophy colleague who published an article on the root of the word "freedom." I was in Norway this summer — I am of Norwegian ancestry — and I brought home a piece of delicious chocolate which has the name *Freia*. A Norwegian goddess (Freia) provides the root of the word freedom. Why? She did not have to marry the king of the gods, but she chose to do so in freedom. Her name gave root to the word "freedom" in the Germanic languages.

Let me look at another aspect of freedom. Luther, in 1520, wrote a treatise on *The Freedom of a Christian*. In that he emphasized that freedom is not the liberty to have choices but in a sense comes when all the choices are over, when we have perceived the will of God. Then we are free. When there are no choices left, when there's one thing to do and we accept that, then we are free from doubt, from double-mindedness; we are free from being Hercules at the crossroad. There is only one thing to do.

BERTRAM   *Freiheit* is the German word.

EVERETT   *Freien* in German is to marry. It's an older word. It is rarely used now, but in the 19th century, it was used a lot.

VAN DER MEER   Is it the same root as *frau?*

EVERETT   I would have to ask my daughter. She is a linguistic specialist.

CROSS   My reflection is also on Father Keefe's mention of freedom and the fact that there is no necessary truth even to science. Science must remain free. The characteristics of empirical science for which I want to speak an apologia among so many theologians, are determinism, parsimony, empiricism, tentativeness — seemingly not freedom. The important thing that theologians can remind empirical scientists of is that these characteristics of science are appropriate and methodological, not ontological.

It's useful for empirical science to adopt a methodological determinism, to assume that everything has a cause and the cause can be discovered, to avoid inventing a *deus ex machina* for those things which can't be explained. It's a useful way to proceed with science; it's not a statement about the nature of reality. Likewise parsimony: things are not perhaps as simple as they might be. It's a very useful rule not needlessly to multiply causes as Ockham reminds us. Empiricism is a wonderful check on rationalism. Things may make a lot of deductive sense, but if we can find direct empirical evidence to support them we're much better off than if we can't. Tentativeness is in fact an essential characteristic not only for empirical science but even more for philosophy and yet more for theology. There is a human tendency to seek confirmation for that which we deduce, to fall in love with our theories and narrow our perception and only see the supporting evidence, not the alternative and disclaiming evidence. In the contemporary world more so than in the past, the source of inspiration for theology is not only in philosophy but in the empirical sciences. That's why we have ITEST.

MULLER   Someone spoke earlier about boundaries. The reference was to Mary Douglas who has done considerable work on this issue of boundaries both in terms of defining individuals and also communities. In Scriptural exegesis this kind of work has been used to look at the Old Testament purity rules. The notion of breaching the boundary creates a condition of impurity, so that running sores and the menstrual cycle will trigger the impurity rules. In every case what is at issue is some sort of movement beyond the boundary of the body. We get comparable insights in defining and transgressing communal boundaries as well. I have found that very helpful in understanding the dynamic of certain scriptural passages.

POUCH   Bear in mind that I am a geologist and this
present topic is largely a theological one. I will probably miss the mark often.
A question has arisen about accounting for the long length of time before the
existence of humans. This is especially true of the Fall. Someone tacked on
the notion that even if we did not have the long length of time there would
be a large amount of space to deal with. This is based on the idea that man
is caretaker of the earth. I am not sure that I see much scriptural support
for that. I see more scriptural support for "the earth being for man, not man
for the earth." God gives dominion to humans over all the earth and uses it
to provide them with all the things they need. Geologically it's a remarkably
convenient planet. I feel more comfortable talking about this than engaging
in a discussion about life possibly arising in other universes.

The earth is unique not only in the solar system but as a self-refining planet.
We have pure quartz sandstone that starts out from igneous rocks that are
a total mishmash of a wide variety of elements. When it's done we end up
with almost nothing but silicon. It's a very convenient planet and it almost
seems to be tailor-made for a technological civilization. Humans arose shortly
after the glaciations that provided such an absolutely wonderful soil. That
seems to be too odd a coincidence to support a claim that the earth is simply
here by chance. It looks as if it was planned, and it looks as if it was planned
for humans to inhabit. That statement might get some sparks flying.

I am interested in going back to one of the original aims of the workshop,
a theology of the human body, to some understanding of the human body.
Pragmatically, in the very near future we will see a lot of ethical decisions
based on what's appropriate to do to the human versus to a non-human.
This is going to be a very hot topic. As we manipulate DNA, we'll get into
some very grey areas. We have some clear white and black areas, but we'll
need to try to stake out some of the gray. We pretty much all agree that the
offspring of a human by standard methods should be considered a human.

We have almost complete and universal agreement that a child is a human
after they reach voting age, and in the Catholic Church, from the moment
of natural conception. I think we're pretty much in agreement that a bacter-
ium that is modified to produce human insulin isn't entitled to human rights.
Somewhere in between there we have to draw a line, not because we want
to draw a line, but because we are going to have to draw that line — soon,
sometime in the next five to ten years. People will cross it, but that's been
true since the time of Cain and Abel.

We're trying to "define" the human body. I think Carolyn Schneider hit the
nail on the head with her list of criteria. We often end up with the situation
where we have a list of criteria we expect all humans to meet. There's a

problem with that. Not every human being will meet all these criteria. Perhaps we need not go with the simple taxonomy of a single definition where each person has to meet all its criteria. Perhaps we'd be better off going with something more typical of what we see in soil sciences where we could meet any of several different criteria. Anything which has speech and language and culture should be considered human, or at least equivalent to human, until we have reason to consider it otherwise. We might have additional criteria as well, such as the normal offspring of a human. This avoids some of the issues of dehumanizing certain aspects or portions of humanity by having *the* definition of humanity. Rather let it be any of several things.

This has worked well for soil sciences and it almost works for geologists. Of course, it gets us into endless debates on actual cases. This brings me to one of my favorite quotes. I ran across it in a ground water geology book and it is apparently from the science fiction writer Paul Anderson. It can be stated briefly: "there is no problem which, viewed from exactly the right angle, fails to become vastly more complicated." We have one of the better ones here.

We keep bouncing off the issue of the Fall. While I am not so sure how important from a pragmatic point of view the Fall is, when deciding whether something is human or not human, we're going to have to make moral distinctions on a practical basis for it. My reading of Genesis suggests that the orders to Adam in the Garden, "you will not eat of the fruit of this tree" is pretty definite. Eve's explanation of it to Satan is, "we're not supposed to eat of the fruit of this tree." Implicit in that is a firm knowledge in the sense of the German *wissen*. There is the clear sense of knowledge of good and evil. The actual sin might be the decision, classifying things as good and evil against what we've already been directly told by God. Given that, I'm referring to the Yahwist (Eloist) interpretation. There is a large element of word-magic in it. Maybe he doesn't mean "know" the way we would use it in the philosophical sense — a matter of culture. It may mean "decide," "give name to." I wonder to what extent it is the strict knowledge of good or evil that should be identified with the Fall. Maybe it's trying to re-write God's definition of good and evil that should be so identified.

BERTRAM   You didn't ask for an answer and I'm not about to give one. All I can do is say to you is that in some exegetical traditions the translation of that term in Genesis is precisely the one you've asked about. It means knowing by experience as, for example, in sexual knowledge where a man knows a woman: *kennen* rather than *wissen*. This brings up a question a lot of us may have been thinking about throughout the weekend. Seeking to understand the body might be a way of rewording our theme for the weekend. If we do, or insofar as we do, understand the body, does that in turn alter the body? For example in marriage, Luther's been quoted in his treatise in 1522, which he wrote before he was married. He said all he had to go by to talk about marriage as a celibate monk was the word, the biblical word. He did the best he could with that. But he did not yet know a woman. He didn't even say yet, because he did not anticipate ever knowing one.

I wonder, when ITEST is assembled to talk about something so close to us as body, allowing that that may very well include mind and soul as well, is it part of our purpose, in trying to gain an understanding of body, to alter the body as well in the process because we understand it better? Karen Horney coined a term psychosomatic, not just to say the *psyche* and the *soma* are closely "intervolved," but that, in understanding the *soma*, the *psyche* can change the quality of the body. I am not arguing for that; I thought that was a procedural question we might have had as we engaged in the discussion.

VAN DER MEER   I'd like to address the question that Charles Ford asked about the Fall. I'll link that with a question of my own. If we look at the narrative of the Fall in the Scripture as something of an historical narrative, where the Fall happens in time — before there was no evil and after there was evil — how can we make sense of that? I have thought a lot about that. Then, I want to make a comment about either dimension of this.

First, it wasn't clear in your question what you meant by the word "death." I'll take it that you mean not just separation from God but also that it has biological implications. I will address this. If as physicist or biologist we try to think about what the creation might be like without biological death, we end up saying that there is no way of conceptualizing what that might look like. If we conceive of the narrative in the way that you did, we would end up looking at the description of the situation before the Fall as something unreal or mythical or at least not capable of conceptualization. I would regret that, because what we can learn from that is very important theologically.

This raises the other question that I want to put on the table, maybe not for an answer now, but as something for everyone to reflect on. The question came out of a particular way of looking at the passage as an historical narrative. We've had comments that express other ways of looking at it. I remember Father Keefe saying that we have to consider revelation as a given. I'm not exactly sure what that means but it certainly sounds different from historical narrative, or maybe the two are compatible. We've also heard conceptions of revelation as explanation seen from a human point of view. How do we explain the things we experience in life? The explanation can be in terms of a religious framework. One way or another, if we want to develop a theology of the human body, that sees the human body in a religious perspective, we also need to look at how the scriptures function in understanding that human body. This was the thrust of my paper. If I may summarize what has been done in the workshop, we've observed various ways of looking at the understanding of the body but we really have not struggled with the question. I would leave that as something for us to consider as "homework."

BERTRAM   Peggy Keilholz had also referred to the question of death following on the fall. There had been death long before there had been humans.

STREETER   I'd like to mention another idea that we might fruitfully pursue. We are a group of western thinkers. There is no one here with what we would call an Eastern cosmology. I'm talking about the Far East, the Sino-religious, the Indic-religious. We westerners have our categories by which we view body and bodiliness. What would the dialogue have been if we had someone here of the Indic tradition for whom there are three ways of looking at the body? Within the Indic system — my knowledge is limited — there is the "gross body," the "subtle body" and I think it is called the "pneumenist body." They look at embodiment from those three facets. The gross body is that which is left behind in death; the subtle body is that which changes and is really the object of re-incarnation; and the "pneumenist" body which does not change. Does this have something to do with what we would call "form" in a Greek causal framework? I don't know; we haven't talked that much with them. We've just opened up to another. That will produce another way to look at this. I don't want to do any more with this, beyond noting that it's out there for us to investigate.

BERTRAM   Some studies of Gnosticism have shown that, in most of the Gnosticisms that we know about in late antiquity and early Christianity, contrary to what we formerly thought, the enlightened mind of the knower was not non-particular, was not non-bodily. It was a highly refined form of matter. Remember that Father Keefe challenged the notion, the traditional misconception of *pneuma*, as necessarily being insubstantial.

KUHL   I want to speak to the discussion about death, pre-death, post-fall, those issues. I tend to talk about it this way with my parishioners who are scientifically minded these days. When we study Genesis this question always comes up. I think of a human being as a steward. I think of death as the end of one's stewardship. There are two ways we can think of this in our own culture. A person can go to work on Monday morning and the boss can come to his or her desk and say "you're no longer needed at this job. You did such a good job that we are going to retire you. You can go home now. Well done, good servant." That person's stewardship is ended. It is a moment of joy that the work no longer needs to be done. I assume that most of us in our culture long for that day when our stewardship might come to that end.

The same person can come to work on Monday morning. The boss comes in and says, "you're no longer needed for your stewardship. You've botched up everything you've touched. You're simply not needed." That person has completed his or her stewardship but it would not be a moment of joy. It would be a leaving of the post, an utter judgment on him or her.

One has to talk about death and then death. What does death mean, post-fall. Is death now a signal that our stewardship is being terminated because we are not able to give glory to God in what we do? Father Keefe talked about theological death as opposed to biological death. They are connected, but they are certainly different dimensions. Post-fall death has a different meaning for fallen creatures. Let's talk about freedom with regard to that. Dying in Christ is a dying in which the old passes away, but there's a continuation. It's freedom in that we no longer have to continue to do something to get something out of it. In this case, it's like retirement. I tell this to senior citizens and they all rejoice: "Now that you're retired you no longer have to work to make a living. You're now free to do those things nobody in the society wants to do but need to be done, because you don't need to be remunerated for it." That is an exercise of freedom. Death and freedom, service, stewardship are bound together. When we distinguish what these are, what seems like a mess takes on some clarity. That metaphor helps us understand the human being before God and the experience we have in the body, of the body and of the world.

BERTRAM   It's not that we have to do it but that we get to do it. When it comes to losing our stewardship, the fall is a kind of death. I thought of Father Keefe's talk of abandoning headship.

SCHNEIDER   I want to emphasize what Bob Bertram said about psychosomatic healing and what Carla Mae Streeter said about world views of the non-western world. I made a trip to a Buddhist monastery in San Antonio. A monk spoke to our group after the worship and told us a story about a trip he made to Thailand; while there he got malaria and was dying. The head of the monastery he was visiting put him in a little room by himself to lie there and meditate. So he meditated and began to focus on the pain and identify its source. He did that; he thought more and more about that particular place in his body. He tried, as it were, to enter into his cells through meditation. When he got down to the cell, inside the innermost part of his body, the fever broke and he was cured. He felt tired for a few hours; after a while he was able to get up and didn't have malaria anymore. That was the way he understood what had happened to him through that meditation on the pain itself. We see that mind and body are closely connected. Carla Mae's mention of non-western peoples brought this event to mind.

BERTRAM   I had a specific example in mind which I didn't mention when I posed that question to Jitse van der Meer: does our attempt to understand the body have a reciprocal effect on the body? The example I had in mind is an ancient one in the Christian tradition. I alluded to it in my mention of Luther's treatise on marriage. Does the twain becoming one flesh in the free nuptial unity gain from having the couple know that's what they are? It has been a prevailing tradition in the Christian tradition that it does indeed make a difference whether the two who become one flesh know that's what they're doing. Maybe it would have to be biological or bodily activity where freedom is involved for the understanding to affect the bodily act. I understand that early on in the plighting of troth, the exchange of vows, that the partners in the wedding ceremony may be talking about more than the marital act but they're also certainly talking about that. They're not promising to do something that would not be done otherwise. That's often what we make of it — a contractual arrangement.

Even the continental understanding of marriage often leaves it at that. On the contrary, they're exegeting, to use Jitse van der Meer's term. They have a hermeneutic involved and they're exegeting what in fact happens when two people enter into sexual intercourse. They're reading all that is encapsulated, encoded, in intercourse, "This is the truth about what we do when we go to bed." It has long range effects, "keeping only unto thee from this day forward through hell and high water, till death do us part." That is implied already in the biological operation. So it's a kind of acknowledgement of a truth. They're not just creating something by an act of will. It's a truth-statement. That's the example I had in mind. I wasn't thinking so much of healing, but I know that's prominent nowadays. We dis-embody the marital act. The reigning term in American parlance now for marriage, is I think, — it's one of the better ones, alas — that marriage is a commitment. Not for a moment would I suggest that it isn't that; but it's as if one is not really married until, by two wills, committing themselves to one another would take place. Au contraire! Something takes place bodily and the commitment is simply a recognition of what takes place.

VAN DER MEER   Early on the comment was made that it's hard to see the connection between biological knowledge of the body and theological knowledge. Dr. Bertram just made a wonderful connection. I would like to add one that relates back to Charles Ford's question about death before the Fall. I think personally that it is well possible — this relates to Steve Kuhl's remarks about stewardship too — to conceive of, say, biological death existing before the Fall without any of the negative connotations that we attach to it. Rather, in Pastor Kuhl's words, we can conceive of it as an acknowledgement that stewardship on earth is done. We have to be moved to another place where something else continues. This would be a transition from one existence to another that, maybe as a consequence of the Fall, has become negative. There we have, I think, another connection between the theology and the biology of the human body that we were looking for.

BRUNGS   Tykva Frymer-Kensky wrote a book called *In the Wake of the Goddesses*. In that book she remarked that in pagan religions we had god, nature, mankind — in that order. Nature was the mediator between the gods and mankind. She remarked the Jewish religion proclaimed that that was wrong: it's God, mankind and nature. Mankind mediates between God and nature. To extend the argument a bit, this is what Saint Paul may have meant by the "elemental forces" he mentions in Galatians and elsewhere. Dr. Greg Pouch's stated that this planet seems designed particularly for us. He said that the planet was made for man, not man for the planet. I think this is true. In graduate school, back in the Sputnik days, we used to joke about an alien space craft coming near earth and taking their readings about the properties of the earth. They would conclude that the planet is uninhabitable. There's too much silicon and no life-forms in nature are silicon based. That would be a logical deduction for them to make. But we're here and in the age of electronic we need silicon.

I'd like particularly to concentrate on one word that Father Keefe mentioned once and no one else picked up. We are involved in a study of the human body, of the nature of Christ's body. I am dealing with corporeality. Jesus Christ is *extremely* specific. His body is extremely specific. We read in the Gospels, "In the fifteenth year of Tiberias..." That situates him in terms of the history of the humanity. It situates him in terms of the Roman Empire, in terms of the local potentates. More than that, we have a double reporting of the genealogy of Christ. We tend to overlook this more than we should. Those lists give ancestors, not all of them, but some of them. One genealogy goes so far as to mention Tamar, Ruth, Rahab and Bathsheba. The evangelists were not adverse to mentioning even the more dubious of Christ's ancestors. It's part of his inheritance. He carried some of them with him.

Like me, like you, Jesus Christ could not have been conceived except when He was conceived. Jesus, I guess, could have been born in another maternal cycle but it would have required still another miracle. God could have managed that since the conception was miraculous anyway. But in the natural course of events this was the appropriate time and Mary's egg in that particular cycle was also appropriate. In our case, we would not have been conceived in any other cycle. We had a forty-eight to seven-two hour opportunity to be conceived — in the history of the universe. That was it. We, too, are specific; we, too, are special. Either we are totally an accident or we are specifically wanted. I prefer to think it's the latter.

We cannot understand Christ in his specificity until we understand a little better what the Jews thought the Messiah would be. This also is part of Christ; He is Messiah. We have to have an idea of what they thought the Kingdom was like and the King would be like, because He is also King. We have to have some notion, better than we do, of the fulfillment of all the prophecies, because Jesus was highly conscious of those and directed his life toward them. I am not saying that He manipulated them, but his life was spelled out in those prophecies.

Father Keefe also used the word "particularity." The Gospels stress the uniqueness of the Christ — corporeally. But Scripture also stresses the communitarian aspects of the Kingdom, of the Messianic times, of the fulfillment of the prophets, and so on. We have to hold these things in tension all the time — the communitarian aspects of Christ's life and the uniqueness of his life.

I am writing a book on corporeality but it's a long term operation. Those who are writing it with me should be here but they're not. They have insights I don't have because all three are women. So we'll have an "ecumenical" product. In terms of Christ Jesus, the important thing is to pay very close attention to his uniqueness as a person, that He has a body corporeally; it is also necessary to treat the communitarian (that is sacramental) effects of his Messiahship, his Kingship and so on.

I want to thank the essayists, Dr. Michael Hoy, Father Donald Keefe, S.J., Father Earl Muller, S.J., Dr. Carolyn Schneider and Dr. Jitse van der Meer for their insights and provocative (in the best sense of the word) statements. I want to thank them also for their charity and patience with us lesser lights. We deeply appreciate their contributions to the ongoing discussion on the human body. I want also to thank the attendees for their patience in waiting to "have their say." I want to thank them as well for their charity. Without that, a meeting like this could have become a battleground. So, thanks much for all your attention and for the relaxed atmosphere that's developed here.

Finally, I want to thank Sister Marianne Postiglione, RSM and Sister Rose Marie Przybylowicz, OSF for their many contributions both in preparing for this weekend and attending to the many organizational tasks. Some of these contributions were small and thoughtful; some were quite large and equally thoughtful. It is a commonplace to say that we could not have held this convocation without their work. Commonplace though it may be, it has the virtue of being true. So thank you, Sister Marianne and Sister Rose Marie. It's an inadequate return for what you've done, but we really appreciate it.

Finally, Godspeed on your way home.

INDEX

PARTICIPANTS

ESSAYISTS

Rev. Michael Hoy, PhD, Dean
Lutheran School of Theology
2030 Union Road
St. Louis, Missouri 63125

Fr. Donald J. Keefe, SJ, PhD
St. Joseph's Seminary, Dunwoodie
201 Seminary Avenue
Yonkers, New York 10704

Fr. Earl C. Muller, SJ, PhD
Sacred Heart Seminary
2701 Chicago Blvd.
Detroit, Michigan 48206-1799

Carolyn Schneider, PhD
Fairway Manor #M2
1048 Country Club Drive
Seguin, Texas 78155

Jitse Van Der Meer, PhD
Pascal Center - Redeemer College
777 Garner Road, E.
Ancaster, Ont. L9K 1J4 Canada

PARTICIPANTS

Prof. Benjamin F. Abell
3268 January - Apt. 2
St. Louis, Missouri 63139-1737

Dr. Frank A. Andrews
2004 Homewood Road
Annapolis, Maryland 21402

Dr. Dimitry A. Bayuk
Inst.: History of Sci/Tech
Staropanski per 1/5
Moscow, Russia 103012

Dr. Robert Bertram
611 Eckrich Place
Webster Groves, Missouri 63119

Fr. Robert Brungs, SJ,
Director: ITEST
3601 Lindell Blvd. - Jesuit Hall
St. Louis, Missouri 63108

Dr. John F. Cross
221 N. Grand - St. Louis Univ.
St. Louis, Missouri 63103

Dr. Armgard Everett
3223 Landria Drive
Richmond, Virginia 23225

Dr. Charles Ford
221 N. Grand - St. Louis Univ.
St. Louis, Missouri 63103

Dr. Robert Greenley
544 Oak Valley
St. Louis, Missouri 63131

Ms Peggy Keilholz
9700 Cisco Drive
St. Louis, Missouri 63123-5405

Rev. Dr. Steven Kuhl
211 Main Street (Box 8)
Mukwonago, Wisconsin 53149

Dr. John Matschiner
10341 Manchester Road
St. Louis, Missouri 63122

Fr. Frederick G. Mc Leod, SJ
St. Louis University
3601 Lindell Blvd
St. Louis, Missouri 63108

Sr. Marianne Postiglione, RSM
ITEST
3601 Lindell Blvd.
St. Louis, Missouri 63108

Dr. Gregory Pouch
P.O. Box 5112
Bloomington, Illinois 61702

Sr. Rose Marie Przybylowicz, OSF
Treasurer General
335 Kirkwood Road
St. Louis, Missouri 63122

Mr. Thomas D. Quinn
3108 Savoy Drive
Fairfax, Virginia 22031-1019

Dr. Thomas Sheahen
52 Wanderer Lane
Deer Park, Maryland 21550

Ms Fiorella Simoni
8906 Garden Gate Drive
Fairfax, Virginia 22031

Mr. James Squire
3519-L Sugar Crest Drive
St. Louis, Missouri 63033

Dr. Carla Mae Streeter, OP
Aquinas Institute
3642 Lindell Blvd.
St. Louis, Missouri 63108-3396

Fr. Robert Zinser
Pastor: St. Teresa of Avila Church
3636 North Market
St. Louis, Missouri 63113